ABSTRACTS *of* GILES COUNTY TENNESSEE

COUNTY COURT MINUTES, 1813–1816
and
CIRCUIT COURT MINUTES, 1810–1816

Carol Wells

HERITAGE BOOKS
2019

HERITAGE BOOKS

AN IMPRINT OF HERITAGE BOOKS, INC.

Books, CDs, and more—Worldwide

For our listing of thousands of titles see our website
at
www.HeritageBooks.com

Published 2019 by
HERITAGE BOOKS, INC.
Publishing Division
5810 Ruatan Street
Berwyn Heights, Md. 20740

International Standard Book Numbers
Paperbound: 978-0-7884-0372-9
Clothbound: 978-0-7884-8464-3

TABLE OF CONTENTS

FOREWORD

Family historians can hardly find a better way to add life to genealogical records than by reading county court minutes. On these pages can be found references to remarriages, heirs, apprenticeships, orphans, transients, indigents, and the insane. Here are mentioned the laying out of roads, licensing of officials, mills, ferries, and ordinaries, as well as suits for assault, trespass, debt, paternity, land, and other county matters.

Minutes vary from county to county in the amount of detail the clerk and justices wrote. Even minutes that omit details may provide information crucial to piecing together an idea of the living conditions and problems of our ancestors. The reader will please make allowances for variations in spelling, and the oddities of handwriting. Names appear as they seemed to be written. Pickens may be Perkins; double t may be double l; in some writing u and n look alike; s, r, and t may be confused. When in doubt about the reading of a name, observe its appearance in the original document.

Giles County was cut from Maury County in 1809. By this time, Indian problems were in the past, and the area was filling rapidly with settlers. Some families farmed only for a season or two before going elsewhere. Depositions and powers of attorney show connections to counties in South Carolina, North Carolina, Virginia, and Kentucky.

Meeting at first in private homes, the court had a courthouse built, which soon burned. This book was abstracted from the Tennessee State Library's microfilm of two surviving county court minute books and one circuit court minute book dating from before 1820. In the absence of census records for early Tennessee, and considering the destruction of many other early records, these three small books have great importance to genealogists.

ABBREVIATIONS

A&B	assault & battery
ac	acres
acct	account
ackd	acknowledged
addl	additional
agt	against
apptd	appointed
atty	attorney
br	branch
B/S	bill of sale
commrs	commissioners
compy	company
cr	creek
ct	court
dam	damages
decd	deceased
dft	defendant
D/G	deed of gift
DS	deputy sheriff
exn	execution
fk	fork
judgt	judgment
No	North
P/A	power of attorney
plf	plaintiff
rd	road
recd	received
retd	returned
sd	said
sec	security, or securities
shff	sheriff
TAB	trespass assault & battery
v	versus
will	last will and testament
wit	witness, witnesses

GILES COUNTY COURT

MINUTES COMMENCING

NOVEMBER COURT

1813

p.1   Court of Pleas and Quarter Sessions holden for County of Giles at the Courthouse in the town of Pulaski On Monday the 15th day of November 1813. Present Somerset Moore, John Dabney, & Thomas Westmoreland, Esqrs.

Ordinary licence granted to John B Prendergast who gave bond & security.

One black poll taken from John Temples list of taxable property.

Ruth McCormack v Thomas Goff. Debt. Plf orders suit dismissed & pays costs.

Bill/sale John White to Wm More[?] acknowledged.

p.2   Appoint Jonathan Berry overseer Weakleys Creek road from Dry fork to John Blazengames fence; hands of Jesse Foster, Robert Lyon, Peter Lyon, Alexander Campbell, Anthony Seals, Tho McBride, Jas Harris, Andw Puget, Levi Lewis, Lazs Stuart, Spencer Roach, Tho Blazingame, David Baker, Benjn Fipps, Elijah Melton, Jonathan Berry & Robert Brashers work thereon.

James McCraven admr/estate of David Stewart decd returns account/sales.

Grand jurors: Charles Buford foreman, William McDonald, Joseph McDonald, William Phillips, Joseph Knox, Jesse Weathers, John Powell, William Giddens, William Henderson, Timothy Ezell, William Pickens, Robert Anderson, Edmund Gatlin.

Order Pleasant New overseer/road in room of James Paxton resigned.

p.3   At least five Justices present, David Flat produced two wolf scalps supposed to be more than four months old which was ordered to be burnt.

[Similar wording for Levi Lewis one wolf scalp; Saml Wright one wolf scalp; Benjamin Chesher one wolf scalp; Wm McKinney one wolf scalp]

Order County trustee pay Alfred M Harris County Solicitor Fifty Dollars for exofficio services for one year prior to this time.

p.4   Nathan Hooker v Christopher Best[Bert?]. Plf in proper person assumes all costs and directs suit be dismissed; plf to pay dft his costs of defence.

Appt Somerset Moore, Nathaniel Moody & Ralph Graves or any two commissioners to let to lowest bidder the building of a bridge across Moores Creek where the Weakleys Creek road crosses same & report to next Court.

Order County trustee pay William Dabney Forty three dollars ninety nine cents for keeping James Dickson for one year ending September last.

Order County trustee pay German Lester ten dollars for one minute book and

p.5   writing paper furnished for use of this Court.

Add John Whites and James Donaldsons hands to hands of Ralph Graves

1

overseer/road from Pulaski to Dry fork of Pidgeon roost creek.

Order County trustee pay Bernard M Patteson Deputy Sheriff Eight dollars for furnishing guard & guarding negro man John while confined for Grand Larceny.

Order County trustee pay Henry Scales One dollar for arresting and guarding negro man John while in confinement for Grand Larceny.

Order County trustee pay James Buford Sheriff Three dollars for furnishing guard and guarding John Howell while in confinement for Petit Larceny.

p.   Order County trustee pay Robert Lewis late constable Twelve dollars for arresting and conveying John Bryant to jail of Williamson County.

Order William Philips, Guston Kerney, William Purnell, Samuel Woods, James Bumpass, Jarret Manefee, John Temple or any five view a road nearest & best way from Manifees ford on Elk river to intersect road lately cut from Huntsville to state line in a uirection to Pulaski; report to next Court.

John Easley Esq resigned as Justice of the Peace for this County.

Commissioners of Pulaski pay Alfred M Harris Eleven dollars for writing 100 blank bonds & notes and carrying the chain one day while sd commrs was laying off [last line cut off this page]

p.   Commrs/Pulaski pay to German Lester $10 for writing one hundred notes and title bonds for use of sd commissioners.

James Trimble assee v Philip Parchman. Debt. Dft having assumed and paid costs in this behalf expended, plf by atty directs this suit be dismissed.

John McCracken v William H Murrah. Case. Plf having assumed & paid costs in this behalf expended directs suit be dismissed.

James Kimbrough v Elijah Anthony. Case. Referees to whom were refered the

p.   final determination return their award: Plf recovers agt dft $10. Signed J Buford, Wm Caldwell, Lewis Brown, M H Buchanan, J J Ward, William Wells. Therefore plaintiff recovers against defendant $10 & his costs of suit. Plf acknowledges in writing full satisfaction of the above award.

Court adjourns till tomorrow 9 Oclock. N Patteson Pleasant Moore Jas Dugger

p.   Tuesday 16 Novr 1813. Present Nelson Patteson, Pleasant Moore, James Dugger

Aaron Lancaster v Robert Willson. Appeal. Plf in proper person assumes costs & directs suit be dismissed; plf pays dft his costs of defence.

Exempt Lewis Kirk from serving on jury this day.

William Sawyers v Martin Friley. Judl att. Continued till next Court.

Henry Scales recognizance, to give evidence behalf State agt Bernard M

p.   Patteson for assault & battery on sd Scales.

Henry Scales recognizance, to give evidence behalf State agt Bernard M Patteson for A&B on sd Scales.

Archibald Alexander recognizance, to give evidence behalf State against

p.   Reuben Manefee for A&B on sd Alexander.

Court adjourns to meet instanter at house of John B Prendergast in Pulaski. Court met. Present Somerset Moore, Nathaniel Moody, Pleasant Moore Esqrs.

Executors of will of Josiah Maples decd returned inventory of estate.

John Dickey Esqr was elected County trustee & took oaths required.

Order County trustee pay Richard Briggs constable $20 for furnishing guard & guarding Thomas Davis to Nashville Jail.

p.   Aaron Lancaster v Isaac Wilson. Appeal. Plf in proper person assumes all costs & 75¢ to defendants attorney and diresta that this suit be dismissed.

2

Aaron Lancaster v Ralph Graves. Appeal. Plf assumes all costs & 75¢ to dfts atty and directs that this suit be dismissed.

Brice M Mayfield v William M Kerley & Nathan Davis. Trover. Continued.

p.13 William M Mayfield v Nathan Davis & William M Kerley. Trover. Defendants being on a tour of duty to Creek nation, order cause be continued till next Court.

Brice M Mayfield v Nathan Davis & William M Kerley. Trover. [as above] Motion of Isaac Lann by atty John White; Isaac Lann paid as security for John Forgey $11.23 on an execution issued in pursuance of judgmt rendered at last term in favour of William Ball agt sd Forgey & Lann. Plf recover agt dft sd sum & p.14 his costs.

Power/atty Robert Kimbrough to John Campbell ackd.

Grand Jury bills/indictment: State v Bernard M Patteson, true bill; same v same, true bill; same v Reuben Manefee, true bill.

William Steele v Daniel Woods. Debt. Jury Wm Fullerton, Jesse West, Thomas p.15 Hall, Wm Graves, Wm Brown, Jos Lann, Washington G L Foley, Jas Giddens, Wm Kindle, Thos Smith, Jno Abernathy, William Jones. Plf recovers agt dft $94.66¼ his debt and his damages and his costs of suit.

James Anderson v Daniel Woods. Debt. Jury[above]. Plf recovers agt dft p.16 $115.50 debt, his damages and his costs.

p.17 Andrew Jackson, Alfred Balch & Thomas Crutcher exrs of Wm T Lewis decd v David Woods. Debt. Jury[above] say dft hath not paid debt, assess plfs damage to $16.87½ besides their costs.

Appt Samuel Avett overseer/road from Camp Branch to Robert Gordons; hands of Thomas Aiken, John Akin, John Roberts, Moses Evetts, James McCullock, Robert p.18 McCullock, David McCullock, Jeremiah Galaspie, Nicholas Grigs, John Chapman, Tho Capuran, Benjn Chapman, Jeptha Moore, Asa Moore, French Moore & Asa Moore & all hands on W T Lewis's Quarter Plantation work thereon under his direction.

William McNeil v Daniel Woods. Debt. Jury[above] say dft hath not paid debt & assess plfs damage by detention to $18.63 beside his costs.

p.19 Lewis Kirk v Archibald McKissack. Debt. Jury[above] say dft hath not paid debt; plfs damage by detention $2.25 beside his costs.

p.20 Samuel Craig v Daniel Woods & Gideon Pillow. Debt. Jury[above] say debt not p.21 paid. Plf recovers agt dfts debt $100, damages, & costs.

James Stewart & Co v Gabriel Bumpass [This item X'd out]

p.22 Court adjourned to meet at the Court house tomorrow morning 9 Oclock.

John Dickey John Hillhouse Robt Oliver

p.23 Wednesday 17th Novr 1813. Present Somerset Moore, John Dickey, Robt Oliver. Court adjourned to meet instanter at house of Jno B Prendergast in Pulaski.

James Buford Esq Sheriff & Collector for Publick & County Tax for 1813 returned list of delinquencies:

James Agnew, 1 white poll .25	Robert Anderson, 1 white poll .25
Robert Anderson, 1 slave .50	Nathl Armstrong, 1 wh poll .25
Richard Armstrong, 1 wh poll .25	Anderson & Strother, 477 acres $1.19¼
James Babb, 1 white poll .25	Jno Baldridge, 160 acres .40
Edward Baker, 1 white poll .25	Jno Baker, 1 white poll .25
Clayton Buckanon, 1 white poll .25	Jno Black, 1 white poll .25
James Brown, 1 white poll .25	John Bigham, 5000 acres $12.50
James Bright, 247 acres .61¼	Buncomb Heirs, 638 acres $1.59

3

NOVEMBER 1813

p.24
George W Campbell, 5000 acres $12.50
John Childress, 4700 acres $11.75
William Cockran, 1 white poll .25
Nathaniel Kimbro, 1 white poll .25
Stephen Condray, 1 white poll .25
Andrew Donaldson, 3 slaves $1.50
John Dabney, 930 acres $2.32½
George Doherty, 2500 acres $6.35
George Doherty, 4969½ acres $12.42½
Daniel Davis, 1 white poll .25
Joseph East, 200 acres .50
John Follis, 1 white poll .25
John Frazier, 1 white poll .25
Thomas Glasgow, 1 white poll .25
David Graham, 1 white poll .25
Joseph Greer, 1000 acres $2.50

p.25
Richd Hightower, 230 acres .50½
Hightower & Haywood 1100 acres $2.75
Andrew Harvey, 1 white poll .25
John Howell, 1 white poll .25
John Hutchinson, 1 white poll .25
Joseph Haynes, 1 white poll .25
James Hunt, 2 slaves $1.00
Thos Jenkins, 1 white poll .25
William M Kerley, 1 white poll .25
George Keltner, 1 white poll .25
Robert Lanier, 500 acres $1.25
Peter Lyon Sr, 6 slaves $3.00
Heirs Saml Lockheart, 3561½ ac $8.90¼
Eli Lancaster, 1 white poll .25
William B Lewis, 300 acres .75
Alexr McKinney, 1 white poll .25
James Morrison, 200 acres .50
James C & David W McRee, 840 ac $2.10

p.26
State, Hardy Murfree, 640 acres $1.60
Thos McNeal, 400 acres $1.00
Jno Oxford, 1 white poll .25
George Poteet, 1 white poll .25
Joseph Paine, 1 white poll .25
William Phillips, 1 white poll .25
Andrew Prather, 1 white poll .25
Hiram Peeler, 1 white poll .25
Thos Polk, 3768 acres $9.42
Saml Polk & Z Alexander, 1060 ac $2.65
Saml Polk, 300 acres .75
Saml Rodgers, 1 white poll .25
James Read Jr, 1 white poll .25
James Read Jr, 4657 acres $11.64¼
William Rodgers, 1 white poll .25
Thos Stanford, 1 white poll .25

Heirs Landen Carter 4000 ac $10
John Childress, 1000 acres $2.50
John Crowson, 1 white poll .25
Francis Childs, 3000 acres $7.50
Andrew Donaldson, 1 wh poll .25
Andrew Davidson, 1 white poll .25
Wm Dulin, 1 white poll .25
George Doherty, 5000 ac $12.50
George Doherty, 640 acres $1.60
John Doherty, 1 white poll .25
John Faris, 1 white poll .25
Abram Follis, 1 white poll .25
John Garner, 1 white poll .25
John Gamble, 1 white poll .25
Brice M Garner, 171½ acres .42
Richd Hightower, 640 acres $1.60
Richd Hightower, 100 acres .25
Hightower & Haywood 500 ac $1.25
Harvey Harvey, 1 white poll .25
James Hutchinson, 1 wh poll .25
Simeon Higgs, 1 white poll .25
James Hunt, 1 white poll .25
John Jewell, 1 white poll .25
Wm Johnson Junr 1 white poll .25
Wm M Kerley, 1 stud horse $4.25
Saml Lindsey, 1 white poll .25
Peter Lyon Sr, 1 white poll .25
James Leith, 1 white poll .25
Thos Lancaster, 1 white poll .25
James Lewis, 400 acres $1.00
Robt McKinney, 1 white poll .25
Rolen McKinney, 1 white poll .25
John McDonald, 227 acres .56¾
Jno P Masterson, 1 white poll .25
State, Hdy Murfree 427 ac $1.06¼
William Neal, 100 acres .25
Jacob Pennington, 1 wh poll .25
Jno Potter, 1 white poll .25
Thos Paine, 1 white poll .25
Isaac Price, 1000 acres $2.50
Robert Porter, 1 white poll .25
Thos Polk, 5000 acres $12.50
Thos Polk, 1200 acres $3.00
Jacob Perkins, 4000 acres $10.00
McNiece Rodgers, 1 white poll .25
Wm H Ragsdale, 227 acres .56¾
James Read Jr, 1 slave [blot]
Tyree Robertson, 1 white poll .25
James Reed Jr, 1 white poll .25
John Smart, 1 white poll .25

4

NOVEMBER 1813

p.27 Thos Shelton, 1 white poll .25
Benj Samuel, 1 stud horse $2.25
George Sherley, 1 white poll .25
Carlus Sharpe, 1 white poll .25
James Stewart, 1 white poll .25
Jno Strother & H Hightower, 300 ac .75
Strother & Bright, 105 acres .26½
William Travis, 1 white poll .25
James Trumbull, 1 white poll .25
James Temple, 300 acres .75
James Temple, 26 acres .06½
Edward Thursby, 10 acres .02½
Israel Woods, 1 white poll .25
Joel Williams, 1 white poll .25
Henry Youngblood, 1 white poll .25
Aaron Youngblood, 1 white poll .25

Benj Samuel, 1 white poll .25
William Stephenson, 1 wh poll .25
Leml Simmons, 1 white poll .25
David Stewart, 1 stud horse $1.75
Walter Simms, 5000 acres $12.50
Strother & Bright, 95 ac .23¾
Strother & Bright, 50 ac .23½
Lewis Taylor, 1 white poll .25
Richd Tutt, 1 white poll, .25
James Temple, 39 acres .09¾
James Temple, 86 acres .21½
Thos Whitson, 140 acres .35
James Williams, 1 white poll .25
[blot] Wilson, 5000 acres $12.50
Hy Youngblood, 1 stud horse $1.75

One hundred and seventeen dollars forty five and one fourth cents is due to the
p.28   County and one hundred and twenty five dollars forty five cents is due to
the State.   Allow Sheriff a credit for afsd sums respectively.
    Reuben Manefee recognizance, to give evidence behalf State against
Archibald Alexander for assault & battery on sd Manefee.
p.29   James Buford, Sheriff & Collector, list of insolvents for 1812 [all white
polls except where noted.]: Jonathan Adams, William Ashmore, George Barns, Jeral
Brashear, Jno Baldridge, Azariah Bone, George Broor, James Brown, Joshua Barns,
Paul Bratton, William Barnet, William Cannon, Danl Cox, Jno Campbell, Wm Carwood,
Alexander Dickey, Benjamin Flat, David Flat, James Joslin, Jas Joslin 1 slave .50,
Jacob Graves, Joshua Glover, Fresh Garner, Jno Herrington, [blot] Howell, Solomon
Hobbs, Andrew Heskins, Hugh Hadden, Robert Hillhouse, Saml Hadden, Thos Hann, Thos
p.30   Hadden, Coleman Harday, Jeremiah Gerco[?], Leonard Jones, Willie Jones,
Mary Jones 2752 acres $6.88, William Knox 2 white polls .50, William Knox 1 slave,
Humphreys Leech, Jno Lacefield, Peter Lemmons Senr 2 slaves $1, Saml Lewis, Lazarus
Masterson, Andw McCrary, Jeptha Moore, Jno Miller, Joseph McCool, Shaderick Mader-
ell, Shaderick Morfet, Henry Morgan, William Morton, William Majors, Jno Nodd, Saml
Oxford, Jonathan Penray[Pemay?], Joseph Fipps, William Prince, Jorden Fipps, Jorden
Fipps 1 slave .50, Tho Rubey, Wm Rust, Paul Rodgers, Wm Rutledge, John Rosen, John
p.31   Rosen 1 slave .50, Wm Rosack, Jno Reynolds, Jos Sally, Jno Scott, David
Shannon, Robert Steel, Abram Starks, Joseph Starks, Jno Starks, Jno Stanley, James
Smith, Wm Starks, Jno Smallwood, Oliver Thompson, Joseph Taylor, Wm Farnney, Rolen
Tanksley, Levi Madderwood, Richard Wilson, Moses Williams, Jno Wilsford, Wm White,
p.32   amounting to $28.88. Sheriff allowed a credit for sd sums on settlement.
    Aaron Lancaster v William W Crittenton. Appeal. Parties in their persons,
dft assumes $2 of costs and plf assumes balance and directs that suit be dismissed.
    John Boyd recognizance to give evidence behalf State against Robert Taylor
p.33   for assault & battery on sd Boyd.
    State v John Crittenton. Retailing spiritous liquors without licence. Dft
in proper persons pleads guilty. Fined $1 and pay costs of prosecution.
    State v Aaron Lancaster. Gambling. Dft in proper person pleads guilty. Fine
p.34   Five dollars and pay costs of prosecution.
    John Easley & Douglass Blue surrender Jacob Crowson and are discharged from
their obligation.

NOVEMBER 1813

Bond Fanny Osburne, John Counts, Joseph Wallace, condition Fanny Osburne
p.35   keep free from charge of this County her daughter Peggy Osburne.
[Similar bond]... keep free from charge of this County her son Frederick Osburne.
Indenture from Betty free woman/colour to Wm Mabry proven by James Perry.
Alexander Miller admr estate of Andrew Miller decd returned acct/sale.
Appoint John Dickey, John Hillhouse & James Ashmore to settle with Alexander Miller admr of estate of Andrew Miller decd.
p.36   State v Jacob Crowson. Bastardy. Discharge of recognizance on payment of
costs he has assumed to pay.
State v Bernard M Patteson. B&A on Henry Scales. Dft in proper person
pleads guilty; fined $3 and pay costs of prosecution. Fine & costs paid.
p.37   State v Bernard M Patteson. A&B on Henry Scales. Dft pleads guilty; fined
$2 and pay costs of prosecution. Paid.
State v Philip Yancy. Affray. Dft in proper person pleads guilty. Fined $10
and pay costs of prosecution.
p.38   Grand Jury bills/Indictment & Presentment: State v Archibald Alexander true
bill; Same v William Murrah, presentment; Same v Patsey Owens, presentment.
State v John Kimbrough. Affray. State no further prosecutes.
p.39   State v Minor Winn. Affray. Dft in proper person pleads Guilty. Fined 12½¢,
committed to jail till adjournment of Court this evening, & pay prosecution costs.
State v Samuel Cox. A&B on John Boyd. Jury Wm Fullerton, Thos Hall, William
p.40   Graves, William Brown, Jesse West, Lewis Kirk, John McNite, John Graves,
John Thompson, Ralph Graves, William Jones, Joel West find dft not guilty.
Appt German Lester overseer of First Street in Pulaski in room of Joseph S
McCormack; hands of Thomas Beal added to hands that work on said street.
p.41   Recognizance Samuel Budd, condition he attend next term to give evidence
behalf State against Samuel Cox Junr for A&B on sd Budd.
Court adjurned till tomorrow morning 9 Oclock.
                                        Somerset Moore N Patteson Robt Oliver

p.42   Thursday 18th Novr 1813. Present Somerset Moore, Nelson Patteson, Robert
Oliver Esqr.
Recognizance, John Boyd, to appear next term to give evidence in behalf
State against Robert Taylor for assault & Battery on sd Boyd.
State v Thomas Smith. Gaming. Dft in proper person pleads guilty. Fined $5
p.43   and costs of this prosecution.
State v Reuben Menefee. A&B on Archd Alexander. Jury Wm Fullerton, Thomas
Hall, Wm Graves, Wm Brown, Jesse West, Lewis Kirk, Marcus Mitchell, Alexr Miller,
Wm Jones, Wm Steel, Henry Tucker, Alexr Jones find dft guilty; assess his fine to
$50.12½ besides cost of prosecution.
p.44   Deed Henry Lester to Lewis Brown 250 acres ackd.
Grand Jury presentment: State v Thomas Smith.
Apprentice indenture between Somerset Moore Esqr chmn of Court and Matthew
Dew was sentered into and filed.
p.45   State v Archibald Alexander. A&B on Reuben Manefee. Dft in proper person
pleads guilty; fined 6½¢ and pay costs of prosecution.
Motion of David Woods & Wm Kindle, they having paid as security for Thomas
Shelton $68.44 on an execution issued by virtue of judgmt rendered at last term in
favour of John McCracken, therefore considered by Court that David Woods & William

6

p.46   Kindle recover agt Thomas Shelton afsd sum and their costs of motion.
John McIver v Caleb Friley. Debt. Capias returned last Court Not Found,
alias not having been ordered by plf, suit is discontinued and plf pays costs.
James Coursey v Francis Adams. Trespass. [as above]
p.47   Court adjourned till tomorrow morning 9 Oclock. Somerset Moore, N Patteson,
John Hillhouse.

p.47[again]   Friday 19th November 1813. Present Somerset Moore, Nelson
Patteson, John Hillhouse, Esquires.
        Appt Nathaniel Moody to take List/Taxable property in Capt Smith's company.
[same wording: Wm Mayfield Esqr in Capt Hendersons; John Hillhouse Esqr in Capt
Perkins; Robt Oliver in Capt Paxtons; Maxamilian H Buchanan Esq in Capt Bensons;
p.48   Robt Buchanan Esq in Capt Harwells; John Dickey Esq in Capt Hills; Jarret
Manefee Esq in Capt Starks; Thos Westmoreland Esq in Capt Phillips; Pleasant Moore
Esq in Capt Reads; Samuel Sheilds Esq in Capt Campbells; Samuel Jones Esq in Capt
Gordons; Robt Steele Esq in Capt Newlands; John Henderson Esq in Capt Youngs; James
p.49   McDonald Esq in Capt Marx's company.
        John Forgey v John Cabe. Case. To determination of Wm Simpson, Walter Lock,
Israel Pickens, John Dickey, Wm Wisdom or a majority of them, whose award is to be
made the judgment of the Court.
        Grant ltrs/admn on estate of John Davis to Thomas Goff. Inventory returned.
p.50   Order of last Court appointing Hardy Hightower, Robert Alsup, John Kennedy,
John Elliss, John Young, Enoch Davis or any five to mark out a road from where road
from Fayetteville by way of McCullins intersects the line dividing Giles & Lincoln
countys, thence nearest & best way to Pulaski until it intersects road from Robert
Alsups to Pulaski, be revived and that they make report to next Court.
        John G Powell v William Creamer. TA&B. Orpha Black, summoned to give evi-
dence, came not. Sci facias issue against her returnable to next Court.
        John G Powell v William Creamer. TA&B. Dft by atty; plf came not. Dft re-
p.51   covers agt plaintiff his costs about his defence expended.
        John Bryant v Washington Croft. Case. Continued till next Court.
        James Walker v Nelson Patteson. Debt. Continued till next Court.
        John Black & wife v William Creamer. A&B. Continued till next Court for
want of the testimony of Isaac Reynolds Jr who is in the army.
p.52   Grand Jury presentments: State v John Counts; same v Henry[?] Been.
        William Steele v John McCabe. Case. Dft withdraws his plea and does not
gainsay action of plff. Plf recovers agt dft his damages by nonperformance of
assumption in declaration mentioned. Damages to be ascertained by jury: William
Fullerton, Thomas Hall, Wm Graves, Wm Brown, Jesse West, Lewis Kirk, Gray Edwards,
Thos Atkinson, Jas Parham, Thos Goff, John Graves, Henry Roberts. Plf recovers agt
p.53   dft $106 damages and costs of his suit.
        Jurors to next Circuit Court: Jacob Byler, Marcus Mitchel, Buckner Harwell
Sr, Lewis Brown, Thos Westmoreland, Joseph Anthony, Elijah Anthony, James Bumpass,
Buckner Harwell Junr, Robt McDonald, Alexr Barron, Robt Gordon, John White Jr, John
Barnett, John McCracken, Nathaniel Moody, Caleb Hill, Robt McNairy, John Clack[or
Clark?], Wm Giddens, Jno Paul Senr, Peter Swanson, Ralph Graves, Jno Graves, Trion
p.54   Gibson, Wm McDonald.
        Jurors to next term this Court: Israel Pickens, Wm Welch, Walter Lock,
Nicholas Welch Jr, Jas Lindsey, John Hannah, Andw Keith, John Tacker, Wm Purnell,

Wm Dabney, John Hicks, John Temple, David Campbell, John Manefee, John Jones,
George Malone, Alexr Jones, David W Porter, Thomas McKissack, Adam Burney, Hardy
Hightower, Early Benson, Thomas Wilkinson, Joseph German, John Young, Wm Stovall.
Court adjourned till tomorrow morning 9 Oclock. Somerset Moore, John
Hillhouse, N Patteson.

p.55   Saturday 20th Novr 1813. Present Somerset Moore, Nelson Patteson, John
Hillhouse, Esquires.
        Andrew Jackson, Alfred Balch & Thos Crutcher exrs of Wm T Lewis. Debt. Plfs
recover agt dft $150 debt, damages, costs. Dft granted appeal to Circuit Court.
p.56   Henry Scales v Gray Edwards. Trespass. Continued till next Court.
        Recognizance of Somerset Moore Esqr, to give evidence this day in behalf
State against William R Davis for gaming.
        Recognizance, Henry Hagen & Lusk Colville, attend next term & give evidence
behalf State against William R Davis for gaming.
p.57   Joseph Boyd v Absolum Boren. Debt. Capias returned Not Found, alias not
being ordered by plf, suit is discontinued & plf pays costs.
        Robert Wilson v Thomas Smith. Plf not appearing, suit is dismissed, plf to
pay the costs.
        Recognizance George Taylor to give evidence next term in behalf State
p.58   against John Hamblin for fornication.
        Recognizance James Harwell to appear next term to give evidence behalf
State against John Hamblin for fornication.
        Recognizance George Taylor to appear next term to give evidence behalf
p.59   State against Sally Doolin for fornication.
        Recognizance James Harwell to attend next Court to give evidence behalf
State against Sally Doolin for fornication.
        Recognizance Nelson Patteson Esqr to attend next term to prosecute in
p.60   behalf State against William R Davis for gaming.
        Grand Jury Indictments: State v John Hamblin, true bill; State v Sally
Doolin, true bill; State v William R Davis, true bill.
        Nathl Taylor v James Ashmore & Robert Campbell. Continued till next Court.
        Court adjourned till Court in Course. Somerset Moore, N Moody, N Patteson.
[blank page]
[p.60 is repeated here without the adjournment and with the following suit]
        William Parker v Jesse Kirkland. Attachment. Defendant came not. Plfs
p.61   declaration being unanswered, plf recovers agt dft the debt with legal
interest computed according to specialty, and his costs of suit.
        Ordered that Court be adjourned till Court in Course.

p.62   Court of pleas & quarter Sessions holden for Giles County at the courthouse
in Pulaski, first Monday in March 1814. Present John Dickey, John Henderson, and
Pleasant Moore, esqrs.
        Deed Buckner Harwell Senr to John B Goldsbury 250 acres ackd.
        Jonathan Richards v Philmer Green. Trespass. John Evans Senr security for

appearance of Philmer Green surrenders him to Court. William Fullerton bail for sd Philmer.

Release John Bigham from tax on 1800 acres wrongly listed to him for 1813.

Deed/gift Polly Graves to Frances Yancy Graves, Sally Yancy Graves & Eliza Patteson Graves proved by Gabriel Bumpass and Thomas Barnet subscribing witnesses p.63   thereto, ordered registered together with certificate of William Riddle the present husband of sd Polly approving the execution of sd deed.

Grand Jurors: John Temple foreman, Wm Welch, David W Porter, Alexr Jones, John Young, Thos McKissack, Geo Malone, David Campbell, John Menifee, John Hanna, Adam Burney, James Lindsey, Walter Locke.

Order William Wells, Wm Abernathy, Thos Westmoreland, Lewis Brown & Marcus Mitchell or any four of them view site whereon John Butler wishes to build a mill on Richland creek.

p.64   Appoint Mathew Benthall overseer/road in room of Walter Locke resigned.

Appt John Elliott overseer/road in room of John Hannah resigned.

Appt Martin Shaddon overseer/road in room of Robert Wilson resigned.

Deed Abel Olive to Joel Lane 600 acres proven by Samuel Shields & Solomon Tuttle subscribing witnesses thereto.

Deed David W McRee & James C McRee to James Haynes Senr 155 acres proven by John Henderson and James S Haynes subscribing witnesses thereto.

Deed David W McRee and James C McRee to Andrew Haynes 50 acres proven by John Henderson and James S Haynes subscribing witnesses thereto.

p.65   Appt Micajah Ezel overseer/road in room of William B Brooks resigned.

John Henderson esqr returned list/taxable property in Capt Youngs Company. [As above: Samuel Shields in Capt Campbells company; Maximillion H Buchanan in Capt Bentsons company]

Brice M Garner & Jared Manifee admrs/estate of Alexander Laughlin deceased returned account of sale of sd estate.

Commissioners apptd to let to lowest bidder the bridge across Moore Creek made report: Nathaniel Moody one of the commrs undertakes same for $128 and has completed sd bridge which is received: Ralph Graves, Somerset Moore. Commrs also returned Nathaniel Moodys obligation to keep sd bridge in repair for five years.

p.66   Order County Trustee pay Nathaniel C Moody $128 for building bridge across Moores Creek and keeping same in repair for five years.

Recognizance Nancy Postin, to give evidence behalf State against John Gregory for A&B on her by sd John Gregory.

Appt Samuel Woods overseer/road in room of William Stanford resigned.

p.67   Order hands of John Lee, John Williams & [blank] Simms be added to hands that work under William Nail overseer of Montgomerys Gap road from Richland Creek to Parks Baileys.

John Doe lessee of John Strother & James Bright v Jacob Winterbower & George Winterbower. Dfts in proper person say they cannot deny they are guilty of trespass. Plf recovers agt dfts their Term yet to come in the messuage & tract in declaration mentioned, and also recover agt dfts their costs of suit.

p.68   Recognizance Washington Croft to prosecute & give evidence behalf State against William B Brooks for assault & battery on sd Croft.

Recognizance Washington Croft to prosecute & give evidence behalf State against Robert Paine for assault & battery on sd Croft.

Recognizance Washington Croft to prosecute & give evidence behalf state against Robert Williams for assault & battery on sd Croft.

p.69   Grant ltrs/admn on estate of William G Pickens decd to Andrew Pickens and Israel Pickens.

Grant ltrs/admn on estate of John G Pickens to Isreal Pickens.

Lunsford M Bramlett Esqr produced licence to practice law; qualified & is admitted to practice in this court.

Order Thomas Westmoreland Esqr to take a list of taxable property in Captain Butlers company.

Will of Mary Maxwell decd proven by oath of Andrew M[in binding] one of the witnesses thereto. On application of John Henderson & Andrew McMekin, order letters of admn on estate of Mary Maxwell decd with will annexed issue to sd John Henderson
p.70   & Andrew McMekin they having qualified & given bond and security. Inventory of estate returned.

James Stewart & Co assee vs Gabriel Bumpass. Dft in proper person confesses he is justly indebted to plfs $26.40 and costs. Plfs recover agt dft sd sums.
p.71   Order Caleb Hill, David Flint, Charles Robertson, Jonathan Moody, Phillup Huggins Tyree Rhodes & John Hannah or five of them view the part of Little Tombigby road which lies between James Lindseys & Joseph Fannings and turn road if they think proper; make report to next Court.

At least five Justices present, William McKinnsy produced a wolf scale more than four months old which was ordered to be burnt.

Deed William Webster & Catherine his wife to Jesse Clark for their interest in a tract of land in Orange County North Carolina ackd by Wm Webster.

Appt Robert Buchanan & Pleasant Moore esqrs to take privy examination of
p.72   Catherine Webster touching her execution of deed to Jesse Clark.

Robt Buchanan & Pleasant Moore examined Catherine Webster apart from her husband and she executed ss deed freely without constraint of her husband.

Deed John Wheeler to Joseph Smith 99 acres in Sulivan County was proven by Robert Birdwell one of the subscribing witnesses thereto.

Appt Thomas Alsup overseer/road in room of Josiah Stoval resigned.

Appt Isaac Johnston overseer/road in room of John Yancy resigned.
p.73   Appt Larken Webb overseer/road in room of John Resenhover resigned.

Appt Solomon Stone Jr overseer/road in room of John G Russel resigned.

Order James Starks James Neal Duncan McIntire Samuel Smith William Ragsdale & Gabriel Bumpass or five of them view a road from Huntsville Road near Doctor Bumpasses through Elkton on Reality to intersect Huntsville road in Madison County.

Alexander Black, Hardy Hightower, Thomas Welch & James Bumpass qualified according to law as Justices of the Peace in this County.

Licence William Price to keep ordinary for one year.

Order Alfred M Harris, Henry Hagen & German Lester superintend the making a paper press for use of the clerk of this Court, the price of which is not to exceed
p.74 $75 and make report to next Court.

Andrew Clark & wife v Leanna Franks. Case. Plf in proper person assumes all costs and directs that this suit be dismissed; pay defendants costs of defence.

Appoint James Stark, Douglas Blue, Maximillion H Buchanan, James Neil, James Williams, John Easley, John Ray, Nelson Patteson, George Brown, Thomas Harwood, Alexander Hood, John Hawkins or five of them to view a road from Manifees ford on Elk river to intersect a road lately cut from Huntsville to state line in a direction to Pulaski and make report to next Court.

Court adjourned till tomorrow ten Oclock. Jacob Byler, John Dabney, J Henderson, Robert Buchanan.

p.75 Tuesday 8th March 1814. Present Jacob Byler, John Dabney, John Henderson.
Andrew Pickens & Israel Pickens admrs/estate of William G Pickens decd
returned an inventory of sd estate.
Robert Buchanan Esqr returned list/taxable property in Capt Harwells comy.
[Similar item for James McDonald in Capt Marks company]
Appt Douglass Blue constable in Capt Starks company.
Maxamilian H Buchanan Esqr elected Sheriff; Buchanan took oaths required by
law, and entered bond and security.
p.76 Deed William Wells to Robert Adams 100 acres ackd.
Deed Jno Averett to Jno Pate 59 acres proven by Martin Lorance & Wm Steele.
Appt John B Walker constable in Capt Campbells company.
Appt William Stoval constable in Capt Paxtons company.
Appt Campbell Mayfield constable in William Hendersons company.
Appt Harrison Hicks constable in Capt Smiths company.
Appt Thomas Marks constable in Capt Marks company.
p.77 Appt Robert Campbell overseer/road in room of James Ashmore resigned.
Samuel Jones Esq returned list/taxable property in Capt Newlins and Capt
Gordons companies.
Order County trustee to pay Nelson Patteson Esqr $9.71 the amount of
damages sustained by sd Patteson in consequence of the Fayetteville road running on
his land as ascertained by a jury appointed to assess the same.
Grant ordinary licence to David Sims for one year.
Order County trustee pay German Lester Clerk/Court $40 for exofficio
services for one year prior to this time, also $15 for recording tax list of this
p.78 county for 1813.
Recognizance William Noblit & William Caldwell, Wm Noblit to make appearance at next term and to demean himself peacefully towards good citizens and particularly towards John Boyd of this County.
Order County trustee pay James Buford late sheriff $50 for exofficio
services for one year prior to this time.
Deed George Breckenridge to John Hughes 150 acres proved by Thos Cavnas and
Nedom Cavnas witnesses thereto.
p.79 Will of James Johnston decd proven by [blank] Abernathy one of the witnesses thereto, & Matthew Johnston & John Johnston executors therein named qualified.
John Forgey v John Cabe. Case. Referees return award: Dft to pay plf $16
and all costs. Signed by John Dickey, Israel Pickens, Walter Lock. Order plf re-
p.80 cover agt dft afsd sum and his costs of suit.
Order John Kenneday with hands under his direction open & keep in repair
the road lately marked out beginning where road from Fayetteville by way of
McCullins intersects the line dividing Giles & Lincoln counties thence towards
Pulaski uintill it intersects road from Robert Alsups to Pulaski, and when opened,
the road from which this is turned to be discontinued as a public highway.
Commrs apptd to settle with Alexander Miller, admrs/estate of Andrew Miller
decd, report they allowed Alexr Miller $159.80 his claim against the estate; signed
p.81 by John Dickey, John Hillhouse, James Ashmore.
Excuse Joseph Jerman from further service as a juror this term.
Nathaniel Moody Esqr resigned as Justice/peace.
Court adjourned till tomorrow 10 Oclock. William Mayfield, Pleasant Moore,
N Patteson.

p.82   Wednesday 9th March 1814. Present John Dickey, Nelson Patteson, Pleasant Moore, Esquires.
        Thos Westmoreland Esqr returned list/taxable property Capt Phillips compy.
[Similar entries for Pleasant Moore in Capt Reeds company; Wm Mayfield in Capt Hendersons company; John Hillhouse in Capt Pickens company]
        Mortgage Zacheus Hurt & Elizabeth his wife to John B Prendergast ackd.
        Order Nelson Patteson & Jacob Byler Esqrs take privy examination of Elizabeth Hurt touching her execution of a mortgage to Jno B Prendergast.
        Nelson Patteson & Jacob Byler returned they examined sd Elizabeth apart
p.83   from her husband; she executed same freely without threats of her husband.
        Mortgage from Zacheus Hurt & Elizabeth his wife to Jno B Prendergast ackd.
        Order Nelson Patteson & Jacob Byler Esqr take privy exmn of Eliz Patteson who report she executed same voluntarily without pursuasions of her husband.
        Order Sheriff summon Mathew Brown & Thomas Marks to attend Court next term.
        Order Shff summon Campbell Mayfield & Harrison Hicks two constables of this County to attend Circuit Court at the next term.
p.84   State v John Counts. Fornication. Dft in proper person pleads guilty; fined $1.66¾ and pay costs of prosecution.
        Nathaniel Moody Esq returns list/taxable property in Capt Smiths company.
        State v William H Murry. Fornication. Dft being on tour of duty to Creek nation, order cause continued till next Court.
        State v Patsey Owens. Fornication. State no further prosecutes.
        Grant ordinary licence to Thomas Smith for one year.
p.85   State v Thomas Smith. Gaming. Jury Israel Pickens, John Hicks, Alexander Tarpley, Ralph Graves, John Yancy, Lester Morris, Samuel Cox Sr, Claibourn McVay, Jacob Crowsen, William Crittenton, Lewis Brown, Wm B Brown find dft guilty. Fined $4 and pay costs of prosecution.
        John Black & wife v William Cremore. A&B. Parties in proper persons; final determination of this case refered to John B Prendergast, Wm Mayfield Esqr, German Lester, Henry Hagen, Samuel Y Anderson whose award to be judgmt of Court.
p.86   William Cremer & wife v John Black & wife. Case. Parties in proper persons, case refered to final determination of John B Prendergast, Wm Mayfield Esq, German Lester, Henry Hagen, Saml Y Anderson whose award to be judgment of Court.
        William Cremer & wife v John Black. A&B. Parties in proper persons, final final determination of case refered to John B Prendergast, Wm Mayfield Esq, German Lester, Henry Hagen & Saml Y Anderson whose award to be judgment of the Court.
        William Cremer & wife v John Black & wife. A&B. Parties in proper persons;
p.87   case refered to determination of Jno B Prendergast, Wm Mayfield Esq, German Lester, Henry Hagen & Saml Anderson whose award to be judgment of the Court.
        Grand jury returned Bill/Indictment: State agt Wm B Brooks, Robt Williams & Robt Paine a true bill.
        State v William R Davis. Gaming. Dft in proper person pleads guilty; fined $5 and pay costs of prosecution. Recognizance Nelson Patteson to give evidence behalf the State against Thomas Wilkison.
p.88   Recognizance Nelson Patteson, to attend from day to day & prosecute and give evidence in behalf of the State against Thomas Wilkinson.
        [Second and third recognizances, worded as above]
p.89   State v William B Brooks. Keeping the peace. Sd defendant discharged from his recognizance.
        State v Robert Paine. Keeping the peace. Sd defendant discharged from his

recognizance.
    Ordered tax list of Philips & Harris 1400 acres on Richland & Elk be received and the double tax be remitted.
p.90   State v Robert Williams. Keeping the peace. Defendant discharged from his recognizance.
    State v William B Brooks. A&B on Washington Croft. Pleaded not guilty.
    State v Robt Paine. A&B on Washington Croft. Pleaded not guilty.
    State v Robt Williams. A&B on Washington Croft. Pleaded not guilty.
p.91   Recognizance Alfred Yancy to attend day to day to give evidence behalf State against Thomas Wilkinson for petit larceny.
    Recognizance Alfred Yancy to attend day to day to give evidence behalf State against Thomas Wilkinson for neglect/duty as overseer/road.
    Recognizance, William B Brooks & Robert Paine to attend day to day to
p.92   answer State for A&B on Washington Croft by sd Brooks.
    Robert Paine and William B Brooks recognizance, condition sd Robert Paine attend day to day to answer State for A&B on Washington Croft.
    Robert Williams and John Butler recognizance, condition Williams attend day to day to answer State for A&B on Washington Croft.
p.93   Appt John Samuel overseer/road in room of Matthew Anderson resigned.
    State v Robert Taylor. Continued to next Court in consequence of the absence of the prosecutor who is on a tour of duty to the Creek nation.
    Court adjourned till Tomorrow 9 Oclock. John Hillhouse, James Bumpass, Pleasant Moore.

p.94   Thursday 10th March. Present John Hillhouse, James Bumpass, Pleasant Moore.
    State v William B Brooks. A&B on Washington Croft. Jury Thos Wilkison, John Hicks, Wm Brown, John McKissack, Thos Crenshaw, Spencer Clack, Rolen Brown, Wm B Pepper, Thos B Hainie, William Hamby, David Read, Robt McNairy. Dft acquitted.
p.95   Grand Jury Bills/Indictment: State v Thomas Wilkinson, true bill; Same v Same, not true bill; Same v Same, not true bill.
    Francis Adams v James Coursey. Trover. Continued till next Court.
    Grand Jury bill/Indictment: State v Thomas Wilkinson, true bill.
    Appt William Kindel overseer/road in room of John Graves resigned.
p.96   State v Robert Paine. A&B on Washington Croft. Jury Israel Pickens, Thos Smith, John Clack, John Anderson, Robt Shane, Wm Fullerton, Andw McPeters, Caleb Friley, Wm L Campbell, Elisha Mayfield, Wm Kindel, Tobias Miller. Dft acquitted.
    Court adjourns till tomorrow 9 Oclock. Jno Dickey, Jas Bumpass, N Patteson.

p.97   Friday March 11th. Present John Dickey, James Bumpass, Nelson Patteson.
    State v Robert Williams. A&B on Washington Croft. Defendant acquitted.
    State v Thomas Wilkinson. Neglect duty as overseer of road. Jury Israel Pickens, Jno Hicks, Thomas C Stone, Wm L Campbell, Thos Wells, David Read, Alexr Miller, John McKissack, Robt Campbell, Brice M Mayfield, John Gregory, Caleb White find dft not guilty. Defendant acquitted.
p.98   State v William B Brooks. A&B on Washington Croft. Motion of Robert Mack defts counsel, order Washington Croft pay costs of prosecution. Counsel for state obtained appeal to Circuit Court.
    State v Robert Paine. A&B on Washington Croft. On motion of Robert Mack

dft's counsel, order Washington Croft pay costs of prosecution. Counsel for state
obtained appeal to Circuit Court.
p.99   State v Robert Williams. A&B on Washington Croft. Order judgment entered up
for all costs.
        Appt William Neal overseer of Fayetteville Road from East end of Madison
Street in Pulaski to fork of road near Solomon Assbels, hands to work thereon:
Nelson Patteson, James Patteson, Robert McNairy, Joseph Dickson, David Dickson,
John Anderson, Alfred Yancy, sd Neals.
p.100   Order County tax for 1814 be as follows:

On each hundred acres of land		.18¾
" town lot		.37½
" Free poll		.12½
" Slave		.25
" Stud horse		.25
" Merchants licence		5.00
" 4 Wheel pleasure carriage		2.00
" 2 wheel do		1.00

Rates for Ordinary Keepers:

Breakfast Dinner & Supper	.25
Horse to corn & fodder 12 hours	.25
Single Horse feed	.12½
Lodging	.08
Rum by the half Pint	.37½
Brandy do	.12½
Whiskey do	.12½

        Jurors to next Court: Joseph Lann, Eli Tidwell Senr, Alexander Miller,
p.101   Edward J Bailey, Wilton F L Jenkins, William Woods, William Graves, John
Stephens, William Ezell, Humphrey Tompkins, Larkin Conden, Henry Steele, Stephen
Anderson, William Beaty, Caleb Hill, David Flint, James Knox, Rolin Brown, William
Maples, Aquilla Wilson, Daniel Molloy, David Baker, Major Harrolson, John Kenan,
Drury Stovall, John Paul Senr.
        James Buford Sheriff & Collector of publick & County tax for 1813 reports
taxes remaining unpaid and that he cannot find any goods & chattels to owners
thereof whereon he can distrain for same: [amount of tax due is here omitted]
John Baldridge 160 Elk River; John Childers 4700 Richland Creek & 1000 Elk River;
heirs of Landon Carter 4000 Richland; Francis Childs 3000 Richd; Joseph East 200
p.102   Pidgeon Roost Cr; Joseph Greer 1000 Richland; Richard Hightower 640 Richland & 230 Bradshaws Cr & 100 Buchanans Cr; Hightower & Haywood 1100 Robertsons
fork; Robert Lanier 500 west of Elk river; Hightower & Haywood 500 Richland Cr 2½
miles below Pulaski; James Lewis 400 acres saved out of a 2000 acre entry; William
B Lewis 300 south side Elk River; James Morrison 1200 acres Buchanans Creek; John
McDonald 227 Buchanan Cr; James C McRee & David W McRee 840 Robertsons Cr; Est of
Hardy Murphey 640 &* 427; William Neal 100 Richland Cr; Isaac Price 1000 mouth of
Ricd Cr; Jacob Perkins 4000 Richland Cr; Thos Whitson 140 Elk River; James Temple
300 Elk River & 39 Reynolds Cr & 126 ditto & 86 Sinking Cr; James Read Junr 4657
Richland Cr & 1 white poll & 1 black; Edward Thursby 10 part of an Old Grant to
p.103   Stokely Donaldson; John Wilson 5000 Blue Cr; Order judgment enter agt
owners of sd land repectively; land or so much thereof as will be sufficient, to be
sold at the Courthouse in Pulaski.
        James Buford Sheriff & Collector reports land not listed for taxation for

MARCH 1814

1813 and therefore subject to double tax: John Drake 80 acres North side Elk River fractional section in range 1. Order judgment agt owner of sd tract.
p.104   George W Scott an orphan bound an apprentice to James H Pickens, an indenture to that effect between John Dickey Esq chmn/Court & sd James H Pickens.
Order John Dickey, Pleasant Moore & John Hillhouse Esqrs let to lowest bidder the keeping of Samuel Scott & Edney Scott two orphan children for one year after giving publick notice of time & place previous to sd letting.
p.105   State v Thos Wilkinson. Neglect of duty as overseer/road. Judgment entered according to act of assembly for all costs.
State v John Gregory. A&B on Nancy Postin. Nancy Postin came not. Sci Fa issues agt her returnable to next Court.
p.106   Order German Lester oversee clearing out of Madison Street from east end of sd street to first street in Pulaski, and sd Lester oversee building of a bridge across Pleasant run where Madison Street crosses same, and all hands within bounds of town of Pulaski work on sd street & bridge under direction of sd Lester.
Deed Thomas Goff to Walter Lock 300 acres ackd.
Grand Jury presentment, State v Jessee Vinsent. Same v Levi Cooper.
p.107   State v John Read Junr. Same v William Holt. Same v Tyree Rodes.
State v Tyree Rodes. Neglect of duty as overseer/road. Dft in proper person; fined 6½¢ and pay costs of prosecution.
Court adjourned till tomorrow at Ten Oclock. N Patteson James Bumpass Pleasant Moore.

p.108   Saturday March 12. Present Nelson Patteson, James Bumpass, Pleasant Moore.
Order Robert Gordon, John McCanless, Martin Franks, John Clark, Richard Mc-Gee, John Ross, Joseph German view part of the Shelbyville road near Widow Hainies plantation & see if it be proper to turn sd road agreeable to wish of Mrs. Hainie.
John Doe lessee of William Shepperd v Thomas Taylor & Abraham Byler. Ejectment. Plf dismisses suit and pays costs.
Thomas Goff v Absolom Boren Junr. Trespass. Capias retd Not Found by Sheriff; alias not having beenordered by plf, order suit dismissed. Plf pays costs.
State v Thomas Wilkinson. Petit Larceny. Grand Jury returned Not a true
p.109   Bill; judgment according to act of assembly for all costs.
State v Thomas Wilkinson. Grand Jury retd Not a true Bill[as above]
Appt Thomas C Stone overseer/Second Street in Pulaski in room of Archibald McKissack removed and all hands residing on Second & Third Street work thereon.
p.110   Order Thos C Stone overseer/Second St have leave to call on hands bound by law to work on first Street for one days work to work on sd Second Street.
Ordered that German Lester overseer of First Street in Pulaski have leave to call on hands bound by law to work on Second St for one days work on First St.
Reuben Smith v Lawson Hobson. Certiorari. Plf came not. Suit dismissed; dft recovers of plaintiff his costs about his defence expended.
p.111   Grand Jury Presentments: State v George Agnew. Same v Richard Conway. Same v Nathaniel Moody. Same v Thomas Smith. Same v William R Davis. Same v Henry Hagen. Same v Thomas Killebru.
Grand Jury Bill/Indictment: State v John Gregory, not a true bill.
p.112   Order all hands that live within the bounds where Matthew Benthal is overseer work on said road under his direction.
State v John Gregory. A&B on Nancy Postin. Judgment according to act of

15

JUNE 1814

assembly for all costs.

John Black & wife v William Creamer. A&B. John Black directs this suit be dismissed & defendant recovers of plf his costs of defence.

p.113   William Creamer & wife v John Black & wife. Case. Parties in proper persons; Dft assumes all costs whereupon plf directs suit be dismissed.

William Creamer & wife v John Black. A&B. Parties in proper persons; dft assumes all costs whereupon plf directs suit be dismissed.

p.114   William Creamer & wife v John Black & wife. A&B. Parties in proper persons; dft assumes all costs; whereupon plf directs suit be dismissed.

Court adjourned till Court in Course. James Bumpass, N Patteson, Pleasant Moore.

p.115   Court of pleas & Quarter Sessions met at the place where the Courthouse formerly stood on Monday 6th June 1814. Present Nelson Patteson, James Bumpass, John Dickey, John Hillhouse, John Henderson, Samuel Smith, William Mayfield, Esq.

The Courthouse being burnt It is ordered that Court be adjourned to meet instanter at the house of Deery & Martin in the town of Pulaski. Present Nelson Patteson, Samuel Smith, James Bumpass, Esquires.

Excuse William Woods from further service as a juror at this term.

At least five justices present, Drew Benson produced six wolf scalps under four months old which was ordered to be burnt.

p.116   At least five justices present, Samuel Wright produced one wolf scalp over four months old which was ordered to be burnt.

Grant ordinary licence to John Gough.

Grant ltrs/admn on estate of Joel M Alsup to John Alsup Senr.

Tax lists received & double tax thereon remited: Saml Chambers 1 white poll & 1 slave. James Brown 79¼ acres, 1 white poll.

Andrew Pickens admr of Wm G Pickens decd returned account/sale of estate.

Admrs of Mary Maxwell decd returned account/sale of sd estate.

p.117   Appt William Maples overseer/road in room of Drury Alsup resigned.

Appt George Watters[Matten?] overseer/road in room of Wm Stovall resigned.

Appt Adam Burnett overseer/road in room of Saml Chambers resigned.

State v William Noblet. Keeping peace. William Caldwell bound last court for appearance of William Noblet surrenders sd Noblet who is committed to custody of the sheriff.

Order County trustee pay Nathaniel Moody $1.50 the balance due for building the bridge across Moores Creek.

p.118   Deed George Brown to Richard Atkins 100 acres ackd.

State v John Hamlin. Fornication. William Caldwell surrenders sd John Hamlin who is committed to the custody of the sheriff.

State v Sally Doolin. Fornication. Elisha Kimbro surrenders sd Sally Doolin

p.119   who is committed to the custody of the sheriff.

Appt John Young overseer/road in room of John Kenneday resigned.

Deed Andrew Erwin to William Nelson 88 acres proven by Saml Smith & Eliab Vinson two of the subscribing witnesses thereto.

Deed Andw Erwin to John Nelson 172 ac proven by Eliab Vinson & Saml Smith.

16

JUNE 1814

Deed Andrew Erwin to Samuel Smith 281 acres proved by Eliab Vinson.

p.120   Deed/gift Ambrose Foster to Polly Winn and others proven by Aquilla Wilson and Abraham Brown.

Ltrs/admn on estate of Minor Winn decd issued to Isham Brown.

Grand Jury: William Maples foreman, David Baker, Henry F Steele, Stephen Anderson, John Stephens, William Graves, Humphrey Tompkins, Wilton F L Jenkins, James Knox, Eli Tidwell Senr, Caleb Hill, John Paul Senr, Drury Stovall.

Petit Jury: David Flint, John Keenan, Larkin Cardin, William Ezell, Daniel Molloy, Alexander Miller, Edmd J Bailey, Rowlin Brown, Major Harrelson, Aquilla Wilson, Joseph Lann.

p.121   Ordered to be under Larkin Webb overseer/road: Thomas Bullman, John Reasonhover, Benjamin Ishmael Shadrack Cross, Henry Cross, John Wright McNite, Samuel McNite, Bennett Creesy, Abraham Brown, Stroud McCormack, Joshua Fitch, James Brown, William Watson.

Grant ltrs/admn on estate of Ambrose Foster decd to Isham Brown.

Order road lately marked out from Huntsville road near Doct Bumpass by Elkton to Madison County line to be opened.

p.122   Order Nelson Patteson, Wm Mayfield, Samuel Y Anderson, Maxamilian H Buchanan & German Lester or three of them let to lowest bidder the building of a temporary jail not to exceed sixteen feet square.

Henry Wilcher v Solomon Asbell. Debt. David Dickson & Joseph Dickson surrender Solomon Asbell who is committed to custody of the sheriff.

Order County trustee pay Saml Y Anderson & German Lester $25 for a paper press & mountain built by an order of last court.

p.123   State v John Linn[Lum?]. Grand Larceny. Court having no furisdiction & dft being discharged from recognizance, order judgmt entered favour of those entitled for all costs, & Fred. Harwell be allowed $5.25.

Court adjourned till tomorrow 9 Oclock to meet at the House of Thomas Smith in Pulaski.   John Dickey, James McDonald, Richard Flynt.

p.124   Tuesday 7th June. Present John Dickey, James McDonald, Richard Flynt, Esqs.

Recognizance of John Dewaser to prosecute and give evidence behalf state agt Thos Goff for assault on John Dewaaser.

Recognizance of John Dewaser to prosecute and give evidence behalf state against Thomas Goff for assault on William Dewaser.

Recognizance of John Dewaser to prosecute and give evidence behalf state
p.125   against Thomas Goff for malicious mischief.

Appt Robert McMeekin constable in Capt Youngs company.

Order Larkin Cardin oversee part of road lately marked which lies between Doct Gabriel Bumpass's to the plumb orchard gap; hands in following bounds to work thereon, begin at NW corner land of Doct Bumpass, running S to include two William Crittentons and Hugh Adams, thence to Butlers ford to Indian line leaving Thomas Westmoreland on west thence with sd line to include Aaron Brown to mouth of Buchanans creek thence N & W to beginning.

p.126   Appt John Gordon constable in Capt Gordons company.

Appt John Buchanan constable in Capt Bensons company.

Noncupative will of William Smith decd proven by Wm Stovall & Joshua Finch.

Recognizance William Dewaser to give evidence behalf State agt Thomas Goff for assault on John Dewaser.

17

Recognizance Wm Dewaser to give evidence behalf State against Thomas Goff
p.127   for assault on William Dewaser.

Recognizance William Dewaser to give evidence behalf State against Thomas Goff for malicious mischief.

Recognizance William L Campbell to prosecute & give evidence behalf State against William Kindall for assault & battery on Wm L Campbell.

p.128   Appt James Ashmore constable in Capt Hills company.

Appt Richard McGehee overseer/Shelbyville Road, the part lately viewed near the plantation of Mrs. Haynie.

John Bryant v Washington Croft. Case. Plf failing to give additional security for prosecution as ordered, suit dismissed; dft recovers agt dft his costs.

p.129   John Alsup v Caleb Friley. Certiorari. Grant plf leave to amend original attachment and cause continued till next Court.

At least five justices present, David Wilcockson produced one wolf scalp over four months old which was ordered to be burnt.

Order James Graham overseer/road in room of Nicholas Welch Junr resigned.

At least five justices present, John Wisner produced eleven wolf scalps under four months old which was ordered to be burnt.

Order James Neile oversee road from Elk River near Elkton to Madison County line, hands in bounds to work thereon: all living between Madison line and road through upper Elkton and south of Elk river and East of Indian line.

p.130   Recognizance, John Dewaaser to prosecute & give evidence next term on behalf State against Thomas Goff for assault on sd Dewaaser.

Recognizance, William Dewaaser[as above] on John Dewaaser.

Recognizance, John Dewaaser to[as above] on William Dewaaser.

p.131   Recognizance, William Dewaaser[as above] on William Dewaaser.

Recognizance, John Dewaaser[as above] malicious mischief.

p.132   Recognizance, William Dewaaser[as above]

Deed John Childress to Stirling C Robertson 2027 acres proven by Alfred M Harris and Peter R Booker the subscribing witnesses thereto.

Deed John Childress to Washington L Hannum 101¾ acres proven by Alfred M
p.133   Harris and Peter R Booker the subscribing witnesses.

John Childress to Eldridge B Robertson deed for 508¾ acres proven by Alfred M Harris and Peter R Booker the subscribing witnesses thereto.

James Walker v Nelson Patteson. Debt. [This item X'd out]

p.134   James Walker v Nelson Patteson. Debt. Plfs atty producing a certified copy of a record from County Court of Cumberland in Virginia. Dft abandons his plea. Plf recovers of dft £25.14.6 Virginia currency equal to $85.75 US currency with interest thereon from 25 Dec 1802 till paid, and further sum of $11.54 costs by plf about his suit in Cumberland Court expended together with his costs in this Court.

p.135   State v Benjamin Naile. Dft in proper person. Nancy Naile not wishing to bind dft farther, he is discharged from recognizance, & assumes payment of costs.

Samuel Craig v Daniel Woods & Giddeon Pillow. Debt. Pillow voluntarily con-
p.136   fesses judgment in favour of plf; execution stayed six months.

Porter & Spencer assee v Nicholas Welch. Debt. Jury John Keenan, Larkin Condin, William Ezell, Daniel Molloy, Alex Miller, Edmd J Bailey, Rolan Brown,
p.137   Major Harrolson, Aquilla Wilson, Joseph Lawn, Thomas C Stone, Alexander Tarpley. Plf recovers against dft $26 the balance of debt & costs of suit.

Release William Batey from serving on jury at this term.

Order Edney Scott a minor girl be bound to James Tinnen, an indenture between sd Tinnen & chmn of this Court having been entered into.

p.138 Grand Jury Bills/Indictment: State v Thomas Goff, true bill; same v same, true bill; same v same; true bill, same v William Kindle, true bill.

State v George Agnew. Affray. Eli Tidwell Junr surrenders George Agnew who is committed to custody of the sheriff.

p.139 Commission James Bumpass & Robert Buchanan Esqrs to take examination and relinquishment of dower of Susannah Barnett to 318 acres in Spartenburg District in South Carolina deeded by Richard Barnett her husband to Daniel White & Isaac Smith.

Spencer Roach v Hugh Gibson. Appeal. Jury David Flint, Andrew McPeters, Simpson Lee, Jas Kimbro, Giddeon Pillow, Spencer Clack, Gabriel Fowlks, Kenson McVay, David Woods, David Read, Thomas Philips, Duncan Brown. Plf recovers of dft
p.140 $10.25 and his costs before the majistrate as in this court expended.

Charlotty Fork[Fort?] v William Davis. Debt. Jury John Keenan, Larkin Condin, Wm Ezell, Danl Molloy, Alex Miller, Edmd J Bailey, Rowlin Brown, Major Harrolson, Aquilla Wilson, Joseph Lann[Lunn?], Thos C Stone, Alexr Tarpley. Plf
p.141 recovers of dft $100 debt, damages $47.25, and her costs of suit.

At least five justices present, Dennis Harty produced a wolf scalp over four months old which was ordered to be burnt.

Recognizance George Agnew, Lewis Kirk, Jno Elliott, John Davis and Sampson McConn, condition George Agnew attend day to day to answer State for affray.

p.142 Israel Pickens admr/estate of John G Pickens decd returned inventory.

William Sawyers v Martin Friley. Attachment. Parties in proper persons; case refered to determination of James Bumpass, John Birdwell, Duncan Brown, Roland McKinney, Mason Moss, Edward Davis & John Hawkins, to make award 5 July next.

William Robertson v James Read, Isaac Bond, Henry M Newlin. Debt. Comes
p.143 into Court William Bottom & Wm Nixon security for Isaac surrender him whereupon Wm Bottom & Robert Wilson special bail.

Brice M Mayfield v Nathan Davis & William M Keiley. Trover. Jury[above except Thomas Wilkinson for Thos Stone]. Plf recovers agt dft his damages $46.25
p.144 and his costs about his suit in this behalf expended.

Court adjourned till tomorrow morning 9 Oclock. John Dickey, N Patteson, Jacob Byler

p.145 Wednesday 8th June. Present Jno Dickey, James Bumpass, Wm Mayfield, Esqrs.

Deed George Shields and Alexr Barron to Alexr Barron Jr 105 acres proven by Robert Stephenson and John Barron.

Order this Court in future try State cases on fourth day of each term.

Recognizance William Creamer to attend day to day to prosecute & give evidence behalf State against Charles Simpson, Wm McGill & Isaac Reynolds.

p.146 Andrew Pickens v Quinton Shannon. Case. Case refered to determination of John Dickey, Saml Sheilds, George Malone, Nelson Patteson, Lewis Brown, John Clark who will meet at house of John McAnally on fourth Saturday in July.

William Noblet v John Boyd. A&B. Plaintiff to appear at next Court to shew
p.147 cause why he should not give additional security for prosecution of suit.

State v Richard Connway. Affray. Dft in proper person pleads guilty. Fined 50¢ and pay costs of this prosecution.

State v William R Davis. Gaming. Dft in proper person pleads guilty. Fined
p.148 $5 and pay costs of this prosecution.

State v George Agnew. Affray. Dft in proper person pleads guilty. Fined 50¢

and pay costs of this prosecution.
p.149   State v William Ferrell. Affray. Wm Brown and Wm F Cunningham surrender Wm
Ferrell who is committed to custody of the sheriff.
State v Thomas Smith. Gaming. Dft in proper person pleads guilty. Fined $5
p.150   and pay costs of prosecution.
Charloty Fort v William Davis. Debt. Thomas Smith and Gilbert D Taylor sur-
render William Davis who is committed to custody of the sheriff.
State v Thomas Killebru. Affray. Dft in proper person pleads guilty. Fined
p.151 $1 and pay costs of this prosecution.
State v Levi Cooper. Affray. Dft in proper person pleads guilty. Fined $1
and pay costs of this prosecution.
State v William Ferrell. Affray. Dft pleads guilty. Fined 6¼¢ and pay costs
p.152   of this prosecution.
Grand Jury Bills/Indictment: State v Oliver Woods, true bill; Same v James
H Williams, true bill; Same v Isaac Reynolds & others, true bill.
State v Robert Taylor. A&B on John Boyd. Dft pleaded not guilty. Jury John
p.153   Keenan, Larkin Cardin, Wm Ezell, Daniel Molloy, Elisha Kimbro, Edmund J
Bailey, Rolin Brown, Major Harrolson, Aquilla Wilson, Joseph Lann, George Malone,
Robt McNairy find dft guilty. Fined $5 and pay costs of this prosecution.
Order Robert Buchanan, Henry Hagen, M H Buchanan settle with Thomas West-
moreland executor of Jesse Westmoreland decd and make report to this Court.
p.154   Grant ltrs/admn with will annexed on estate of William Smith decd to Alexr
McDonald, he having been qualified & given bond & security.
State v John Read Jr. Affray. Dft in proper person pleads guilty. Fined 6¼¢
and pay costs of this prosecution.
Recognizance Robert Taylor, Wm W Crittenton & John Hammons, condition sd
p.155   Robert Taylor appear 4th day next term; in meantime demean himself peace-
ably towards good citizens & particularly towards John Boyd of this County.
Recognizance John Caldwell, Edmund J Bailey, Thos Read & Hardin Taylor
indebted to Elizabeth McKinney, condition sd John Caldwell pay sd Elizabeth McKinney
$25 annually for five years (provide infant sd to be begotten on sd Elizabeth
McKinney by sd John Caldwell live so long) and further that sd John Caldwell keep
sd infant free from becoming a charge to this County.
p.156   State v William Kindle. A&B on Wm L Campbell. Dft in proper person pleads
guilty; fined $1 and pay costs of this prosecution.
State v Wm H Murrah. Fornication. Dft hath died since finding of this bill.
Cause is not farther prosecuted for the State.
p.157   State v John Hamblen. Fornication. George Taylor prosecutor came not;
judgment Ni-si entered agt him.
State v John Hamblen. Fornication. State no further prosecutes.
State v Sally Doolin. Fornication. George Taylor bound in recognizance to
p.158   prosecute came not; judgment Ni-si entered against him.
State v Sally Doolin. Fornication. State no further prosecutes dft.
State v William Holt. Affray. Dft in proper person pleads guilty. Fined $1
p.159   and pay costs of this prosecution.
Henry Scales v Gray Edwards. Trespass. Parties in proper persons; plf
assumes half costs and directs suit be dismissed; dft assumes other half of costs.
Perry Cohea v Philip Parchman. Plf by his atty assumes all costs and
directs suit be dismissed; dft recovers against plaintiff his costs of defence.
p.160   John G Powell v Orpha Black. Sci Fa. Plf releases dft from forfeiture on

JUNE 1814

the payment of all costs.
State v Nathaniel Moody. Betting on a game of cards. Upon arrainment
pleaded not guilty.
Court adjourned till tomorrow morning nine Oclock. John Dickey, N Patteson,
Jacob Byler.

p.161   Wednesday 9th June. Present Jno Dickey, Nelson Patteson, Jacob Byler Esqrs.
State v Patsey Owens. Fornication. Nole Prosequi entered last Court; judg-
ment entered in favour of those entitled for all costs.
State v William H Murrah. Fornication. Nole prosequi entered[as above]
p.162   State v John Hamblen. Fornication. Nole prosequi [as above]
State v Sally Doolin. Fornication. Nole prosequi [as above]
State v Nathaniel Moody. Gaming. John Turner summoned to give evidence
p.163   behalf State came not; Sci fa issue returnable to next Court.
State v Nathaniel Moody. Gaming. Dft in proper person. Jury John Keenan,
Larkin Condin, William Ezell, Danl Molloy, Edmd J Bailey, Rolin Brown, Major
Harrolson, Aquilla Wilson, Joseph Lann, Lewis Kirk, Joseph Anthony, Thomas C Stone
say dft is guilty; fine $5 and pay costs of this prosecution.
p.164   At least five justices present, Andrew Blythe produced three wolf scalps
over four months old which was ordered to be burnt.
State v Henry Hagen. Gaming. Jury[above] say dft is guilty. Fine $5 and pay
p.165   costs of this prosecution.
Deed Thomas Britton to John Elliss and wife for 250 acres ackd.
Deed/gift Thomas Britton to John Elliss and wife ackd.
Deed Thomas Britton to John Kenneday and wife 250 acres ackd.
Deed/gift Thomas Britton to John Kenneday & wife ackd.
p.166   Deed Reese Porter to heirs of Rees Porter Junr 366½ acres ackd.
Deed Rees Porter to John Porter 279½ acres ackd.
Deed Rees Porter to Robert Weakley 611 acres ackd.
Appt Joseph Johns overseer/Prewetts Gap road in room of John McAnnally.
p.167   Order Tyree Rodes overseer/Little Tombigby road have following hands to
work thereon: Isaac Moody, Matthew Richards, David Smith, Solomon Dearman, Thos
Dearman Jr.
State v William Noblet. Keeping peace. Dft in proper person. John Boyd the
prosecutor not wishing to rebind dft any farther, order he be discharged from his
recognizance.
Grand Jury Bills/Presentment: State v Saml Chambers; Same v German Lester.
p.168   State v German Lester. Neglect of duty as overseer of first street in
Pulaski. Dft in proper person pleads guilty. Fine $1 and pay costs of prosecution.
State v Samuel Chambers. Neglect of duty as overseer/road. Dft in proper
p.169   person pleads guilty. Fine 6¼¢ and costs of prosecution.
John Dickinson assee v William M Marr. Debt. Dft in proper person ack he is
in debt. Plf recovers agt dft $600 debt, $82.78 damages by detention, and costs.
Plf by attorney agrees to stay execution till next Court.
p.170   Petition of William B Lewis & Margaret his wife, John H Eaton & Mira his
wife, and Charlotte Lewis praying division of tract of land Grant No 120 dated July
1788 granted by North Carolina to Micajah G Lewis, as heirs and representatives of
sd Micajah. It appearing that Thomas A Claibourne father of Ferdinand L Claibourne,
Mary Claibourne and Micajah Claibourne who are infants & in right of their mother

21

are entitled to one fifth part of sd land was duly notified on 29th April last that sd Wm, Margaret, John & Mira & Charlotte would petition for division of tract of 5000 acres, therefore order that Samuel Jones, William Woods, Robert Gordon, John Dabney, and William Dabney be commissioners to lay off and divide sd tract equally between Margaret Lewis, Mira Eaton, Charlotte Lewis, and Thomas A Claibourne father
p.171   & guardian of his infant children, Ferdinand, Mary & Micajah Claibourne.

Thos Washington & Capinan[Capusan?] White exrs of Thos Masterson decd v William M Marr. Debt. Dft in proper person ack he is indebted. Plfs recover agt dft $55.62 debt, $2.16 damages of detention and their costs of suit. Execution stayed till next Court.

p.172   Robert Cummins v John Yancy. Debt. Dft in proper person ack he is indebted. Plf recovers $340 debt, [blank] damages and costs. Plf by atty acknowledges satisfaction of above judgt to amount of $130 of which dft is released. Plf by attorney stays execution till next Court.

p.173   Wm Mayfield v Nathan Davis & Wm M Kerley. Trover. Continued to next Court.

William Ferrell v William Ball. A&B. Jury John Keenan, Larkin Condin, Wm Ezell, Danl Molloy, Edmd J Bailey, Rolin Brown, Major Harrolson, Aquilla Wilson, Thos Wilkinson, Joseph Anthony, Thos C Stone, John Newton say plf did not commit
p.174   first assault upon dft and that dft did not gently lay his hands upon the plf; they assess plaintiffs damages to 6¼¢ besides costs.

State v Thomas Wilkinson. Neglect/duty as overseer/road. Jury David Flint, Alexr Miller, John Graves, John B Prendergast, David Reed, Tyree Rodes, Isaac Mayfield, Matthew Dew, Wm Cunningham, John Waldrop, Caleb White, & Simpson Lee cannot agree. With assent of Court, jurors disperse to meet again tomorrow morning.

p.175   Francis Adams v James Coursey. [item X'd out]

p.176   William Creamer recognizance, to attend next term & give evidence against Isaac Reynolds, Wm McGill and Charles Simpson.

Court adjourned till tomorrow morning 9 Ock. John Dickey, James Bumpass, James Dugger.

p.177   Friday 10th June. Present John Dickey, Nelson Patteson, James Bumpass.

Thomas Smith v Archibald McKissack. Case. Plf came not. Dft recovers his costs about his defence in ths behalf expended.

Plummer Willis admr of William Plummer decd v Edmund J Bailey, Thomas Westmoreland, & Wm Wells. Debt. Plf came not. Dft recovers agt plf their costs.

p.178   Nathaniel Taylor v James Ashmore. Case. Jury William Ezell, Larkin Condin, Danl Molloy, Rolin Brown, Major Harrolson, Aquilla Wilson, Joseph Lann, Wm Riddle, Lewis Kirk, Zacheus Hurt, Eli Snow, Robert Wilson find dft not guilty. Dft recovers agt plf his costs of defence. Plf obtains appeal to Circuit Court.

p.179   Nathaniel Taylor v James Ashmore & Robert Campbell. Case. Jury[above] find dfts not guilty of publishing libel. Dfts recover of plf their costs of defence. Plf granted appeal to Cirucit Court.

p.180   Brice M Mayfield v Nathan Davis & Wm M Kerley. Trover. Jury Wm Ezell, Danl Molloy, Larkin Condin, Rolin Brown, Major Harrolson, Aquilla Willson, Joseph Lann, Wm Riddle, Lewis Kirk, Zacheus Hurt, Eli Snow, James Hammons say dfts are guilty;
p.181   assess plfs damage to $6.25 & costs. Dfts granted appeal to Circuit Court.

Grant ltrs/admn on estate of Somerset Moore decd to Charlotte Moore & James Buford, they having given bond and security. Charlotte Moore and James Buford admrs of estate of Somerset Moore return inventory of sd estate.

JUNE 1814

Grand Jury Bills/Presentment: State v John Gregory; Same v Gray Edwards.
p.182   Commissioners appointed to settle with Thomas Westmoreland exr of Jesse
Westmoreland decd made report which was ordered to be recorded.
William Ball v Henry Scales. Appeal. Jury Edmund J Bailey, Jas Patteson,
Saml Cox, Wm Kindle, Leonard Brown, Jno Anderson, Robt McNairy, Samson McCown,John
Yancy, Wm Bratton, Jas Bunch, Wm Martin. Plf recovers agt dft and Ransom Wells his
security on the appeal the sum of $17.21¾ debt, costs before & in this court.
p.183   Charloty Fort v William R Davis. Debt. William R Davis, Edmund J Bailey &
Ralph Graves acknowledge themselves indebted to Charloty Fort $200, condition Wm R
Davis appear here at return of Ca Fa should one issue against him in this case.
State v Gray Edwards. Affray. Dft in proper person pleads guilty. Fine $1
p.184   and pay costs of this prosecution.
Jurors to next Circuit Court: Nelson Patteson, Arthur Hicks, Alexr Black,
Jas McDonald, Geo Hillhouse, Quinton Shannon, Wm Lyon, Wm Mayfield, Samuel Shields,
Jno Henderson, Robt Oliver, Walter Lock, Thomas Westmoreland, James Buford, Andrew
Elliott, John Yancy, John Dickey, Thos Welch, Richard Flint, Buckner Harwell Junr,
Robt Buchanan, Jno Dabney, Tyree Rodes, Giddeon Pillow, Jas Dugger, William Neal.
Jurors to next County Court: John Graves, Nathan Bass, John Birdwell, John
Webb, Timothy Ezell, Thos McCearly, Wm Brown, Jas Forbes, Wm Nut, Wm Wisdom, Elias
Tidwell Junr, John Clack, Thos Harwood, Thos Rea, Buckner Harwell Sr, Lewis Brown,
p.185   Hugh Campbell, William Phillips, Wm M Marr, Wm Dabney, John Laird, Thos K
Gordon, Allen Abernathy, Lester Morris, William Smith, Joseph Knox.
Order Isaac Oxford with hands under his direction open & keep in repair the
part of Little Tombigby road lately marked by a jury leaving the road near where
George Ruff formerly lived, crossing the creek below Bylers powder mill to intersect old road near Big Creek; when so opened, that part from which this is turned
is to be discontinued as a publick highway.
Order Robert Anderson with hands under his direction open & keep in repair
p.186   the part of Little Tombigby road marked out to leave present road at foot
of ridge dividing Richland from Pidgeon Roost break at a beach marked I.B. to
follow round a knob with the blazes to old road at a beach marked R.
Brice M Mayfield v Nathan Davis & William M Kerley. Trover. Dfts granted
appeal to Circuit Court for Giles County.
William Kindle v Henry Scales. Appeal. Jury John Keenan, Jas Moore, Christopher Wright, Thos Wilkinson, Joseph Anthony, Ralph Graves, Samuel Hurt, Nathaniel
p.187   Moody, Jas H Williams, David J Robertson, Spencer Clack, Larkin Mayfield.
Plaintiff recovers agt dft and Claibourne W McVay his security $40 debt and his
costs as well before the majistrate as in this Court expended.
Court adjourned till tomorrow 9 Oclock. John Dickey, James Bumpass, James
Dugger.

p.188   Present John Dickey, James Bumpass, James Dugger, Esquires.
Francis Adams v James Coursey. Trover. Jury John Keenan, Larkin Cond, Wm
Ezell, Danl Molloy, Edmund J Bailey, Rolen Brown, Major Harrolson, Aquilla Wilson,
Thos Wilkinson, Joseph Anthony, Thos C Stone, John Newton. Plf by his attorney
tendered to Court the following Bills of Exceptance
            Francis Adams v James Coursey. June Term 1814. Plf proved by
Samuel Burton the subscribing witness to the agreement hereto attached the
execution of sd writing by defendant to plf and thereupon plf offered the same in

JUNE 1814

evidence to jury which was objected to by counsel for dft, sd objection sustained
p.189   by Court, to which opinion the plf begs leave to except and prays that his
bill of Exceptions be made part of the record which is ordered accordingly. John
Dickey, James Bumpass, John Hillhouse. Jurors afsd upon oaths say defendant is not
guilty. Dft recovers of plf his costs about his defence in this behalf expended.
Plf prays writ of error to Circuit Court which is granted.
p.190   John Paul Senr v Kinchen T Wilkinson. Deposition of John Paul Junr of Rockbridge County Virginia to be taken in behalf defendant.
     Samuel Cox v John Boyd. Case. Jury Larkin Condin, Wm Ezell, Danl Molloy,
Rolin Brown, Major Harrolson, Aquilla Wilson, Jos Lann, Elisha Mayfield, John
Abernathy, Wm Riddle, Green McCafferty, Saml Hurt assess plfs damages to $150. Plf
p.191   recovers damages and his costs of suit.
     Order County trustee pay Maxamillion H Buchanon Sheriff $17.50 for furnish-
ing guard and guarding prisoners committed to his custody during present Term.
     Order William Purnell oversee Hurtsville Road.
p.192   Wm M Kenley v Margaret Allison & Halbert Allison exrs of Frank Allison
decd. Plf in proper person assumes all costs & directs that suit be dismissed.
     Ralph Graves assee v Halbert Allison. Appeal. Plf in proper person assumes
all costs and directs that this suit be dismissed.
     Order following tax list be received, double tax thereon be remitted: Henry
Scales, 1 white poll, 1 slave.
p.193   Charlotte Moore and James Buford admrs of estate of Somerset Moore decd
returned additional inventory of sd estate. Order/sale issue to sell perishable
part of estate of Somerset Moore decd.
     Appoint Charles Buford, Joseph Anthony, German Lester to allot to Charlotte
More widow of Sommerset More decd a sufficient portion of stock corn and dead
victuals of the goods and chattels of sd deceased as will be sufficient to maintain
her and her children for one year.
     James C & David W McRee v James McCraven admr of David Stewart. Sci Fa. Dft
came not. Judgment according to Sci Facias revived against defendant in favour of
p.194   plaintiffs for sum of $290 debt, $29.36¼ damages with interest thereon from
November 1811 till paid besides their cost of suit.
     James C & David W McRee v James McCraven admr of David Stewart. Sci Fa. Dft
came not. Judgt in favour plfs for $290 with interest thereon of six percent per
annum from 12 March 1810 together with their cost of suit.
     Order William Fish oversee opening road from Plumb Orchard gap to Elkton
with hands in bounds: all between land settled by Doct Bumpass & friends and Elk
River, from Indian line north to include hands liable to work by Esqr Philips.
p.195   State v Gilbert D Taylor. Gaming. Dft in proper person pleads guilty. Fine
$5 & pay costs of this prosecution.
     Order County trustee pay Elisha Mayfield & Spencer Clack $8 for conveying
Daniel Woods to jail in Maury County at instance of Wm McNeil agt sd Woods.
p.196   Grand Jury Bills/presentment: State v William Ball; same v Gilbert D Taylor; same v Nelson Patteson; same v Henry Hagen; same v William Ball; same v Thomas
Smith; same v William Kindle; same v Charles Conway; same v Ezekiel McKirley; same
v Martin Shaddon.
p.197   Order Sheriff summon Constables Robert McMicken & John B Walker to attend
at the next term of this Court to assist him.
     Augustine Carter v John Pate. Caveat. Considered by Court that for insuffi-
ciencies in sd caveat that same be quashed; dft recovers of plf costs of defence.

24

Appoint John Keenan overseer/Madison Street in Pulaski in room of German Lester, resigned.

p.198   Nathaniel Moody v John McIver. Attachmt. Dft came not. Plf recovers agt dft his damages by reason of nonperformance of promises in declaration; damages to be enquired into by jury at next term of this Court.

Wm Ball v Henry Scales. Appeal. Dft is granted appeal to Circuit Court.

p.199   Attendance of but two witnesses to be taxed against John Boyd in the suit of Samuel Cox against him.

William Kindle v Henry Scales. Appeal. Dft is granted appeal to Circuit Ct.

Deed Levin Grace to Daniel Woods 500 acres porven by Robert Steele one of the subscribing witnesses, having been proven in Maury County by William Pillow.

Court adjourned till Court in Course. N Patteson, James Bumpass James Dugger.

p.200   Court of Pleas and Quarter Sessions met at the house of Thomas Smith in Pulaski on Monday, 5th September. Present John Dickey, William Mayfield, and Pleasant Moore, Esquires.

Power/attorney Benjamin French to James Kimbro acknowledged by sd French.

Deed Abel Olive to Robinson Johnston and Daniel Johnston heirs of Alexander Johnston decd for 300 acres proven by Samuel Shields and Joel Lane.

Order John Birdwell oversee/road in room of Isaac Lamb, resigned.

Order Richard Stewart oversee/road in room of John Montgomery, resigned.

Deed Martin Flynt to Berry Dearing 120 acres ackd by sd Martin Flynt.

p.201   Deed Richard Flynt to William Dearing 120 acres ackd by sd Richard Flynt.

Grant ltrs/admn on estate of George Goff decd to John Goff. John Goff admr of George Goff decd returned inventory/estate of sd George Goff decd.

Will of Mereday Flynt decd proven by John Laird. Perry Flynt, one of exrs therein named was qualified according to Law.

Power/atty James Wright to Wm H Ragsdale proven by John Kelly & John Isom.

p.202   Deed Archibald Young to Ambrose Yarboro 100 ac proven by Britton Yarboro.

Deed Guston Kearney to Washington Croft one lott in Elkton ackd.

Will of Jeremiah Perry decd proven by [blank]; John Perry & William Standford two of executors therein named qualified according to Law.

At least five Justices present, David Flatt produced six wolf scalps over four months old which was ordered to be burnt.

Appoint John Goff guardian for Peggy Goff, James Goff, and John Goff, orphan children of George Goff decd.

At least five Justices being present, John Anderson produced in Court two wolf scalps under four months old which were ordered to be burnt.

p.203   Deed William B Lewis to John Hawkins 300 acres proven by William Purnell and Gilbert D Taylor and Guston Kearney.

Deed Guston Kearney to William Purnell one Lott in Elkton ackd.

Deed Guston Kearney to Adaline C M Purnell one Lott in Elkton ackd.

Deed Guston Kearney to Hortensius Q Purnell one Lott in Elkton ackd.

p.204   Deed Guston Kearney to Amanda Ann Purnell one Lott in Elkton ackd.

Will of Larkin Cleveland decd proven by Thomas Lane, Martin Lane and James

Perry; German Lester one of executors therein named qualified.

Power/atty John Evans to Thomas T Armstrong proven in Court.

At least five Justices present, George McKinny produced one wolf scalp over four months old which is ordered to be burnt.

Power/atty John Tacker & others to Thomas Clarke proven in Court.

Order County Trustee pay to May Richardson $39.50 for keeping James Dickson a poor person of this County for one year ending first day of this month.

p.205   Appoint John Hicks, Charles Buford & Ralph Graves let to lowest bidder on this day on the Public Square in Pulaski the keeping of James Dickson a poor person of this County for one year from this time.

Grand Jury: John Clack foreman, William Nutt, Thomas McCarley, William Wisdom, Nathan Bass, Hugh Campbell, John Graves, Timothy Ezzell, Joseph Knox, Buckner Harwell Senr, Allan Abernathy, William Phillips, John Birdwell.

At least five Justices present, Joseph Dickson produced one wolf scalp under four months old which is ordered to be burnt.

[as above] Thomas Gamble, two wolf scalps over four months old.

[as above] John Rowsey, two wolf scalps under four months old.

Appoint James Lindsey overseer of the Little Tombigby road in room of Robert Anderson, resigned.

p.206   Order Ralph Graves, Henry Hagen, Lewis Kirk, William Parker, Thomas C Stone, and German Lester & William M Kerley or any five of them view the shoals of Richland Creek and see if it be proper to turn the road from where it now crosses sd creek and make return to this Court.

Appt Joseph Robertson overseer of the Shelbyville road in room of James S Haynes resigned.

Order William Henderson, James McCravens, James Mitchell, Andrew McMicken, Alexander Stinson & John Andrews or any five view the Shelbyville road near the plantation of James S Haynes and see if it be proper to turn sd road agreeable to the wish of sd Haynes and make report to next Court.

A majority of this Court present, order that Double County Tax of such persons as were in the army and service of the United States at the time they should have listed their Taxables be remitted on application and giving satisfaction that they were in sd service.

Ordered following tax list be received by Court & double tax thereon be remitted: Isaac Wilson one white poll; Henry Steele, one white poll, one slave; Andrew Keith fifty acres of land, one white poll.

p.207   Order/sale issues to executors of Mereday Flynt decd to sell property directed in the will of sd decd to be sold.

Order William Donald, William Neal, Quinton Shannon, James Berry, Lewis Kirk & Alexander McDonald or any five of them view & mark out a road from where Huntsville road crosses Pleasant run thence to Nelson Pattersons South east corner on the north line of Doherty's 5000 acre tract thence to intersect Fayetteville road near Solomon Asbells, and make report to present Term of this Court.

Rowland McKinney v John Caldwell. Trespass. William Caldwell and Elisha L Kimbrough bound for appearance of John Caldwell surrender him to Court; thereupon Joseph Anthony and James Harwell bail.

p.208   Thomas Webb recognizance to attend day to day to prosecute in behalf State against Samuel Criswell for A&B committed on Julius Webb by sd Criswell.

Recognizance Nathaniel Alman, condition he attend day to day to prosecute & give evidence behalf State agt William Ball for A&B on Nathaniel Alman by sd Ball.

SEPTEMBER 1814

William Maples and John Easley exrs of will of Josiah Maples decd return account/sales of perishable estate of sd deceased.

Fine Christopher Wright One Dollar for contempt of Court and he remains in custody of the Sheriff untill paid.

p.209   State v John Tinnen. Nonattendance as witness agt Nathaniel Moody. Dft in proper person is discharged from any forfeiture on his paying all costs.

Fine James Read Two Dollars for contempt of Court; also fined One Dollar for profane swearing in presence of Court, he is to remain in custody untill paid.

Appt William Phillips overseer/road in room of Guston Kearney resigned.

Order/sale issued to John Goff admr/estate of George Goff decd commanding him to sell the perishable part of sd estate, Negroes excepted. Order/sale issued to John Goff guardian to Peggy Goff, James Goff, and John Goff, orphans of George Goff decd commanding him to sell house & Lott in Pulaski belonging to sd estate.

Exhonerate Thomas Harwood for serving as a juror this Term.

p.210   Grant Ltrs/admn on estate of William Crowson decd to Mary Crowson, Richard Crowson, and Moses Crowson, they having entered bond with security.

Deed Andrew Erwin to Samuel Smith 281 acres proven by John Crowson.

Court adjourned till tomorrow morning 9 Oclock. John Dickey, Thomas Welch, Saml Shields.

p.211   Tuesday Sept 6th. Present John Dickey, Thomas Welch, Samuel Shields, Esqrs.

Recognizance Allan Moore to attend day to day to prosecute & give evidence behalf State against Tobias Millar for Assault on Allan Moore by sd Millar.

Allan Moore [as above] evidence agt Wm Ball, assault on sd Allan by Ball.

Recognizance, Thos Webb to attend day to day & prosecute in behalf State agt Saml Criswell and others for assault on Julius Webb by sd Criswell & others.

p.212   Exhonerate James Brown from paying double county tax on 78 acres and one white poll, he being in the army and service of the United States at time of listing taxable property.

Julius Webb recognizance to attend day to day to prosecute behalf state against Samuel Criswell & others for assault on sd Julius Webb.

Commission heretofore apptd to divide land of Micajah G Lewis to be allowed as follows: R Gordon 8 days $16; J Dabney 6 days $12; Will Dabney 6 days $12, S James 5 days $10, William Woods 9 days $18; and further sum of $17 allowed for

p.213   expences incured in surveying, chane carrying & marking, the sd W B Lewis, Jno H Eaton, & Charlotte Lewis to pay sd sums in equal proportion.

Grant Ordinary licence to Robert Gordon for twelve months.

Deed Rees Porter to David W Porter 283 acres proven by Thomas McKissack and John McKissack the subscribing witnesses thereto.

Deed Jno Porter to Jno Sappington proven by Thos McKissack & Jno McKissack.

p.214   Deed David W Porter to John Sappington ¼ acre land ackd.

Julius Webb recognizance attend day to day to give evidence behalf State against Samuel Criswell and others.

James P Downs v Nathan Hooker. Debt. Jury: Thomas Ray, Elias Tidwell Jr, John Webb, Lewis Brown, Lester Morris, Elijah Anthony, Elisha L Kimbro, John Abernathy, Samuel Hemphill, Nathan Farmer, John Paul, David Bunch assess plfs damages

p.215   by reason of detention of sd Debt to $8.12½ besides cost. Plf recovers $125 debt together with damages and costs.

Henry Wilcher v Solomon Asbell. Debt. Jury[above]. Plf recovers agt dft $80

27

p.216   debt and his damages and costs.

Commissioners of Pulaski v John Paul and William F Thompson. Debt. Dfts in proper person cannot gainsay plfs action. Plfs recover of dfts $171 together with
p.217   their damages and costs.

Deed James C McRee and David W McRee to William Henderson 25 acres ackd.

Edmund Pulle v William R Davis. Debt. Jury Thos Rea, Eli Tidwell Junr, John Webb, Lewis Brown, Lester Morris, Elijah Anthony, Elisha L Kimbrough, John Abernathy, Saml Hemphill, Nathan Farmer, John Paul, David Bunch. Plaintiff recovers agt
p.218   defendant $150 debt with his damages and costs of suit.

Edmund Pulle v William R Davis. Debt. Defendant surrenders in discharge of John Waldrop and Zacheus Hurt who were bound for his appearance.

David W Porter admr of Elias Porter decd returned amt/sale of sd estate.
p.219   John M Taylor v Thomas Smith. Debt. Jury Thos Rea, Elias Tidwell Jr, John Webb, Lewis Brown, Lester Morris, Elijah Anthony, Elisha L Kimbrough, John Abernathy, Saml Hemphill, Nathan Farmer, John Pall, David Bunch. Plaintiff recovers agt defendant $140 debt, his damages and his costs of suit.

Order/sale issued to Charlotte Moore and James Buford to sell perishable part of the estate of Sommersett Moore deceased, the Negroes excepted.
p.220   Order German Lester, Henry Hagen & Nathaniel Moody allott to Charlotte Moore, widow of Sommersett Moore decd a sufficient portion of the stock, corn and deal victuals of the goods & chattels of sd decedent as will be sufficient to maintain her and her children for one year.

Grand Jury Bills of Presentment: State v Matthew Richards; Same v John Fanning; Same v Jonathan Richards; Same v George Fanning.

Deed William Polk to Aaron Brown 3830½ acres proven by George Malone and Lewis Brown two of the subscribing witnesses thereto.
p.221   Grand Jury Bills/Indictment: State v Samuel Criswell & others, not a true bill. Same v William Ball, true bill; same v Tobias Millar, true bill; same v William Ball, true bill; same v John Welch, true bill; same v William Welch, true bill; same v Joseph Wallace, true bill.

Order Thomas Westmoreland, John Dickey & Arthur Hicks esqrs settle accounts between David W Porter admr/estate of Elias Porter decd and the Legatees.
p.222   Order Thomas Westmoreland released from payment of double tax on 100 acres which was wrong listed.

Appoint Jacob Byler overseer of Little Tombigby road in room of Isaac Oxford resigned.

Appt Thomas B Haynie overseer/road in room of Drury Stovall resigned.

William F Thompson v Anthony Samuel. Appeal. Jury Thos Rea, Elias Tidwell Jr, John Webb, Lewis Brown, Lester Morris, Elijah Anthony, Elisha L Kimbrough, John Abernathy, Saml Hemphill, Nathan Farmer, John Pall, David Bunch. Plf recovers of dft $22.75 and his cost as well before the Magistrate as in this Court expended.

Nuncupative will of William Smith deceased devising to John Brown the amount of his wages as a soldier in the service of the United States as one of the Militia of the State under the command of Major General Jackson was produced in open Court and proven by the oath of David Brown a subscribing witness thereto.
p.223   A majority of Court present, order Justices appointed to take lists of Taxable property for present year have leave to correct any errors which they may have made in the lists returned by them.

Court adjourned till tomorrow morning 9 Oclock. John Dickey, B Harwell, Pleasant Moore.

p.224 Wednesday September 7th. Present Alexander Black, Pleasant Moore & John Hillhouse.

Recognizance John Boyd to attend day to day to prosecute & give evidence behalf State against John Yancy for retailing spiritous liquors without licence.

Recognizance John Caldwell to attend day to day to prosecute & give evidence behalf State against Rowland McKinney for gaming.

Recognizance Tyree Roads to attend day to day to prosecute & give evidence behalf State against Daniel T Woods for sending sd Roads a written challenge to

p.225 fight a duel, and not depart without leave of the Court.

Recognizance Tyree Roads to attend day to day to prosecute & give evidence behalf State against Oliver Woods for bearing a written duel challenge from Daniel T Woods to sd Roads.

State v George Fanning. Affray. Dft in proper person pleads guilty. Fine 6½¢ and pay cost of this prosecution.

State v John Fanning. Affray. Dft in proper person pleads guilty. Fine 6½¢

p.226 and pay costs of this prosecution.

State v Jonathan Richards. Affray. Dft in proper person pleads guilty. Fine 6½¢ and pay costs of this prosecution.

State v Mathew Richards. Affray. Dft in proper person pleads guilty. Fine 6½¢ and pay costs of this prosecution.

p.227 Will of William H Murry decd proven by George Earnest and Thomas Standford the two subscribing witnesses thereto. William Phillips and Thomas Phillips the executors therein named qualified according to Law.

Deed Buckner Harwell Senr to Buckner Harwell Junr 115 acres ackd.

Deed Buckner Harwell Senr to Thomas Harwell 115 acres ackd.

William S Gaynes and Francis A Cash Esqrs produced their licences to practice law; qualified agreeable to Law and authorized to practice.

Bill/sale Parkes Bailey to Charles C Bailey for sundry property ackd.

p.228 Grand Jury Bills of Indictment: State v Oliver Woods, true bill; Same v John Yancy, true bill; Same v Rowland McKinney, true bill; Same v Larkin Mayfield, true bill; Same v William McGill, true bill; Same v Daniel T Woods, true bill.

Commissioners apptd to settle with David W Porter admr/estate of Elias Porter decd made return of settlement.

Order County Trustee pay Micajah Ezzell $44.74 for building the temporary jail let by commissioners appointed at last Court for that purpose.

p.229 Thomas Goff administrator of the estate of John Davis decd returned an account of sale of sd estate.

Executors/will of William H Murry returned inventory of sd estate.

Order/sale issued to executors/will of William H Murry to sell perishable estate of sd decedent agreeable to law.

Deed James Winters to John Pate 16 acres ackd.

John Caldwell, recognizance, to attend next Term to prosecute & give evidence behalf State against Rowland McKinney for gaming.

p.230 William Mayfield v Nathan Davis & William M Kearly. Trover. Jury Thos Rea, Elias Tidwell Jr, John Webb, Lewis Brown, Lester Morris, Jas Paine, John McKissick, John Pall, Wm Jones, Green McCafferty, Jas Moore, Jas Wilkinson. Plf recovers of dfts $55 damages assessed by jury and his costs of suit.

John Kelly Esq recognizance, attend day to day to prosecute & give evidence behalf State against Washington G L Foley for A&B on sd John Kelly by sd Foley.

p.231 Appt Thos Goff overseer/Prewits Gap Road in room of Isaac Wilson resigned.

SEPTEMBER 1814

Commissioners apptd by Court to allott to heirs of Micajah Green Lewis their proportions of 5000 acres granted by North Carolina to sd Lewis made report of division among Mira Eaton, Margaret Lewis, Charlotte Lewis, Ferdinand L
p.232 Claiborne, Mary Claiborne, Micajah Claiborne, that is to say John H Eaton and Mira Eaton his wife are entitled to [land description here omitted] and Lott two belongs to William B Lewis and Margaret Lewis his wife [land description here omitted], Lott No. 3 to Charlotte Lewis [land description here omitted]; Lott No. 4
p.233 to Ferdinand L Claiborne, Mary Claiborne and Micajah Claiborne [description of land here omitted]
       Expences incured by surveying $8, chain carrying 7 and marking 2. R. Gordon 8 days, W Woods 9 days, J Dabny 6 days, W Dabny 6 days, S Jones 5 days, Samuel Jones, William Woods, Robert Gordon, William Dabney, John Dabney.
p.234 Andrew Pickens v Quinton Shannon. Case. Referees returned their award: Subscribers met at house of John McAnally, find for dft. [signed] John Dickey, Saml Shields, Geo Malone, N Patterson, Lewis Brown, John Clack. Therefore dft recovers agt plf his cost about his defence in this behalf expended.
       William Sawyers v Martin Friley. Referees conclude that the heifer or value
p.235 thereof shall be equally divided between parties and each shall pay half the costs. [signed] John Hawkins, Duncan Brown, James Bumpass, John Birdwell, Edward his X mark Davis, Mason his M mark F Moss, Rowland his L mark McKinny.
       Order William Wells, William Abernathy, Thomas Westmoreland, Lewis Brown and Marcus Mitchell or any four of them to view the scite whereon John Butler wishes to build a mill on Richland creek to assess damages; Buckner Harwell Senr to appear at next Court to shew cause &c.
       Deed Zenas Alexander and Samuel Polk to John Young 171 acres proven by Alfred M Harris and Peter R Booker.
p.236 Deed William Bradshaw sheriff of Maury County to Alfred M Harris proven by Robert Mack and Peter R Booker.
       Resignation of Samuel Smith Esqr is accepted by the Court.
       Court adjourned till tomorrow morning 9 Oclock. John Dicky, B Harwell, Pleasant Moore.

p.237 Thursday Sept 8th. Present John Dickey, Buckner Harwell, Pleasant Moore.
       State v William Ball. Gaming. Dft in proper person pleads guilty. Fine $5 and pay costs of this prosecution.
       State v Henry Hagen. Gaming. Dft in proper person pleads guilty. fine $5 and pay costs of this prosecution.
p.238 State v Nelson Patterson Jr. Gaming. Dft in proper person pleads guilty; fine $5 and pay costs of this prosecution.
       State v William Kindell. Gaming. Dft in proper person pleads guilty. Fine $5 and pay costs of this prosecution.
       State v Thomas Smith. Gaming. Dft in proper person pleads guilty. Fine $7 and pay costs of this prosecution.
p.239 State v Charles Conway. Affray. Dft in proper person pleads guilty. Fine 6¼¢ and pay costs of this prosecution.
       State v Larkin Mayfield. Affray. Dft in proper person pleads guilty. Fine $5 and pay the costs of this prosecution.
       State v John Welch. Assault. Dft in proper person pleads guilty. Fine $1 and pay costs of this prosecution.

SEPTEMBER 1814

p.240   State v Joseph Wallace. Assault. Dft in proper person pleads guilty. Fine
$1 and pay costs of this prosecution.
          State v William McGill. Affray. Dft in proper person pleads guilty. Fine $5
and pay costs of this prosecution.
          State v John Gregory. Affray. Dft in proper person pleads guilty. Fine $1
and pay costs of this prosecution.
p.241   State v Jno Yancy. Retailing spiritous liquors. Dft in proper person pleads
guilty. Fine 6½¢ and pay the costs of this prosecution.
          State v Gabriel Faulks. Neglect/duty as overseer/road. On arraignment dft
pleads not Guilty. Jury Thos Rea, Eli Tidwell Jr, Jno Webb, Lewis Brown, Lester
Morris, Joseph Hart, Herod Fowlks, Nathan Henderson, Joseph Riley, Leonard Brown,
Burton Beasley, Saml Cox find dft not guilty.
p.242   State v Thomas Goff. Assault on John Dewaaser. Dft arraigned, pleads not
guilty. Jury[above] find dft guilty. Fine 12½¢ and pay costs of prosecution.
          State v Thomas Goff. Assault on Wm Dewaaser. On arraignment, dft pleads not
guilty. Jury Wm Brown, Jno Laird, Nathan Davis, Jno McKissick, Gray Edwards, Gideon
Pillow, John Anderson, Wm Pullen, Saml Y Anderson, Thos C Stone, Thomas Wilkinson,
p.243   Joseph Dickson find dft not guilty.
          State v Joseph Kelly. A&B. Dft in proper person pleads guilty. Fine $5 and
pay costs of this prosecution.
          Appoint Washington G L Foley overseer of Little Tombigby road in room of
Tyree Roads resigned; he is to have hands in the following bounds: from between sd
Roads's boundary & Robert Andersons, running to Pleasant Moores, thence to John
Roops[Rooss?] thence to Amos and Moses McLemores, to Hugh Cooks and John Gilberts,
to Solomon Dearmans, south to ridge between Pigeon roost and Richland creek, with
ridge to beginning including all hands that formerly worked on sd road and all
within above described bounds.
p.244   Grand Jury Bills/Indictment: State v Washington G L Foley, a true bill;
Same v Joseph Kelly, a true bill.
          Appt William Dearing overseer/road in room of Gabriel Fowlks resigned.
          Power/atty Thomas McKissick to William McKissick ackd.
          Deed Richard Hightower to William McDonald was partly proven heretofore,
fully proven at this court by oath of James Benham.
          Samuel Smith v Edward Davis. Case. Parties in proper persons, and dft
having paid costs, plf directs his suit be dismissed.
          Order William Phillips, overseer/Huntsville road, have under his direction
hands in following bounds: from mouth of Indian Creek to Thomas Maxwell then between John Perry and Enoch Scratches plantation then to strike sd road above M H
p.245   Buchannon then along road westward to dividing ridge between Richland and
Elk Rivers, along ridge to McIntire's branch leaving McIntire to the right and
Vinson's house the same including Mr Austin and strike Elk river opposite Reynolds
Island, then up Elk river to the beginning.
          Bill/sale Archibald McKissack to Nathan Davis a certain Negro girl proved
by German Lester.
          Grand Jury Bill/Indictment: State v Washington G L Foley, not a true bill.
          Appt Joseph Roe overseer/road in room of Larkin Cardin[Condin?] resigned.
          Appt David W Porter overseer of the Weakleys Creek road in room of Charles
Dever resigned.
          Appt Robert Clarke overseer/road in room of Richard McGee resigned.
p.246   Appt John Temple overseer/road in room of Robt Hunnecut resigned.

31

Appt John Campbell overseer/road in room of Daniel Vinson resigned.

Appt Matthew Johnston overseer of Montgomerys Gap road in room of Phillip Parchman, resigned.

Order Robert Campbell overseer/road have under his direction the following hands: Robert Bogle, Joseph South, Thos Stewart, Hamilton C Campbell, Jas Ashmore, James Hannah, Thomas Rea, Joseph Rea, William Rea, Jesse Kirklin, Robert Reece.

Joseph Kelly v John Manifee. Deposition of Thomas Kelly to be taken to benefit of plaintiff.

James P Downs v Nathan Hooker. Debt. Richard Hooker and Douglas L Blue sur-
p.247 render Nathan Hooker to Court; he is committed to custody of the Sheriff there to remain untill discharged therefrom by due course of Law.

Court adjourned till tomorrow 9 Oclock. John Dickey, Pleasant Moore, John Hillhouse.

p.248   Friday 9th September. Present John Dickey, Pleasant Moore, John Hillhouse.

Appt Andrew Turnbow overseer of Bigbigby road from John Normans to Maury County line in room of Edward Baker resigned.

Recognizance of William Ball to attend day to day to prosecute & give evidence behalf State against Allan Moore for gaming.

Recognizance of William Ball [same wording as above]

Release Archd McKissack from double tax on one white poll, one black poll.
p.249   State v Thomas Goff. Throwing down a fence. Upon his arraignment Goff pleads not guilty. Jury Thos Rea, Eli Tidwell Jr, Jno Webb, Lester Morris, Archd McKissack, John Crittenton, Martin Shadden, Odell Garret, Thomas Phillips, Leonard Brown, Thos McKissack, John Paul find dft guilty. Fine $10 and pay costs of this prosecution, imprisoned for ten days.

Recognizance of Mary McGee to attend day to day to prosecute & give evidence behalf State against Solomon Wilbourn for assault & battery on sd Mary.

Grand Jury Bills/Indictment: State v Allan Moore, true bill; Same v Same, true bill; Same v Solomon Wilburn, true bill.

Grand Jury Bills/Presentment: State v William L Campbell; Same v Charles Conway; Same v Riley Finney; Same v Ezekiel McKerley.

Account/sale estate of Ambrose Foster decd returned by administrator.

Account/sale estate of Minor Winn decd returned by the administrator.
p.251   State v Charles Conway. Affray with Riley Finney. Dft in proper person pleads guilty. Fine 6¼¢ and pay costs of this prosecution.

Isham Brown admr/estate of Minor Winn decd returns additional inventory. Order/sale issued to Isham Brown to sell additional estate of sd decedent.

State v Thomas Smith. Gaming. Dft in proper person pleads guilty. Fine $5 and pay costs of this prosecution.
p.252   State v Charles Simpson & William McGill. Riot. Dfts plead not guilty. Jury Wm Brown, Jno Laird, Lewis Brown, Fountain Lester, Jno Tinnen, Lawson Hobson, Jas C Burney, Jno Anderson, Jno Elliott, Jas Kimbrough, Jas Egnew, Andrew McPeters. State recovers agt dfts $66.66 damages assessed and pay costs of this prosecution.

State v Ezekiel McCarley. Assault on M H Buchannon. Dft in proper person pleads guilty. Fine $1 and pay costs of this prosecution.
p.253   Recognizance of John Kelly to attend next County Court to prosecute & give evidence in behalf State against Washington G L Foley for A&B on sd Kelly.

State v Samuel Riley. A&B on John Alsup Junr. Dft in proper person pleads guilty. Fine $1 and pay costs of this prosecution.

State v Allan Moore. Gaming. Dft in proper person pleads guilty. Fine $5
p.254 and pay the costs of this prosecution.

State v Allan Moore. Gaming. Dft in proper person pleads guilty. Fine $6
and pay costs of this prosecution.

State v Ezekiel McCarley. Affray. Dft in proper person pleads not guilty.
Jury Thos Rea, Eli Tidwell Jr, Jno Yancy, Lester Morris, Archd McKissack, Jno Crittenton, Martin Shadden, Odel Garret, Thos Phillips, Leonard Brown, Thos McKissack,
p.255 John Paul find dft guilty. Fine 6¼¢ and pay cost of this prosecution.

Inventory/estate of William Smith decd returned by administrator. Grant
leave for admr to sell perishable part of sd estate except the dividents divised in
the nuncupative will heretofore proven.

Remit double tax on lists: Nathan Davis, one white poll, 357 acres on
Buchannons creek, 10 acres on Pigeon roost. Also Jesse Webb, one white poll.

Jurors to next Court: George Gibson, Jas Hannah, John Robertson, Wm Beaty,
Joseph Rea, Peter Swanson, Hamilton C Campbell, James Pickens, James Boran, Leander
Sheilds, Robt Anderson, Jno Johnston, Robt Willson, Elisha Melton, Archd McKissack,
Isaac Lann, Ralph Graves, John Hicks, Lazarus Stewart, Joseph Lann, Thomas C Stone,
John Thompson, John Barnett, Absalom Harwell, Duncan Brown, Aquilla Wilson.
p.256 State v Daniel Woods. Sending a written duel challenge to Tyree Rodes. Thos
Goff, David Woods, Wm McCabe surrender dft, thereupon Lewis Kirk, David Woods, Wm
McCabe special bail.

William Henry v David Smith. Case. Plf in proper person assumes payment of
all costs & directs that this suit be dismissed.

State v Samuel Criswell & others. Grand jury having returned "not a true
bill" order judgment in favour of those entitled for all costs.
p.257 State v Thomas Goff. A&B on William Dewaaser. Dft being acquitted, ordered
judgment be entered in favour of those entitled for all costs.

State v Washington G L Foley. Affray. Grand Jury having returned "not a
true bill" order judgment in favour of those entitled for all costs.

Grand Jury returned into Court Bill/Presentment: State v Samuel Riley.

State v Thomas Goff. A&B on John Dewaaser. Dft granted appeal to Circuit
Court having filed reasons and entered bond and security.
p.258 State v Thomas Goff. Maliciously throwing down the fence of John Dewaaser.
Dft granted appeal to Circuit Court having filed reasons & entered bond & security.

State v Charles Simpson & William McGill. Riot. Dft is granted appeal to
Circuit Court having filed reasons and entered bond and security.

Ordered Court adjourned untill tomorrow morning 9 Oclock. Pleasant Moore
Robt Buchanan, William Mayfield.

p.259 Saturday Sept 10th. Present Buckner Harwell, Wm Mayfield, Nelson Patterson.

Recognizance of Abel Oxford to attend next term to prosecute and give
evidence in behalf State against William Welch for A&B on sd William Welch.

Recognizance of Robert Dowdle, Jeremiah Parker, Eli Joiner, Carol White, to
attend next Term to give evidence behalf State against William Welch for A&B on
Abel Oxford by sd William Welch.

Recognizance of Wm Welch to attend next Term to answer indictment against
p.260 him for assault on Abel Oxford.

State v William Ball. Gaming. Dft pleads not Guilty. Jury Wm Brown, John

SEPTEMBER 1814

Laird, Thos Rea, Eli Tidwell Jr, Lester Morris, Wm Kindell, Thos Wilkinson, Herod
Foulks, Wm Jones, Joseph Shadden, John McDonald, Lewis Kirk find dft not guilty.
    State v William Ball. A&B on Allan Moore. Dft pleads not Guilty. Jury
p.261   [above] find dft guilty. Fine $20 and pay costs of prosecution.
    State v Tobias Millar. False Imprisoning of Allan Moore. Dft pleads not
guilty. Jury Lewis Brown, John Webb, Thomas C Stone, Isaac Mayfield, Andw McPeters,
Leonard Brown, Larkin Mayfield, John Beshers, Robt Shane, Joseph Lann, James Paul,
Thomas Wills find dft not guilty.
p.262   State v William Ball. Gaming. Dft being acquitted, order judgment entered
in favour of those entitled for all costs.
    State v Nancy Poston. On sci fa for not attending to prosecute & give
evidence in behalf state against John Gregory. Dft came not. Judgment acainst her
for $100 beside costs and execution awarded agt her accordingly.
    Ralph Graves v Halbert Ellison. Plf in proper person assumes payment of all
costs and directs his suit be dismissed.
p.263   James & David W McRee v James McCraven admr of David Stewart decd. Debt.
Dft came not. Plffs recover agt dft $99.50 debt with legal interest thereon from
first of May 1812 untill paid, to be levied of goods & chattels & lands of David
Stewart decd in hands of James McCraven admr together with their costs of suit.
    Recognizance of Nicholas Welch and William Welch, condition Wm Welch appear
at next Court to answer State for assault on Abel Oxford.
p.264   Order road at Shoals of Richland Creek be turned agreeable to report of
Jury apptd this Court to view same. William Kindle with hands under his direction
open & keep in repair the part on north side of sd creek; Samuel Burney with hands
under his direction open & keep in repair part on south side of sd creek.
    State v Tobias Millar. False imprisonment of Allan Moore. Dft being acquit-
ted, order judgment entered in favour of those entitled for all costs.
    State v William L Campbell. Affray with Zacheus Hurt. Dft in proper person
pleads guilty. Fine $2 and pay costs of this prosecution.
p.265   Grand Jury Bills/Presentment: State v Nathan Davis & Thomas Smith; Same v
William Ball; Same v Charles Hudspeth.
    State v Daniel T Woods. Sending written duel challenge to Tyree Rodes.
Lewis Kirk, David Woods & Wm McCabe surrender dft to Court.
    Recognizance of Daniel T Woods, David Woods, William Ball, condition that
p.266   Daniel T Woods appear next Term this Court to answer charge of sending a
written duel challenge to Tyree Rodes.
    State v Nathan Davis. Affray with Thomas Smith. Dft in proper person pleads
guilty. Fine 50¢ and pay costs of this prosecution.
    State v Thomas Smith. Affray with Nathan Davis. Dft in proper person pleads
guilty. Fine 50¢ and pay costs of this prosecution.
p.267   Recognizance of Nathaniel Alman to attend next Term to prosecute & give
evidence behalf State agt William Ball for assault on Nathaniel Alman by sd Ball.
    Order double tax remitted on tax list: James Patterson one white poll,
three black polls.
    Appoint John Hawkins guardian for Elizabeth Barret Lockhart.
    Sheriff to summon John Buchannon and Harrison Hicks constables to attend
next Circuit Court.
    Sheriff to summon John C Walker and Robert McMecon constables to attend
next County Court.
p.268   William Noblet & wife v John Boyd. Case. Order Robert Mack be received as

additional security for prosecution of this suit.
Court adjourned till Court in Course. William Mayfield, Pleasant Moore, Robt Bucanan.

p.269   At a Court of Pleas and Quarter Sessions holden for Giles County at the house of Thomas Smith in Pulaski on Monday 5th December 1814. Present James Bumpass, Alexander Black, Jarrett Manifee, Esquires.
Grant lts/admn on estate of George Earnest decd to Mary Earnest.
Mary Earnest admx of Geo Earnest decd returns inventory of estate.
Grand Jury: John Hicks Foreman, Joseph Lann, Robt Wilson, Leander Shields, Joseph Rea, Absalom Harwell, Thomas C Stone, Aquilla Wilson, James H Pickens, John Robertson, Duncan Brown, Isaac Lann, John Barnett.
Grant Ordinary Licence to William Kindell for twelve months.
p.270   At least five Justices present, James Kimbrough produced one wolf scalp over four months old which is ordered to be burnt.
Deed Alexander McDonald to Joseph Riley 100 acres ackd.
Assignment of platt and certificate of survey from Alexander McDonald to William McDonald for fifty acres ackd.
Assignment of platt and certificate of survey from Alexander McDonald to William McDonald for thirty acres ackd.
Admrs of estate of Somerset Moore decd return account of sales of estate.
Appt James Bumpass, Wm Phillips, Duncan McIntire to allott to Mary Earnest widow of late George Earnest decd a sufficient portion of provisions as will maintain herself and family for one year from time Geo Earnest departed this life.
p.271   Rowland McKinney v John Caldwell. Trespass. Parties in proper persons. Dft having assumed and paid costs, plf directs suit be dismissed.
Extrs estate of Jeremiah Perry decd returned inventory of sd estate.
Issue order/sale to extrs of Jeremiah Perry decd to sell perishable estate.
Will of James Haynes decd proved by Andrew Haynes and John Haynes.
Order County Trustee pay Alfred M Harris Solicitor/County $50 for exofficio services for one year prior to this time.
p.272   State v Gabriel Fowlks. Neglect of duty as overseer/road. Defendant being acquitted, order judgment in favour of those entitled for all costs.
James Buford late Sheriff and Collelctor/tax for 1813 returned list of Insolvents for sd year amounting to $40.89¼ which was allowed him, $21.07¼ of which is due to State and $19.82 is due to county. Order credit be allowed.
Jonathan Richards v Philmer Green. Case. Plf is in the army & service of the United States; order this cause be continued.
p.273   Deed John Haynes to James S Haynes 53 acres ackd.
Order/sale issued to Mary Earnest admx/estate of George Earnest decd to sell perishable part of the estate of sd decedent.
Adjourned till tomorrow 9 OClock.   Wm Mayfield, Pleasant Moore, B Harwell

p.274   Tuesday Dec 6th 1814. Present Buckner Harwell, Pleasant Moore, Wm Mayfield.
Recognizance of John Boyd, prosecute & give evidence behalf State against

DECEMBER 1814

Jacob Crowson for A&B on sd John Boyd.

Commissioners of Pulaski v Phillip Parchman. Judicial attachment. Jury John Thompson, John Birdwell, John Paul, Wm Riddle, Archibald Alexander, Charles G Abernathy, James Kimbrough, Zacheus Hurt, Thomas B Haynie, Wm Brown, Wm Phillips,

p.275 Thos Maxwell assess plfs damages by detention of debt to $37.39 besides costs. Plfs recover of dft $277 debt, their damages and their costs.

Commrs of Pulaski v Philip Parchman. Debt. Jury[above] say dft hath not

p.276 paid debt. Plfs recover of dft $200 debt, $27 damages, and costs of suit.

John Stokes assee v Jeremiah Woodward. Debt. Jury[above]. Plf recovers agt

p.277 dft debt $115, damages $6.00¾, and costs of suit.

David L Jones v William Parker, Thomas Smith, Thos Goff. Debt. Jury [above]

p.278 Plf recovers agt dfts $100 debt, $5 damages of detention, & costs of suit.

Isaac Thomas Senr v John Crowson. Debt. Jury[above]. Plf recovers agt dft

p.279 $161.50 debt, damages $10.49¾, and costs of suit.

p.280 Deed Samuel Paxton to Robert Oliver 20 acres ackd.

Deed Richard Hightower to James W Paxton 100 acres proven by Samuel Paxton and Pleasant New.

Deed Guston Kearney to Edward O Chambers lot 97 in Elkton proven by Henry Hagen and Gray Edwards.

Deed Guston Kearney to Edward O Chambers lot 98 in Elkton proven by Henry

p.281 Hagen and Gray Edwards.

Deed Guston Kearney to Edward O Chambers lot 117 in Elkton proven by Henry Hagen and Gray Edwards.

Admrs/estate of William Crowson decd returned inventory. Richard Crowson one of admrs of estate of William Crowson decd protests against return of Joe, one of the slaves in the inventory of sd estate, returned at this Court, which slave he claims as his own property.

p.282 Order/sale issues to administrators of the estate of William Crowson decd to sell the perishable part of sd estate.

Bond of Jacob Crowson and James Caldwell, condition sd Jacob Crowson keep free from charge to this county Lorenzo Dow Williams and Pleasant Williams two bastard children said to have been begotton on Sarah M Williams by Jacob Crowson.

Deed Shadrack Howard to James Temple 100 acres proved by John Easley and James Stark.

p.283 Grand Jury Bill/Indictment: State v Jacob Crowson, true bill.

Pettway & Maury v Oliver Woods & Samuel Woods. Debt. Jury[above]. Plfs re-

p.284 cover agt dfts $149.58 debt, damages $4.86¾ and costs.

Deed James Temple to John Rhea 26 acres proven by Jno Temple & Jno Manifee.

William W Cooke v James Read. Debt. Dft surrenders himself in discharge of Andrew Neal & Daniel T Woods who were bound for his appearance at this Term.

p.285 Appt Mary Crowson guardian of Jonathan Crowson.

Appt Mary Crowson guardian to Jane Crowson.

Maxamilian H Buchanon Esqr sheriff protests agt sufficiency of the jail.

Deed James Ireland to John Samford 415 acres proven by Thomas Maxwell and Samuel Woods.

Grant Ordinary Licence to John Shoemaker for twelve months.

Appt Edward O Chambers overseer/Huntsville road in room of Marcus Mitchell.

p.286 Grand Jury Bills/Presentment: State v Henry Roberts. Same v Zacheus Hurt.

Appt Joseph Murphy overseer of the Shelbyville Rd in room of James S Haynes resigned.

36

DECEMBER 1814

Deed William Bond to Ransom H Wells 100 acres proven by Henry Scales and Absalom Harwell.

Order William Wells have direction of following hands to work under him on road: Buckner Harwell Senr, Henry Loyd, John B Goldsberry, Hugh A Dany[Dary?], Richard Harwell and Shadrack Harwell.

Court elected William M Kerley Coroner who gave bond and qualified.

p.287   Thomas C Stone v William F Thompson. Case. John Paul and James Paul surrender Wm F Thompson; thereupon Joseph Anthony & John Yancy bail for sd Thompson.

Jury apptd last Court to view cite whereon John Butler wishes to build a mill made return: valued two acres on Richland creek belonging to Buckner Harwell Senr to $3; the acre belonging to John Butler to $5. Signed William Abernathy, William Wells, Thomas Westmoreland, Lewis Brown.

p.288   John Boyd v Edmund J Bailey. Debt. Jury John Thompson, John Birdwell, John Paul, William Riddle, Archibald Alexander, Charles C Abernathy, James Kimbrough, Zacheus Hurt, Thomas B Haynie, William Brown, William Phillips, Thomas Maxwell. Plf recovers of dft $74 the balance of debt, damages $3.14, and his costs of suit.

p.289   Giles County v Henry Cross. Complaint made to Court by Gabriel Bumpass in behalf Eby Estess[Estep?] that she has been ill treated by Henry Cross to whom she was bound; subpenas issue.

Court adjourned till tomorrow 9 Oclock. Pleasant Moore, Hardy Hightower, J Henderson.

p.290   Wednesday 7th December. Present Pleasant Moore, John Henderson, Hardy Hightower, Esqrs.

Order John Temple overseer/road have under his direction the hands in following bounds: from below Capt Starks up river to include Wm Manefee thence with road to State line, to Burges Trace including George Brown to beginning.

Pettway & Maury v Thomas Tarpley. Appeal. Jury Robt Anderson, Geo Gibson, Lewis Kirk, John Isom, Wm Parker, Geo Harrison, Herod Foulks, Jno Graves, James Wilkinson, John Birdwell, Martin Shadden, Wm Riddle. Plfs recover of dft $36.43

p.291   damages and costs of their suit.

Nathaniel Moody v John McIver. Judicial attachment. Plf in proper person assumes all costs and dismissed suit; dft recovers of plf his costs of defence.

p.292   Order County trustee pay Wm Ball $72.37½ for furnishing prisoners, guard, meat, drink, candles & house room during April Term of Circuit Court in this city.

Grant ltrs/admn on estate of James Harwell decd to Buckner Harwell Senr.

Appt Archibald McKissack overseer/road in room of Jonathan Berry resigned.

Order County trustee pay Gabriel Bumpass $6.75 for services in settling with County Trustee and Sheriff of this County.

Order County trustee pay Tyree Rodes $7.50 for five days service in
p.293   settling with the County trustee and Sheriff of this County.

Order County trustee pay John Jones $7.50 for five days [as above]

Order County trustee pay William M Kerley, John McKissack, Larken Mayfield, Elisha Mayfield, Eli Tidwell, Hardin Paine each $4.50 for guarding Edwards and Shawley during April Circuit Court last.

Order County trustee pay Micajah Ezell $1.50 for cutting window in the temporary jail built by order of this Court.

Appt James Paine commissioner to settle with County trustee and Sheriff.
p.294   Reappt John Jones a commr to settle with County trustee & Sheriff.

37

DECEMBER 1814

Reappoint Tyree Rodes to settle with County trustee and Sheriff.

Deed Ransom H Wells to Aquilla Wilson 162½ acres proven by Daniel McCallum and Duncan Brown.

p.295 Appt John Graves, Edmund J Bailey, Henry Hagen to settle with executors of Zacheus Hurt decd and make report to present term of this Court.

Appt John Henderson, Jno Dabney, Samuel Shields Esqrs to settle the account current of James McCraven admr of David Stewart decd and make return to next Court.

Grant letters of admn with will annexed on estate of James Haynes decd to James Haynes, he having been qualified and given bond and security. James Haynes admr with will annexed of estate of James Haynes decd returned inventory.

p.296 Order William McDonald, William Neal, Quinton Shannon, James Berry, Lewis Kirk, Alexander McDonald, James McDonald or any five of them mark out a road from where Huntsville road crosses Pleasant Run to Nelson Pattesons south east corner, with north line of Dohertys 5000 acre tract, thence to intersect Fayetteville road near Solomon Asbells; make report to next Court.

Order road near plantation of James Haynes be opened at expence of sd Haynes agreeable to report of jury apptd for that purpose; when opened, Joseph Murphey to oversee said road, keep same in repair with hands under his direction.

p.297 Deed Gideon Pillow and Ann his wife to Paul Dismuke for land in Davidson County ackd by sd Gideon Pillow.

Order Wm Mayfield and Pleasant Moore Esqrs examine Ann Pillow touching her free consent in execution of a deed from Gideon Pillow and wife Ann to Paul Dismuke for land lying in Davidson County.

Admr/estate of Minor Winn decd returned account/sale of sd estate.

Henry Scales v Bernard M Patteson. Jury Robt Anderson, George Gibson, Lewis p.298 Kirk, John Isom, William Parker, Herod Fowlks, Jno Graves, James Wilkinson, John Birdwell, Shadrack Cross, Harden Paine, James Kimbrough say dft is not justified in A&B and false imprisonment. Plf recovers of dft damages $150 and costs.

On petition of Mary Crowson widow of William Crowson decd, order sheriff summon twelve disinterested freeholders to set off to sd Mary one third part of the p.299 land, unless sd widow agrees to take less, including mansion house in which sd Wm Crowson usually dwelt together with out houses &c; make return next Court.

Order James Ford, Samuel Smith, Thomas Westmoreland, Aaron Brown, Wm Price divide & appropriate between Richard Crowson, Moses Crowson, John Crowson, Abraham Crowson, Isaac Crowson, Thomas Crowson, Jonathan Crowson, Jane Crowson children & legatees of Wm Crowson decd two tracts of land of which Wm Crowson died seized & possessed as mentioned in the petiton, one containing 325 acres, other 106 acres.

p.300 Thursday 8th December. Present James Bumpass, Richard Flynt, Alexr Black.

Sheriff to summon Frederick Harwell & John Gordon, constables, to attend next term of this County Court.

Sheriff to summon Harrison Hicks & Campbell Mayfield, constables, to attend next Circuit Court.

Jurors to next County Court: Jas Tinnen, Gideon Pillow, Duncan McIntire, Wm Phillips, Wm Standford, Larkin Webb, Jno Paul, Jacob Templen, Samuel Pearson, David Campbell, David W Porter, Richd Bently, Buckner Harwell Sr, Jas Robertson, William Ezzell, John Simms, Archibald Crocket, Robert Alsup, Jno McNight (Bradshaw), James Kimbrough, Elijah Anthony, Shadrack Harwell, Saml Harwell, Joseph McDonald, Thomas Gordon, Nathan Farmer.

p.301   Jurors to next Circuit Court: Tyree Roades, Nelson Patteson, Jas Bumpass, Robert Buchanon, James McDonald, Samuel Jones, Hardey Hightower, John Montgomery, Pleasant Moore, John Dickey, Arthur Hicks, William Mayfield, Saml Sheilds, Jarrett Manifee, Thomas Harwood, William Price, James Paine, Joel Lane, William McDonald, Nathaniel Moody, Charles Buford, Thomas Westmoreland, Robert McNairy, Robt Oliver, Buckner Harwell Jr, James Dugger.

Plummer Willis admr v Edward J Bailey, Thos Westmoreland, Wm Wells. Debt. p.302   Dfts withdraw plea. Plf recovers agt dfts $132.02 debt, damages $39.23 and his costs of suit in this behalf expended.

Appointments of Justices to take lists of taxable property: John Dabney in Capt Youngs Company; Richard Flynt in Capt Shields Company; Thomas Welch in Captain Pickens Company; Jacob Byler in Capt Bylers Company; Arthur Hicks in Capt Herraldsons Company; John Henderson in Capt McVays Compy; Hardy Hightower in Capt Paxtons Compy; James Bumpass in Capt Bensons Compy; James Bumpass in Capt Phillips's Compy; Jarrett Manifee in Capt Starkes's Company; Buckner Harwell in Capt Bentleys Compy; p.303   Nelson Patteson in Capt Smiths Company; Alexr Black in Capt Cocks's Compy; James Dugger in Capt Markes's Company; Thomas Westmoreland in Capt Butlers company; Richard Flynt in Capt Allens Company.

State v Danl T Woods. Sending written duel challenge to Tyree Rodes. Dft arraigned and pleaded not Guilty.

Grant ltrs/admn on estate of Josiah Eddy decd to William Anderson.

Grant ltrs/admn on estate of Nicholas Welch decd to Sarah Welch. p.304   Sarah Welch admx/estate of Nicholas Welch decd returned inventory of said estate; order of sale issued to sell articles contained in the inventory.

Recognizance of Abel Oxford, condition he appear next Term & prosecute & give evidence behalf State against William Welch.

Recognizance of Eli Joiner, Jeremiah Parker & Robert Dowdle condition they p.305   appeal next Term & give evidence behalf State against William Welch.

State v Samuel Cox Junr. A&B on Samuel Bird. Counsel for State no further prosecutes; dft discharged.

State v Samuel Cox Junr. Nole proseque entered. p.306   State v Samuel Cox Junr. Samuel Bird[Bud?] came not; Judgment agt him for $100; scire facias issued against him, returnable to next Court.

State v Henry Bean. Fornication. Counsel for State unwilling to prosecute; nole proseque entered. p.307   State v Henry Bean. Fornication. Judgment entered in favour of those entitled for costs.

State v Thomas Wilkison. Neglect/duty as overseer/road. Counsel for state is unwilling to prosecute.

State v Thomas Wilkinson. Nole proseque entered. p.308   State v Jesse Vinsent. A&B on Francis Hicks. Counsel for State saith he is unwilling to prosecute.

State v Jesse Vinsent. A&B on Francis Hicks. Judgment entered in favour of those entitled for all costs.

Appt Jeremiah Parker, James Graham, John Hillhouse to allot to Sarah Welch p.309   widow of Nicholas Welch decd sufficient provisions on hand as will support herself and family for one year from death of sd decedent.

State v Oliver Woods. Affray. Dft in proper person pleads guilty. Fine $3 & pay costs of this prosecution. p.310   State v William Horn. Keeping the peace. Counsel for State is unwilling to prosecute. Judgment in favour of those entitled to costs.

Commrs to settle account current of exrs of Zacheus Hurt decd made return.

State v William Ball. Assault on Nathl Almon. Jury John Thompson, William Pullin, John Yancy, Wm F Cunningham, Archd Alexander, Dudley Smith, Wm Ruddle, John
p.311 Crittenton, Thos Tarpley, James Paul, Andrew McPeters, William Hendry find dft guilty. Fine $20 and costs of this indictment.

John Butler having paid into Court the amount of the value of one acre layed off for the purpose of building a mill across Richland creek agreeably to order heretofore made as appears by return of Jury for that purpose; order sd John Butler have a fee simple in sd acre of land.

State v Riley Finney. Nole Proseque entered.

p.312 State v Riley Finney. Counsel for State is unwilling to prosecute.

State v Zacheus Hurt. Affray. Dft in proper person pleads guilty. Fine $1 and costs of this prosecution.

State v Henry Roberts. Affray. Dft in proper person pleads guilty. Fine $1
p.313 and pay costs of this prosecution.

Sheriff to notify James J Ward to appear next Term to shew cause of why a bastard child in his possession should not be bound out.

Indenture between Thomas Westmoreland chmn/Court pro-tem and German Lester, conditionally binding Elizabeth Stegall minor girl to sd Lester.

Indenture between Thomas Westmoreland chmn/Court Pro-tem and William F Thompson conditionally binding Lucinda Stegall a minor girl to sd Thompson.

p.314 On petition of William Riddle and Polly Riddle his wife late Polly Graves and widow of John Graves decd admx of estate of John Graves decd, order Sheriff summon twelve disinterested freeholders to allott to sd Polly and William one third part of land including the mansion house which which John Graves most usually dwelt & put sd Polly and William possession of same, and sd Jury divide personal estate of John Graves decd into three equal parts amongst the two children of sd John Graves decd and sd petitioners.

Court adjourned untill tomorrow 9 Oclock. William Mayfield, Pleasant Moore, Hardy Hightower.

p.315 Friday Decr 9th. Present Wm Mayfield, Pleasant Moore, Hardy Hightower.

Grant Ordinary Licence to Zacheus Hurt for twelve months.

On petition of Thomas Smith order stay proceedings to remove to this Court papers relative to a judgment which Archibald McKissack obtained agt sd petitioner before Arthur Hicks Esqr November 1814 for $45.37½.

John Edwards v Henry Scales. Certiorari. Dft in proper person. Plf recovers against dft $3 the amount of judgment rendered by Justice/Peace with legal interest
p.316 thereon from 20 May 1814 with damages and his costs.

William Hendry v Washington G L Foley. Case. Order Commission issue to two Justices of the Peace of Lincoln County, North Carolina, to take deposition of William Graham behalf plaintiff.

Reuben Higginbotham v William Ball. Case. Henry Hagen and William F Cunningham surrender William Ball to Court.

Reuben A Higginbotham v William Ball. Case. Henry Hagen & Wm F Cunningham
p.317 surrender William Ball to Court.

Reuben A Higginbotham v William Ball. Case. Commission issues to two Justices/Peace of Madison County, Mississippi Territory, to take deposition of

Benjamin L Sanders behalf plaintiff.
  Deed/release German Lester & Fanny Cleveland to Carter H Cleveland proven
by Oliver C Cleveland.
p.318   Henry Scales v Bernard M Patteson. Grand dft appeal to Circuit Court.
State v Wm Ball. A&B on Nathl Almon. Grant dft appeal to Circuit Court.
Commrs of Pulaski v Phillip Parchman. Debt. Grant dft appeal to Circuit Ct.
p.319   Commrs/Pulaski v Phillip Parchman. Debt. Grant dft appeal to Circuit Court.
  On Petition of Charlotte Moore widow of Somerset Moore decd. Order Sheriff
summon twelve disinterested freeholders to set off to Charlotte Moore one third
part of the land together with one third of the crop on hand including the mansion
house together with out houses &c & put petitioner in possession of the same.
p.320   William Robertson v James Read, Isaac Bond, Henry M Newland. Debt. Plf in
proper person assumes all costs and directs suit be dismissed.
  James Maxwell v David McMicken & John Henderson exrs. Case. On motion of
Plffs atty, original writ amended by striking out word executors and inserting the
word administrators and plaintiff pays costs of this amendment.
p.321   Grand Jury Bills/Presentment: State v Pleasant New. Same v John Young. Same
v Robert Campbell.
  William F Thompson v William Hamby. Appeal. Jury George Gibson, Robt Anderson, Andrew McPeters, Benjamin Essman, James Kimbrough, Matthew Dew, George Harrison, Henry Roberts, Nicholas Nail, Samuel Cox, Larkin Mayfield, William Hendry. Plf
p.322   recovers of dft $21.50 debt, costs before the magistrate and in this Court.
  Court adjourned untill tomorrow morning 9 Oclock. John Dickey, B Harwell,
Ar Hicks

p.323   Saturday Decr 10th. Present Buckner Harwell, Pleasant Moore, John Dickey.
  Reuben A Higginbotham v William Ball. Case. Green McCafferty & Zacheus Hurt
bail for William Ball.
  Reuben A Higginbotham v William Ball. Case. [worded as above]
p.324   Maxamilian H Buchanon Sheriff & Collector of Public and County Tax for 1814
reports taxes unpaid on following tracts of land:

Reputed owners	No of acres
Hardy Askews heirs	50 Indian creek
Heirs of Buncomb	638 Richland creek
David Berry	100 Indian creek; 50 ditto
James Conner	600 Robertsons fork
John Childress	1464 Robertsons fork
ditto	4700 Richland creek
ditto	1000 Elk River
Carters heirs	4000 Richland creek
John Edwards	100 Buchanons creek
Robert Fenner	4030[?] "
Joseph Greer	1000 Buchanons creek
Lewis Green	100 mouth of Richland
Charles Gerrard	250 Robertsons fork
Richard Hightower	640 Richland creek part of a 5000 acre grant to John Haywood by conveyance
ditto	400 part of 5000 acres granted to Wm T Lewis held by conveyance

	John Haywood & Richd Hightower	800 part of 5000 granted Wm T Lewis, held by conveyance
	ditto	6000 Richland Creek
	Isaac Hooser	30 Sinking creek
p.325	John Lester	10 Richland creek entry
	William Lytle	640 Sinking creek
	David McRee	140 Robertsons fork
	John McIver	5000 Robertsons fork
	Robert Nelson	5000
	Pallas Neal	300 Richland
	Thomas Porter	200
	John Purviance	303 Indian creek joining Lockhart
	Thomas H Perkins	50 by entry on Indian creek
	Walter Simms	5000 Richland creek
	James W Smith	500 ditto
	Robert Weakley	500 ditto
	Hezekiah Wright	200 Buchanons creek
	Daniel Adams	20 Bradshaws creek.

State and County to recover against owners or claimants of tracts the amount of tax costs & charges due thereon.

p.326   Maxamilian H Buchanon Sheriff & Collector of Public & County Tax reports following land not listed for taxation for 1814:

	Reputed owners	Acres
	George Simpson	152 North side Elk River Grant # 1779
	Chapman White	400 Elk River adj George Simpson
	Henry Tormer[Former?]	1010 Robertsons fork granted by North Carolina #24 dated 14 July 1812.
	Nathl Taylor assee of Robert Campbell	1000 incl Town of Pulaski, grant #4 dated 14 July 1812.
	Thomas Taylor Junr & James P Taylor	640 on Pigeon roost creek granted by No Carolina #38 14 July 1812 [descr omitted]
	John Drake	80 North side Elk River Warrant 835 Entry 630 [description here omitted]
p.327	Thomas H Perkins	100 Indian Creek, Warrant 318
	William Purnell	100 South side Elk river, certificate 1514 for 286 acres joining James Bright
	William Purnell	86 North side Elk River warrant 1514 for 286 acres joining Samuel Lockhart & Wm Phillips
	Henry Cearby	500 Richland creek held by deed
	Adam Lowery	35 Pigeon roost adj J White
	Thomas Polk	5000 Buchanons Creek, Pigeon roost & Bradshaw adj Micajah Green Lewis & others
	Thomas Greer	1000 Richland cr adj Isaac Prices grant
	Jeremiah Guilford	300 Richland & Buchanons cr by entry 799
	Jeremiah Guilford	200 Buchanons by entry 799
	ditto	200 begin NE corner of grant to Martin Armstrong on Buchanons cr, by entry 923
p.328	James Ruby	300, entry 807 on Richland cr of Elk R begin at Thos Polks SE corner on Richld.

DECEMBER 1814

Daniel Waters   400, Entry 804 Buchanons creek.
State & County to recover against owners or claimants the amount of double tax with costs & charges due thereon.

John Paul v Henry Hagen. Trover. Jury George Gibson, Robert Anderson, Green McCafferty, John McCracken, Nathaniel Moody, Spencer Clack, Zacheus Hurt, Eli Tidwell Sr, Wm Brown, Wm Hendry, James Kimbrough, John Keenan. Plf recovers of dft $32
p.329   damages together with his costs about his suit in this behalf expended.

Grant Ordinary Licence to Archibald Alexander for twelve months.

John Boyd v Edmund J Bailey. Debt. Grant dft appeal to Circuit court.

Indenture between John Dickey chmn of Court and Samuel Pearson binding Isabella otherwise called Eba Estep a minor girl to sd Pearson was entered into.
p.330   Buckner Harwell Senr admr estate of James Harwell decd returns inventory.

Order/sale issued to Buckner Harwell to sell perishable part of sd estate.

Nelson Patteson v William Hamby. Dft in proper person agrees that judgmt rendered agt him Feb 1813 be revived agt him for $87.50 with legal interest thereon from 20 February 1813 untill paid beside costs.

Maxamilian H Buchanon Sheriff & Collector for 1814 returned list of insolvents for sd year amounting to $6 which was allowed him, $3 of which is due to State and $3 to County.
p.331   Charles Rawson v Holbert Ellison. Certiorari. Dft recovers of plf his costs by him about his defence in this behalf expended.

State v George Taylor. Recog to appear behalf State agt John Hamblin. Dft came not. Execution awarded agt him for amount of his recognizance.

State v George Taylor. Upon recognizance to prosecute behalf state agt Sally Doolin. Dft came not. Execution awarded against him for amt of recognizance.
p.332   Deed Samuel McGee to Andrew Highsaw land in Overton County fully proven by Alfred M Harris and ordered to be certified.

Order Charles Conway committed to jail there to remain till adjournment of Court this Evening.

Samuel Sheilds Esqr resigned as a justice of the peace for this county.

Court adjourned till Court in Course.

Pleasant Moore, Wm Mayfield, B Harwell

p.333   Court of Pleas and quarter Sessions at house of Thomas Smith in Pulaski 6 March 1815. Present Samuel Jones, Buckner Harwell, William Mayfield, Justices.

Peter Bass v Nelson Patteson. Case. Plf assumed & paid all costs and directs suit be dismissed.

Grant Ordinary Licence to William Phillips for one year.

Executors of Jeremiah Perry decd returned account of sales of sd estate.

Appt Burton Beasley overseer of Fort Hampton road in room of Isaac Johnston resigned.
p.334   Appt Nathaniel Young overseer/road in room of Pleasant New resigned.

Deed Alexander McDonald to Joseph German 120 acres proved by Kinchen Baldwin and Francis Beard.

Appt Wm Mayfield & Pleasant Moore Esqrs to take privy examination of Elizabeth Perkins touching her free consent to exn of deed from Samuel Perkins & Eliza-

43

beth his wife to Jonathan Taylor for 283 acres in Anson County, North Carolina.
Deed Joseph McDonald to Rolly Brown 125 acres ackd.
p.335   Bill/sale Rolly Brown to Joseph McDonald negro man James ackd.
Deed Alexander McDonald to Francis Beard 25 acres proven by William New and Pleasant New.
Deed Thomas Marker[Markes?] to Timothy Ezzell 25 acres proven by James Dugger and Kenson McVay.
Appt John Henderson and John Dabney esqrs to settle account current between estate of David Stewart decd and James McCraven admr; make return to this Court.
p.336   Grand Jury: Duncan McIntire foreman, Shadrack Harwell, Samuel Pearson, Wm Standford, Archd Crockett, Jos McDonald, Wm Ezzell, Nathan Farmer, John Paul, James Kimbrough, Richard Bentley, Larkin Webb, William Phillips.
Deed William McDonald to William Davidson 52 acres 35 poles proven by John McNight and James McDonald.
Grant ltrs/admn on estate of Isaac Oxford decd to Jonathan Moody.
James Perry qualified as deputy sheriff during present Term of this Court.
p.337   Grant ltrs/admn on estate of William Horn decd to Nancy Horn.
Order/sale issued to Jonathan Moody admr/estate of Isaac Oxford decd.
Grant Ordinary Licence to John Yancy for one year.
Grant ltrs/admn on estate of John Lee decd to Elizabeth Lee & William Lee.
p.338   Order County trustee pay Maximilian H Buchanan $50 for exofficio services for one year prior to this time.
Order County trustee pay German Lester Clerk of Court $40 for exofficio services for one year prior to this time. Also $20 for recording the tax list. Also $15 for books furnished up to this date.
Appt Thomas Lane overseer/road in room of John Samuel resigned.
Deed William Lytle to John Vance 100 acres proven by Ephraim Parham and
p.339   Buckner Harwell Junr.
Revive order of last Court appointing Wm McDonnald, Wm Neal, Quinton Shannon, James Berry, Lewis Kirk, Elexander McDonnald, James McDonnald or any five of them to mark out a road from near where Huntsville road crosses Pleasant run thence to Nelson Pattesons SW corner on north line of Dohertys 5000 tract thence to intersect the Fayetteville road near Solomon Asbells.
p.340   Deed Isham Brown to Joshua Finch 105 acres ackd.
Grand Jury bills/Indictment: State v John McCabe Junr, true bill; Same v Same, true bill.
Lewis Lunsford recognizance, attend day to day to give evidence & prosecute behalf State against John McCabe Junr.
Nancy Boner[Bauer?] recognizance, attend day to day to give evidence behalf
p.341   State against John McCabe Junr for assault on Mahulday Lunsford.
Lewis Lunsford recognizance, to attend day to day and prosecute & give evidence behalf State against Jno McCabe Junr for assault on Nancy Boner.
Nancy Boner recognizance, attend day to day to give evidence behalf State agt Jno McCabe Jr for A&B on Nancy Boner.
p.342   Deed Spencer Griffin to Jacob Scott 300 acres in Maury County partly proven by Brice M Garner, certificate of sd probate being made by Clerk of Lincoln County & fully proven by oath of Wm Woods a subscribing witness thereto.
Deed Isham Brown to Benjamin Benson 130 acres ackd.
Deed Isham Brown to Early Benson 342 acres ackd.
p.343   Appoint Jacob Cannamore overseer/road in room of Abner McGanha[M Gauha?]

resigned.
Deed William Bond to Isham Brown 2219.3 acres proven by William Paine and
Larken Webb.
County trustee to pay Nathaniel Moody $21.06 the amount of his account.
p.344   Appt Major Harraldson overseer/road in room of Robert Reed resigned.
Appt Henry M Newland, Walter Fraser & William Fraser to allot to Alizabeth
Lee widow of John Lee decd sufficient portion of stock & provisions as will main-
tain her & children if any for one year from date of her husband's decease.
Deed Aquila Wilson to Mathew Montoreft[?] 105 acres ackd.
Deed Abel Olive to Green Ham Dotson 100 acres proven by Winnifred Simmons
and Martha Simmons.
p.345   Jarret Manifee returned list/taxable property in Capt Stark's company.
Order Joseph German, Pleasant New, Enoch Davis, Kinchen Baldwin, John
McKnight, George Waters & Samuel McKnight view situation of ground near Nathaniel
Youngs and see if Huntsville road can be turned agreeable to petition of sd Young.
Exrs of Will of William H Murrah decd returned account of sale of estate.
Will of Samuel Smith decd partly proven by William Ramsey.
Deed William Lytle to John Vance 100 acres proven by Ephraim Parham and
p.346   Buckner Harwell.
Deed John Jones to James Wilson 270 acres ackd.
Order William Henderson, Britton Yarborough, John Gordon, John Maxwell,
Enoch Davis, John Elliss & Joseph German mark a road from Hightowers Mill on Brad-
shaws creek to Cockrells gap or to intersect road from Robert Gordons to sd gap.
Agreeably to order of last Court, on 23 Decr a jury allotted to Mary
p.347   Crowson widow of William Crowson decd, her dower. Signed Aquila Wilson,
Richard Barnett, W Manifee, Thos Maxwell, Samuel Smith, Gabriel Bumpass, Wm Price,
Isaac Atkins, James J Ward, Wm Phillips, James Bumpass, Samuel Woods. The sd Mary
Crowson is perfectly satisfied. The above Jurors were qualified. James Bumpass JP.
Admrs/estate of William Crowson decd returned account of sale of sd estate.
John Temple recognizance to attend day to day to prosecute & give evidence
p.348   behalf State agt William Ball for A&B on sd John Temple.
[Another recognizance worded as above.]
Will of Buckner Harwell Senr proven by Edmond Cooper.
Power/atty Margaret Ellison and Holbert Ellison exrs/estate of Frank Elli-
son decd to William M Kearby proven by sd Margaret Ellison & Holbert Ellison.
p.349   At least five justices present, David Wilcox produced a wolf scalp over
four months old which is ordered to be burnt.
State v David McMicken. Keeping the Peace. Dft in proper person. Prosecut-
or not being desirous to rebind dft, he is released on his paying all cost.
Court adjourned untill tomorrow morning 9 O'clock. J Henderson, S Jones, J
Hillhouse, Hardy Hightower.

p.350   Tuesday March 7th. Present John Henderson, Samuel Jones, John Hillhouse,
Hardy Hightower, Esquires Justices.
John Hawkins recognizance, attend day to day to prosecute behalf State
against John Garrett.
Appt. Sterling Brown constable in Capt Brooks's company.
Appt Enoch Davis constable in Capt Paxtons company.
Appt Jesse Marlow constable in Capt Cock's company.

45

p.351   Appt Jeremiah Parker constable in Capt. Pickens's company.

Appt Carter H Cleveland overseer of Whites Mill road in room of William W Walton resigned, and that he have direction of following hands: Wm W Walton, Jesse Walton, Larkin C Walton, Willis Walton, Saml Jones, David Jones, Fanny Cleveland, Carter H Cleveland, Oliver C Cleveland, Samuel Evets, and James Read.

Deed Richard Hightower to James McDonald 70 acres ackd.

Appt William Lyon overseer of Weakley Creek road in room of Archibald McKissack removed.

p.352   James Dugger esqr returns list/taxable property in Capt Markes's company.

John Henderson esqr returns list/taxable property, Capt McVays company.

William Purnell v John Easley. Appeal. James J Ward security for defendant.

Appt Jonathan Berry constable in Capt. Herraldsons company.

Appt Thomas Phillips constable in Capt. Phillips's company.

p.353   Appt Richard Briggs constable in Capt. Adams Company.

Appt Frederick Harwell constable in Capt. Butlers Company.

Jacob Byler esqr returns list/taxable property, Capt Bylers company.

Buckner Harwell esqr returns list/taxabke property, Capt Bentleys Company.

Grand Jury Bills/Indictment: State v William Ball, true bill; Same v Same, true bill; State v John Garrett, true bill.

p.354   County Tax for 1815: On each hundred acres   .18¾
                          On each town lott   .37½
                          On each free pole   .12½
                          On each Slave   .25
                          On each stud Horse   .25
                          On each Merchants Licence   5.00
                          On each four wheel pleasure carriage 2.00
                          On each two wheel   do   1.00
        Ordered Ordinary Keepers be governed by following rates:
                          For breakfast dinner and supper   .25
                       " Horse to corn and fodder 12 hours .25
                       " Single horse feed   .12½
                       " Lodging   .08
                       " Rum by the half pint   .37½
                       " Wine by   ditto   .37½
                       " Brandy   ditto   .12½
                       " Whiskey   ditto   .12½
        Arthur Hicks esqr returned list/taxable property, Capt Reads company.

p.355   Grant ltrs/admn on estate of James Newell decd issue to Alexander Millar.

Admr/estate of James Newell decd returned inventory of sd estate.

Order/sale issues to Alexr Millar admr/estate of James Newell decd to sell the perishable part of sd estate and make return to next Court.

Grant Ordinary Licence to John Yancy for one year.

Grant Ordinary Licence to Isaac Smith for one year.

p.356   Admrs/estate of John Lee decd returned inventory/sd estate. Order/Sale issued to admrs/estate of John Lee decd to sell perishable part of sd estate.

John B Prendergast v David Woods. Appeal. Jury John McNight, Robt Alsup, Jas Tinnen, Elijah Anthony, Jacob Templen, Jesse McAnally, Spencer Clack, John Alsup Jr, Early Benson, Joseph Johns, Matthew Dew, Joseph Dickson. Plf recovers of dft $16.37½ and his costs before the magistrate as in this Court expended.

p.357   Court elected register for this County in room of Thomas Westmoreland decd;

Fountain Lester was elected, who took oaths and entered bond & security.
Grant Ordinary Licence to Thomas Smith for one year.
White & Conn v William Ball. Debt. Jury Jno McNight, Robt Alsup, James
Tinnen, Elijah Anthony, Jacob Templen, Jesse McAnally, Spencer Clack, John Alsup
Jr, Early Benson, Joseph Johns, Matthew Dew, Joseph Dickson. Plfs recover of dft
p.358 $68.52½ debt, together with damages $10.71 besides costs of suit.
Court adjourned untill tomorrow morning 9 O'clock. N Patteson, James
Bumpass, A Black

p.359   Wednesday March 8th. Present Nelson Patteson, Jas Bumpass, Alexander Black.
Will of Thomas Westmoreland decd proven by Gabriel Higginbotham and William
Price the subscribing witnesses, whereupon Sally Westmoreland and William Ragsdale
two executors therein named qualified according to Law.
Will of William Fish decd proved by Gabrael Higginbotham and William Howe,
subscribing witnesses; Duncan McIntyre and William Price qualified as executors.
Appt Thomas K Gordon, Richard Mc[binding], William Chapman, Joseph Luker,
Thomas Mac[binding], Lemuel Linsey and Samuel Criswell to view a road the best way
p.360   from Pulaski to Robert Gordons and make report to next Court.
William W Cook v James Read. Debt. Dft came not. Plf recovers of dft $50
debt, $2.17 damages and his costs of suit.
Appointments of Justices to take lists of taxable property for 1815: John
p.361   Dabney, Captain Allens Company; John Henderson, Captain Shields Company;
Alexander Black, Captain Cox's company.
John Boyd v Samuel Cox. A&B. Jury Jas Tennin, Jno MacNight, Robt Alsup, Wm
Tollis, Jessee MacAnally, Alexander Tarpley, Thomas Bratton, Wm W Crittenton, John
Macininch, Wm Cubley, Saml Woods, Micajah Ezell cannot agree. Samuel Woods one of
p.362   the jurors is withdrawn and the cause continued untill next Court.
Deed Fountin Lester & Harriett S T Lester his wife to George Looftin, land
in Christian County, Kentucky, ackd.
Order Saml Jones & Hardy Hightower Esqrs take privy examination of Harriett
S F(sic) Lester touching execution of deed from Fountin Lester & Harriett S T
Lester his wife to George Looftin, and make return to this Court.
Samuel Jones & Hardy Hightower Esqrs report Harriett S T Lester examined a-
p.363   part from her husband said she freely signed deed to George Looftin.
Will of Robert Williams decd proven by James Pain & Gabriel Bumpass.
Grand Jury Bills/Presentment: State v Archibald Alexander; Same v John
Bryant; Same v Phillip Parchman; Same v Isaac Johnson.
p.364   Thomas Washington & Chapman White exrs v Nelson Patterson. Case. Jury Jacob
Templen, Elijah Anthony, Jno Clack, Spencer Clack, Thos C Stone, Gray H Edwards,
Jno Crittenton, David Campbell, Moses Grissom, Andw McPeters, Ely Tidwell, Danl
Baker. Plfs recover of dft $103.49 besides their costs of suit.
Reuben Higginbotham v William Ball. Motion of Plf by attorney, order two
p.365   Justices/Peace of Madison County, Mississippi Territory, take deposition of
Benjamin Sanders in behalf of the plaintiff.
Hardy Hightower returns list/taxable property, Capt Packstons Company.
John Alsup Junr v Caleb Friley. Certiorari. Jury[above] say dft doth owe
plf $23.25 besides costs. Plf recovers of dft and James Doran his security afsd sum
p.366   together with six percent damages and his costs of suit.
Order of last Court directing allottment of dower to Charlotte Moore widow

of Somerset Moore decd not having been acted on, the Petition of John Hicks and
Charlotte Hicks late Charlotte Moore and widow of Somerset Moore decd, order
Sheriff to summon twelve disinterested freeholders to set off to John and Charlotte
one third part of land described in the petition including the mansion house &c and
p.367   one third of the personal estate of sd Somerset decd.
        Deed James C McRee and David W McRee to Archibald Young 164½ acres ackd.
        Deed Richard Hightower to Archibald Crockett 95 acres ackd.
        Deed Samuel Sheilds to John Childress 168¼ acres ackd.
p.368   Deed William M Marr to William McClure Junr 125 acres proved by William
Jones and William Dabney.
        Appt William Price overseer/road in room of William Fish, decd.
        Deed Adam Lowry to Fountain Lester 35 acres ackd.
        Commrs apptd to allott to Elizabeth Lee widow of John Lee decd a portion of
provisions on hand belonging to the estate made report thereof.
        Admrs/estate of John Lee decd return inventory/estate.
        Deed John Childress to Thomas Stewart 30 acres proven by Samuel Shields and
Richard S Stewart.
p.369   Deed Thomas Westmoreland to Henry McKey 110 acres proven by Henry Scales
and John Butler.
        Deed John Childress to Richard S Stewart 71¼ acres proven by Samuel Shields
and Thomas Stewart.
        Deed John Childress to Samuel Shields 84¼ acres proven by Thomas Stewart
and Richard S Stewart.
        Deed Isaac Tidwell to Permelia, Vinson, Isaac, David, Gazeway, Elizabeth
and Nancy Tidwell for certain property ackd.
p.370   Appt John Yancy guardian for Fanny Y Graves orphan of John Graves decd.
        Appt John Yancy guardian for Sally Y Graves orphan of John Graves decd.
        Court adjourned untill tomorrow morning 9 O'clock. Wm Mayfield, Hardy
Hightower, Pleasant Moore.

p.371   Thursday March 9th. Present Wm Mayfield, Hardy Hightower, Pleasant Moore.
        State v William Welch. Assault on Abel Oxford. Jury Elijah Anthony, Wm Ten-
nen, Danl T Woods, Nichs Naile, Zacheus Hurt, Tyree Rodes, Jno McKissack, Saml Harwell, Jacob Crowson, Alexr Tarply, John Young, Martin Shadden find dft not guilty.
p.372   State v James H Williams. Affray. Dft in proper person pleads guilty. Fine
$3 & pay costs of this Indictment.
        State v Alexander Angus. Assault on James Hall. Dft came not. Judgment ac-
cording to his recognizance entered against him $100; scire facias issues agt him.
        State v Alexander Angus. John McCabe bound for appearance of Alexander
p.373   Angus came not. Judgment agt him $100 according to his recognizance.
        Nancy Horn admx/estate of William Horn decd returned inventory of estate.
        Appt David W Porter, Tyree Rodes, Wm Woods to allot to Nancy Horn widow of
William Horn decd stock & provisions sufficient to maintain her and her children
for one year from day of her husbands death.
        State agt William Welch. Assault on Daniel White. Dft in proper person
p.374   pleads guilty. Fine $5 and costs in this suit expended.
        Order/sale issued to exrs of will of Samuel Harwell decd to sell perishable
part of sd estate, Negroes excepted.
        Grant Ordinary Licence to William W Crittenton for one year.

48

MARCH 1815

State v Daniel T Woods. Sending a written duel challenge to Tyree Rodes.
p.375   Jury Jacob Templen, John McNight, Nathl Moody, David Reed, Andw McPeters, Saml Cox, Jno McAninch, Stephen Anderson, Parks Bailey, David W Porter, David Campbell, John McKissick find dft guilty. Considered by Court that dft shall forever be incapable of holding any office or appointment in this government whether of honor or profit, and shall moreover be incapable of giving testimony in any Court of record or serving as a Juror, and that he pay costs of prosecution.
State v Robert Harrison. Gaming. Dft came not. Judgt according to recognizance $100; scire facias issued agt him returnable to next Court.
State v Robert Harrison. Gaming. John Harrison bound for appearance of Robert Harrison came not & neither did he deliver sd dft. Judgment according to his
p.376   recognizance $100; scire facias against him returnable to next Court.
State v Noah Hampton. Gaming. Dft came not. Judgment according to his recognizance $100; scire facias issues agt him returnable to next Court.
State v Robert Cotton. Gaming. [worded as above]
p.377   State v Robert Cotton. Gaming. Isaac Purvis bound for appearance of Robert Cotton came not & neither did he deliver sd dft; Judgmt according to recognizance.
State v Noah Hampton. Gaming. John Harrison bound for appearance of Noah Hampton came not nor did he deliver sd dft; Judgment according to recognizance.
p.378   William Purnell v George Sanders. Appeal. John Easley security for dft.
William Purnell v Abraham Cole. Appeal. John Easley security for dft.
William Purnell v James Starke. Appeal. John Easley security for dft.
William Purnell v Benjamin Osburn. Appeal. John Easley security for dft.
p.379   William Purnell v James Niel. Appeal. John Easley security for defendant.
William Purnell v Amos Vernon. Appeal. John Easley security for dft.
John Kelly Esqr recognizance, attend next Term of Court to prosecute behalf
p.380   State against Washington G L Foley.
Will of Samuel Harwell decd produced; both witnesses being dead, handwriting of testator and one of the witnesses being proven, ordered same be admitted.
Noncupitive will of Gardner Harwell decd proven in part by Samuel Harwell.
John Caldwell recog., attend next Term behalf State v Rolin McKenny[?]
Court adjourned untill tomorrow morning 9 O'clock. Wm Mayfield, N Patteson, Ar Hicks.

p.381   Friday, March 10th. Present Nelson Patteson, Wm Mayfield, Arthur Hicks.
Washington Croft v Henry Hagen. A&B. Plf came not. Dft recovers of plf his costs about his defence in this behalf expended.
Appt Acquilla Wilson, Duncan Brown, Daniel MacCollum, Gabrael Bumpass, Richard Barnett, Samuel Woods, William Phillips or any five of them lay off a road if practicable from fork of road on north side Elk River to cross at Shoemakes ferry and intersect Huntsville road.
p.382   On petition of German Lester, Exr/will of Larkin Cleaveland decd, there being nine magistrates present, setting forth that sd Cleaveland requested his exrs to procure the emancipation of a mulatto woman named Milly otherwise Milley Cole and her two children Doctor Franklin and Amelia on account of meritorious services of sd Milly, ordered and required by sd Court that sd German Lester give bond with security in penalty of $1000; whereupon German Lester, Henry Hagen, Fountain Lester, Thomas Smith and Carter Cleaveland bond, condition sd Milley and her children Doctor Franklin and Amelia become not chargeable to this county.

Thereupon John Dickey chairman of sd Court reported sd petition is granted and signed his name to same. Milly otherwise called Milley Cole & her children Doctor Franklin and Amelia are emancipated.

p.383   State v John Young. Neglect duty as overseer/road. Jury John Graves, Martin Shaddon, Ralph Graves, Wm W Crittenton, Lewis Kirk, David Campbell, John Boyd, Millinton Tidwell, Geo Harrison, Wm Brown, Thos C Stone, Henry Robards find dft guilty. Dft by his attorney moves Court for arrest of judgment.

p.384   State v Pleasant New. Neglect duty overseer/road. Jury Green MacCafferty, David W Porter, William Henry, Spencer Clack, Joseph Lann, Sampson McCown, Reuben Smith, Jesse Kirkland, David Read, John Read, Thos B Haynie, Larkin Mayfield find dft not guilty.

State v John Smith. Assault on Elijah Milton. Jury John Macnight, Robert Alsup, Jacob Templin, Elijah Anthony, Nathl Moody, Jas Tennin, Thos Harwell, Gray H

p.385   Edwards, John Powell, Saml Burney, Washington G L Foley, Samuel Paxton say dft is guilty. Fine $5 with costs of prosecution.

State v Jacob Crowson. A&B on John Boyd. Jury Andw McPeters, Washington Croft, Gideon Pillow, Tyre Rodes, Thos Bratton, Jno Keenon, Lewis Kirk, Jas Wilkinson, Moses Grissom, Wm Henderson, Spencer Clack, Oliver Woods cannot agree. A juror

p.386   is withdrawn, and a new Trial is to be held at next court.

Order Kinchen Baldwin, Pleasant New, Wm New, Joseph Jerman, Nathaniel Young, Francis Beard, William Hays or any five view situation of the road near John Youngs plantation and make return to next Court.

William Ball v Lewis Kirk. Appeal. Parties in proper person; each having assumed payment of his own cost, plaintiff dismissed his appeal.

Lewis Kirk v William Ball. Appeal. [worded as above]

p.387   Grand Jury discharged from further services during this Term.

Admx of Nicholas Welch decd returned account/sale of sd estate.

Deed Samuel MacGee to George Coulter 150 acres ackd.

Power/attorney Robert R Alsup and Lois his wife to Robert Oliver proven by H Hightower Esqr & John Kenady.

Order Wilson Collier overseer/road in room of Micajah Ezell resigned, and that he have all hands within bounds north of a line across land of Doctor Gabrael Bumpass so as to leave the Bradleys on the north.

p.388   Order all hands on the tract settled by Doctor Gabrael Bumpass south of line work under Joseph Rowe overseer/road.

Will of Odell Garrett decd proven by Arthur Hicks and Charles Simpson; David Campbell and Thomas McKissack executors therein named, qualified.

Executors of will of Odell Garret decd returned inventory/estate.

Deed Ezekiel Polk to Peter Lemmonds 150 acres proven by Isaac Atkins and Hugh Campbell.

State v Oliver Woods. Bearer of a duel challenge from Daniel T Woods to Tyree Rodes. Councel for State with assent of Court sayeth he is unwilling to prosecute further. Dft is dischanrged; dft in proper person assumes payment of costs.

p.389   State v Thomas McKerly. Neglect/duty as overseer/road. Dft pleads guilty. Fine 6½¢ and pay costs of prosecution.

State v Charles Hudspeth. Gaming. Dft came not. Judgment according to his bond, $200; scire facias issues agt him returnable to next Term.

p.390   State v Charles Hudspeth. Gaming. John Yancy bound for appearance of Charles Hudspeth came not nor did he deliver sd dft. Judgment according to his bond, $200; scire facias issues against him returnable to next Term.

MARCH 1815

State v Charles Hudspeth. Gaming. Benjamin Naile bound for appearance of Charles Hudspeth came not nor did he deliver sd dft. Judgmt according to his bond.
State v Abraham Sequers. Gaming. Dft came not. Judgment according to recognizance $100; scire facias issues agt him, returnable to next Court.
p.391   State v Abraham Sequers. Gaming. Thomas Smith bound for appearance of Abraham Sequers came not nor did he deliver dft. Judgment according to recognizance $100; scire facias issues against him returnable to next Court.
Court adjourned untill tomorrow morning 9 Oclock.
                              N Patteson, Robt Buchanan, Pleasant Moore.

p.392   Saturday March 11. Present Nelson Patteson, Pleasant Moore, Robt Buchanan.
Thomas Smith v Archibald McKissack. Supercedeas. Plaintiff in proper person assumes all costs and directs this suit be dismissed.
Archibald McKissack v Thomas Smith. Certiorari. [worded as above]
Robert Buchanon esq returns list/taxable property, Capt Butlers company.
Order Commissioners of Pulaski or a majority of them lay off Prison bounds.
William Steele v Thomas C Stone & others. Continued untill next Court.
p.393   John McCracken v Nicholas Naile, Wm Ball, Zacheus Hurt. Order motion entered to obtain judgment agt dfts on their bond for sd Nicholas Nailes keeping within the Prison bounds. Motion continued untill next Court.
William Hendry v Washington G L Foley. Case. Depositon to be taken of William Graham by Justices of Lincoln County, North Carolina, behalf of plaintiff.
Motion of John Yancy guardian of Fanny Y and Sally Y Graves orphans of John Graves decd, Court orders that William Riddle and Polly his wife appear at next Term and shew cause why they should not give security for forthcoming redelivery of distributive share or dower claimed by sd Riddle in right of his wife, which property is conveyed by his sd wife during her widowhood to sd infants.
p.394   Order that order of last Court granted on petition of William Riddle and Polly his wife late Polly Graves and widow of John Graves decd be revived.
p.395   Benjamin Benson v William Purnell. Appeal. Dft came not. Judgment of the Justice below for sum $18.46 is affirmed together with legal interest thereon from 17 Decr 1814 untill paid, together with costs before Magistrate and in this Court. Dft obtained appeal to Circuit Court.
Executors/will of William Fish decd return inventory/ estate. Order/sale issues to exrs of will of William Fish decd to sell perishable estate.
p.396   James Cunningham v John Millar. Case. Commission to two Justices of Madison County, Mississippi Territory to take deposition of John Craig, behalf dft.
State v Daniel T Woods. Sending a written duel challenge to Tyree Rodes. Dft granted appeal.
Constables Frederick Harwell and Enoch Davis to attend next Circuit Court.
Constables Richard Briggs and Sterling Brown to attend next County Court.
p.397   Jurors to next County Court: Henry Ross, Israel Pickens, Jas Hannah, Daniel White, David Maxwell, Robt Wilson, Oliver Woods, John Temple, Thos Harwood, Timothy Ezell, Daniel McCollum, Hugh Campbell, Samuel Newton, William Bradley, Hugh Adams, John Abernathy, Henry Terry, James Forbes, Thomas Rhea, Samuel McNight, Elisha Melton, John Hamm, Samuel Y Anderson, Thos McKissack, Nathan Bass, Nathaniel Moody.
Levi C Roberts v Washington Croft. Appeal. Plf in proper person having assumed payment of all costs directs his suit be dismissed; ordered accordingly.
Adjourned till Court in Course. N Patteson, Pleasant Moore, Robt Buchanan.

JUNE 1815

p.398 At Court of pleas and Quarter Sessions at house of Thomas Smith in Pulaski, Monday 5th June. Present Samuel Jones, William Mayfield, Buckner Harwell Esqrs.
Order Court adjourned to meet instanter at Isaac Smith's house in Pulaski.
Court met. Present James Dugger, Robert Buchanan, William Mayfield Esqrs.
At least five Justices present, John Graves produced a wolf scalp over four months old which was ordered to be burnt.
Appt Hightower Parten overseer/road in room of John Young resigned.
Appt William Watson overseer/road in room of Joshua Rickman resigned.
p.399 Remit double tax on John Dewaaser 440 acres; Andrew Rogers 1 white poll, 7 slaves.
At least five justices present, Samuel Ramsey produced one wolf scalp over four months old & one wolf scalp under four months old; ordered to be burnt.
[Worded as above] John Reasonhover, 9 wolf scalps under four months.
Appt James Brown, Thomas Sturt[Stuaht?] and William Jones to allot to [blank] Walker widow of Henry Walker decd a portion of estate as will be sufficient for maintenance of herself & family for one year from the death of sd decedent.
p.400 Authorize Justices to correct mistakes they may have made in Lists of taxable property; also to receive lists from persons who have not turned them in.
Grand Jury: James Forbes, Thos McKissack, Hugh Campbell, John Hamm, Israel Pickens, Samuel Newton, Elisha Melton, David Maxwell, Thomas Rea, Nathaniel Moody, Nathan Bass, Samuel Y Anderson, Hugh Adams.
Deed Buckner Harwell Junr exr of Buckner Harwell decd to George Brown 135 acres ackd.
p.401 Deed Drury Stovall to Buckner Harwell Senr 135 acres proven by Richard Barnett and James Kimbrough.
Deed Joshua Rickman and Thomas Westmoreland to James Graham 98 acres proven by George Brown and John Crittenton.
Deed Thomas T Armstrong to John Laird 185 acres proven by Perry Flynt and James H Evans.
p.402 Deed James Bright to Thomas Williams 35 acres proven by John Manefee and Saml Fain.
Deed Peter Ussery to Joseph Perkins 52 acres ackd.
Deed Thomas T Armstrong to James Hampton Evans 171 acres proven by Perry Flyntt and John Laird.
Deed Thomas T Armstrong to John Fry 325 acres proven by John Laird and Thomas Moody.
p.403 Deed H Grove attorney in fact for Andrew Erwin to James Caldwell 215 acres proven by J Ford and William Caldwell.
Deed Henson Grove attorney in fact for Andrew Erwin to James Wilson 100 acres proven by J Ford and James Caldwell.
Deed Jacob Bogard to Robert Carlton 150 acres ackd.
p.404 Deed Jacob Bogard to John Hughs 72 acres ackd.
Deed Jacob Bogard to John Calahan 107½ acres ackd.
Deed John Calahan to William Staples 30 acres ackd.
Deed Peter Ussery to Samuel Perkins 132 acres ackd.
Deed Isham Brown to Valentine Huff and John Shoemaker trustees in trust for Baptist Church on Indian creek one acre ackd by Isham Brown.
p.405 Deed Aaron Brown to John Besheers 320 acres ackd.
Deed Peter Ussery to Jacob Bogard 450 acres ackd.
Deed Peter Ussery to William Ussery 120 acres ackd.

Deed Peter Ussery to William Jones 100 acres ackd.

Deed Peter ussery to William Boils 58 acres ackd.

p.406 Deed Jacob Bogard to Peter Ussery 848 acres ackd.

Deed James Stark to William Redus[Reders?] 100 acres proven by Douglas Blue and James Hodges.

Deed Isham Brown to Jesse Lamb 172 acres ackd.

Appt Allan Abernathy overseer of upper Fayetteville road in room of Thomas McKerley resigned.

p.407 George Standford recognizance, attend day to day, prosecute & give evidence behalf State against John Perry for A&B on sd George Standford.

John Standford recognizance, attend day to day, give evidence behalf State agt John Perry for assault & battery on George Standford.

Grant ltrs/admn on estate of Nathan Henderson decd to Sally Henderson.

p.408 Grant ltrs/admn on estate of Henry Walker decd to Archer Jordan and Henry Walker. Administrators return inventory of sd estate. Order/sale issues to Archer Jordan and Henry Walker to sell perishable part of estate.

Grant ltrs/admn on estate of Jeremiah Gillespie decd to Elizabeth Gillespie and James McColloch. Admrs return inventory of said estate; order/sale issues to admrs to sell perishable part of said estate.

p.409 Grant ltrs/admn on estate of William F Thompson to Levi F Thompson. Admr returns inventory. Order/sale issued to sell perishable part of said estate.

Appt John Dabney and John Henderson Esqrs to settle accounts of David Stewart decd with James McCraven admr of sd estate.

Appt Charles Adkins overseer of Huntsville road in room of William Wells resigned.

Grant ltrs/admn on estate of George Poteete decd to Job Poteete. Admr

p.410 returns inventory of said estate.

Appt William Cubley overseer/road in room of John Elliott resigned.

Admrs/estate of John Lee decd return account of sales of sd estate.

Grant ltrs/admn on estate of William McClure decd to Willliam McClure. Admr returns inventory. Order/sale issued to Wm McClure admr/estate of William McClure decd to sell perishable part of the estate.

Grant ltrs/admn on estate of Charles Easley decd to John Easley and Joseph Bolin. Inventory of sd estate returned. Order/sale issues to John Easley & Joseph

p.411 Bolling admrs/estate of Charles Easley decd to sell the perishable part of sd estate.

Will of Odell Garrett decd partly proven at last Court now fully proven by Charles Simpson one of subscribing witnesses thereto. Polly Garret, David Campbell and Thomas McKissack extrs therein named qualified according to Law.

Appt Jordan Solomon overseer of part of road where George Waters formerly was, having direction of following hands and all others living at their houses or plantations: George Waters, John Wisener, Hardy Hightower, Joseph Roper, Samuel Ramsey, Jesse Young, Robert Alsup, Andrew Neil, James Perry, Jordan Solomon.

p.412 Appt Levi F Thompson guardian to Nancy B Thompson, Beriah K Thompson, Ebenezar E Thompson and Calvin L Thompson heirs and legatees of William F Thompson.

Order of last Court apptg Kinchen Baldwin, Pleasant New, Joseph German, Nathaniel Young, Francis Beard, William Hays and William New or any five of them to view situation of road near John Youngs plantation is revived.

State v Charles Hudspeth. Gaming. Dft in proper person pleads guilty. Fine $5 and pay costs of this prosecution.

p.413   John Birdwell recognizance, attend day to day, prosecute & give evidence behalf State agt Rebeccah Seay and Mary Seay for trading with a slave or slaves.

John Samford recognizance, attend day to day, give evidence behalf State agt Rebeccah Seay and Mary Seay for trading with a slave or slaves.

State v Charles Hudspeth. Scire facias. Dft in proper person. Forfeiture

p.414   heretofore taken agt dft set aside upon payment of costs.

State v John Yancy. Scire facias. Dft in proper person. Forfeiture heretofore taken agt dft set aside upon payment of costs.

Appt Thomas K Gordon overseer/road in room of Richard McGee resigned.

Court adjourned till tomorrow morning 9 Oclock. N Patteson, Ar Hicks, John Dabney.

p.415   Tuesday 6th June. Present Nelson Patteson, Arthur Hicks, John Dabney Esqrs.

Appt James Bumpass, Duncan McIntyre, and William Phillips to Let to Lowest Bidder the keeping of an orphan child named Thomas Cyler now in possession of Wm Arrington for term of twelve months.

Upon application of William B Lewis and John H Eaton setting forth that they have claim to two tracts of 2000 acres each in Giles County granted to James Martin Lewis by grant 20 Decr 1796. Warrant directed to John Dabney, John Henderson and Saml Jones Esqrs or any two of them to attend sd Lewis & Eaton upon above men-

p.416   tioned lands and to examine witnesses touching premises, such examination in writing signed with names of witnesses, to perpetuate boundaries of sd land.

Admx of estate of Nathan Henderson decd returned inventory of sd estate.

John B Prendergast v Isaac Johnston. Debt. Dft in proper person saith he doth owe $108.40 debt and that plf hath sustained damages of detention $2.88. Plf

p.417   recovers debt, damages, and costs of suit.

William W Cook v Quinton Shannon. Debt. Dft in proper person cannot gainsay plfs action. Plf recovers of dft his debt $50, damages $2.50, and costs of suit.

p.418   Revive order of last court apptg Thomas K Gordon, Richard McGee, William Chapman, Joseph Luker, Thomas McKerley, Saml Lindsey and Saml Criswell to view the nearest and best way from Pulaski to Robert Gordons.

Appt Joseph Knox overseer/road in room of Matthew Benthall resigned.

Will of Herbert Harwell decd proven by Rowley Harwell and Samuel Harwell, the other subscribing witnesses being dead, handwriting of decd witnesses being proved, order admitted to record. Nancy Harwell & Coleman Harwell extrs qualified.

Exrs of will of Herbert Harwell decd returned inventory of estate.

p.419   Grand Jury Bills/Indictment: State v John Perry true bill; Same v John B Williams true bill; Same v George Stanford, true bill.

Nuncupative will of Gardener Harwell decd fully proven by Rolly Harwell whereupon Rolly Harwell executor therein named qualified according to Law. Exr of Nuncupative will of Gardner Harwell decd returned inventory of estate.

p.420   At least five justices present, John Smallwood produced one wolf scalp over four months old and four wolf scalps under four months old; ordered burnt.

Order County trustee to pay William M Kerley $11.87½ for keeping Samuel Scott an orphan boy for twelve months let by order of this Court.

Order Samuel Scott an orphan boy be bound an apprentice to William M Kerley untill he shall arrive to age of twenty one years.

Exempt John Dickey from payment of $1 part of tax on one stud horse listed by him for taxes of the present year.

Exrs of will of Samuel Harwell decd returned account of sale of sd estate.

p.421   Exempt William Baley from $4.25 tax on one stud horse listed by him.

Exempt James Simmons from tax on property & lotts listed by him, sd property not taxable.

Order William Henderson, Britton Yarborough, John Gordon, John Maxwell, Enoch Davis, John Elliss, Joseph German, William New, George Waters, Francis Beard, Robert Oliver or any five of them mark out a road from Hightowers mill on Bradshaws creek to Cockrells Gap, intersecting road from Robert Gordons to sd gap.

p.422   Order Moses Evetts oversee the road from Camp branch to Gordons, directing hands: John Roberts, John Akin, Thomas Akin, Jeptha Moore, Asa Moore, French Moore, Lamb Moore, John Chapman, Benjamin Chapman, Thos Chapman, William Chapman, Benjamin Wheeler, Moses Evetts, John Wilson and hands, Harris Burges, John Grigs, Nicholas Grigs, James McCulloch, Robert McCulloch and David McCulloch.

Grant ltrs/admn on estate of James Quinn decd to Amos Quinn.

Stephen Williams v John Lee. Attachment. Samuel Cooper, garnishee, saith he gave his note to dft for $109 due 25 Decr next and hath not paid same. Simpson Lee, garnishee, saith James Hooks is indebted to dft more than $10.

p.423   Appt Edmond Gatlin overseer/road in room of Adam Burney resigned.

Appt John Manifee overseer/road in room of William Purnell resigned.

Grant ltrs/admn on estate of Holbert Ellison decd to Jane Allison, Jacob Templen, German Lester, they having been qualified.

Will of Buckner Harwell decd partly proven last Court now fully proven by William Cox, whereupon Sarah Harwell and Buckner Harwell Junr exrs therein named were qualified according to Law.

Admr/estate of Isaac Oxford decd returned account/sales of sd estate.

Admr/estate of Isaac Oxford decd returned additional inventory.

p.424   Deed Rees Porter to James B Porter 320 acres proven by John McKissack and John Evans.

Deed John Samford to Buckner Madry 131½ acres ackd.

Deed Thomas Brittian to Hardy Hightower 250 acres proven by John Kennedy and William Bolding.

Deed Buckner Madry to John Birdwell 37 acres 60 poles ackd.

p.425   Grand Jury Bills/Presentment: State v William Holt; Same v Rebecca Seay and Mary Seay.

Jenkins Whiteside v Daniel T Woods. Debt. Dft in proper person saith he

p.426   doth owe plf $100 debt, $7.08 damages together with his costs.

Nancy Odell v Benjamin Naile. Certiorari. Jury Samuel McNight, William Bradley, Henry Terry, Timothy Ezell, John Abernathy, William Brown, Thomas Wilkinson, Caleb White, Alexander Jones, Nathan Davis, Gray Edwards, Richard Bent-

p.427   ly. Plf recovers of dft her debt, damages, and costs of suit. Dft obtained appeal to Circuit Court.

Stephen Cantrill v James McCraven. [This suit X'd out]

p.428   Thomas Wilkinson v Nelson Patteson. Appeal. Jury[above except Jesse Weathers & James Egnew in place of Thos Wilkinson & Alexr Jones]. Plf recovers $4.12½

p.429   and his costs of suit.

Assignment of platt & certificate of survey from Joshua Hadley to William McDonald acknowledged by sd Joshua Hadley.

Exrs of will of Herbert Harwell decd returned account/sales of estate.

Thomas Taylor Junr v Thomas Smith. Case. Plf in proper person assumes payment of all costs and directs suit be dismissed.

p.430   Court adjourned till tomorrow 9 Oclock. N Patteson, Jas Dugger, Wm Mayfield

p.431   Wednesday 7 June. Present Nelson Patteson, James Dugger, William Mayfield.
Henry Minor Esqr having produced Licence as attorney and having taken Oaths prescribed by Law is admitted to practice as such.
Thomas Wilkinson v Nelson Patteson. Appeal. Jury: Daniel McCollum, Henry Terry, Wm Bradley, Timothy Ezzell, Geo Harrison, Chas Conway, Lawson Hobson, Tyree Rodes, Saml Coxe, Henry Roberts, John Easley, Jacob Crowson. Plf recovers of dft
p.432 $15.25 and his costs before the magistrate as in this Court expended.
Exrs/will of Buckner Harwell decd returned inventory.
Deed William Polk by attorney Samuel Polk to David L Jones 50 acres proven by Alfred M Harris and Peter R Booker.
Admx/estate of William Horn decd returned account/sales of sd estate.
Deed Joshua Hadley, Maxamillian H Buchanon & Gabriel Bumpass to Aquila Wilson 160 acres proven by Henry Scales and Robert Buchanon.
p.433   Stephen Cantrell v James McCraven admr/estate of David Stewart decd. Debt. Jury Saml McNight, Wm Bradley, Henry Terry, Timothy Ezzell, Jno Abernathy, William Brown, Caleb White, Nathan Davis, Gray Edwards, Richd Bentley, Jesse Weathers, Wm B
p.434   Brooks. Plf recovers agt dft debt and damages and his costs of suit.
At least five justices present, John Welch produced two wolf scalps over four months old, which were ordered to be Burnt.
Commrs apptd to allott to Nancy Horn, widow of Wm Horn decd, a portion of provisions on hand belonging to the estate made report thereof.
State v Butler Hale. A&B on David Tuttle. Dft in proper person assumed and paid costs; nole proseque entered.
p.435   John Boyd v Samuel Coxe. A&B. Jury Danl McCollum, Henry Terry, Wm Bradley, Timothy Ezzell, John Brashers, Chas Conway, Lawson Hobson, Jacob Crowson, Daniel Baker, Robt Campbell, John Nave, Robert Paine. Plf recovers of dft his damages $13 and costs of suit.
p.436   Grand Jury Bills/Presentment. State v Charles Conway; Same v Richard Conway; Same v Jas Conway; Same v Jas Bunch; Same v Wm Holt; Same v Robt Steele.
p.437   Order County Trustee pay William Arrington $21 for keeping orphan child for six or seven months last past.
Jurors to Circuit Court: Wm H Ragsdale, Humphrey Tompkins, Aquilla Wilson, Wm Price, Robt Paine, Robt Buchanan, Thos Steele, Willis S McLaurine, Wm Maples, Drury Alsup, Wm Neale, Alexr Black, Ralph Graves, John Phillips, Saml Y Anderson, Nelson Patteson, Wm Mayfield, John Dickey, Walter Loch, Jacob Byler, Alexr Miller, Wm Pickens, John Jones, Robt Read, John Knox, Arthur Hicks.
Constables Enoch Davis & Jeremiah Parker to attend Circuit Court.
p.438   Jurors to next County Court: John Yancy, David W Porter, Lester Morris, Chas Buford, Jos Dickson, John Elliott, Major Harrolson, David Baker, Thos McBride, John Blazingame, John Robertson, Danl Allen, Hamilton C Campbell, Jos Rea, John Gibson, Thos Meredith, Wm Rose, Wm Brown, John Butler, John Barnett, Robt McNairy, Wm B Pepper, Earley Benson, John Kenneday, Elijah Anthony, Joseph Anthony.
Constables Thos Marx & Thos Phillips to attend next term of this Court.
Order Nelson Patteson, James Buford, John Hicks to superintend the election of Governor, member of Congress and members of General Assembly in Pulaski on first Thursday and Friday in August next.
p.439   John Hillhouse, Matthew Benthall, Jacob Byler apptd judges to superintend

56

election at house of John Dickey Esqr on first Thursday & Friday in August next.
Order George Malone, John Laird, Anthony Samuel superintend election at the house of Martin Lane on first Thursday and Friday in August next.
Order John Hawkins, Thos Harwood, Wm Price superintend election at house of William Phillips on first Thursday & Friday in August next.

p.440   State v Robert Campbell. Neglect/duty as overseer/road. Dft in proper person pleads guilty; fine 6½¢ and costs of prosecution.
Order William Neal with hands under his direction together with hands at Edward O Chambers, Judith and Samuel Hurts, William Abernathys, John Abernathys and Alexander Tarpleys open road lately marked out from Huntsville road beyond Chambers fence thence to Cooks Bear pen Hollow thence by Solomon Asbells across creek to intersect Fayetteville road near John Webbs. When opened, the road from Solomon Asbells to fork at William Neals fence to be discontinued as a publick highway.

p.441   Court adjourned till tomorrow morning 9 Oclock. John Dickey, Pleasant Moore, Ar Hicks.

p.442   Thursday 8th. Present John Dickey, Pleasant Moore, Arthur Hicks, Esqrs.
Eldridge B Robertson Esqr having produced licence to practice law on being qualified was admitted to practice in this Court.
State v Isaac Reynolds. Riot. Counsel for State no further prosecutes.
State v Isaac Reynolds. Riot. Judgment entered in favour of those entitled.
p.443   State v John Garrett. Trading with a Negro. Dft hath departed this Life.
State v John Garrett. Judgment entered in favour of those entitled.
State v John B Williams. Trading with a negro. Dft came not. Judgment ac-
p.444   cording to recognizance $200; scire facias agt him returnable next Court.
State v John B Williams. Trading with a Negro. John Manifee being required to bring dft came not; judgmt according to recognizance $100; scire facias issues.
State v Charles Conway. A&B on Henry Roberts. Dft in proper person pleads
p.445   guilty. Fine $2 and pay costs of prosecution.
State v John Perry. A&B on William Standford. Dft in proper person pleads guilty. Fine $5 and pay costs of prosecution.
p.446   State v Washington G L Foley. A&B on John Kelly. Jury Timothy Ezell, John Abernathy, Samuel McNite, Leonard Brown, Spencer Clack, James Reddus, Samuel H Dodson, William Dabney, Jacob Cody, Charles Dever, William Hendry, Thomas Brown. Dft acquitted, plf John Kelly the prosecutor in this case to pay costs of prosecution.
p.447   State v William Ball. A&B on Thos Marks. Dft in proper person assumes payment of all costs; nole prosique entered.
State v Edwin Denton. Keeping the peace. Dft in proper person. No person appearing to rebind sd defendant, he is discharged from his recognizance.
p.448   Grand Jury Bills/presentment: State v James Paine; Same v Same; Same v Wm Straughan; Same v Nathl Messer; Same v Henry Roberts; Same v Nicholas Naile; Same v Elisha Shelton; Same v William Adams; Same v William Kindle; Same v William Ball; Same v Henry Hagen; Same v Thomas Smith.
p.449   State v Spencer Clack. [blank]
State v John Bryant. Affray with Archibald Alexander. Jury Daniel McCollum, Thos K Gordon, Henry Terry, Jas Hannah, Chas Conway, Thos Wilkinson, Jos Johns, Jas Agnew, Phillip Parchman, Wm Giddens, John Yancy, John Alsup Junr. Dft acquitted.
p.450   State v Phillip Parchman. Affray with John Jones. Jury Danl McCollum, Thos K Gordon, Henry Terry, Jas Hannah, Chas Conway, Jos Johns, Wm Giddens, John Yancy,

JUNE 1815

John Alsup, Samuel McKnight, John Abernathy, William Hendry. Dft acquitted.
    State v Martin Shadden. Neglect/duty as overseer/road. Jury[above] find dft
guilty; fine $2.50 and pay costs of prosecution.
    State v Isaac Johnston. Affray with Jno Jones. Jury Timothy Ezzell, William
p.451   Bradley, Spencer Clack, Leonard Brown, James Reddus, Saml H Dodson, Charles
Devers, James Agnew, Robert Anderson, John Waldrup, John Maxwell, Joseph Shadden
p.452   find dft not guilty.
    State v Richard Conway. Affray with Henry Roberts. Dft in proper person.
Jury Daniel McCollum, Henry Terry, James Hannah, Jno Phillips, Joseph Johns, Elijah
Anthony, Robt Brashers, Saml McNight, Jno Abernathy, Moses L Moon, Wm Hendry, Archd
Alexander find dft guilty. Fine $2 and pay costs of prosectuion.
p.453   State v Archibald Alexander. Affray with John Bryant. Dft in proper person
pleads guilty. Fine $1 and pay costs of this prosecution.
    State v John McCabe Jr. A&B on William Brown. Dft in proper person pleads
guilty. Fine $5 and pay costs of this prosecution.
p.454   State v William Perry. Dft in proper person pleads guilty. Fine $1 & costs.
    State v Henry Hagen. Gaming. Dft in proper person pleads guilty. Fine $5
and pay costs of this prosecution.
p.455   State v Spencer Clack. Gaming. Dft in proper person pleads builty. Fine $5
and pay costs of this prosecution.
    State v Thomas Smith. Gaming. Dft in proper person pleads guilty. Fine $5
and pay costs of this prosecution.
p.456   State v William Kindell. Gaming. Dft in proper person pleads guilty. Fine
$5 and pay costs of this prosecution.
    State v John Bryant. Affray with Archibald Alexander. Dft being acquitted,
judgment entered up in favour of those entitled for all costs.
p.457   State v Phillip Parchman. Affray with John Jones. Judgment entered up in
favour of those entitled for all costs.
    State v Samuel Rose. Keeping peace. Dft came not. Judgment according to
tenor of his recognizance, $100 with costs.
p.458   State v Moses Hamilton. Security for Saml Rose for keeping the peace. Dft
came not; judgment according to recognizance, $100 besides costs.
    State v Isaac Purvis. Scire facias. Dft in proper person. Forfeiture agt
dft set aside upon the payment of costs.
p.459   John Caldwell recognizance, to attend next Term to prosecute & give
evidence behalf State against Rowland McKinney for gaming.
    Grant Ltrs/admn on estate of Isam Hammonds decd to John Hammonds.
    State v Valentine Choate. Keeping the peace. Defendant in proper person, no
person appearing to rebind dft, order he be discharged of payment of all costs.
p.460   Commissioners apptd to mark out the Prison bounds made report: Bounds for
all unfortunate debtors to take air exercise containing near six acres as follows:
Lotts 67 and 66 on which the Jail stands, the whole Public Square & thirty feet
back on every Lott & street adjoining same, Lott 51 including the Spring, thence to
Public Square. Gab Bumpass, N Moody, S Jones, Tyree Rodes, M H Buchanon.
p.461   State v Alexander Angus. Council for State is unwilling to prosecute
further; James Angus in proper person assumes payment of all cost.
    State v Alexander Angus. Forfeiture agt dft set aside; James Angus assumes
payment of all costs.
p.462   State v John McCabe. Dft in proper person, forfeiture set aside upon
payment of costs.

JUNE 1815

State v Isaac Johnston. Affray with John Jones. Judgment entered in favour of those entitled for all costs.
p.463 Court adjourned till tomorrow morning 9 Oclock. John Dickey, Pleasant Moore, Wm Mayfield.

p.464 Friday 9th June. Present John Dickey, Pleasant Moore, William Mayfield. Admrs/estate of Holbert Allison decd returned inventory of sd estate. Deed/gift John Hicks to Harrison Hicks for certain property ackd. Deed/gift John Hicks to Francis Hicks for certain property ackd. Deed/gift John Hicks to Mary Hicks, Parkey Hicks, and Sally Hicks for certain property therein named ackd.
p.465 Jonathan Richards v Philmer Green. Case. Jury Henry Terry, William Bradley, Washington G L Foley, Wm Riddle, Robert Brashers, Wm Hendry, Robert McCulloch, Wm R Cox, Thomas C Stone, John Yancy, Herod Foulks, Joseph Johns. Plf recovers of dft damages $89.50 and costs of suit.
p.466 Order following tax lists received and double tax thereon remitted

Nelson Patteson	100 acres head of Leatherwood
&	20 ditto
Nathan Davis	40 ditto
	30
	60 acres, ridge dividing Buchanons & Leatherwood
	10 head of Pigeon roost
	20 ditto
Nathan Davis	183 acres Leatherwood Creek
	37½ acres ditto
John Nelson	100 acres Richland Creek
	1 white pole
	1 Black pole
	1 Stud horse at $2
Lydia Nelson	80 acres Richland creek
	1 black pole
Elizabeth Smith	280 acres Richland Creek
	2 black poles
James Rainey	3000 acres Richland creek
Lemuel Simmons	1 white pole
Thomas Beal	1 white pole
John Bryant	1 white pole
John Elliott	1 white pole
James McGill	1 white pole
Benjamin Tutt	1 white pole
Richard McLemore	1 white pole
Andrew Elliott	1 white pole
Caleb White	53 acres
	1 white pole
	1 black pole

p.467 Thomas C Stone v Wm F Thompson. Case. Dft hath departed this Life. John Dabney Esqr resigned as Justice/Peace for this County. Order Samuel Jones, Alexr Black and William Mayfield Esqrs settle with M H Buchanon surviving admr/estate of Clayton S Buchanon decd.

JUNE 1815

Commissioners apptd to settle estate of David Stewart decd in hands of
James McCraven admr made return of their settlement.

p.468   Remit double Tax on following Tax lists:

Stephen Anderson	1 white pole	1 black pole
Matthew Anderson	1 white pole	1 black pole
James Brown	1 white pole	
Robert Bell	1 white pole	
Charles C Baley	1 white pole	1 black pole 3 lotts
Richard Bailey	1 white pole	
William Chapman	1 white pole	
John Chapman	1 white pole	
Martin Lorance	40 acres Robertson fork 1 white pole	1 black
	1 Stud horse at $5	
Asa Moore	1 white pole	
Japtha Moore	1 white pole	
Robert McDaniel	1 white pole	
John Milroy	1 white pole	
Joshua Hadley	2424 acres by grant & entry	
M H Buchanon	50 acres by entry 1 white pole	
William Pullin	1 white pole 1 black pole	
Moses Pullin	78 acres Robertsons fork	
Andrew Pickens	1 black pole	
Phillip Parchman	4 black poles	
Joseph Riley	100 acres Leatherwood cr 1 white pole	
Walter Simms	5,000 acres	
Alston Waters Jr	184 waters Robertsons fork	
Matthew Wilson	1 white pole	

p.469   Nelson Patteson v Thomas Wilkinson. Trespass. Jury Lewis Kirk, Danl McCollum, Timothy Ezzell, John Abernathy, Thos Beal, Sampson McCown, James Agnew, Samuel Pearson, Spencer Clack, William Arnett, John Elliott, David Campbell. Dft recovers against plaintiff his costs about his defence in this behalf expended.

p.470   Remit double tax on following lists:

Coleman Harwell	1 white poll	2 slaves
Est Samuel Harwell decd	10 slaves	
Nancy Harwell	8 slaves	
Thomas Wells	1 white poll	
William Kyle	1 do	10 slaves
Thomas Alsup	40 acres head Buchs; 25 acres Indian Cr	
James Morphos	1 white poll	
George M Gibson	1 do	
John Oxford	1 do	
Peter Swanson	1 do	
Absolom McCormack	1 do	
Richard Connway	1 do	
Alfred Donaldson	1 do	
Richard Johnston	1 do	2 slaves
John Johnston	1 white poll	1 slave
Matthew Johnston	1 white poll	1 slave
Jesse McAnally	1 white poll	
George Coalter	80 acres Elk River	

60

JUNE 1815

James Paine   1 stud Horse
John Anderson   1 white pole
Isaac Anderson   1 do
p 471   Grand Jury Bills/presentment: State v Henry Hagen; Same v William Kindle;
Same v Henry C F Cyrus.
        Court adjourned till tomorrow morning 9 Oclock. N Patteson, James Bumpass,
Pleasant Moore

p.472   Saturday 10th June. Present Nelson Patteson, James Bumpass, Pleasant Moore.
        State v Henry Hagen. A&B on Lewis Kirk. Dft in proper person pleads guilty.
Fine $1 and pay costs of this prosecution.
        State v William Kindell. A&B on John Romack. Dft in proper person pleads
guilty; fine $5 and pay costs of this prosecution.
p.473   John Paul v Kinchen T Wilkinson. Judicial attachment. Jury Wm Bradley, John
Abernathy, Henry Terry, Wm Riddle, John Yancy, Charles Hudspeth, Wm Abernathy, Saml
Chambers, Wm Steele, Herod Fowlks, Saml Burney, Wm Hendry. Plf recovers of dft
damages by reason of false & defamatory words to $30.66½ and costs of suit.
p.474   Order Ralph Graves oversee road from junction of First and Second in
Pulaski to dry fork of Pigeon roost, calling on all hands residing east of Third St
for two days work to assist hands now under his direction to put in repair that
part of sd road which lies between sd junction and Thomas Wilkinsons fence.
        John Paul v Kinchen T Wilkinson. Judicial attachment. Bond of James Buford
in room of Henry Hagen who was original security.
        Petit jurors not now in service are discharged.
p.475   Grand Jury Bills/presentment: State v John Bryant; Same v Jelly Pemberton;
Same v Milley Cole; Same v William W Crittenton.
        Order Grand Jury discharged from further service at this Term.
        Appt Thomas Phillips overseer/road in room of Martin Shadden resigned.
        William Hendry v Washington G L Foley. Case. Order two Justices/peace for
Lincoln County, North Carolina, take deposition of William Graham behalf plf.
p.476   At least five justices present, John S Bailey produced a wolf scalp over
four months old which was ordered to be burnt.
        Jonathan Richards v Philmer Green. Case. Grant Dft appeal to Circuit Court.
        Order William Henderson, John Porter and Wm Mayfield allot to Jane Allison
widow of Halbert Allison decd provisions belonging to estate as will be sufficient
for support of herself and family for one year from time of his death.
p.477   State v William Welch. A&B on Abel Oxford. Dft acquitted; Judgment entered
up in favour of those entitled for all costs.
        State v Pleasant New. Neglect/duty as overseer/road. Dft acquitted; judg-
ment entered up in favour of those entitled for all costs.
p.478   Order admr of estate of John Graves make sale of sufficient portion of sd
estate as will pay debts due from said estate.
        Order that order heretofore granted for division of estate of John Graves
decd be revived and jury make report to next Court.
        John Paul v Kinchen T Wilkinson. Judicial attachment. Dft obtains appeal to
Circuit Court.
        State v John Young. Neglect/duty as overseer/road. Dft fined 6¼¢ and pay
costs of this prosecution.
p.479   John Paul v Kinchen T Wilkinson. appeal. Order two Justices/peace for

SEPTEMBER 1815

Augusta County, Virginia, take deposition of John Paul Junr on behalf plf.
    Appt Henry P Crittenton overseer/road in room of Samuel Cox resigned.
    Qualify John Buchanan to act as Deputy Sheriff.
p.480   Remit double tax on following tax list:
Joseph Dickson	1 white pole
Isaac Reynolds Jr	1 do
Wm B Lewis	1420½ ac part of 5000 acres granted Micajah G Lewis
John H Eaton	1421½ ac part of above mentioned tract
Charles Ho Lewis	1421½ ac part of above mentioned tract

Ferdinand, Mary and McCajah Claibourne 1066 acres part of the above
                mentioned tract.
    Heirs of William T Lewis 3000 acres the residue of two tracts of 2000
                acres each granted to Wm T Lewis
    Order John McCracken overseer of Second Street in Pulaski in room of Thomas
C Stone removed, given leave to call on all hands subject to work on first street
for one days work to work on Second Street.
    Court adjourned till Court in Course. N Patteson, James Bumpass, A Black

p.481   [blank]
p.482   Court of Pleas and Quarter Sessions at house lately occupied by Isaac Smith
it being the place of holding Court at Last term, Monday 4th September. Present
John Dickey, John Hillhouse, Pleasant Moore, Esquires, Justices.
    Admrs of estate of Henry Walker decd returned account of sale of sd estate.
    Allow George Brown $38.75 for keeping James Dickson a poor person for
twelve months prior to this time, let by order of Court at last September Term.
    Court adjourned to meet Instanter at Court house in Pulaski.
    Court met. Present John Dickey, Alexr Black, Pleasant Moore, Jacob Byler.
p.483   Power/attorney Anthony Samuel to Thomas B Haynie ackd.
    Power/attorney David Cooke to John Cooke and Lemuel Cooke ackd.
    Power/attorney Walter Fraser and James Fraser to William Fraser ackd.
    Executors/will of William H Murrah decd returns additional account/sale.
    Deed Richard Hightower to John Hughs 15 acres 10 poles land ackd.
p.484   Deed Samuel Paxton to Robert Oliver 5½ acres ackd.
    Deed Maxamillion H Buchanon to Henry Nave 103¾ acres ackd.
    Deed John Hughs to David Hill 51 acres 90 poles land ackd.
    Mortgage George Harrison to William Mayfield ackd.
    Deed/gift John Black to John Henry Black and others proven by Alfred M
Harris the subscribing witness thereto.
p.485   Grand Jury: Jno Yancy foreman, Jno Butler, Thomas H Meredith, Thos McBride,
Elijah Anthony, Lester Morris, Earley Benson, John Elliott, Joseph Rea, John Blazingame, Joseph Anthony, William B Pepper, Hamilton C Campbell.
    Constable Douglass L Blue sworn to attend Grand Jury this Term.
    Deed Richard Hightower to George Walters[Watters?] 60 acres ackd.
    Grant Ltrs/admn on estate of James Robertson decd to Martha Robertson and
Richard Darby; inventory returned. Order/sale issued to Martha Robertson & Richard
p.486   Darby admrs/estate of James Robertson decd to sell perishable estate.

62

Order William Henderson, Archibald Young & Brittain Yarborough allot to Martha Robertson widow of Jas Robertson decd sufficient portion of estate to maintain herself & family for one year from the time Jas Robertson departed this life.

Order Robert Buchanon & James Bumpass Esqrs settle account current of Isam Brown admr/estate of Minor Winn decd; report to next Court.

Order Robert Buchanon & James Bumpass Esqrs settle account current of Isam Brown admr estate of Ambrose Foster decd.

Following persons who were summoned as Jurors this Term are exhonerated therefrom: Daniel Allen, John Kenneday, John Barnett, Charles Buford.

p.487 Jurymen sworn as original panel this Term: Robert McNairy, John Gibson, David W Porter, William Brown, Joseph Dickson, William Rose.

Grant Ordinary Licence to John Thompson for one year.

Grant Ordinary Licence to Nathaniel Moody for one year.

Grant Ltrs/admn on estate/George Williams decd to Rebeccah Williams. Order of sale issued to Rebeccah Williams to sell perishable part of sd estate.

Grant ltrs/admn on estate of Robert Birdwell decd to Jane Birdwell and John
p.488 Birdwell. Inventory of estate returned.

David McMicken v William White. Trespass. Edward Lee and William Lee bound for appearance of William White surrender him to Court. Thos Acres and William Lee bail for William White.

Grant ltrs/admn on estate of Randal Cheek decd to Valentine Cheek. Inventory of estate returned by admr.

Order Nelson Patteson, Jas Buford & Ralph Graves let to lowest bidder the keeping of James Dickson a poor person of this County for one year from this time.

State v Benjamin Naile. Failing to produce Charles Hudspeth. Dft in proper person; forfeiture agt dft set aside upon payment of costs.

p.490 Order Nathan Davis, Allen Abernathy, James Dugger, Thomas Mark, Thomas McKerley & Samuel Caswell or any five of them view Fayetteville road near plantation of Austin Smith and see if it be proper to turn sd road agreeable to wish of Smith.

At least five Justices present, David Flatt produced three wolf scalps over four months old which was ordered to be burnt.

At least five Justices present, William Metcalf produced one wolf scalp over four months old and seven under four months old which was ordered to be burnt.

At least five Justices present, John Rea produced two wolf scalps over four months old which was ordered to be burnt.

Appt Samuel Perkins overseer/road in room of John Hughs resigned.
p.491 Appt Reuben Smith overseer of Weakleys creek road in room of David W Porter resigned.

Order Wm Pullen oversee Montgomery Gap rd in room/Mattw Johnston resigned.

Will of John Black decd proven by Elizabeth McGee subscribing witness; whereupon Richard McGee executor therein named qualified as executor.

Deed Josiah Temple to John Menifee 37½ acres proven by Simon Williams and Daniel Martindale.

Deed Samuel Bradley to George Winterbower 20 acres ackd.
p.492 Deed Josiah Temple to James Williams 30 acres proven by Simon Williams & Daniel Martindale.

Deed John Lester to James Williams 10 acres proven by Simon Williams and Daniel Martindale.

Deed Archibald Young to Ambrose Yarborough 100 acres partly proven at Last Court is now fully proven by Brittain Yarbrough.

Deed Isham Brown to Abraham Brown 246 acres ackd.
p.493   Deed Isham Brown to Larkin Webb 45 acres ackd.
Deed Aaron Brown to Reuben Westmoreland 640 acres ackd.
Deed Alexander McDonald to William New 100 acres ackd.
Deed Samuel Paxton to Robert Oliver 15 acres ackd.
Deed Richard Hightower to Pallis Niel 300 acres ackd.
p.494   Order John McNight oversee road from Pleasant News to ridge towards Indian creek directing following hands: John McNight, Michael Gooden, Pleasant New, Kinchen Baldwin, Saml Wright, Charles Browning, Jas Paxton, Enoch Davis, Saml McNight.
William McClure admr/estate of Wm McClure decd returned acct/sale.
Order John Dabney, Ephraim Patrick & William M Marr allott to Fanny McClure widow of Wm McClure decd sufficient portion of estate to maintain herself and family for one year from time Wm McClure departed this life.
Order William McDonald, Thomas Alsup, Josiah Stovall, John McNight, Samuel McNight, Robt Oliver, Pleasant New or any five of them to view situation of ground where Isaac Williams wishes to turn the road from Rock Spring to foot of ridge and if practicable to turn sd road agreeable to petition of Isaac Williams.
p.495   Deed Robert Henderson by atty William S Henderson to Thomas Chatman 270 acres having been partly proven last Court is now fully proven by Thomas Lane.
Order Alfred M Harris Esqr be allowed five percent on monies by him in capacity of agent and attorney for commissioners collect or pay over to commrs.
Order Nelson Patteson, Edward O Chambers and William Neale let to lowest bidder the building of bridge across Crooked Creek where road from Pulaski to Elkton crosses same.
p.496   Appt Charles Robertson overseer/road in room of Jacob Byler resigned.
Appt Henry Abernathy overseer/road in room of Joseph Rowe[Reeve?] resigned.
Order John McNight, Samuel McNight, John Wisener, James Madry, Samuel Ramsey view that part of road from Hightowers mill to Cockrells gap near Robert R Alsups plantation and see if it be proper to turn said road or if it should run as it now does, and assess damages Alsup may sustain.
Order that part of Fayetteville road near John Youngs plantation which has been opened by order of this Court be established as a public highway and that Hightower Partin oversee keeping same in repair with hands under his direction.
Deed Alexander McDonald to Moses Kindell 100 acres ackd.
p.497   Order Joseph Anthony, Elijah Anthony, Jesse Beasley, John Yancy and James Buford let to lowest bidder the building of a bridge across creek that runs through John Yancys lane where the road from Pulaski to Fort Hampton crosses same.
Appt John Maxwell overseer/Shelbyville road in room of Jos Murphy resigned.
Appt Maj Richardson overseer/road in room of Ephraim Partrick resigned.
Mary Earnest admx of George Earnest decd returned account/sale of estate.
Jas Bumpass, Duncan McIntire & Wm Phillips apptd last Ct to let to lowest bidder the keeping of orphan child Thomas Cyler for twelve months report the child let to Joseph Stovall for $25.
p.498   Will of Isaac Meadows decd proven by Joshua Nichols and Coleman Hutcheson; Anderson Meadows and Elijah Meadows, exrs therein named were qualified.
Daniel T Woods v Joseph Johns. Case. James Brownlow and Richard H Allen surrender dft. Nelson Patteson & Nathan Davis bail for dft.
p.499   John Gilbert v Moses Kindell. Certiorari. Parties in proper persons; dft assumes payment of clerks cost; plf assumes constables cost; plf dismisses suit.

SEPTEMBER 1815

Stephen Williams v John Lee. Attachment. Simpson Lee recognizance, condition John Lee appear at next Term. Samuel Cooper & James Hooks, garnishees and
discharged & property attached replevied.
p.500   Amos Williams & Betsey Williams v Thomas Williams. Issue whether James
Williams late of this County deceased died testate or intestate.
        Court adjourned till tomorrow morning 9 Oclock. Jacob Byler, Hardy High-
tower, Robt Buchanan.

p.501   Tuesday 5th Sept. Present Jacob Byler, Robert Buchanon, Hardy Hightower.
        Appt Thos Baily overseer/Fayetteville rd in room of Thos B Haynie resigned.
        Noel Patterson v John Braden & Jacob Montgomery. Debt. Jury Robert McNairy,
Jno Gibson, Wm Brown, Jno Graves, Thomas Steele, Robt Anderson, Reuben Smith, David
Campbell, Wm(sic) Brown, Thomas Harwell, Robt McLaurin, William Hendry. Plaintiff
p.502   recovers of dfts $113 debt, damages $4.52 and costs of suit.
        Order Jesse West, Martin Shadden, Elisha Dodson, Wm B Cocke, Saml H Dodson,
Jno Phillips, Wm Woods, Jesse Marlow or any five mark out a road from William Giddens to intersect the Columbia road at James Tinnens; make return to this court.
        Charles Smith for benefit of Josiah Alderson v Nelson Patteson. Debt. Jury
p.503   [above] say dft hath not paid debt fifty pounds nine shillings eleven pence
one farthing Virginia currency, value $168.33. Plf recovers debt, damages $58.80,
and costs about is suit in this behalf expended.
        Order County trustee pay John Goff $4.30 for boarding guard while guarding
John Boyd who was ordered into custody of sheriff at June Term 1814.
p.504   Amos Quinn admr/estate of James Quinn decd returned inventory of sd estate.
Order/sale issues to Amos Quinn to sell perishable part of sd estate.
        John Alsup recognizance, attend day to day to prosecute & give evidence
behalf State agt John Perry for A&B on sd John Alsup.
        William Caldwell recognizance, attend day to day to prosecute & give
evidence behalf State agt Rowland McKinney for A&B on sd Wm Caldwell.
        Appt Abijah Flynt constable in Capt Pickenses company.
p.505   John Easley and Joseph Boling admrs/estate of Charles Easley decd returned
account of sale of sd estate.
        Grant Ordinary Licence to Nathan Farmer for one year.
        William ONeal v Gideon Pillow. Debt. Jury[above]. Plf recovers of dft his
p.506   debt; damages assessed by jury to $9, and costs.
        John Temple v James McCormack. Debt. Jury[above]. Plf recovers of dft $215
debt, damages $10.75, and costs of suit.
p.507   John Boyd v Zacheus Hurt. Debt. Jury David W Porter, Joseph Dickson, William Rose, Wm B Brooks, Alexr Tarpley, William L Campbell, John Abernathy, Featherston Harwell, William R Cox, Samuel H Dodson, Matthew Dew, Bernard M Patteson. Plf
recovers of dft $72 debt, $4.84 damages, and his costs of suit. Marginal note:
Execution stayed by Bill/Injunction granted 14 Octr 1815.
p.508   John Boyd v Edward O Chambers. Debt. Jury Robt McNairy, Jno Gibson, Robert
Anderson, Reuben Smith, William Brown, Thomas Harwell, Robert McLaurine, Wm Hendry,
Thos C Stone, Edward M Brown, Robt Black, David W Porter. Plf recovers of dft $120
debt, damages $7.66 and his costs of suit. 1816 June 15 Recd of G Lester the amt
of the above Judgment. John Boyd.
p.509   Will & A Trigg v William Ball & Gilbert D Taylor. Debt. Jury Joseph Dickson, William Rose, Wm B Brooks, Alexander Tarpley, Gray H Edwards, John Abernathy,

65

Featherston Harwell, Wm R Cox, John Keenan, Matthew Dew, Bernard M Patteson, David Campbell. Plfs recover of dfts $180.21¼ debt, damages $9.65, & their costs of suit.

p.510   Reuben Hampton v Caleb Fraley. Debt. Jury Joseph Dickson, Wm Rose, Wm B Brooks, Alexander Tarpley, Gray H Edwards, Jno Abernathy, Featherston Harwell, Wm R Cox, Jno Kenan, Matthew Dew, Bernard M Patteson, David Campbell. Plf recovers of dft $432 debt, damages $19.89, and costs of his suit in this behalf expended.

Deed William M Marr to Micajah C Davis 76 acres ackd.

p.511   Thomas Taylor v James Austin admr. Appeal. Jury[above] say dft fully administered estate of Thomas Dillon, further say intestate Thomas Dillon in his lifetime was indebted to sd Thomas Taylor sum [blank] which hath not been paid, and assess his damages to [blank]. Plf recovers of dft debt and damages to be levied of goods of sd Thomas Dillon.

p.512   Wm Henderson, Jno Porter & Wm Mayfield report they allotted to Jane Allison widow of Halbert Allison decd a portion of sd estate for her & family's support for one year: allowed $53 exclusive of 2 barrels of corn and 25 weight of bacon.

Power/atty James Wilson to Maxwell Wilson proven by Samuel Jones.

Will of Isham Fuqua decd proven by Alexander Jones & Samuel Jones subscribing witnesses thereto; Peter Fuqua & Jesse Fuqua exrs therein named were qualified.

Appt Moses Crowson guardian to William Crowson, Mary Crowson, Hightower Crowson, orphans of William Crowson decd.

p.513   Will of James Willson decd proven by Henry F Steele and Samuel Jones; Matthew Wilson & David L Jones exrs therein named were qualified according to Law.

William Smith v William W Crittenton. Case. Justices/Peace of [blank] County, Georgia, to take deposition of Walker Fitts to be read in behalf plf.

p.514   Dudley Smith v William W Crittenton. Case. Deposition of Walker Fitts to be taken by Justices of [blank] county, Georgia, to be read in evidence behalf plf.

Court adjourned untill tomorrow morning 9 O'clock. Robt Buchanan, Jas Dugger, Thomas Welch.

p.515   6th Sept. Present Robert Buchanon, James Dugger, Thomas Welch, Esquires.

Deed Nathan Hooker & Ann his wife to John Lucus and Thomas Cornish 120 acres proven by Wm Cornish and Richard Hooker.

Deed Nathan Hooker and Ann his wife to William Cornish 100 acres proven by William Cornish and Richard Hooker.

Appt John Hillhouse & Wm Mayfield Esqrs to take privy examination of Ann

p.516   Hooker touching her free execution of deed to John Lucus & Thomas Cornish.

Appt John Hillhouse & William Mayfield to take privy examination of Ann Hooker touching her free execution of a deed to William Cornish.

Matthew Dew v John Paul. Appeal. Jury David W Porter, Joseph Dickson, Wm Rose, Leonard Brown, Tobias Miller, Thomas K Gordon, Isaac Purvis, Edmund J Bailey, Samuel Chambers, Sampson McConn, Joseph Shadden, Joseph Lann. Plf recovers of dft

p.517 $50.54 and his costs before the majistrate as in this Court expended.

Grant Ordinary Licence to Wilson Jones for one year.

Will of Samuel Smith decd proven by Wm Ramsey and John Campbell.

Order hands that formerly worked on forthampton road under Samuel Cox late overseer work under Henry P Crittenton the present overseer of sd Road.

p.518   John Gregory v Robert McDow. Trespass. Robert McDow surrendered. John Crowson becomes bail for Robert McDow.

John Hillhouse & Wm Mayfield report they examined Ann Hooker apart from her p.519   husband; she executed deed to John Lucus & Thomas Cornish voluntarily.

John Hillhouse & Wm Mayfield report they examined Ann Hooker apart from her husband; she executed deed to William Cornish freely & without compulsion.

Deed Fountain Lester & Harriott S T Lester his wife to Francis Boyd land in [blank] County, Kentucky, acknowledged.

p.520   Order Samuel Jones & James Bumpass Esqrs take privy examination of Harriott S F Lester touching her execution of deed to Francis Boyd.

Samuel Jones & James Bumpass Esqrs return they examined Harriott S F Lester apart from her husband; she voluntarily executed deed to Francis Boyd.

p.521   Exrs/will of Thomas Westmoreland decd returned inventory of sd estate.

Exrs/will of Thomas Westmoreland decd returned inventory of sd estate.

Order James Buford, Edmund J Bailey, & Jas Bumpass divide personal estate of Thomas Westmoreland and allot to Sally Westmoreland widow of sd Thomas Westmoreland decd her share thereof agreeable to the Will.

Order/sale issued to Sally Westmoreland and William H Ragsdale extrs of will of Thomas Westmoreland decd to sell balance of personal estate after the widow gets her distributive share.

Commrs apptd to mark out a road from William Giddens to Columbia road at James Tinnens report they marked, beginning at Giddens then by Conways, Dodsons, p.522   passing by a large spring then by Shaddens to intersect road from Pulaski to Columbia at the corner of Marlows field.

Appt Jesse McAnally to cut out & oversee new road from Wm Giddens to James Tinnens and that he have direction of following hands to open sd road: Chas Conway, Richard Conway, Jas Conway, Jas Finney, Samuel H Dodson, Jesse West, John Phillips, John McNight, Wm Woods, William B Cocke, Thos Dearman, Elisha Dodson, John Shadden, Martin Shadden, Danl Kilpatrick, Jos Shadden, Jno Marlow, Jesse Marlow, Silas Littlejohn, Solomon S Dearman, James Tinnen and all others living within sd bounds.

Jurors apptd last Court to mark out a road from Hightowers mill on Bradshaw creek to Cockrells gap made return: from Hightowers mill by John Kenedy leaving Widow Ritchie on right, then striking creek above sd widows then to head of creek crossing the ridge at a gap near Charles Littletons, crossing Richland creek at mouth of Robertsons creek, up sd creek passing John Thompson and intersecting p.523   Fayetteville road near Capt Youngs, then to Cockrells gap.

Appt John Littleton to cut out & oversee road from Littletons Gap to Capt Youngs and have direction of all hands that now work under Brittain Yarborough and William Steele to open same.

Appt Tryon Gibson to open that part of road from Hightowers mill to Littletons gap and have direction of hands now under direction of Hightower Parten with addition of Robert R Alsup & Hardy Hightowers hands & all living in his house.

Appt William Fannon overseer/road from Lincoln line to William Hendersons thence to Shelbyville road to Cockrells gap in room of Brittain Yarborough.

William Hendry v Washington G L Foley. Parties in proper person agree to withdraw suit and leave it to arbitration of James Buford, James Bumpass and Samuel p.524   Y Anderson, their award to be the judgment of this Court.

Grant Ltrs/admn on estate of Thomas Crenshaw to Rebeccah Crenshaw. Admx of estate of Thomas Crenshaw decd returned inventory of said estate.

Appt Joseph Dickson overseer of new road from where it turns off Huntsville road near Chamberses to where it intersects old road at Solomon Asbells, and have following hands: all at James Pattesons, Solomon Asbells, Robert McNairys, Joseph Dicksons, John Rowseys, John Crittentons, Custus Killams, Alexander Tarpleys, John

Abernathys, Wm Abernathys, David Dicksons.

p.525   Thomas Wilkinson v Nelson Patteson. Case. Jury Robert McNairy, John Gibson, Jas Paine, John Phillips, Green McCafferty, William Hendry, Francis Hicks, Jesse Kirkland, Stephen Anderson, Absalom Harwell, Marcus Mitchell, Jno Isham. Dft recovers of plf his costs about his defence expended.

Court adjourned untill tomorrow morning 9 Oclock. James Dugger, James Bumpass, Pleasant Moore.

p.526   Thursday 7th Septr. Present James Dugger, James Bumpass, Pleasant Moore.

William Follis recognizance, attend day to day to prosecute & give evidence behalf State agt William Kendell for A&B on sd William Follis.

State v James Connway. A&B on Henry Roberts. Dft in proper person pleads guilty. Fine $5 and pay costs of prosecution.

p.527   Robert Taylor recognizance, attend day to day to prosecute & give evidence behalf State against John Boyd for Petit Larceny.

Grant Ordinary Licence to Samuel Pearson for one year.

State v Jacob Crowson. A&B on John Boyd. Jury Wm Brown, Jos Dickson, Jno K Gibson, Simpson Lee, John Sims, David L Jones, Wm W Crittenton, Davis Brown, Archd p.528   Cunningham, David Campbell, Edward Davis, Jas Kimbrough find defendant not guilty.

State v Thomas Smith. Sci fa for not producing Abraham Sequirs. Dft in proper person; forfeiture set aside upon his payment of costs.

p.529   State v Abraham Sequirs. Sci Fa for not appearing. Dft in proper person; forfeiture agt dft set aside upon his payment of costs.

State v James Paine. Gaming. Jury David W Porter, Robert McNairy, Benjamin Bennett, Jno Manefee, Thos Tarpley, Wm Straughn, Jos Bennett, Wm Hamby, Jas Cald- p.530   well, Richd Lann, Saml Chambers, Enoch Bryant say defendant is not guilty.

State v Butler Haile. Gaming. Council for State sayeth he wishes no further to prosecute in this case. Nolle Prosequi entered.

State v Butler Haile. Gaming. Judgmt entered for those entitled for costs.

p.531   State v Nathaniel Messer. Gaming. Nolle Prosequi entered.

State v Nathaniel Messer. Judgmt in favour of those entitled for costs.

State v Jacob Crowson. A&B on John Boyd. Judgment entered in favour of those those entitled for all costs.

p.532   State v Rowland McKinney. Gaming. Jury[above but Caleb White for Jas Caldwell] find defendant not guilty.

State v John Perry. Dft in proper person pleads Guilty. Fine $1 and costs.

p.533   State v Archibald Alexander. Affray with Conway. Dft in proper person. Jury Wm Brown, Jno K Gibson, David L Jones, Archibald Cunningham, David Campbell, Edward Davis, Jas Kimbrough, Danl Molloy, Jno McDonald, Jas McDaniel, Thos Tarpley, Thomas Brown say defendant is not guilty.

State v Archd Alexander. Judgment in favour of those entitled for costs.

p.534   State v Robert Hanson. Gaming. Dft came not. Judgment according to recognizance rendered absolute against him for $100 beside costs; execution accordingly.

State v John Harrison. Gaming. Dft came not. [as above]

State v Noah Hampton. Gaming. Dft came not. [as above]

p.535   State v Jno Harrison. Gaming. Judgmt accdg to recognizance $100 & costs.

State v Robert Cotton. Gaming. Dft came not; judgt absolute $100 & costs.

p.536   State v Rebeccah Seay & Mary Seay. Trading with Negro Slaves. Jury Wm Brown,

Jno K Gibson, David L Jones, Archd Cunningham, David Campbell, Edward Davis, James Kimbrough, Daniel Molloy, Jno McDonald, James McDaniel, Thos Tarpley, Thomas Brown find dfts guilty. Fine $10 and pay costs of this prosecution.

Brand Jury Bills/Indictment: State v John Boyd true bill; Same v William Kindell true bill; Same v James Long & Elizabeth Lark true bill.

p.537   John Hammonds admr/estate of Isham Hammonds decd returned inventory. Order of sale issued to John Hammonds to sell perishable part of sd estate.

Grant ltrs/admn on estate of Raleigh Dodson decd to Mary C Dodson. Mary Dodson admx returned inventory. Order/sale issued to sell perishable estate.

Appoint Isaac Adkins, Wm Phillips & Thomas Phillips to allot to Mary Dodson
p.538   as much of sd estate as will be sufficient to maintain herself & family for one year from date of death of sd Raleigh Dodson.

State v James Bunch. Affray with Henry Roberts. Jury: William Brown, John K Gibson, David L Jones, Archibald Cunningham, David Campbell, Edward Davis, Jas Kimbrough, Daniel Molloy, John McDonald, James McDaniel, Thomas Tarpley, William Neale find defendant guilty. Fine $5 and pay costs of this prosecution.

p.539   State v Abraham Isaac. Recognizance as security for Samuel Rose. Forfeiture heretofore taken against dft set aside on his payment of costs.

Jurors to mark a road from Pulaski to Robt Gordons report they had done so.

Appt Samuel Criswell overseer/road Pulaski to Robert Gordons from Pulaski to fork of Leatherwood cr with hands in bounds from Columbia road incl Allen Abernathys hands, Wm Giddens, M Scott and hands on Strothers Branch.

p.540   Appt Richard Bently overseer/part of road from Pulaski to Robt Gordons from Leatherwood cr to head of Pigeon roost cr with hands in bounds from David Maxwells on Pigeon roost incl him, all settlers on Pigeon roost to head, thence to William Buchanons on Long cr, thence to John Edwards, thence to Thomas Baileys incl Peyton Herring, to Timothy Ezzells to beginning.

Appt Thomas Barton overseer to open road from head of Pigeon roost where Bently works to Thomas Bartons with following hands: from Richland creek below Hawkins Gunters, running south to ridge thence eastward to Huntsville road, to Wm Grays incl Gray, to beginning incl Eli Snow and Thomas Barton and all hands west of the branch Barton lives on and all hands within sd bounds.

Appt Thomas K Gordon overseer/road from Thos Bartons to fork near Alexr Thompsons with hands in bounds from Richland at mouth of branch Thos Barton lives
p.541   on, up creek incl Widow Barton & Robt Gordon thence east so far as incl Samuel McAndless and all settlers on branch he lives on thence to Richland cr incl Robert Cox & Andrew Clark, thence down to the beginning.

State v John Dewaaser. Keeping Peace. Dft in proper person is discharged from his recognizance.

State v William Dewaaser. Keeping Peace. Dft in proper person [as above]

State v William Ball. A&B on John Temple. Deposition of John Paul to be taken tomorrow morning benefit plaintiff.

p.542   State v William Ball. A&B on John Temple. Continued.

James Long, John Manifee, John Perry, Benjamin Tutt, Joseph Kelly, Nicholas M Fane recognizance, condition James Long attend day to day to answer charge of Lewdness.

State v William White. Keeping Peace. Dft in proper person is discharged.
p.543   State v Jesse Pratt. Keeping Peace. Dft in proper person is discharged.

State v William Adams. Keeping Peace. Dft in proper person is discharged.

State v Robert Jordan. Keeping Peace. Dft in proper person is discharged.

p.544 State v Lewis Lunsford. Recognizance. Motion of Alfred M Harris Solicitor of this County; it appearing to Court that Lewis Lunsford bound in sum $100 to appear at last term to prosecute John McCabe Jr for A&B on Nancy Boner came not, Ni Si ordered agt him which was not entered by Clerk. Sd Lewis Lunsford forfeits to state the amount of his recognizance; scire facias issues.

State v Lewis Lunsford. Recognizance. [worded as above, except the A&B was on Mahuldah Lunsford]

p.545 State v Nancy Boner. Recognizance. Alfred M Harris Solicitor for County; Nancy Boner bound to appear last Term & give evidence against John McCabe Jr for A&B on Nancy Boner came not. Nancy Boner forfeits to State her recognizance.

State v Nancy Boner. [as above, but A&B on Mahuldah Lunsford]

p.546 State v John McCabe Jur. A&B on Nancy Boner. Council for State sayeth he wishes no further to prosecute in this case.

State v John McCabe Jr. A&B on Nancy Boner. Judgment entered up in favour those entitled for all costs.

State v John McCabe Jr. A&B on Mahuldah Lunsford. Council for State sayeth he wishes no further to prosecute in this case.

p.547 State v John McCabe Jr. A&B on Mahuldah Lunsford. Judgment entered up in favour of those entitled for all costs.

Jurors to next Term: Shadrack Harwell, Micajah Ezzell, Richard Bentley, Wm Ezzell, Andrew Haynes, Craven Belcher, Holmon Fowler, Abner McGaughy, Wm Garrett, Peter Lyon, Andw Elliott, Anthony Seal, David Campbell, John Robertson, James Knox, Jas Hannah, Jno Barnett, John Wills, Jesse Lamb, Richd Barnett, Jno Porter, William Henderson, Robert Anderson, James Agnew, William Woods, Simpson Lee.

Bond of Simpson Lee, Ralph Graves and Lunsford M Bramlett $120, condition he faithfully pay unto Fanny Hooks $10 every six months for three years from this time, it being for Bastardy.

Court adjourned untill tomorrow morning 9 Oclock. N Patteson, Pleasant Moore, James McDonald.

p.548 Friday 8th Sept. Present Nelson Patteson, Pleasant Moore, James McDonald.

Appt Nathaniel Moody overseer to open Jefferson Street from Publick Square till it intersects Madison St, with all hands residing in Pulaski east of Third St.

Appt William McCracken overseer to open Madison St in Pulaski from publick Square till it intersect Jefferson St; all hands east of Thrd St work thereon.

Grant Ltrs/admn on estate of Lileston Meadows decd to Rebeccah Meadows & p.549 John Davis. Rebeccah Meadows & John Davis admrs/estate of Lileston Meadows decd returned inventory. Order/sale issued to sell perishable part of sd estate.

Order Wm Henderson, Britton Yarbrough, & Archibald Young allot to Rebeccah Meadows widow of Lileston Meadows decd such portion of sd estate as will support herself & family for one year from time sd Lileston Meadows departed this Life.

Thomas Tarpley recognizance, to attend day to day to prosecute, and that p.550 wife Eliza S Tarpley attend day to day & give evidence behalf State agt William Parker for A&B on sd Eliza S Tarpley.

Jacob Crowson v Archibald McKissack. Appeal. Order Buckner Harwell Esqr bring all papers relative to matter in dispute.

Jane Allison, Jacob Templin & German Lester admrs/estate of Halbert Allison decd returned account of sale of sd estate.

p.551 State v Henry Roberts. Affray. Dft in proper person. Jury David W Porter,

SEPTEMBER 1815

Robert McNairy, Enoch Bryant, David Crook, Gray H Edwards, George Harrison, John Arnett, William L Campbell, William Steele, John Brashers, Samuel Chambers, Quinton Shannon find defendant not guilty. Dft acquitted.

State v Henry Roberts. Affray. Judgmt entered in favour of those entitled.

p.552 State v William Ball. Assault on Gabl Bumpass. Jury John H Gibson, Joseph Dickson, Robt Bigham, Wm Caldwell, Lemuel Lindsey, Wm B Brooks, Wilson Jones, John Perry, Archd McKissack, Thos Wells, Jno Black say dft is not guilty. Acquitted.

p.553 State v William Ball. Assault on Gabl Bumpass. Order Judgment be entered in favour of those entitled for all costs.

Grant ltrs/admn on estate of Charles Tchoat decd to James Ashmore.

p.554 State v William Perry. A&B on John Birdwell. Jury David W Porter, Robert McNairy, Enoch Bryant, David Crook, Gray H Edwards, Geo Harrison, John Arnett, Wm L Campbell, William Steele, Quinton Shannon, Jno Brashers, Jas Paine Jr cannot agree. Quinton Shannon withdrawn and cause continued till next Court.

Jenkin Whiteside v Daniel T Woods. Debt. William Ball and William Hendry surrender Daniel T Woods to Court.

p.555 Grand Jury Bills/Presentment: State v Pryor Kyle; Same v Andw Lewis; Same v Green McCafferty; Same v Henry Scales; Same v William Follis; Same v Jno McCabe Jr.

Grand Jury Bill/Indictment: State v William Parker, true bill.

p.556 Appt James McDonald guardian to Martin Flynt, Sally Flynt, & Susannah Flynt minor orphans of Hasten Flynt decd.

State v Wm W Crittenton. Assault on Gabl Bumpass. Jury Wm Brown, Jno K Gibson, Jos Dickson, Wm Caldwell, Wilson Jones, John Perry, Duncan Brown, John Foulks, Thos Wells, Rowland Brown, William Jones, Archibald McKissack find dft not guilty.

p.557 State v Wm W Crittenton. Judgt in favour of those entitled for all costs.

Grant Ordinary Licence to John Birdwell for one year.

State v John Bryant. Lewdness. Jury[above, but Bernard Patteson for Wilson Jones]. Dft guilty. Fine $10, ten days in County jail, & pay cost of prosecution.

State v Jilly Gibson alias Jilly Pemberton. Lewdness. Dft in proper person

p.559 pleads guilty. Fine $10, ten days in County jail, pay cost of prosecution.

Silas Flournoy v James Austin. Debt. Dft in proper person saith he doth owe $656.28¼, damages $41.87½ beside costs. Plf recovers of dft.

p.560 James Long, Joseph Kelly, John Manefee, Thomas Williams and John Dillon recognizance, condition James Long attend next Term on charge of Lewdness.

Julius K Lark recognizance, to attend next Term to prosecute agt James Long and Elizabeth Lark for lewdness.

Gabriel Joslin v George Harrison. Certiorari. Jury David W Porter, Robt McNairy, Gray H Edwards, Simon Williams, Enoch Bryant, David Crook, John Arnett, Wm L Campbell, John Brashers, Quinton Shannon, Samuel Cox, James Paine. Plf recovers of dft $39 & costs before magistrate & in this behalf.

p.561 Gabriel Joslin v George Harrison. Certiorari. Thomas Bratton summoned as witness behalf Dft came not. Geo Harrison recovers agt Thos Bratton $125 according to the tenor of his subpoena.

Jilley Pemberton otherwise called Jilley Gibson, John Crowson & William R Cox recognizance, condition Jilley Pemberton otherwise Jilley Gibson to answer in

p.562 Circuit Court a charge of Lewdness.

John Bryant, John Crowson, William R Cox recognizance, condition John Bryant appear at Circuit Court to answer charge of Lewdness with Jilly Pemberton otherwise called Jilly Gibson.

Order Joseph Knox oversee/road, directing hands James Knox, Walter Lock,

71

SEPTEMBER 1815

John K Gibson,George M Gibson, William Beaty, George Hogue, John Hogue, Robert Ross, William Brown, Andrew McCutchen, Samuel Gibson, Joseph Knox.

p.563   Appt William Price overseer/road from Doctr Bumpasses to Elkton, the part from Wrights Branch to Elk river, directing William Price, Gabriel Higginbotham, John Shoults, Charles Pendleton, Alexander McKinney, [blank] Jamison, Duncan Thompson, William Green, Ezekiel Buckaloo, Elijah Wright, Isaac Crowson, Joseph Love, James Owens, Wm Owens, Smallwood Owens, Winlock Wright.

Appt Ica Adkins overseer/road from Doctr Bumpass's to Elkton the part from Wrights Branch to Plumb Orchard with following hands: Robt Anderson, Isham Adkins, Isaac Adkins, Ica Adkins, Peter Lemmons, William Dodson, Richard Martin, Theophilus Singleton, Isaac Gibson, Phillip Snipes, Robt Harvey, Jas Phillips, Hugh Campbell, William Harvey, Alexander Harvey, Stephen Arrington.

State v John Bryant. Lewdness. Dft is granted appeal to Circuit Court.

p.564   State v Jilley Pemberton otherwise called Jilly Gibson. Lewdness. Dft is granted appeal to Circuit Court.

Court adjourned till tomorrow Morning 8 Oclock.

p.565   Saturday 9th September. Present Nelson Patteson, Pleasant Moore, William Mayfield, Esquires, Justices.

James Austin v Edward Keeling & John Anderson. Motion of Alfred M Harris attorney for James Austin suggesting Silas Flournoy had obtained judgment at present term agt plf as security for dfts for $628.56¼ and $41.87½ damages and $6.77½ costs, as security on a note for the above defendants. It not appearing to Court from sd note whether sd Austin was security for sd dfts, jury sworn: David W Porter, John Rea, Thomas McKissack, Lemuel Lindsey, John Hammonds, Wm L Campbell, Nathl Alman, Henry Roberts, Zacheus Hurt, Green McCafferty, Freeman Crenshaw. Jury find Austin was and is only security for sd defts. Austin recovers agt Edwd Keeling & John Anderson $704.93¼: debt, damages, costs, and cost of this motion.

p.566   John Dillon recognizance, condition he and his wife Polly Dillon attend next Term to give evidence behalf State agt James Long & Elizabeth Lark.

John Dabney and John Henderson apptd to perpetuate testimony relative to boundaries of two tracts of land of 2000 acres each on Richland Creek of Elk river originally granted to James M Lewis by grant 331 and 332 dated 20 December 1796, returned depositions of James M Lewis and Robert Weakley; publication has been made twice in Western Chronicle that heirs of William T Lewis decd intended to have testimony perpetuated, therefore ordered sd depositions be recorded.

p.567   Power/atty William Craig to Joseph Shadden proven by Alfred M Harris.

Amos Williams & Betsey Williams v Thomas Williams. Whether James Williams decd died testate or intestate. Jury[above but William Brown for Robt McNairy] say James Williams did die testate making his will in writing. Sd will is admitted to probate, and plaintiffs recover of dft their costs in this behalf expended.

p.568   Will of James Williams decd was proven by Freeman Crenshaw, John Manifee, John Crowson, & John D Stokes the subscribing witnesses thereto, whereupon came Betsey Williams and Amos Williams the exrs therein named who qualified.

Solomon Graves v John Graves. Debt. Plaintiff by his attorney directs this suit be dismissed; plf pays costs.

p.--   Cravens Belcher v William Kyle. Debt. Dft came not; plf recovers of dft $252.06¼ debt, $13.65 damages of detention, and his costs of suit.

Cravens Belcher v William Kyle. Debt. Dft came not. Plf recovers of dft

72

$252.06¼ debt, $10.29 damages of detention, and his costs of suit.

p.-- David Smith v William Hendry. Certiorari. Plf came not. Dft recovers agt plf his costs of his defence in this behalf expended.

James Austin v George Keeling. Debt. Dft came not. Plf recovers of dft $1000 debt, $120 damages of detention, and his costs of suit.

Appt Robt Bigham overseer/Prewitts gap road in room of Jos Johns resigned.

p.569 Motion of William Riddle by his attorney, an order heretofore made for sheriff to have a jury lay off the dower of sd Polly is revived.

Motion of John Yancy guardian of Fanny Y Graves and Sally Y Graves infant heirs of John Graves decd, order Lewis Brown, Aaron Brown, John Butler, William Wells, Lester Morris or a majority of them divide that part of the personal estate of sd John Graves decd which belongs to sd infants equally between them.

Deed Gideon Pillow to Daniel T Woods 500 acres proven by William Woods and Nathan Davis.

Deed Daniel T Woods to Robert Bigham 500 acres proven by Nathan Davis and William Woods.

p.570 Thomas C Stone v Levi F Thompson admr of William F Thompson. Sci Fa. Dft came not. Plf recovers agt dft sum[blank] debt and his costs.

John Boyd and William Caldwell recognizance, condition John Boyd attend next Term to answer charge of Petit Larceny.

p.571 State v John Manefee. Not producing Jno B Williams. Dft in proper person. Forfeiture heretofore taken agt dft is set aside upon payment of costs.

Thomas Wilkinson v Nelson Patteson. Case. Plaintiff is granted appeal to the Circuit Court.

p.572 Levi F Thompson admr/estate of William F Thompson decd returned account of sale of sd estate.

William Ball v Levi F Thompson admr of Wm F Thompson decd. Sci Fa to revive a suit. Dft came not. Suit revived.

Amos Williams and Betsey Williams exrs/will of James Williams decd return inventory of sd estate. Order/sale issued.

p.-- James Maxwell v John Henderson & Andrew McMicken admrs. Case. Jury John Yancy, John Butler, Thos McBride, Elijah Anthony, Lester Morris, Earley Benson, John Elliott, Jos Rea, John Blazengame, Jos Anthony, Wm B Pepper, Hamilton C Campbell. Dfts recover of plf their costs/defence. Plf obtains appeal to Circuit Court.

p.-- Maxamilian H Buchanan sheriff & collector/public & county tax for 1815 reports taxes remain due on following tracts:

Reputed owners	No. of acres, situation
Joel Lewis	33[3311?] Richland creek
William Thomas	150 Indian Creek
James Conner	600 Robertsons fork
George Doherty	2500 Elk River
Thomas Polk	3758 Elk waters
do	5000 do
Saml Polk	300 Robertsons fork
Saml Polk & Zenas Alexander	860 waters Bradshaws creek
Robert Steele	640 Robertsons fork
Wm T Lewis heirs	1210 west fork Bradshaws creek grant
Benjamin McCullock	50 acres west fork Bradshaws creek
Wm H Ragsdale	40 west fork Bradshaws creek entry
Alexander Brannon	100 acres

	The heirs of Landon Carter	4000
p.573	Estate of Suvion Elliott	700 Weakleys cr
	Thomas Greer	1000 near mouth of Richland creek
	Joseph Greer	1000
	Thomas Hudson	540
	John McIver	5000 Robertson fork
	Hugh Elliott	400 Weakleys creek by grant
	Abner Pillow	500
	Wm White	65
	Jas Wells	228 Indian Creek
	Ro [blank]	

p.574   Maxamilian H Buchanon Shff and Collector of publick and county taxes
reports following land was not listed for taxation for 1815.

Henry Toomer 2020 both sides Robertsons fork granted by North Carolina
No.24 dated 14 July 1812.

Nathaniel Taylor assignee of Robert Campbell. 1000 including town of
Pulaski grant No 4 dated 14th July 1812.

Thomas Taylor Jr & James P Taylor. 640 acres Pigeon roost creek granted by
No Carolina No 38 dated 14 July 1812.

Thos H Perkins. 100 said to be on middle fork Indian creek warrant 318.

Henry Cearby. 500 on Richland cr held by deed.

Jeremiah Guilford 300 on waters of Richland & Buchanans cr.

Jeremiah Guilford. 200 on waters of Buchanans creek beginning at the
northeast corner of grant to Martin Armstrong.

p.575   James Raley. 300 acres Entry 807 on waters of Richland cr of Elk River
beginning at Thos Polks southeast corner.

Daniel Waters. 400 Entry 804, Warrant No [blank] east side Buchanans creek.

Jeremiah Guilford. 200 on waters of Buchanans Creek.

Gabriel Joslin v George Harrison. Certiorari. On motion, order judgment
against George Harrison & Wm Mayfield his security for $39 and costs of suit and
that execution be awarded accordingly.

Court adjourned till Court in Course. N Patteson, A Black, Pleasant Moore.

p.576   Court of Pleas and Quarters Sessions at the Court House in Pulaski, first
Monday, 4th December 1815. Present James Dugger, Hardy Hightower, Arthur Hicks.

Deed Maxamilian H Buchanon to Edmund Shelton 100 acres ackd.

Deed Joshua Hadley and Gabriel Bumpass to Maxamilian H Buchanon 480 acres
porven by Edmund Shelton and John Buchanon.

Executors/estate of James Williams decd returned account/sales.

p.577   Exr/estate of Isaac Meadows decd returned inventory.

Admr/estate of James Newell decd returned account/sale.

Admr/estate of James Brown decd returned inventory of sd estate.

Grant Ltrs/admn on estate of John White decd to Elizabeth White, James
Dugger and Fountain Lester. Inventory returned. Order/sale issued.

p.578   Richard Ramsey, John Nelson & Elizabeth Smith exrs named in will of Samuel
Smith decd which was fully proven last Term entered bond and qualified.

74

Executors/will of Samuel Smith decd returned inventory/estate.

Order/sale issued to Richard Ramsey, John Nelson, & Elizabeth Smith, exrs/will of Samuel Smith decd to sell perishable part of sd estate.

Grant ltrs/admn on estate of William Caldwell to John Caldwell and Joseph Loony. The Administrators returned an inventory of said estate.

Deed Gabriel Bumpass to Maxamilian H Buchanon 10 acres 12 poles proven by Edmund Shelton and William B Brooks.

p.579   Deed Henry Nave to William B Brooks 103¾ acres ackd.

Deed Isham Brown to Adam Bell 48 acres ackd.

Grand Jury: William Woods foreman, Shadrach Harwell, Jas Agnew, Jesse Lamb, Richard Barnett, John Wells, John Robertson, Holmon Fowler, James Knox, Richard Bently, William Henderson, William Ezzell, William Garrett.

Admrs/estate of James Robertson decd returned account of sale.

Britton Yarbrough, Archd Young & William Henderson report they allotted to Martha Robertson widow of James Robertson decd one years provisions.

p.580   Grant Ltrs/admn on estate of Thos Ussery decd to Peter Ussery.

Deed Gabriel Bumpass to William B Brooks 145 acres proven by Maxamilian H Buchanon and Edmund Shelton.

Deed Maxamilian H Buchanon to Gabriel Bumpass 134 acres ackd.

Deed William H Ragsdale to Maxamilian H Buchanon 105 & 1 pole land ackd.

Bill/sale Charles Anderson to John White for Negro girl Grace proven by Simpson H White.

p.581   Appt Jesse Craft guardian to Sally Williams minor orphan of James Williams decd, he having entered into bond with security in sum $150.

Order Nelson Patteson & William Mayfield Esqrs settle account current of John Goff admr of estate of George Goff decd; report to present Term.

Order John Dickey & John Hillhouse Esqrs settle account current of Israel Pickens admr of estate of John G Pickens decd; report to next Court.

William Henderson, Britton Yarbrough & Archd Young report they allotted to Rebeccah Meadows widow of Lileston Meadows decd one years provisions.

Admrs/estate of Lileston Meadows returned account/sale of sd estate.

p.582   Appt Rowland Brown overseer/road in room of Josiah Stovall resigned.

At least five justices present, Eli Seals produced one wolf scalp over four months old which is ordered to be burnt.

At least five justices present, John Caldwell produced one wolf scalp over four months old which is ordered to be burnt.

Grant ltrs/admn on estate of Levi Cooper decd to Lavinah Cooper.

Appt George Watters overseer/road in room of Jordan Solomon removed.

Order Elisha Dodson, Robt Wilson & James Donaldson allott to Elizabeth White widow of John White decd sufficient provisions of sd estate as will maintain her and family for one year from the date of death of John White.

p.583   Daniel Puryear v Phillip Parchman. Parties in proper persons; final determination refered to Nelson Patteson Esqr whose award shall be judgment of Court.

State v William Bolen & Joseph Bolen. Pettitt Larceny. [blank] surrender to Court the defendant who is committed to custody of Sheriff.

Appt William McDonald guardian to Joseph Birdwell minor son and orphan of Robert Birdwell decd.

p.584   William Bolen, Joseph Bolen, Lunsford M Bramlet & Thomas Simpson recognizance, condition Wm Bolen & Jos Bolen appear at present Term to answer charge.

Allow Alfred M Harris Esqr County Solicitor $50 for exoficio services for one year prior to this time.

Robert Buchanon & James Bumpass Esqrs report they settled account current of Isham Brown admr/estates of Minor Winn and Ambrose Foster decd.

John Dabney, Wm M Marr & Ephraim Patrick report they allotted to Fanny McClure widow of William McClure one years provisions.

p.585   Daniel Puryear v Phillip Parchman. Referee returned award: plf recovers of dft $5 & costs. N Patteson.

Bill/sale William Birdwell to Matthew Cunningham Negro Rhody proven by Edward Mercer.

Appt Robert Buchanon guardian to Minor Winn and John Winn minor orphans of Minor Winn decd.

p.586   Power/attorney Daniel Hughs to Muntilear Richardson proven by Hardy Hightower and James Adair.

Appt William Swain overseer/road from Hightowers mill to Cockrells Gap in room of Tryon Gibson resigned.

Appt Aquila Wilson overseer/road in room of Samuel Woods resigned.

On petition of Gilly Love wife of Joseph Love and widow of William Crowson decd, order at last Term appointing Moses Crowson guardian to William Crowson, Mary Crowson and Hightower Crowson orphans of Wm Crowson decd be revived, and Joseph Love be apptd guardian to sd children in room of Moses Crowson.

Order road near plantation of Robert R Alsup be turned agreeable to return of jury appointed for that purpose.

p.587   Thomas K Gordon and Daniel Allen commissioned by the governor as Justices/Peace were qualified according to Law.

Order road near plantation of Isaac Williams be turned agreeable to return of jury appointed for that purpose.

William Calloway, owner & keeper of a cotton gin, gave bond and security.

Court adjourned untill tomorrow morning 9 O'clock. Jarrat Menefee, Thos K Gordon, Hardy Hightower.

p.588   Tuesday Decr 5th. Present Jarret Manefee, Thomas K Gordon, Hardy Hightower.

Lemuel Meade produced licence to practice law, and on being qualified is admitted to practice in this Court.

Order Jas Buford, Edmund J Bailey & Jas Bumpass apptd last term to divide personal estate of Thos Westmoreland decd proceed as ordered.

Order John Dickey & John Hillhouse Esqrs settle account/admn with Andrew Pickens & Israel Pickens admrs of William G Pickens decd.

On petition of Sally Williams by Jesse Craft her guardian, order Jarrett Manifee, Freeman Crenshaw & John Rhea allott to sd Sally one third part of the household furniture of James Williams decd & deliver same to her sd guardian who shall proceed to sell same & make return of his proceedings to next Court.

Order admrs of Robert Birdwell sell whole personal estate & make return.

State v Moses Hamilton. Enoch Davis garnishee being sworn says he owes
p.589   Hamilton $8.37½. State to recover sd sum of sd Enoch Davis.

Lumm[Lemon?] Grace v Gideon Pillow. Debt. Jury Micajah Ezzell, Andrew Haynes, Peter Lyons, Andw Elliott, Anthony Seale, Jas Hanna, John Barnett, Marcus Mitchell, James Wilkinson, Tryon Gibson, John Anderson, Saml Harwell. Plf recovers agt dft balance of debt & damages $25.99 & his costs of suit.

Henry Roberts v Zacheus Hurt. Debt. [illegible]

p.590   John Walker v Edmond J Bailey. Debt. Jury[above]. Plf recovers agt dft $245.69 and his costs of suit.

Order Robert Buchannon & James Bumpass Esqrs settle with admrs of William Crowson decd and make return to next term.

Admrs of William Crowson decd return additional inventory & acct/sales.

Admr of George Williams decd returned inventory; order of sale issued.

p.589[again]   Order Thos Mitchell, Wm Wells & Lewis Brown allott to Rebecca Williams widow of George Williams one years provisions out of his estate.

Reuben Higginbotham v William Ball. Depositions of John M Taylor & Benjn S Sanders to be taken. Cause continued.

Executor/John Black returned inventory of personal estate.

Admx of Levi Cooper returns inventory of personal estate.

Order William Henderson, William Mayfield & Simpson Lee allott to widow of Levi Cooper one years provisions out of his estate.

Duncan McIntire, Joseph Rea, James Leach, William Cooke, & John C Walker commissioned under great seal of Tennessee Justices/Peace for Giles County appeared and severally took prescribed oaths & took their seats as Justices of this Court.

p.590[again]   William Wallace v John Thomson. Appeal. Jury Micajah Ezzell, Andw Haynes, Peter Lyons, Andw Elliott, Anthy Seal, James Hannah, John Barnett, Marcus Mitchell, Jas Wilkinson, Tryon Gibson, Jno Anderson, Samuel Harwell. Dft recovers agt plf his costs of defence in this behalf expended.

Deed Hardy Hightower to William H Ragsdale 300 acres ackd.

Deed Maxamilian H Buchanan to Richard Barnett 227 acres ackd.

Appt Edmund Shelton overseer/Huntsville rd in room of Wm Phillips, resgnd.

p.591   Deed Maxamilian H Buchanan to Duncan McIntire 90 acres ackd.

At least five justices present, David Flat produced two wolf scalps over four months old which was ordered to be burnt.

Revive order of last Court apptg James Buford, John Yancy, Elijah Anthony, Jos Anthony & Jesse Beasley to let to lowest bidder the building of bridge across creek running through John Yanceys land where the road from Pulaski to Fort Hampton crosses same.

Order County Trustee pay Nelson Patteson $65 for building bridge across Crooked Creek near Edward O Chambers plantation, let by Court order at last Term.

p.592   State v Reuben Manefee. A&B on Archd Alexander. Fine heretofore assessed remitted upon payment of all costs. George Coalter assumes payment of all costs.

Appt Isreal Pickens overseer/road in room of James Graham, resigned.

Reelect John Dickey County Trustee, who took oaths & entered bond.

Elect Thomas Brown constable in Capt Wm Pickens company.

p.593   Elect Nicholas Welch constable in Capt Hailes company.

Grant ltrs/admn on estate of Willson Jones decd to Rebeccah Jones, Thomas McKissack, and Edmund L Bailey; qualified and gave bond & security.

Order David W Porter, James Porter, & Lawson Hobson allot to Rebeccah Jones widow of Wilson Jones decd, one years provisions out of sd estate.

James Ashmore admr/estate of Charles Tchoat decd returned inventory.

p.594   Issue order/sale to James Ashmore admr/estate of Charles Tchoat decd to sell personal part of sd estate.

Appt John Dickey, John Hillhouse, & Jas Hannah to allot to Letty Tchoat widow of Chas Tchoat decd provisions sufficient to maintain herself and family for one year from time sd Charles Tchoat departed this life.

Nelson Patteson & Wm Mayfield Esqrs report they settled account current of

John Goff admr of George Goff decd.
Deed John Easley to Thomas Whitson 140 acres ackd.

p.595   Appt Wm Rose overseer/Huntsville road in room of Edwd O Chambers resigned.
On petition of James B Lockhart that he is entitled to one sixth part of
two tracts, one of 2000 acres, other of 3000 acres of which sd last tract belongs
to the Locator which sd land was granted by North Carolina to Samuel Lockhart now
dead, and that he sd James B Lockhart is one of the heirs of sd Samuel Lockhart
decd, and that there are five other heirs of sd Saml decd to wit, John Lockhart,
Thomas Lockhart, Benjamin Lockhart, Wm B Lockhart & Matthew S Lockhart amongst whom
sd tracts (after deducting 1000 acres out of the sd 3000) ought to be equally
divided. Sd intention of division was advertised 6 months prior to petition, order
p.596   Wm H Ragsdale, Wm Phillips, Guston Kearney, Jas Austin, Jas Patteson divide
sd lands in six equal parts according to quantity and quality and allot same to
persons herein named.
Court adjourned till tomorrow morning 9 Oclock. Duncan McIntyre, Arthur
Hicks, Robt Buchanan.

p.597   Wednesday 6th Decr. Present Duncan McIntyre, Arthur Hicks, Robt Buchanan.
James Tremble v James Paine. Debt. Plfs attorney excepts to sufficiency of
the bail taken in this case by the sheriff; sheriff notified.
On petition of David Flatt, order writs supercedeas & certiorari issue relative to an execution from Jacob Byler Judge advocate Second Regiment agt sd Flatt.
Joseph Kelly v John Manefee. Case. Parties in proper persons; each assumes
payment of his costs & plf directs that suit be dismissed.
p.598   William W Parham v William Ball. Case. Jury Andw Hayne, Peter Lyon, Andrew
Elliott, Anthony Seals, James Hann[torn], John Barnett, William Parker, Rober[torn]
derson, James Kimbro, William W[torn] John Manefee, William B Brooks. Plf recovers
of dft damages by occasion of defts nonperformance to $80[torn]
p.599   Grand Jury Bills/Indictment: State v Christopher Hobbs, not true bill; Same
v Wm & Jos Bolling, true bill.
State v Moses Allen. Keeping peace. Dft in proper person; discharged from
his recognizance; dft assumes payment of costs.
Grant ltrs/admn on estate of Edmund [torn] decd.
p.600   Marshall Franks admr/estate of Edmund Franks decd returned inventory. Issue
order/sale to Marshall Franks to sell estate of Edmund Franks dec.
Order John Kenneday, Robt R Alsup, Geo Waters, John Elliss, John Wisener,
Hardy Hightower, Joseph German, & Wm New or any five of them mark out a road from
Hightowers mill towards Huntsville to Lincoln county line.
Order road near plantation of Austin Smith be turned agreeable to report of
jury and [blank] overseer of the part from which this is turned open and keep in
repair the same with hands under his direction.
p.601   Admrs/estate of Henry Walker decd returned account/sales of sd estate.
State v William Ball. A&B on Jno Temple. Dft in proper person. Counsel for
state wishes no further to prosecute. State recovers of dft costs expended.
State v William Ball. A&B on Jno Temple. Dft in proper person. State no
p.602   further prosecutes. Dft assumes payment of all costs.
John Temple v William Ball. Trespass A&B. Dft in proper person assumes
payment of all costs; plf directs suit be dismissed.

Deed Aaron Brown to John Barnet 254 acres ackd.

p.603   Philip Parchman v Thomas Cheatham. Case. Plf in proper person assumes payment of all costs & directs that this suit be dismissed.

Appoint John Graves overseer/Prewets Gap road from Haywoods creek to Tinnens point, and have under his direction hands of Robert Scott, John G Russell, Wm McAnally, John McAnnally, [blank] Ross, Joseph Abernathy, William Pullin, & Robert Abernathy, and sd Graves own hands.

p.604   Dudley Smith v William W Crittenton. Case. Jury Andrew Haynes, Peter Lyon, Andw Elliott, Anthy Seals, Jas Hannah, John Barnett, Robt Anderson, Jas Kimbro, Wm Webb, John Manefee, Wm Brooks, Nathaniel Almon. Plf recovers of dft his damages by reason of nonperformance $70.50 and his costs of suit.

p.605   Court adjourned till tomorrow morning 9 Oclock.

James Bumpass, Robt Buchanan, A Black.

p.606   Thursday 7th Decr. Present James Bumpass, Robert Buchanan, Alexander Black.

James Tremble v James Paine. Debt. Dft came not. Plf recovers of dft $150 debt $4.05 damages of detention, and his costs of suit.

State v Christopher Hobbs. Petit Larceny. Not a true bill.

p.606   State v Christopher Hobbs. Petit Larceny. Judgment entered up in favour of those entitled for all costs.

p.607   State v Solomon Kilburne. A&B on Mary Magee. Council for State no farther prosecutes. Nolle Prosequi entered.

State v Solomon Kilburne. A&B on Mary McGee. Order judgment entered up in favour of those entitled for all costs.

p.608   State v William Holt. Affray with James Finny. Dft in proper person. Dft pleads guilty. Fine $2 and pay costs of this prosecution.

State v William Holt. Affray with Henry C F Cyrus. Dft in proper person pleads guilty. Fine $2 and pay costs of this prosecution.

Order Hightower Partain oversee Fayetteville road with hands in following bounds: Francis Bean and James Garrett and all hands southwardly of them that was in his former bounds with the addition of Hardy Hightowers hands.

p.609   State v James Paine. Gaming. Dft came not. Judgment according to tenor of his bail bond against him.

State v James Paine. Gaming. Nathaniel Mercer who was bound for appearance of James Paine came not nor did he deliver sd dft. Judgment according to tenor of his obligation against him.

State v James Paine. Gaming. Butler Haile who was bound for appearance of

p.610   Jas Paine came not nor did he deliver dft. Judgmt according to obligation.

State v Elisha Shelton. Affray. Dft in proper person pleads guilty. Fine $2 and pay costs of this prosecution.

State v Pryor Kyle. Affray. Dft in proper person pleads guilty. Fine $2 and

p.611   pay costs of this prosecution.

State v Green McCafferty. Presentment. Dft in proper person pleads guilty. Fine $5 and pay costs of this prosecution.

Admx/estate of Raleigh Dodson decd returned accouant/sale of sd estate.

Grand Jury Bills/Indictment: State v John Kerby, true bill. Same v Isaac Mayfield, true bill.

p.612   Grant Ltrs/admn on estate of Lewis Paine decd to Rosannah Paine. Rosannah Paine returned inventory of sd estate. Order/sale issued to sell perishable estate.

DECEMBER 1815

Henry Roberts v Zacheus Hurt. Debt. Dft granted appeal to Circuit Court. Direct sheriff to bright to next term a child of colour named Ned or Neddy now at house of Samuel Coxe of this County.

p.613   State v Henry C F Cyrus. A&B on Wm Holt. Jury Micajah Ezell, Andrew Haynes, Peter Lyon, Andw Elliot, Anthy Seals, Jas Hannah, Jno McKissack, Dudley Smith, Robt Black, Alexr Tarpley, Wm Riddle, Wm Parker say dft is guilty. Fine $5 and pay costs of this prosecution.

State v William Perry. A&B on John Birdwell. Dft in proper person. Jury
p.614   Archd Alexander, John Barnett, Thos Tarpley, Moses L Moon, Robert Anderson, Jno Graves, Elijah White, Wm R Coxe, Jno Newton, Elijah Kimbrough, Jas J Ward, Edwd M Brown say dft is guilty. Fine $5 and pay costs of this prosecution.

John Walker v Edmond J Bailey. Debt. Dft granted appeal to Circuit Court.

State v Etheldred Bunn. Keeping/Peace. Dft in proper person discharged from his recognizance.

p.615   State v John Boyd. Petit Larceny. Jury Micajah Ezzell, Andrew Haynes, Peter Lyon, Andw Elliott, Anthy Seals, Jas Hannah, Mattw Dew, Jno Perry, Green McCafferty find dft not guilty. On motion of Robert Mack, dfts atty, order Robert Taylor the prosecutor pay costs of this prosecution.

George Coalter v James D Breckenbridge. Caveat. Facts agreed by parties to be true: John Drake assignee by virtue of part of warrant No 835 made entry in his own name in office of the Principal Surveyor of Second Survey Dist on 26 Sept 1807
p.616   of 80 acres in Sec No 1 range No 1 on north side Elk river [land descr here omitted]. That sd entry in name of John Drake was on 13 Octr 1814 levied on by M H Buchanon Sheriff by virtue of an execution in favour of James Walker agt John Drake and sold by sd sheriff in pursuance thereof on 18th Feby 1815 and purchased by sd George Coalter the Caveator. That sd John Drake on 21st March 1815 withdraw sd Entry, that M H Buchanon Sheriff did in pursuance of sale made to George Coalter afsd assign sd entry to George Coalter. That sd entry was surveyed on 1st Novr 1814 by James Bright D Surveyor and a platt & certificate thereof returned 3d January 1815. Same was withdrawn by John Drake on 21st March 1815 and that M H Buchanon Sheriff did in pursuance of sd sale assign sd platt & certificate to Caveator.
p.617   Caveator by virtue of same warrant by virtue of which John Drake made entry No.630 on 21 March 1815 made an entry of 80 acres as in caveat set forth & obtained a survey to be made thereon on 12th May 1815 and returned to office of Principal surveyor as in caveat set forth.

Court adjourned untill tomorrow morning 9 Oclock.

N Patteson, Thos K Gordon, James Bumpass

p.618   Friday 8th Decr. Present Nelson Patteson, Thomas K Gordon, James Bumpass.

Jurors to next Circuit Court: John Henderson, John Dabney, John C Walker, James Leach, Alexr Thompson, Thomas K Gordon, Oliver C Cleveland, Thos Lane, Saml Jones, Geo Malone, Wm Cook, John Laird, Daniel Allen, Jos Rea, Jno Hillhouse, John Dickey, Jacob Byler, Thomas Harwood, Buckner Harwell, William Brown esqr, Willis S McLaurine, Jas Dugger, James McDonald, Tyree Rhodes, Robt Oliver, Hardy Hightower.

Jurors to next County Court: Jas Austin, Daniel McCollum, Jno Reasonhover, Wm Maples, John Butler, Henry Loyd, Wm Wells, John Abernathy, John Newton, William Giddens, Chas Buford, Ralph Graves, Robt Williams, Wm B Cocke, Wm Pullen, Richard Johnston, Martin Lane Senr, Jno Pate, Charles Littleton, George Sheilds, Jno Cook,

DECEMBER 1815

Andw Pickens, Joseph German, Robert R Alsup, Thomas B Haynie, William McDonald.
p.619   Richard Briggs, recognizance, condition Richard Briggs attend day to day to
prosecute & give evidence behalf State agt John Alsup Junr.
        William McGill, recognizance, condition he attend day to day to prosecute
behalf State against Orpha Black.
        Order Richard Bently apptd to open part of Shelbyville road from Leather-
wood creek to head of Pigeon roost creek have under his direction with hands in
following bounds from David Maxwell, all hands above him to head of Pigeon roost
crk then to Upper Fayetteville road at William Buchanons, thence with road including all on North thereof, to Timothy Ezzells, thence to beginning.
p.620   Jenkin Whitesides v Daniel T Woods. Debt. Robert Campbell and John C
Maxwell surrender dft to Court.
        State v William Boling. Pettitt Larceny. Dft in proper person. Jury John
Barnett, Peter Lyon, Andw Haynes, Anthony Seals, Saml Chambers, Chas Dever, Tobias
Millar, Jos Luker, Saml Coxe, Wm Webb, Wm Parker, Larkin Everett say dft is guilty.
Dft by attorney moves an arrest of judgment. [blank]
p.621   John Alsup Junr & Green McCafferty recognizance, condition sd John Alsup Jr
appear at next Term to answer charge of A&B.
        Grand Jury Bills/Indictment: State v John Alsup Junr, true bill/ Same v
Orpha Black, true bill.
p.622   George Coalter v James D Breckenridge. Caveat. Considered by Court that no
Grant issue to James D Breckenridge on a Platt & certificate returned into Office
of Principal Surveyor on 17th June 1815 for 80 acres which survey was made by James
Bright deputy surveyor on 12 May 1815, further considered by Court that a Grant
issue to George Coalter the caveator for 80 acres on a platt & certificate returned
into Principal Surveyors office on 3d January 1815 in name of John Drake which
survey was made by James Bright Deputy surveyor on 1 November 1814 and was assigned
by M H Buchanon Sheriff to George Coalter as in Caveat set forth. Further, sd
George Coalter recover of James D Breckenridge his costs by him about his caveat
expended.
p.623   John Myers for benefit of Jesse Newland v Philip Parchman. Original
attachment. Robert Willson and Wm Ball bail for dft.
        On motion of Isaac Reynolds Junr, order certified that sd Isaac Reynolds
had his ear bitten off in an affray with William Terrell.
p.624   Court adjourned till tomorrow morning 9 Oclock.
                                        John Dickey, N Patteson, A Black

p.625   Saturday Decr 9th. Present John Dickey, Nelson Patteson, Alexander Black.
        Appointments to take lists of taxable property for 1816: William Mayfield
in Capt Wilkinsons company; Buckner Harwell in Thomas Browns company; Robert Buchanon in Capt Brooks company; James McDonald in Capt Mark[binding]; Robert Oliver
p.626   in Capt Paxtons compy; John Dickey to Capt Bylers compy; James Bumpass in
Capt Willsons compy; Duncan McIntyre in Capt Phillips compy; Pleasant Moore in Capt
Herraldsons compy; Jarrett Manifee in Capt George Browns company; Thos K Gordon in
p.627   Capt McVays compy; John Henderson in Capt Youngs compy; Alexander Black in
Capt Cockes compy; Daniel Allen in Capt Hailes company; Joseph Rea in Capt Pickens
compy; Thomas Lane in Capt Allens compy; William Cook in Capt [blank] company; John
p.628   C Walker in Captain [blank] Company.
        On petition of Rebeccah Williams widow of George Williams deceased, & it

81

appearing to Court that admx of estate of sd George Williams decd had notice of this motion, Order writ issue to Sheriff to summon twelve disinterested freeholders to set off to sd Rebeccah Williams one third part of land including the mansion house and put sd Rebeccah Williams in possession of same, and that sd jury divide personal estate of sd George Williams decd into six equal parts amongst five children of sd George decd and sd petitioner and deliver to sd petitioner one sixth part of same and return proceedings to next Court.

p.629   Dudley Smith v Wm W Crittenton. Case. Dft granted appeal to Circuit Court.

Grant Ordinary Licence to Robert Gordon for one year.

State v Henry Scales. A&B on Green McCafferty. Council for State no farther prosecutes. Nolle Prosequi entered.

State v Henry Scales. A&B on Green McCafferty. Order judgment entered up in favour of those entitled for all costs.

p.630   State v William Kindell. A&B on William Follis. Dft in proper person. Jury Isaac Mayfield, Brice M Mayfield, Jas Kimbrough, Jas Moore, Herod Foulks, Jno Barnett, Peter Lyon, Andrew Haynes, Anthony Seal, Robt Anderson, Jno Abernathy, Dudley Smith find defendant guilty. Fine $25 and pay costs of this prosecution.

p.631   State v William Bowling. Petitt Larceny. Reasons in arrest of Judgment being argued and sustained, dft go hence without day upon payment of all costs. Wm Bowling and Lunsford M Bramlett assume payment of all costs.

State v John Kerby. Dft in proper person pleads guilty. Fine $3 and costs of prosecution.

p.632   Richard Briggs, recognizance, condition he attend next term & give evidence behalf State agt John Alsup Jr for A&B on sd Richard Briggs.

Grand Jury Bills/Presentment: State v Hazel Rodes & Jesse Isaacks; Same v William Kindell.

State v William Kindell. Dft in proper person pleads guilty. Fine $5 and
p.633   pay costs of this prosecution.

State v Orpha Black. A&B on Martha Magill. Dft in proper person. Jury Andw Elliott, Robert Gordon, Robert Black, Samuel H Dodson, John McNight, William Wells, Thos Moore, Jas Hannah, Major Herraldson, Gideon Pillow, Jas Moore, William Riddle say dft is guilty. Fine $1 and pay costs of this prosecution. John Black assumes payment of fine and costs.

p.634   On motion of George Coalter atty for David Dickson, David Dickson has paid as security for Daniel T Woods, keeping the prison bounds when committed to same at instance of Geo Zollicoffer, sum $6.93; judgment obtained agt sd Dickson for same before Wm Mayfield Esqr. Considered by Court that David Dickson recover agt sd Daniel T Woods afsd sum $6.93 together with costs of this motion.

On motion of George Coalter atty for John Keenan. John Keenan hath paid $6.93 as security for Daniel T Woods, keeping the prison bounds to which he was committed as instance of George Zollicoffer and judgment obtained agt sd Keenan for same before Wm Mayfield Esqr. Considered by Court that sd Jno Keenan recover agt sd Daniel T Woods afsd sum of $6.93 together with costs of this motion.

p.635   On motion of George Coalter attorney for Wm Ball [blank]

On motion of George Coalter attorney for Archibald Alexander [blank]
p.636   On motion of George Coalter attorney for Lewis Kirk [blank]

Ordered that Court be adjourned till Court in Course.

                      John Dickey, N Patteson, Robt Buchanan

End of this book.

Minute Book #C [first pages missing; page heavily discolored]

p.-   John Myers for benefit of Jesse Newland v Philip Parchman. Dedimus protestatums issue to two justices of Christian County KY and two justices for [blank] county in Illinois Territory to take depositions of John Barton and others behalf defendant.

Abel Winningham v Archibald Alexander. Debt. Deposition of Nathan Osburne,
p.--   Randolph County, North Carolina, to be taken, benefit plaintiff.

State v Lewis Lunsford. Failing to prosecute A&B on Mahulda Lunsford. Dft came not; judgment against defendant for $100 and costs.

State v Lewis Lunsford. Failing to prosecute A&B on Nancy Boner. [as above]
p.--   State v John B Williams. Failing to answer charge of Petit Larceny. Dft came not; judgment against him for $200 and costs.

William Parker v Maberry Helms & Jesse Kirkland. Debt. Parties in proper persons; dft with Robert Campbell confesses judgment for $200; plf stays execution without interest for nine months and pays half costs.

Court adjourned untill tomorrow morning 9 Oclock.

N Patterson, Thos K Gordon, A Black

p.--   Saturday 9 March 1816. Present Nelson Patteson, Thos K Gordon, Alexr Black.
Isaac Johnston v John C Maxwell. Appeal. Dft came not; judgment of Justice of peace for $17.16 with interest from 30 January 1816 untill paid together with costs as well before the majistrate as in this court expended.

Washington G L Foley v Thomas Creel. Certiorari. Plf came not. Dft recovers of plf his costs about his defence in this behalf expended.

p.--   Mortgage John C Maxwell to John Keenan proven by Archibald Murphey and Harris Johnston.

Robt & William Dickson v Green McCafferty. Attachment. Defendant came not. Plaintiffs recovers of dft $113.87½ debt, $57 damages of detention, and costs.

Levina Cooper admx/estate of Levi Cooper decd returned amount/sale.

p.--   Grand Jury Bills of presentment: State v Henry Hagen; Same v John Jones; Same v Roland Tankersley; Same v Archibald McKissack; Same v Balaam Straughan, Same v William Straughan.

Appt David L Jones overseer/road in room of Carter H Cleveland resigned.

William L Lindsey, Enoch Bryant, Benjamin Burnett, recognizance, condition sd William L Lindsey keep peace toward John Porter for twelve months.

p.7   June Term 1816.
Grand Jury: Henry M Newland foreman, William B Brooks, Thomas Markes, William Maples, Samuel Chambers, James Price, Robert Anderson, Lewis Brown, Peter Satter-field, Lester Morris, James McCutchen, Thomas H Meredith, George Gibson.

Jesse Marlow constable sworn to attend Grand Jury this Term.

Power/attorney Ephraim Davidson to John Jones ackd.

At least five justices present, Benjamin Chisher produced one wolf scalp over four mmonths old which is ordered to be burnt.

Deed John Henderson to James Mitchell 34 acres ackd.
Deed John Henderson to Alexr Hinson 68 acres ackd.
p.8   Grant Ordinary Licence to William Henderson for one year.
Jurors/original panel qualified: Robert Black, James Simmons, James Buford,
George Hillhouse, Early Benson, Jno Porter, Hamilton C Campbell, Wm Hendry, William
Pride, Quinton Shannon, James McCraven, Nathan Farmer.
Order Robt Oliver Esq & William McDonald let to lowest bidder the keeping
of Thomas Cyler an orphan boy for 1 year from 1 July next; make return next Court.
Order County trustee pay Josiah Stovall $25: keeping Thomas Cyler one year.
Appt Jno Hillhouse & Jno Dickey Esqrs to settle with admrs/Jas Newell decd.
p.9   Will of Alexander Barron decd proven by James Alexander and Nathaniel Alex-
ander the subscribing witnesses thereto. Alexr Barron & John Barron, exrs therein
named qualified. Exrs returned inventory of personal estate. Order/sale issued.
Admr of Spencer Lyon decd returned account of sale of sd estate.
Appt Thomas Marks overseer of the upper Fayetteville road in room of Allen
Abernathy, resigned, and order he have same district of hands.
p.10   Allow Justices to correct mistakes in their lists of taxable property.
Mortgage James McClannahan to Henry White proven by William Mayfield.
Grant ltrs/admn on estate of William A Smith decd to Austin Smith. Inven-
tory of estate returned by admr. Order/sale issued to sell perishable estate.
p.11   Admrs/estate of William Caldwell decd returned additional inventory.
Deed Richard Hightower & Mordecai Pillow to Alexr McDonald 216 acres proven
by Peter R Booker and John White two of the subscribing witnesses thereto.
Grant ltrs/admn on estate of John Ackridge decd to John Gregory.
Deed James McKinney to Archibald McKinney 200 acres proven by James McCravens and Robert Cox the subscribing witnesses.
Deed John McKinney to Robert Coxe 74 acres proven by George A McKinney and
James Fraser.
p.12   Benjamin Cash & John M Armstrong merchants v John Tilford. Debt. Dft in
proper person sayeth he doth owe plffs $120 debt, $6.75 damages/detention, & costs.
James Buford v William Parker. Debt. Dft in proper person. Plf recovers of
p.13   dft $200 debt, $5 damages & costs.
Jacob & Abraham Byler v Zacheus Hurt & Archibald Alexander. Debt. Dfts in
proper person. Plfs recover of dfts $238 debt, $5.95 damages, and costs.
p.14   John B Prendergast v Zacheus Hurt. Debt. Dft in proper person. Plf recovers
of dft debt $355, damages $8, and costs of suit.
Archibald Alexander asseignee v Samuel Pearson. Debt. Dft in proper person.
p.15   Plf recovers agt dft $100 debt, $7.50 damages & costs of suit.
Tyree Rodes v William Parker. Debt. Dft in proper person. Plf recovers of
dft debt $200, damages $5, and costs of suit.
p.16   Ira Bradford v Gideon Pillow. Debt. Dft in proper person. Plf recovers of
dft debt $100, damages $5, and costs of suit.
James Kimbrough v William Woods & Tyree Rodes. Debt. Dfts in proper per-
p.17   sons. Plf recovers debt $364, damages $10.75, and costs.
Andrew Jackson, Thomas Crutcher and Alfred Balch exrs v William Ball &
Green McCafferty. Debt. Dfts in proper persons. Plfs recover of dfts debt $185,
damages $8.25, and costs of suit.
p.18   William Sheppard assee v William Price. Debt. Jury Robt Black, Jas Simmons,
Jas Buford, Geo Hillhouse, Early Benson, John Porter, Hamilton C Campbell, William
Hendry, Quinton Shannon, Jas McCravens, Nathan Bass, Edwd M Brown. Plf recovers of

dft $200.24 balance of debt, $6 damages of detention, and his costs of suit.

Allow jurors who divided estate of John Graves decd $1 per day.

p.19   George Peyzer assee v William Purnell. Debt. Jury Robt Black, Jas Simmons, Jas Buford, Geo Hillhouse, Early Benson, Jno Porter, Hamilton C Campbell, William Hendry, Quinton Shannon, Jas McCravens, Nathl Bass, Edwd M Brown. Plf recovers of dft $1098.40 debt, damages $67.27 & his costs of suit.

p.20   Thomas Yeatman v William Purnell. Debt. Jury[above]. Plf recovers of dft $1356.41 debt, $91 damages of detention, and costs of suit.

Admrs/estate of Thomas Ritchie decd returned inventory of sd estate.

p.21   Thomas Franks recognizance, attend day to day to prosecute & give evidence behalf State agt Sterling C Robertson and [blank] Rucker for retailing spirituous liquore by the small measure without Licence.

Robert Oliver recognizance, attend day to day to give evidence behalf State agt James Burns and Joseph Davis for an affray.

Tax lists received: David Maxwell 400 acres Pigeon roost creek, 2 slaves, 1 white pole; Samuel Woods 450 acres, 1 white pole; William M Marr 1500 acres, 15 slaves, 1 white pole; William Bottoms, 1 white pole, 1 slave; James Berry 1 white pole;   Potter Neill, 300 acres Buchanans creek, James Berry agent; John Gregory 1 white pole.

p.22   Andrew Hynes & Thomas H Fletcher merchants v Edmund J Bailey. Debt. Dft in proper person. Plfs recover of dft $189 debt, $11.34 damages, and costs of suit.

Joseph Lann v William Parker. Debt. Parties in proper persons; dft having assumed and paid all costs, plf directs suit be dismissed.

p.23   State v Thomas Franks. [blank] bound for appearance of Thomas Franks surrenders him to court.

Thomas Franks and Gabriel Bumpass, bond for appearance of Thomas Franks for A&B on Negro man property of Sterling C Robertson.

p.24   Brice M Garner v Hugh Campbell. Plf assumes payment of all costs and directs suit be dismissed; dft recovers of plf his costs of defence.

Court adjourned till tomorrow morning 9 Oclock.

                    Hardy Hightower, Duncan McIntyre, Jacob Byler

p.25   Tuesday 4th June. Present Hardy Hightower, Duncan McIntyre, Jacob Byler.

Alexander McDonald v Lawson Hobson & Nelson Patteson. Debt. Parties in proper persons. Lunsford M Bramlett and Alfred M Harris return final determination of this case: Dft to pay plf $160 with interest from 1 Oct 1813 till this time at 6% per annum; Hobson pays costs of suit.

p.26   Isaac N Hobson recognizance, to attend day to day & give evidence half State agt Brice M Mayfield for Assault & Battery on sd Isaac N Hobson.

Charles Conway recognizance, attend day to day & prosecute & give evidence behalf State against John McCracken for A&B on sd Charles Conway.

Charles Conway recognizance, attend day to day to prosecute & give evidence behalf State against Charles Gudrelan[Guerelan?].

p.27   Release Wm Blythe from payment of poll tax, he being over age.

Elijah Anthony v William Riddle & Polly Riddle admrs. Debt. Original writ to be amended from the debitate to the debit & detenate.

Thomas Harwood commissioned as justice/peace appeared and qualified.

Appt John Jones guardian to Robert Jones an orphan of Samuel Jones decd.

Appt Charlotte Jones guardian to Mary Caroline Jones orphan daughter of

Samuel Jones decd.
p.28   Grant Ordinary Licence to Wilton F L Jenkins for one year.
        Deed William M Marr to Thomas Walker 180½ acres ackd.
        Exrs/will of John Reasonhover decd returned account/sale of sd estate.
        Thos Yeatman v William Purnell. Debt. Dft granted appeal to Circuit Court.
        George Peyzer assee v William Purnell. Debt. Dft granted appeal to the
Circuit Court.
p.29   State v James Burns. Affray. Dft in proper person pleads guilty. Fine 6¼¢
and pay costs of this prosecution.
        State v Joseph Davis. Affray. Dft in proper person pleads builty. Fine 6¼¢
and pay costs of this prosecution.
p.30   John Boyd v Robert Taylor. A&B. Jury Robt Black, Jas Simmons, Jas Buford,
Geo Hillhouse, Early Benson, Hamilton C Campbell, Wm Hendry, Quinton Shannon, Jas
McCravens, Jas Austin, Wm M Marr, Adam Burney find dft guilty & assess plfs damage
to $12.50 besides costs. Plf recovers of dft his damages & costs of suit.
p.31   Deed William Fullerton to Richard Lann 2 lotts in Pulaski ackd.
        James Kimbrough v William Woods & Tyree Rodes. Debt. Dfts are granted
appeal to the Circuit Court.
        Grant ltrs/admn on estate of Welcome Hodge decd to Rhody Hodge. Admx re-
turns inventory. Order/sale issued to admx/estate of Welcome Hodge decd to sell
perishable part of sd estate and make return thereof to next Court.
p.32   John McCabe v John McCracken. Certiorari. Parties in proper persons. Dft
assumed and paid all costs; plf directs suit be dismissed.
        Appt James Ashmore constable in Capt Bylers company.
        Deed commissioners of Pulaski to John D Hill Lott 17 proven by Samuel H
Dodson and Jacob Byler.
p.33   Appt Joseph Robertson overseer/road in room of William Long resigned.
        Appt John Walthal overseer/road in room of Edmund Gatlin resigned.
        Appt Wm Phillips, Isaac Atkins, Hugh Campbell to allott to Rhody Hodge as
much of estate of Welcome Hodge decd as will maintain herself and family for one
year from the time of sd Welcome Hodge departed this life.
        Order James Austin and John Barnett be appointed inspectors for Towns of
Upper Elkton and Lower Elkton, they having given bond and security.
        Order County trustee pay Thomas Phillips constable $24.75 for arresting
John Romack and conveying him to Maury Jail.
p.34   Appt Elzey West constable in Capt Robert Pickens company in room of John G
Fowlks resigned, sd Elzey West having been qualified & given bond & security.
        Deed John Childress to William Phillips lots 28 and 56 in upper Elkton
proven by Thos Phillips and Samuel Farrie[Fanie?].
        Deed Alston Jones to James Henderson & others 75 acres proven by Miller
Doggett and James Brown, two of the subscribing witnesses.
        Deed Abner Pillow to Tyree Rodes 500 acres proven by Wm Brownlow and John G
p.35   Russell.
        Deed Solomon Simmons and Mary his wife to Christopher Christopher for land
in Wake County No Carolina ackd
        Appoint Nelson Patteson and Jacob Byler Esqrs to take privy examination of
Mary Simmons touching her consent in execution of deed to Christopher Christopher
for land in North Carolina. Nelson Patteson & Jacob Byler report of Mary's consent.
p.36   John McCabe v John McCracken. Certiorari. Dft in proper person assumes
payment of all costs; plf's attorney directs suit be dismissed.

JUNE 1816

On motion of William Phillips by his atty & with assent of parties, order sd William Phillips be discharged from being security for Joseph Love as guardian in right of his wife Mary, whereupon Enoch Davis and Leonard Partin undertake as securities for sd Joseph Love, and sd William Phillips is discharged.

p.37   Order Hightower Partain oversee part of the road from Pulaski to Fayetteville with hands in bounds from James McCandless, all eastward by John Ellis to top of ridge beween sd Elliss & John Kennedays that was in said Partains former bounds.

Order William Swain oversee road from Hightowers mill towards Cockrells gap with hands in his former bounds above Fayetteville road with addition of Francis Beards and George Garretts hands.

James Kimbrough comes into Court & agrees to maintain and clothe an orphan child Avelina Cobb for twelve months for $24 to be paid at expiration of sd months.

Order 1816 tax list received: Hubbard Saunders 1000 acres on Richland Cr.

p.38   Admrs/estate of Samuel Jones decd returned account of sale.

Commissioners apptd to allott to Peggy Simpson widow of Charles Simpson decd made return of their allotment.

Appt Neil Patterson overseer/Montgomery Gap road in room of Wm Neil resgnd.

Order John Young, Pleasant New, Samuel Paxton, Enoch Davis, John McNight, Robert Devenport, Thomas B Haynie & William Ezzell or any five of them mark out a road from Huntsville road near Samuel Paxtons lane, to intersect Pulaski road near William Ezzells, make report to next Court.

Order Henry F Steel, John Johnston, Matthew Johnston, William Lee, Richard Johnston, William Pullen & John Jones or any five of them view ground near William H Cooks and see if it be proper to turn the road agreeable to wish of sd Cook.

p.39   Order Abraham Brown, Shadrack Cross, John Wright, Stroud McCormack, Larkin Webb, Bennett Creesy & James Brown or any five of them view situation of ground near plantation of Shadrack Cross and see if it be proper to turn the road.

Deed Samuel Duncan & heirs of John Carson[Canon?] to John Henderson 185 acres proven by Alexander Stinson and James Mitchell.

Court adjourned untill tomorrow morning 8 O'clock.

Jacob Byler, Daniel Allen, N Patteson

p.40   Wednesday June 5th. Present Jacob Byler, Daniel Allen, Nelson Patteson.

Admr/estate of Ebby Cobb decd returned account of Sale of sd estate.

Exrs/will of William Jones decd returned account of sale of sd estate.

Order Jarret Menefee & Thomas Harwood Esqrs settle accounts of William Phillips and Thomas Phillips as exrs of will of William H Murrah decd.

Order 1816 tax lists received: Robert Burton 5000 acres Big Creek; estate of John Graves decd 250 acres Richland cr, 7 slaves; Geo W Campbell 5000 Richland Cr; James Bright 220 both sides Elk river, 90 between Richld & Inn[Indian?] Crk; 23 do, 10 head Reynolds creek; John Strother & Jas Bright 50 Scotts Creek; Saml Burton 114 acres Sucking Cr.

p.41   Reuben A Higginbotham v William Ball. Case. Jury Robt Black, Jas Simmons, Geo Hillhouse, Jno Porter, Hamilton C Campbell, Wm Hendry, Wm Pride, Quinton Shannon, Jas McCravens, Nathan Farmer, Tryon Gibson, Christopher Wright assess plfs damage by reason of nonperformance to $117.50 besides costs. Plf recovers agt dft.

p.42   Bill/sale German Lester to James Buford 2 Negroes Anarchy & Mary ackd.

Deed John Vance to Willie Garrett 50 acres ackd.

Bill/sale Charles C Bailey to Parker Bailey, property therein named, ackd.

87

JUNE 1816

At least five justices present, Phenice Cox produced a wolf scalp over four months old which was ordered to be burnt.

Will of John Temple decd partly proven by Freeman Crenshaw one of the subscribing witnesses thereto. John Hawkins and Duncan McIntyre executors therein named qualified according to Law & gave bond and security.

p.43   John Millar v James Cunningham. Certiorari. Jury Jas Buford, Earley Benson, Wm Phillips, Robert R Alsup, John Caldwell, Jno Gregory, Jno Elliss, Thomas Bigham, Rolly Harwell, Chas Dever, Robt Lyon, Jno Vance day dft doth owe plf $16 [blank]

p.44   Exrs/will of John Temple returned inventory of personal estate. Order/sale issued to exrs/John Temple decd to sell perishable part of said estate.

Order Aaron Brown, Thomas Brown, John Butler, John Barnett, Samuel Cox, & Elijah Anthony or any five of them view that part of Forthampton road near Elijah Anthonys plantation and see if it be proper to turn sd road.

Deed Commrs/Pulaski to John Crawford Lott 117 proven by Nathaniel Allman and David Maxwell subscribing witnesses thereto.

p.45   John Dewaaser v John Davidson, James Duprees, John Fowlks. Covenant. Jury Robt Black, Jas Simmons, Geo Hillhouse, Jno Porter, Hamilton C Campbell, Wm Hendry, Wm Pride, Quinton Shannon, Jas McCravens, Nathan Farmer, Wm White, Elias Tidwell say dfts have not performed their covenant. Plf recovers of dfts damages $30 and costs of suit.

p.44[again]   John Elliss v William Richardson. Appeal. Parties in persons, each assuming payment of his own cost, plaintiff directs suit be dismissed.

Order Miller Dogget oversee part of road lately marked out from Robert Gordons to Columbia in Maury County which lies between County line and where sd road crosses Robertsons fork, and that he direct for that purpose hands in following bounds: from County line westward to include Solomon Tuttle, southward crossing Robertsons fork incl John Barron and Wm Barron, eastward up sd Creek incl Samuel Montgomery thence to where Robert Carlton lives, northward including John

p.45[again]   Callahan, John Hughes & Griffis to County line to beginning.

Order Pleasant Jones oversee to open road lately marked out from Robert Gordons toward Columbia which lies between where sd road crosses Robertsons fork and Mr Fishers, directing following hands in bounds from Robert Caltons north to county line, thence east with sd line to include William M Marr, south by Mr Fishers incl Green Vickers, west to James Leitchs including all settlers on north side Blue Creek, north to Samuel Montgomerys, thence up the creek to beginning.

Order David McCullock oversee road lately marked out from Robert Gordons to

p.46   Columbia between Mr Fishers & Robt Gordons, having direction of hands in bounds from Fishers down Blue Creek including settlers on east side of Camp branch, up creek incl Robt Gordons, east to include M Ship, north including John Clark and Samuel Day & John Oxford, thence crossing Richland cr incl Abner McGauhey, thence including farm where Stephen Farmer formerly lived, thence northward to beginning.

Remit double tax on tax lists: Wm & James W Smith 500 acres; John Graves 1 white poll, 2 slaves; Fountain Lester 40 acres, 1 white pole, 3 slaves; Robert Turner[Teniser?] 4030 acres.

p.47   Alexander Jones v Chapman White. Certiorari. Jury Earley Benson, John Caldwell, Rolly Harwell, Andw McPeters, Leonard Brown, Robt Lyon, Nathan Davis, Wm Webb, Alfred Yancy, Joseph Johns, Lewis Conner, Major Harrolson say they cannot agree. Jurors to disperse and to meet again tomorrow morning.

Court adjourned till tomorrow morning 9 Oclock. J Byler, A Black, J Walker

88

p.48   Thursday June 6th. Present Jacob Byler, Alexander Black, John C Walker.
Appt Buckner Harwell Esqr special guardian to Rachel Winn, Nancy Winn, Eliza Winn, William Foster, Mary Foster and Thomas Foster heirs of Ambrose Foster and to Henry Nave heir of Polly Winn.
Order Ralph Graves oversee road from Pulaski to dry fork of Pigeon roost creek with following hands in addition to his former number: all at William Graves, Edward Conway and Elizabeth Whites.
Thomas Wood and Andrew Prater recognizance, condition Thomas Wood appear next Term to answer the State of a charge of Bastardy.
p.49   Jesse Marlow recognizance, condition he attend next Term to prosecute & give evidence behalf State against James Finney for A&B on sd Jesse Marlow.
Alfred Yancy recognizance, condition he attend day to day to prosecute & give evidence behalf State against Edmund J Bailey for A&B on sd Alfred Yancy.
Alfred Yancy recognizance, to attend day to day to prosecute & give evidence behalf State against Moses McWherter for A&B on sd Alfred Yancy.
p.50   James Yancy recognizance, to attend day to day & give evidence behalf State against John Morrison for Pettit Larceny.
James Yancy recognizance, to attend day to day & give evidence behalf State against William Stewart for Pettit Larceny.
State v John Alsup. A&B on Richard Briggs. Jury Geo Hillhouse, Hamilton C Campbell, Wm Hendry, Quinton Shannon, Jas Buford, Jno McKissack, Matthew Anderson, Jno Hicks, Robert Paine, Jno Clack, Wm Jones, Saml Hurt find dft guilty. Fine 6½¢ and committed to county jail without bail for ten days & pay costs of prosecution.
State v Balaam Straughn. Gaming. Jury[above except Harrison Hicks for John Hicks] find dft not guilty.
p.52   State v Balaam Straughn. Gaming. Judgment entered up in favour of those entitled for all costs.
State v William R Coxe. Gaming. Jury[above]. Dft guilty. Fine $5 & costs.
p.53   State v John Bryant. Gaming. Jury Nathan Farmer, Wm Pride, Jas Simmons, Jas McCravens, Eli Tidwell, Isaac Lann, Wm Lyon, John Abernathy, Wm Phillips, Aquila Wilson, John Yancy, James Moore find dft guilty. Fine $5; pay costs of prosecution.
Admrs/estate of Wilson Jones decd returned account of sale of sd estate.
p.54   State v John Bryant. Gaming. Jury Geo Hillhouse, Hamilton C Campbell, Wm Hendry, Quinton Shannon, James Buford, Mattw Anderson, Robert Paine, Jno Clack, Wm Jones, Saml Hurt, Thos McCarley, Edmund Shelton say dft is guilty. Fine $5 & costs.
State v Henry Hagen. Gaming. Dft in proper person pleads guilty. Fine $5
p.55   and pay costs of this prosecution.
John Yancy recognizance, attend next Term to prosecute Anson Taylor for A&B on James Yancy.
State v Nicholas Naile. Affray. It appearing Dft hath not been taken on the alias Plurias writ issued against him and that he hath removed himself ouit of the limits of this State, therefore a Nolle Prosequi is entered in this case.
p.56   State v Nicholas Naile. Affray. Judgment entered up in favour of those entitled for all costs.
State v John McCabe Junr. Affray. It appearing that dft hath not been taken on writ issued against him, and that he hath removed himself out of the limits of this State, order Nolle Prosequi entered in this case.
State v John McCabe Junr. Affray. Judgment entered up in favour of those entitled for all costs.
p.57   State v John Gregory. Gaming. Dft in proper person pleads guilty. Fine $5

JUNE 1816

and pay costs of this prosecution.
State v William Ball. Gaming. Dft in proper person pleads guilty. Fine $5
and costs of this prosecution.
p.58   State v Charles Conway. Dft in proper person pleads guilty as charged in
bill of presentment; Fine $1 and pay costs of this prosecution.
State v Thomas B Haynie. Gaming. Jury Geo Hillhouse, Robt Black, Hamilton C
Campbell, Wm Hendry, Quinton Shannon, Jas Buford, Mattw Anderson, Wm Jones, Samuel
Hurt, Thos McCarley, Edmund Shelton, Aquila Wilson find dft guilty. Fine $5 and pay
p.59   costs of this prosecution.
State v John Gregory. Gaming. Jury Nathan Farmer, Wm Pride, Jas Simmons, Wm
Lyon, Wm Phillips, Jno Yancy, Jas Moore, Wm Webb, Jno Porter say dft is guilty.
p.60   Fine $5 and pay costs of this prosecution.
State v Wm R Cox. Gaming. Dft in proper person. Jury Nathan Farmer, William
Pride, James Simmons, Jas McCraven, Eli Tidwell, Isaac Lann, Wm Lyon, Wm Phillips,
John Yancy, James Moore, William Webb, Jno Porter find dft guilty. Fine $5 and pay
costs of this prosecution.
p.61   State v Jno Bryant. Gaming. Jury[above] say dft is guilty. Fine $5 & costs.
Appt James B Goldsberry overseer/Huntsville road in room of Charles Atkins
resigned; to have some district of hands.
p.62   State v Edmund J Baily. A&B on Alfred Yancy. Dft in proper person pleads
guilty. Fine 6½¢ and pay cost of this prosecution.
State v John Jones. Gaming. Jury[above] say dft is guilty. Fine $5 & costs.
p.63   State v Archibald McKissack. Gaming. Jury Geo Hillhouse, Robt Black, Hamilton C Campbell, William Hendry, Quinton Shannon, Jas Buford, Edmund Shelton, Aquila
Wilson, Thos Wilkinson, Andw McPeters, Early Benson, Caleb White say dft is guilty.
Fine $5 and pay costs of this prosecution.
p.64   State v John Gregory. Gaming. Dft in proper person pleads guilty. Fine $5
and pay costs of this prosecution.
State v Rowland Tankersley. Gaming. Dft in proper person pleads guilty.
Fine $5 & pay costs of this prosecution.
p.65   State v Balaam Straughn. Gaming. Dft in proper person pleads guilty. Fine
$5 and pay costs of this prosecution.
State v Wilson Collier. Neglect as overseer of road. Dft in proper person
pleads guilty. Fine 6½¢ and costs of this prosecution.
p.66   State v John McCracken. A&B on Charles Conway. Dft in proper person pleads
guilty. Fine $5 and pay costs of this prosecution.
At least five justices present, James Wilson produced one wolf scalp over
four months old and one under four months old which were ordered to be burnt.
Power/atty David L Jones and Matthew Wilson executors of James Wilson decd
to Maxwell Wilson ackd by sd David L Jones & Matthew Wilson.
p.67   At least five justices present, John Smallwood produced in open Court one
wolf scalp over four months old and four under four months; ordered burnt.
Receive 1816 tax list of Edmund J Bailey 555 acres west side Richland
creek, 231 ditto, 7 slaves, 1 white pole.
Wade Blasengame, Wm Blasengame, James Wilson, Blasengame Ham, Sarah
English, Thomas McBride recognizance, condition they attend next Term, sd Wade
Blasengame to prosecute & give evidence, others to give evidence behalf State
against William Darnell for pettit larceny.
Court adjourned till tomorrow morning 9 Oclock.
A Black, Wm Mayfield, Wm H Cook

90

p.68   Friday June 7th. Present Alexander Black, William Mayfield, William H Cook. State v William Straughn. Gaming. Dft in proper person pleads guilty. Fine $5 and pay costs of this prosecution.

State v Charles Gudrelan. A&B on Charles Conway. Dft in proper person pleads guilty. Fine $5 and pay costs of this prosecution.

p.69   Bill/sale Robert Rivers to Buckner Harwell negro therein named proven by Thomas Brown and Henry McKey.

Deed Alexander McDonald to John McDonald 138 acres proven by Edward M Brown and Jesse S Buchanon.

State v Elijah Cunningham. A&B on John Duncan. Jury Early Benson, Jas Mc-Cravens, Jas Simmons, Robt Black, Wm Pride, Jno Porter, Jas Buford, Geo Hillhouse, Nathan Farmer, Quinton Shannon, Mattw Montcrief, Henry McKey say dft is not guilty. Dft recovers of John Duncan the prosecutor his costs about his defence expended.

p.70   Jurors to next Circuit Court: Jno Dickey, Robt Buchanon, James Bumpass, Wm Brown, Jarret Manifee, Arthur Hicks, Robert Oliver, John C Walker, John Henderson, Tyree Rodes, Samuel Shields, Peter Swanson, Wm Henderson, Alexr Black, Wm Mayfield, Wm M Marr, Wm Pickins, Thomas Welch, Danl Allen, Jas Cooke, Duncan McIntyre, Hardy Hightower, Thomas Harwood, Alexander Thompson, Britton Yarbrough.

Constables Jeremiah Parker and John Gordon to attend next Circuit Court.

p.71   Jurors to next County Court: Marcus Mitchell, Chas C Abernathy, William W Crittenton, Jason Hopkins, Chas Buford, Jos Anthony, Saml Y Anderson, Lewis Conner, Parks Bailey, Wm McDonald, Robt McNairy, Thos Greenwood, Owen Smith, Elisha White, Jno White, David L Jones, Walter Fraser, Samuel Weir, John Barnett, John McKissack, Alexr Barron, Nathan Bass, Thomas Rhea, George Brown (Capt) and Hugh Campbell.

p.72   Order County trustee pay Archibald Alexander $70 for building an addition to the temporary jail of this County, let by order of this Court at last Term.

Peter Swanson v Halbert Allison & Partrick Long. Certiorari. [blank]

At least five justices present, William McKenney produced one wolf scalp over four months old which was ordered to be burnt.

p.73   State v Edmund Shelton. Neglect/duty as overseer of road. Jury Earley Benson, Jas McCravens, Jas Simmons, Robt Black, Wm Pride, Jno Porter, Jas Buford, Geo Hillhouse, Nathan Farmer, Quinton Shannon, Mattw Montcrief, Henry McKey say dft is not guilty.

State v Edmund Shelton. Dft being acquitted by jury, judgment in favour of

p.74   those entitled for all costs.

State v Aquilla Wilson. Neglect/duty as overseer of road. For manifest informality in the presentment, order same be quashed.

State v Aquilla Wilson. Neglect/duty as overseer/road. Judgment entered up in favour of those entitled for all costs.

p.75   Appoint Baker P Potts guardian for Madison W Caldwell a minor orphan of William Caldwell decd.

State v Brice M Mayfield. A&B on Isaac N Hobson. Jury Earley Benson, Jas McCravens, Alfred Yancy, Robt Black, Wm Pride, Jas Buford, Geo Hillhouse, Nathan Farmer, Quinton Shannon, Mattw Montcrief, Henry McKey, Edmund Shelton say dft is

p.76   guilty. Fine $2.50 and pay costs of this prosecution.

Alexander Thompson appointed a Justice/peace appeared in Court & qualified.

State v Joseph Starkey. Keeping peace. Dft in proper person; no person appearing to rebind sd dft, order he be discharged from his recognizance.

John Boyd recognizance, condition he attend day to day to prosecute behalf

p.77   State against Robert Taylor.

John Boyd, recognizance, condition Elijah Boyd attend day to day to give evidence behalf state against Robert Taylor.

State v Martin Shadden. Keeping peace. Dft in proper person; no person appearing to rebind dft, order he be discharged from his recognizance.

p.78   State v Moses McWherter. A&B on Alfred Yancy. Dft in proper person pleads guilty. Fine $5 and pay costs of this prosecution.

Alexander Jones v Chapman White. Certiorari. Jury say dft doth owe plf $12.

p.79   Plf recovers of dft afsd sum and his costs before Majistrate & this Court.

John B Long v Bernard M Patteson. Debt. Dft in proper person. Plf recovers of dft $40 with interest and his costs which the dft paid to Clerk of Court; the balance of the debt in the declaration mentioned is transfered to the Circuit Court of Giles County for trial.

p.80   State v William Kindell. Gaming. Dft came not. Judgmt entered agt him $300 according to tenor of his bail bond; scire facias issued agt him.

State v William Kindell. Gaming. William Price who was bound for appearance of Wm Kindell came not. Judgmt according to tenor of his bail bond entered against him for $300; scire facias issued against him.

p.81   State v Anson Taylor. Gaming. Dft came not. Judgment against him for $400 acording to tenor of his bail bond; scire facias issued against him/

State v Anson Taylor. Gaming. Robert Taylor, bound for appearance of Anson Taylor, made default. Judgment against him $400; scire facias issued agt him.

p.81[again]   State v Anson Taylor. Gaming. Matthias Richardson bound for appearance of Anson Taylor made default. Judgmt agt him $400; scire facias issued.

State v Anson Taylor. Gaming. Dft came not. Judgment agt him $400 according to tenor of his bail bond; scire facias issued against him.

p.82   State v Anson Taylor. Gaming. Robt Taylor bound for appearance of Anson Taylor made dafault. Scire facias entered against him returnable to next Court.

State v Anson Taylor. Gaming. Matthias Richardson [as above]

p.83   State v William Darnell. Petit Larceny. Benjamin Beeson bound for appearance of Wm Darnell made default. Judgment according to tenor his bail bond $400; scire facias issued against him returnable to next Court.

State v William Darnell. Petitt Larceny. Sampson McCown bound for appearance of Wm Darnell came not; judgment according to tenor of his bail bond $400 agt him; scire facias issued agt him returnable to next Court.

p.84   State v William Darnell. Pettit Larceny. Andrew Elliott bound for appearance of Wm Darnell made default. Judgment according to tenor of his bail bond agt him $200 and scire facias issued agt him returnable to next court.

State v William Darnell. Pettit Larceny. Roland Tankersly bound [as above]

p.85   State v William Darnell. Pettit Larceny. Robert Lyon bound [as above]

State v Charles Atkins. Neglect as overseer/road. Dft in proper person pleads guilty. Fine 6½¢ and pay cost of this prosecution.

p.86   State v James Kettell[Kellett?]. Gaming. Dft came not. Judgment agt him $400 according to tenor of his bail bond; scire facias issued against him.

State v James Keltit. Gaming. Robert McDow bound for appearance of James Kettit came not. Judgment against him $400; scire facias issued against him.

p.87   State v James Keltit. Gaming. Dft came not; judgment $400 according to tenor of his bail bond; scire facias issued against him returnable to next Court.

State v James Kettet. Gaming. Robert McDow bound [as above]

p.88   State v James Keltet. Gaming. Dft came not [as above]

State v James Kellett. Gaming. Robert McDow [as above]

p.89   State v James Kettit. Gaming. [as above]
        State v James Keltet. Gaming. Robert McDow made default. [as above]
p.90   State v James Keltet. Gaming. [as above]
        State v James Kettet. Gaming. Robert McDow made default. [as above]
p.91   State v Nathaniel Mercer. On scire facias for not producing James Payne.
Release dft from forfeiture heretofore taken against him.
        Appoint M H Buchanon esq guardian of Jacob a free person of colour.
        Receive 1816 tax lists: L M Bramlett 1 white pole, 3 slaves; Philmer Green
3 slaves; Andrew Castleman 540 acres on Richland creek; Thomas McNeil 400 do.
p.92   John Gregory v Robert McDow. Trespass. Jury Early Benson, James McCravens,
Jas Simmons, James Buford, John Porter, George Hillhouse, Quinton Shannon, Edmund
Shelton, Thomas Brown, Isaac Atkins, Jno Yancy, Hamner Turner find dft guilty. plf
recovers of dft damages $17.16 and his costs of suit.
        Permit John Yancy former guardian of Frances Y Graves & Sally Y Graves to
correct the return of their estate by him returned to this Court last Term.
p.93   State v Thomas Franks. Counsel for State no further prosecutes dft. Thomas
Franks assumes payment of costs prior to this case being brought to Court and one
half costs since that time; Eldridge B Robertson and Stirling C Robertson assume
upon themselves the payment of the balance of sd costs.
        Court adjourned till tomorrow morning 9 Oclock.

                                        John Dickey, A Black, Alexr Thomson

p.94   Saturday 8 June. Present John Dickey, Alexander Black, Alexander Thompson.
        Polly Covey v William Welch. Appeal. Dft came not. Judgment of the justice
below be in all things affirmed: $1.62½ with legal interest thereon from 9 April
1816 untill paid together with costs before Majistrate as in this Court expended.
        George Harrison v Thomas Bratton. Sheriff returned alias Sci Fa that dft
was not found; dft made default. Judgment interlocutory $125 made final against
p.95   him, and plaintiff has execution thereof.
        Duncan Baker v John C Maxwell. Attachment. Dft came not. Plf recovers of
dft damages by reason of nonperformance of promise. Damages to be enquired of by a
jury at next Term.
        Elisha Mayfield v David Woods. Attachment. Dft made default. Plf recovers
p.96   of dft damages sustained by reason of nonperformance of agreemnt; damages
to be enquired of by a jury at next Term.
        Robert Gordon v Woody Loyd & Jeremiah Woodward. Covenant. Jury Robt Black,
Jas Simmons, Jas Buford, Geo Hillhouse, Earley Benson, Hamilton C Campbell, Wm
Hendry, Jas McCravens, Jno Porter, Wm Pride, Jas Doran, Robt Bigham. Plf recovers
p.97   of dft his damages $100 and his costs of suit.
        State v James Finney. A&B on Jesse Marlor. Richard Conniway, Edward Conni-
way, John Shadden and Thomas Boatwright bound for the appearance of James Finney
surrender him to Court.
p.98   Isaac N Hobson v Brice M Mayfield. A&B. Dft made default. Plf recovers of
dft damages sustained by A&B. Writ of Enquiry to be executed at next Term.
        Deed Joshua Hadley to Maxamilian H Buchanan 190 acres proven by John
Buchanan and Jesse Buchanan.
p.99   David McMecken v William White. Case. Jury Nathan Farmer, Quinton Shannon,
Jas Finnen, William Pullin, Marcus Mitchell, Harrison Hicks, Jacob Templen, James
Patteson, Wm W Crittenton, Saml Y Anderson, John Yancy, Joseph Anthony say dft is

not guilty. Dft recovers of plf his costs of defence in this behalf expended.

Daniel T Woods v Joseph Johns. Continued till next Court. Plf recovers of dft the costs of this Term.

p.100   Order Henry Abernathy overseer of part of Lower Elkton road have under his direction the hands of Davis Brown, Zebulon Raney, Robt Rivers, Richard Harwell and all hands on plantation of Sally Harwell.

Washington G L Foley v Daniel T Woods. Jesse Foster and Joseph Shadden bound for appearance of Daniel T Woods surrender him. Thereupon Robert Bigham and Jno Dewaaser dfts bail.

p.101   Deed Joshua Hadley, Gabriel Bumpass and Maxamilian H Buchanan to Holloway J Maples 150 acres proven by James Buford and Alexr McDonald.

Joseph Pickens v Harrison Hicks. It appearing to Court that dft hath been notified, and he as constable hath failed to pay over to plf $10 which he collected on 22 Novr 1815 of John Bryant by virtue on an execution in favour of plf agt sd Bryant, therefore plf recovers of dft sd sum with interest thereon at rate of 6% per annum from 22d Novr 1815 till this time together with his costs, from which p.102   judgment dft obtains appeal to Circuit Court.

Order part of road over which Richard Bentley is overseer be shortened one pole at southwest end of his bounds.

Charlotty Fort v William Davis. Sci Fa to revive a judgt. Dft in proper person. Plf recovers of dft $100 debt together with $47.25 damages with interest p.103   thereon from 7 June 1814 till paid together with her costs as well in the original suit as in this behalf expended.

David Woods v Richard Briggs. Dft made default. Plf recovers of dft damages. Jury to enquire into damages.

p.104   Andrew Erwin v Mary Crowson & Moses Crowson admrs of Wm Crowson decd. Debt. Dfts came not. Plf recovers of dfts $150 debt, $13.10 damages of detention and his costs of suit to be levied on goods and chattels of sd Wm Crowson decd in hands of sd admrs if any; if none, to be levied of goods, chattels, lands of sd dfts.

p.105   John B Long assee v Bernard M Patteson. Debt. Dft in proper person. Order this cause transferred to Circuit Court.

Order that that part of Shelbyville road over which Samuel Criswell is overseer be extended one pole beyond Leatherwood creek and that sd Criswell with hands under his direction keep the same in repair.

Commrs appointed to settle with John Yancy former guardian of Frances Y & Sally Y Graves made report.

p.106   William Ball v Levi F Thompson admr of Wm Thompson decd. Appeal. Jury Quinton Shannon, Jas Simmons, Jas Buford, Geo Hillhouse, Early Benson, Hamilton C Campbell, Wm Hendry, Jas McCravens, Jno Porter, Wm Pride, Jas Doran, Robt Bigham[blank]

p.107   Andrew Jackson, Thomas Crutcher, Alfred Balch exrs of W T Lewis decd v William Ball & Green McCafferty. Debt. Ralph Graves bound for appearance of Wm Ball surrenders him. Thereupon Edmund J Bailey dfts bail.

p.108   Mary Crowson, Richard Crowson, Moses Crowson admrs v James J Ward & James Caldwell. Debt. Dfts made default. Plfs recover of dfts $268.31 debt with $7.42 damages of detention together with their costs.

Court adjourned till Court in Course. John Dickey, A Black, Alexr Thomson.

p.109   Court of Pleas & Quarter Sessions at the Court house in town of Pulaski on Monday the second day of September. Present Nelson Patteson, Buckner Harwell, Duncan McIntyre, Esquires, Justices.

Grant ltrs/admn on estate of Reuben Naile decd to Rowland Brown.

Constantine Perkins produced his license to practice law, qualified, and is admitted to practice in this Court.

Grand Jury: Charles Buford foreman, John McKissack, Samuel Weir, Walter Fraser, Nathan Bass, William W Crittenton, Parks Bailey, Alexander Barron, Thomas Rhea, Charles W Abernathy, Joseph Anthony, Robert McNairy, Hugh Campbell.

p.110   At least five justices present, David Flat produced three wolf scalps over four months old which was ordered to be burnt.

At least five Justices being present, Charles Conniway produced in Court one wolf scalp over four months old which was ordered to be burnt.

At least five Justices being present, Benjamin Chesher produced one wolf scalp over four months old which was ordered to be burnt.

Deed Guston Kearney to William Phillips Lot 115 in Upper Elkton ackd.

Appt John Redle Senr overseer/road in room of Robert Bigham resigned.

p.111   Deed James McDonald to James Moore fifty acres proven by Thomas B Haynie & John Brown.

Deed/gift Richard Atkins to David Crook negro therein named proven by Maxamilian H Buchanan.

William Kelly Esquire having been licensed to practice law, on being qualified was admitted to practice in this Court.

p.112   Appt Guston Kearney guardian of Tabitha M M A Fish a minor heir of William Fish decd.

Grant ltrs/admn on estate of William Shannon decd to Herod Fowlks. Inventory of sd estate returned. An Order of sale issued to Herod Fowlks admr/estate of William Shannon decd to sell perishable part of sd estate.

p.113   Order Alexander Black & John Dickey Esqrs settle estate of Rees Porter decd in the hands of Sally D Porter, Joseph B Porter and William Whitsett admrs.

The order appointing Roland Brown administrator of the estate of Reuben Naile decd rescinded; Benjamin Naile apptd admr of estate of sd Reuben Naile decd.

Deed Isham Brown to James Brown 105 acres ackd.

p.114   Deed Isham Brown to Elizabeth Brown 102 acres ackd.

Deed Isham Brown to William Watson 99 acres ackd.

Deed Richard Burnett to John Perry 30 acres proven by John Paine and Hartwell Bumpass.

Order hands of Charlotte Jones and James Reed be added to hands that work under John Jones, overseer of the Montgomerys gap road.

p.115   Deed Jacob Cody to Saml Patrick 50 acres ackd.

Deed James Temple to James McCormack 86 acres proven by Amos Williams and Samuel McCormack.

Deed Ransom Wells to Gabriel Bumpass 150 acres ackd.

Appt Jos German overseer/road in room of Hightower Partin[Pontin?] resignd.

p.116   Deed Daniel Adams to George Waters 20 acres proven by John Wisener & William Taylor.

Appt Luke Adams guardian to William L Williams, a minor heir of James Williams decd. Appt Luke Adams guardian to Andrew Jackson Williams, a minor heir of James Williams decd.

Grant ltrs/admn on estate of Archd Cunningham decd to William Cunningham.

p.117 Deed Richard Hightower to John Montgomery 100 acres proven by Samuel Shields and George Shields.

Deed Reuben Hightower to John Montgomery 100 acres proven by Samuel Shields and George Shields.

Grant ltrs/admn on estate of Frances Reasonhover decd to Earley Benson.

p.118 Deed William Woods to Moses Pullin 38 acres ackd.

Assignment of Certificate #1295 from Ebenezer Petty to William Kelly 160 acres in Madison County M. T. ackd.

Return of a settlement between the field officers & Judge advocate of the 52d Redgiment of the Malitia of this State was made by Col Thos K Gordon the commandant of sd Redgt and ordered to be recorded.

Deed Rebeccah Williams to Caleb White for 53 acres proven by William B Pepper and John Williams.

p.119 Executors of will of Alexr Barron Senr decd returned an account of the sale of part of his estate.

Appt James Brown overseer/road in room of William Watson resigned.

Order that the road near plantation of Wm H Cook Esqr be turned agreable to report of a Jury apptd for that purpose and that Henry F Steele oversee opening and keeping in repair the same with the hands under his direction.

William Purnell v James Neile. Appeal. On affidavit of John Rhea stating he had proved three days attendance at June Term as witness in this case which was not entered, it is ordered same be added in the bill of costs.

p.120 William Purnell v John Easley. appeal. On affidavit of John Rhea[as above]

William Purnell v James Starke. Appeal. On affidavit of John Rhea[as above]

William Purnell v Amos Vernon. Appeal. On affidavit of John Rhea[as above]

p.121 William Purnell v Abraham Cole. Appeal. On affidavit of John Rhea[as above]

William Purnell v Benjamin Osburne. Appeal [as above]

William Purnell v George Saunders. Appeal. [as above]

p.122 Order Samuel Ramsey overseer/road in room of John Elliss resigned, and that he have following hands Robert Alsup, Isaac Bridgewater, John Keneday, George Garrett, Robt Glasgow, William Turner, Jesse Hackney, William Keneday, Wm McClanahan.

Order Samuel McNight overseer/road in room of John McNight resigned, & have same hands & work from Gap near Pleasant News to top of ridge toward Indian creek.

Order Stephen Samuel oversee Montgomery Gap road in room of Niel Patterson resigned and have same district of hands.

Appt Henry F Steele to oversee the Montgomery Gap road in room of William Patton resigned and have the same district of hands.

Order Samuel Poteet oversee road in room of Samuel Criswell resigned.

p.123 Elijah Anthony v William Riddle & Mary Riddle his wife admrs &c. Debt. Jury Marcus Mitchell, Saml Y Anderson, John Barnet, Wm Phillips, William Bottoms, David Crook, John Perry, Early Benson, John McDonald, Edward M Brown, Peter Satterfield, Henry Roberts. Plf recovers of dfts $132 debt and damages $37.31 besides costs.

At least five Justices present, John S Bailey produced a wolf scalp over four months old which is ordered to be burnt.

p.124 James Cunningham v John Millar. Case. Plf by attorney directs that this suit be dismissed; defendant recovers of plf his costs about his suit expended.

Court adjourned till tomorrow morning 9 Oclock.

A Black, Thos K Gordon, Joseph Rea

p.125   Tuesday 3d Septr. Present Alexr Black, Thos K Gordon, Joseph Rea, Justices.
Deed Parks Bailey and Mary Bailey his wife to Silvanus Ingram land in Lunenburg County Virginia ackd by sd Parks Bailey.   Appt Duncan McIntire & Alex Black Esqrs to take privy examination of Mary Bailey touching her free consent in execution of deed to Silvanus Ingram. Duncan McIntire and Alexr Black Esqrs report their
p.126   examination of Mary Bailey.
Power/attorney Parks Bailey to Lucas Gee & John E Bailey ackd.
Joseph Hankins recognizance, to attend day to day to prosecute & give evidence behalf State against Levi Fugate for assault on his body.
p.127   Joseph Hankins recognizance, condition his wife Polly Hankins & his daughter Polly Hankins attend day to day to give evidence behalf State agt Levi Fugate.
Admx/estate of Wellcome Hodge decd returned account of sales.
Appt Thomas Harwood & Duncan McIntire to settle account current of Brice M Garner and Jarret Manefee admrs of estate of Alexr Laughlin decd.
Deed David W McRee & James W McRee to Joseph Yarum[?] 150 acres ackd.
p.128   Deed Wm Polk to James Payne 1280 acres proven by Benjn Cross & Geo Beard.
Deed Wm Polk to Henry Cross 1220 acres proven by Benjn Cross & Geo Beard.
Deed Richard Hightower to John McDonald 30 acres 112 poles proven by Robert
p.129   McDonald and Alexander McDonald.
Deed Richard Hightower to Robert McDonald 25 acres nine polls proven by Alexr McDonald and John McDonald.
Deed Edmund Shelton to William B Brooks 50 acres ackd.
At least five Justices present, James McDonnell produced one wolf scalp over four months old which was ordered to be burnt.
p.130   At least five Justices present, Joseph Luker produced a wolf scalp over four months old which was ordered to be burnt.
Court elected by ballot a Ranger in room of Lewis Kirk decd; Presley Ward was elected, who was qualified.
Appt David Crook a constable in Capt Wilsons company, who qualified.
Deed Moses Crowson to John Wright 81 acres ackd.
At least five justices present, Drury Joiner produced one wolf scalp over four months old which was ordered to be burnt.
p.131   Appt Peter Swanson overseer/road in room of Charles Robertson resigned.
Appt Charles C Abernathy overseer of the Fayetteville road in room of Joseph Dickson resigned.
Authorise Fountain Lester to purchase a suitable record book for use of the register of this County.
Grant Ltrs/admn on estate of Mary Ann Finch to Thomas Batey.
Admr/estate of Mary Ann Finch decd returned inventory/estate.
p.132   Order/sale issued to Thomas Batey to sell estate of Mary Ann Finch decd.
Admr/estate of Archd Cunningham decd returned inventory of estate.
Order/sale issued to Wm Cunningham admr/estate of Archd Cunningham decd to sell said estate.
Earley Benson one of the executors/estate of John Reasonhover decd returned additional inventory of sd estate.
Order/sale issued to Earley Benson exr/John Reasonhover decd to sell property contained in the additional inventory by him this day returned.
p.133   Order John Henderson, John Dabney and Archibald Young allot to Charity Cunningham widow of Archibald Cunningham decd so much of sd estate as will maintain her and family for one year from the time sd Archd Cunningham departed this Life.

County Trustee to pay German Lester $5.50 for a state Docket furnished for use of this Court.

Deed James Bumpass to Edmund Shelton 106 acres ackd.

p.134 Deed Maxamilian H Buchanan to James Bumpass 105 acres ackd.

Bill/sale Philip Parchman to Danl McIntire negro boy therein named proven by Malcomb McIntire.

Grand Jury Bills/Indictment: State v Levi Fugate true bill. Same v R Conniway & others true bill.

Admr/estate of Frances Reasonhover decd returned inventory/estate.

p.135 Order County trustee pay Samuel Pearson $30.50 for boarding guard and prisoners &c while guarding Levi Fugate and William Darnell at March County Court and at the April Circuit Court of this county.

Admr/estate of Frances Reasonhover decd returned an inventory of sd estate.

Order/sale issued to Earley Benson admr/estate of Frances Reasonhover decd commanding him to sell the sd estate.

Order heretofore made for division of lands belonging to heirs of Samuel Lockhart decd is in all things revived, returnable to next Court.

p.136 Andrew B Moore v Gabriel Bumpass. Appeal. Jury Marcus Mitchell, Jason Hopkins, John Brashers, John Philips, Peter Satterfield, Samuel Hurt, William Maples, William B Pepper, Isaac Mayfield, Alfred Yancy, William Moore, Isaac Atkins. Plf recovers of dft $4036 and his costs. Dft is granted appeal to Circuit Court.

p.137 Assignment of plat & certificate of survey from Alfred M Harris to Geo Coalter 80 acres in name of James D Breckenridge ackd by sd Alfred M Harris.

Order Miller Doggett oversee road having under his direction hands in the following bounds, from county line including Alston J Waters and Thos Stuart thence west including widow Walker and Wm James thence north, including Bogard, to county line including all hands on Stuarts Branch, thence west to the beginning.

John Myers for benefit of Jesse Newland v Philip Parchman. Debt. On affidavit of Robert Mach[binding] dft's attorney, order cause continued next Term.

p.138 Order Thos Goff, John Laird, Berry Dearing, James Evans & Thos Moody view part of Prewitts gap road which lies between Reddles and Robert Bighams and see whether it be proper to turn sd road and make report next term of this Court.

Court adjourned till tomorrow morning 9 Oclock.

Wm Mayfield, John C Walker, William Brown

p.139 Wednesday Sepr 4th. Present William Mayfield, John C Walker, William Brown.

James Manifee recognizance, condition he attend day to day to prosecute and give evidence behalf State agt James McCormack for A&B committed on him.

Appt John Dicky and John Hillhouse Esqrs to settle account current with Jonathan Moody admr/estate of Isaac Oxford decd; make return next Court.

Order Robert Buchanan & James Bumpass Esqrs settle acct courrent with admrs of William Crowson decd; make return to next Court.

p.140 Order Nelson Patteson, John Hicks & Chas Buford let to lowest bidder the keeping of James Dickson a pauper for twelve months from date hereof.

Order Alexr Black & Wm Mayfield Esqrs settle acct current with Maxamillian H Buchanan surviving admr/estate of Clayton S Buchanan decd; make return next Ct.

Admrs/estate of William Crowson decd returned additional acct/sales.

Admr/estate of Isaac Oxford decd returned additional inventory.

Order James Bumpass, Robert Buchanan, John Williams, Gabriel Bumpass, Wm B

Pepper divide personal estate of William Crowson decd between legatees.
p.141   William Smith v William W Crittenton. Case. Jury Marcus Mitchell, Jason
Hopkins, Jno Vance, Claybourn McVay, Thos Bailey, Joab Campbell, Lester Morris, Jno
Williams, James Neal, Isaac Atkins, Jesse Mitchell, Gideon Pillow. Plf recovers of
dft $49.75 damages besides costs.
    Grand Jury Bills/Indictment: State v James McCormack true bill. State agt
Levy Fugate true bill.
p.142   Grant ltrs/admn on estate of Lewis Kirk decd to Mary Kirk, John Porter, and
David W. Porter.
    Deed William Woods to John Phillips 97 acres 41 poles ackd.
    William Purnell v James Niell. Appeal. On affidavit of John Manifee stating
he had proved three days attendance as witness which was not entered, order same be
added in Bill of costs.
p.143   William Purnell v James Starke. Appeal. [as above]
    William Purnell v Amos Vernon. Appeal. [as above]
    William Purnell v Abraham Cole. Appeal. [as above]
p.144   William Purnell v Benjamin Osburne. Appeal. [as above]
    William Purnell v George Saunders. Appeal. [as above]
    Order John Lucas, Charles Carrol, James Matthews, William Reddish, Thomas
Williams, James Temple, James Niell, William H Ragsdale or any five to mark out a
road from mouth of Richland creek towards Fort Hampton as far as State line.
p.145   Assignment of Certificate #1332 for 628 acres in Madison County M.T. from
Charles Whitson to William Kelly was acknowledged by sd Charles Whitson.
    Commissioners apptd to allot to Rhoda Hodge widow of Wellcome Hodge decd a
years provisions made return of their allotment.
    Deed Thomas E Sumner to Abner Rhea 220 acres proven by Larkin Webb and
Zebedee Weaver two of the subscribing witnesses.
    Appt John Porter guardian to Janette B Porter, Nelly McNeese Porter, and
Reese W Porter, minor orphans of Reese Porter decd.
p.146   Deed Commrs/Pulaski Tyree Rodes, M H Buchanon, Nathaniel Moody, to Edward
Ragsdale, lott #176 proven by Lundsford M Bramlet and Charles Perkins.
    Deed Commrs/Pulaski Tyree Rodes, M H Buchanon, Nathl Moody, to Spencer
Buford, Lott #175 proven by Lunsford M Bramlet and Charles Perkins.
    Deed Commrs/Pulaski Tyree Rodes, M H Buchanon, Nathaniel Moody, to James
Giddens, Lotts #110, 133, 332 proven by Lunsford M Bramlet and Charles Perkins.
p.147   Deed Commrs/Pulaski Tyree Rodes, M H Buchanon, Nathaniel Moody, to Charles
Buford, Lotts #161, 162, 163, 164 proven by Lunsford M Bramlet and Charles Perkins.
    David Woods v Richard Briggs & Samuel Briggs. Richard Briggs assumed pay-
ment of all costs; plaintiff's attorney directs suit be dismissed. Plf recovers of
Richard Briggs his costs of suit.
p.148   Abel Oxford v Charles Whitson. Case. Jury Samuel Y Anderson, John Barnett,
Brice M Mayfield, Alexander Tarply, Thomas Wells, Henry Loyd, Thomas Brown, Robert
Paine, Samuel Cox, Robert Anderson, Elisha Kimbrough, William Webb say they cannot
agree. Samuel Cox withdrawn; cause continued untill next Court.
    Grand Jury Bills/Indictment: State v Joseph Hankins, true bill. Same v
Isaac N Hobson, true till. And the following presentments: State v William
Bratton. Same v Isaac Johnston.
p.149   On application of Moses Crowson, it is ordered [blank]
    Court adjourned untill tomorrow morning 9 Oclock.
               John Dickey, John Hillhouse, Thos K Gordon, A.W.

SEPTEMBER 1816

p.150   Thursday Sept 5th. Present John Dickey, John Hillhouse, Thomas K Gordon.
John Eppler, recognizance, attend day to day to prosecute and give evidence behalf State against Samuel Parmly for A&B on sd John Eppler.
John Eppler, recognizance, attend day to day to prosecute and give evidence behalf State against William Kyle for A&B on John Eppler.
p.151   State v Thomas Loftin. Bastardy. Dft not a citizen of this county; nolle prosequi entered.
State v Thomas Loftin. Bastardy. Judgment entered up in favour of those entitled for all costs.
State v Martin Adams. Gaming. Dft is not a citizen of this County; Nolle prosequi entered.
p.152   State v Martin Adams. Gaming. Judgment entered up in favour of those entitled for all costs.
State v Isaac Johnson. Affray. Dft in proper person pleads guilty. Fine $2.50 and costs of this prosecution.
John Manifee recognizance, attend next Term to prosecute and give evidence
p.153   behalf State agt James McCormack Junr for A&B committed on sd John Manifee.
State v Hasel Rodes & Jesse Isaacks. Affray. Dfts not citizens of this State. Nolle prosequi entered.
State v Hasel Rodes & Jesse Isaacks. Affray. Judgment entered up in faovur of those entitled for all costs.
Wade Blasengame recognizance, condition he attend next Term to prosecute &
p.154   give evidence behalf State against William Darnell for Pettit Larceny.
William Blasengame and Blasengame Ham, recognizance, condition they attend next Term to give evidence agt William Darnell for Pettit Larceny.
Wilson English recognizance, condition Sarah English his wife attend next Term to give evidence behalf State agt Wm Darnell for Pettit Larceny.
p.155   State v Richard Bently. Neglect as overseer/road. Dft pleads not guilty, in proper person. Jury Marcus Mitchell, Jason Hopkins, Wm Parker, Henry Roberts, Larkin Mayfield, Nathaniel Young, Nathan Davis, Alfred Yancy, Andrew Paul, Thomas C Stone, Ransom Wells, Littleton Johnston say dft is not guilty.
State v Richard Bently. Neglect as overseer/road. Judgment entered up in favour of those entitled for all costs.
p.156   State v Archibald Alexander. A&B on Nathan Bass. Jury[above except Rowland Brown for Littleton Johnston] find dft guilty. Fine $12; pay costs of prosecution.
Admr estate of William A Smith decd returned account of sales of sd estate.
p.157   Rachel Foster, orphan girl, bound to Henry Loyd.
State v Wm Kindle. Failing to appear & answer State for Gaming. Dft in proper person; sufficient cause shewn, forfeiture set aside on payment of costs.
State v Wm Price. Failing to produce Wm Kindell. Sufficient cause shewn, forfeiture heretofore taken is set aside on payment of all costs.
p.158   State v Wm Kindle. Gaming. Dft in proper person pleads guilty. Fine $5 and pay costs of this prosecution.
State v James Finney. A&B on Jesse Marlow. Dft in proper person. Jury Thos Jones, Mattw Anderson, Brice M Mayfield, Jas Simmons, Eli Tidwell, Charles Dever, Jos Roe, Patrick Long, Thomas Wilkinson, Humphrey Tompkins, John Barnett, Samuel Y
p.159   Anderson find dft guilty. Fine $1, committed to Jail without bail twenty days, & pay costs.
State v Thomas Woods. Bastardy. Dft in proper person and Andrew Prater and Asa Moore. Bond. Condition Thomas Woods keep free from charge to this County a

100

bastard begotton on body of Nancy Gilbert by sd Thomas Woods, and that he pay sd
p.160   Nancy Gilbert for maintenance of sd child semiannually $20 the first year,
fifteen per year for two succeeding years, making in whole $50.
    State v Asa Moore. Bastardy. Dft in proper person. Dft with James McNees &
[blank] recognizance, to keep free from charge to county a bastard child begotton
on body of Ritta Rea, and that he pay to sd Ritta Rea for maintenance of sd child
$20 first year and $15 a year for two succeeding years making in the whole $50.
p.161   Deed Augustine Carter to Jabez Carter 34 acres proven by Lemuel Cook and
Walter Frazer.
    Sampson McCoun v William C Mayfield. Parties in proper persons; determina-
tion of case is refered to Nelson Patteson, John Dickey, John Clack, James Buford
and Charles Buford. Referees to meet in Pulaski first Saturday in December next.
p.162   Deposition of Charles C Bailey in Lunenburg County, Virginia, to be taken
on behalf plaintiff.
    Wm Smith agt Wm W Crittenton. Case. Dft obtained appeal to Circuit Court.
    Deed William Woods to William Pullin 150 acres ackd.
p.163   Matthias B Minfree surviving obligee v William H Ragsdale. Debt. Dft in
proper person. Plf recovers $207.50 debt, damages by detention $17.06 & costs.
p.164   Matthias B Minfree surviving obligee v William H Ragsdale. Debt. Dft in
proper person said he doth owe $123 part of debt in the declaration mentioned, and
damages of detention $7.38, besides costs. Plaintiff recovers said sums.
p.165   Thomas Jones & Jno A Walker merchts, assignees, v Richard B Walthall. Debt.
Dft in proper person saith he owes $110 debt, damages/detention $3.50. Plaintiffs
recover said sums of defendant besides cost of suit.
p.166   Robert Erwin v James Mitchell. Certiorari. Jury Marcus Mitchell, Jason
Hopkins, John Waldrop, Jacob Templin, Thos C Stone, Leonard Brown, Jas Paine, Wm B
Brooks, Wm Pullin, Enoch Bryant, Samuel Y Anderson find dft indebted to plf $97.88
& costs. Plaintiff recovers, also his costs before the majistrate as in this court.
p.167   William Steele v William Woods. Debt. Dft in proper person. Plf recovers of
dft debt $112.50, damages $3.46, and costs of suit.
p.168   Hinchey Pettiway & Thomas T Maury merchts v Bernard M Patteson. Debt. Dft
in proper person. Plf recovers of dft debt $119, damages/detention $5.95, & costs.
p.169   Ralph Graves and Charles Buford appointed last Court inspectors at Pulaski
appeared in Court and Qualified as Law directs.
    John Barnett appointed last Court inspector at upper Elkton & Lower Elkton
appeared in Court and was qualified as law directs.
    Order Nathaniel Moody, Henry Hagen, and German Lester allot to Mary Kirk
widow of Lewis Kirk decd from sd estate maintainance for herself and family for one
year from time sd Lewis Kirk departed this life; make return to next Court.
    Danl T Woods agt Joseph Johns. Case. On dft's motion, new trial to be held.
p.170   James Kimbrough assee agt Edmund J Bailey. Debt. Dft in proper person. Plf
recovers of dft balance of debt $250, damages/detention $7.50, and costs of suit.
    Grand Jury Bills/Presentment: State v James Conway. Same v Richard Conway.
p.171   William McKinney, Rowland McKinney, Isaac Crowson recognizance, condition
William McKinney appear at next Circuit Court to answer State on charge of having
facilitated the escape of a Negro man named Nace charged with murder of Mason Moss.
    Order Maximilian H Buchanon Sheriff recover of William Riddles and wife
Mary $11 for his services rendered in division of estate of John Graves decd and
allotting to said Mary her dower.
p.172   Mason Crowson assee v Archibald Alexander. Debt. Grant plfs atty leave to

amend his declaration on payment of costs of amendment.

Hayes & Hightower agt Jeremiah Guilford. Caveat. Jury Marcus Mitchell, Jason Hopkins, Jno Waldrop, Jacob Templin, Thos C Stone, Leonard Brown, Jas Paine, Wm B Brooks, Wm Pullin, Robt Devenport, Enoch Bryant, Wm Hendry. True facts: dft p.173 hath not begun his survey on Lynn & Ash 30 chains south of Ancient corner; many Ancient corners in neighborhood of land surveyed & claimed by the caveatter. Ancient corner claimed in caveaters survey stands on Newtons creek is a northwest corner to Ancient survey of 2000 acres granted to Ezekiel Polk, also NE corner of 5000 acre tract granted by North Carolina to Thomas Polk, and beginning corner of caveators entry. That lines around Thomas Polks and Ezekiel Polks tracts for long before date of dfts entry were objects of notoriety. That no part of Newtons creek is within land surveyed for caveater but south of NE corner & wholly within Thomas p.174 Polks tract. Survey of caveatee is wholly within the bounds of the caveators entry. Thereupon Court withholds judgment untill next Term of this Court.

Court adjourned until Court in Course.

Wm H Cook, John Dickey, Thos K Gordon

p.175 Court of Pleas and quarter Sessions, first Monday, Decr 2d. Present William Brown, Alexander Black, Buckner Harwell, Esquires.

Deed John H Eaton to John S Fraser 121½ acres proven by David McCullock and James McCullock.

At least five Justices present, Eli Tidwell produced one wolf scalp over four months old which was ordered to be Burnt.

Appt Richard Brandon overseer/Weakleys creek road from Weakleys creek to Jesse Weathers with same hands former overseer had under his direction.

p.176 Appt Robert Paine overseer/Huntsville rd in room of Aquila Wilson resigned.

Grand Jury: Duncan Brown foreman, Lester Morris, James M Simmons, Robert Black, Alexr Tarply, William B Pepper, John Dabney, Joseph McDonald, John McNight, Thomas Brown, William Phillips, William Henderson, Stephen Anderson.

Constable Jeremiah Parker qualified to attend the Grand Jury this Term.

Deed William Polk to Oliver C Cleveland 40 acres proven by Carter H Cleveland and Keller Walton.

Deed Heirs of David Stewart decd to John McKinney and Archd McKinney 321 acres proven by James Fraser and John Fraser.

p.177 Admr/estate of Reuben Naile decd returned inventory of sd estate.

Order/sale issues to Benjamin Naile admr/estate of Reuben Naile decd to sell perishable part of sd estate.

Deed John H Eaton to James McCullock 370 acres proven by John Wilson and David McCullock.

Assignment of platt and certificate/survey from Isaac Vanhooser to John Austin 30 acres proven by William Anderson and James Craig.

p.178 Admrs/estate of Joseph Moore decd returned inventory of sd estate.

Order Fanny Moore & James Wilkinson admrs/estate of Joseph Moore decd sell perishable part of sd estate.

Grant ltrs/admn on estate of Isaac Johnston decd to Nancy Johnston.

Admx/estate of Isaac Johnston decd returned an inventory of sd estate.

Order/sale issued to Nancy Johnston to sell perishable part of estate of Isaac Johnston decd.

Order John Hicks, John Walthall Senr and Nathaniel Moody to allot to Nancy Johnston widow of Isaac Johnston decd sufficient provisions from estate to maintain herself and family for one year from her husbands death.

p.179 Order John Goff admr/estate of George Goff decd to sell negro man Jack belonging to sd estate for purpose of paying the balance/debts of sd estate.

Commrs apptd to allot to Fanny Moore widow of Joseph Moore decd one years provisions out of said estate report of their allotment.

Deed Hardy Hightower to John Wisenor 60 acres ackd.

Appt George Garrett overseer/road in room of William Swain, resigned.

Appt John Perry overseer/road in room of Edmund Shelton, resigned.

p.180 Grant ltrs/admn on estate of Nicholas Akin decd to Richard Briggs.

Appt Jesse Lamb guardian for Polly Reasonover.

Deed Oliver Cleveland to Thomas Lane 140 acres proven by Martin Lane and James Frasier.

Order Henry M Newlin, John Frasier, Jas McCullock allot to Jane Akin widow of Nicholas Akin as much of sd estate as will maintain her and family for one year from the date of the death of her husband.

Appt John Wisenor overseer/road in room of George Walters resigned.

Exrs/estate of James Williams decd returned account of sale of sd estate.

p.181 Will of Randal Fugate decd produced; proven by Arthur Hicks.

Grant ltrs/admn with will annexed on estate of Randal Fugate decd to Nancy Fugate widow of Randal Fugate.

James Stewart v Jonathan Berry. Two of plfs witnesses did not give evidence at trial; amount of their attendance to be taken from Bill/Costs charged to dft.

p.182 James Stewart v Jonathan Berry. Robert Lyon one of witnesses summoned claimed his attendance as a citizen of Maury County whilst he resided in this County; therefore ordered that bill of costs be rectified and that he be allowed only fifty cents per day for his attendance.

Appoint Rebeccah Meadows guardian to Talitha Meadows, Patsey Meadows, and Lileston Meadows minor orphans of Lileston Meadows decd.

On petition of Rebeccah Meadows widow of Lileston Meadows decd that she hath not received her distributive share of estate; that he left three children;

p.183 order Sheriff summon twelve disinterested freeholders to lay off to Rebeccah Meadows one fourth part of the personal estate of Lileston Meadows decd.

Deed Commrs/Pulaski to David Maxwell, lots 130 & 131 proven by Henry Roberts and James Doran.

Grant Ltrs/admn on estate of Samuel Read decd to Levinah Read & Isaac Bond.

p.184 Admrs/estate of Saml Read decd returned inventory of sd estate.

Order/sale issued to Levina Reed & Isaac Bond admrs/estate of Samuel Read decd to sell personal part of sd estate.

Appt James Price, William Price, William H Ragsdale to allot to Levina Read widow of Saml Read decd so much of sd estate sufficient to maintain her and family for one year from time Saml Read departed this life.

Admr/estate of Frances Reasonhover decd returned additional inventory.

p. Admr/estate of John Reasonhover decd returned amount/sale of sd estate.

Admr/estate of Frances Reasonhover decd retd amount/sale of sd estate.

Order County trustee pay Alfred M Harris Esq $50 County Solicitor for exofficio services for one year prior to this time.

DECEMBER 1816

Order Britton Yarbrough, Alexander Thompson and Thomas K Gordon esqrs settle account current of John Henderson & Andrew McMicken admrs with will annexed of estate of Mary Maxwell decd and make return to next Term of this Court.

p.   Grant Ltrs/admn on estate of Samuel Hurt decd to Buckner Harwell Esq.

Order exrs/will of Isaac Meadows decd sell to highest bidder negro girl belonging to estate of sd Isaac Meadows decd to comply with directions of sd will.

On petition of Joseph Looney one/admrs of William Caldwell decd, appt John Henderson, Britton Yarbrough & William Henderson to settle with sd administrator.

p.185   Will of Mason Moss decd partly proven by John Nelson one of subscribing witnesses; no executor was apptd; admn of estate with will annexed on same being fully proven is granted to Joannah Moss on her giving bond and security.

William New v William Davis. Case. Plaintiff having paid all costs directs that this suit be dismissed.

p.186   James Cunningham v John Duncan. Case. Parties in proper persons; dft having assumed and paid cost, plaintiff directs that suit be dismissed.

Joseph Johns v Robert Bigham. Appeal. Plf in proper person having assumed payment of all costs directs that this suit be dismissed.

Court adjourned till tomorrow morning 9 Oclock.

James Bumpass, Duncan McIntyre, J Henderson

p.187   Tuesday Decr 3d. Present James Bumpass, Duncan McIntyre, John Henderson.

Appt William Henderson overseer/road in room of William Fanning resigned.

Abner Rhea v Joseph Shadden & William Arnett. Debt. Dfts in proper persons say they cannot gainsay plf. Plf recovers of dfts his debt $133.89, damages $5.98, p.188   and his costs in this behalf expended.

Samuel Tait v John Riddle. Debt. Dft in proper person cannot gainsay plf. Plf recovers of dft debt $113.50, damages $4.12½, & costs of suit. [marginal note: Plf by L M Bramlett his attorney assignes all his interest in foregoing judgment to Edmuad S Bailey, 2nd August 1817]

p.189   Samuel Tait v John Riddle. Debt. Dft in proper person canot gainsay plfs action. Plf recovers of dft debt $113.50, damages $4.12½, and costs of suit. [marginal note: Plf in foregoing judgment by L M Bramlett his attorney to Edmund J Baily, 2 August 1817]

At least five Justices present, John Hicks produced one wolf scalp over four months old which was ordered to be Burnt.

p.190   Joseph Lann v Nathan Davis. Debt. Dft in proper person sayeth he cannot gainsay plfs action. Plf recovers of dft debt $106.56, damages of detention $6.36, and his costs by him about his suit expended.

At least five Justices being present James Patteson produced one wolf scalp over four months old which was ordered to be burnt.

p.191   Sally Westmoreland & Wm H Ragsdale exrs of Thos Westmoreland decd v Nelson Patteson & Henry Hagen. Debt. Dfts in proper persons cannot gainsay plfs action. Plfs recover of dfts debt $113.51½, damages/detention $5.81, and costs of suit.

p.192   Deed Adam Bell to John Birdwell 10 acres ackd.

Motion of Tobias Miller by his attorney Alfred M Harris; it appearing that sd Miller paid as security for Zachs Hurt $83 to satisfy judgment that John McCracken obtained agt sd Hurt, and sd Miller became security for the stay of execution and paid the amount to William R Davis a constable on 19 June last. Sd Tobias Miller recovers against sd Zachs Hurt afsd sum $83 with legal interest thereon from 19 June last till paid together with cost of this motion.

Licence Edmund Cornelius to keep Ordinary for one year.

p.193   Grant letters of administration on the estate of Patrick Long decd to Jacob Templin and German Lester.

Order County trustee pay William M Kerley coroner $5 for holding an inquest on body of Patrick Long decd.

At least five justices present, Robert Cooper produced two wolf scalps over four months old which was ordered to be burnt.

Admr/estate of Mary Ann Finch decd returned amount/sale of sd estate.

William F Cunningham appeared & was qualified as Deputy.

p.194   Daniel T Woods v Joseph Johns. Parties in proper persons; dft assumes payment of all costs; plf directs suit be dismissed.

Appt William Brown and Thomas Harwood Esqrs to settle with Duncan McIntyre and William Price admrs/estate of William Fish decd.

Levin Dilling v James Paine. William Straughan & Thomas Johnston surrender James Paine to Court.

p.195   James Tremble v James Paine. Debt. Wm Straughan & Thomas Johnston bound for appearance of James Paine surrender him to Court.

John Myers for benefit of Jesse Newland v Philip Parchman. Debt. Deposition of John Barton of Livingston County, Kentuckey, to be taken behalf defendant.

p.196   John Myers for benefit of Jesse Newland v Philip Parchman. Debt. Deposition of Joseph Harden of [blank] County, Indiana, to be taken behalf defendant.

Grant ltrs/admn on estate of James Donaldson decd to John Dickey and William H Cook Esqrs.

Admrs/estate of James Donaldson decd returned inventory of sd estate.

Order/sale issued to John Dickey & William H Cook admrs/estate of James

p.199   Donaldson decd to sell perishable part of sd estate.

Order John Johnston, John Cook, & Wm Lee allot to Polly Donaldson widow of James Donaldson decd so much of estate as will maintain her and family for one year from time sd James Donaldson departed this Life.

Appt Jarrat Manefee and Thomas Harwood Esqrs settle with the executors of James Williams decd and make return of settlement to next Term.

William M Kerley unanimously appointed Coroner of this County.

p.200   William Hendry v Washington G L Foley. Case. By consent of parties, the deposition of Sampson McCoun to be taken tomorrow morning in Pulaski.

Peter Swanson and Robert Reese recognizance, condition Franky Helms keep free from charge to this County a bastard child begotten on her by William Swanson.

Bill/sale Joel Cooper to Thomas Gill, a negro girl, proven by John Butler and Henry Melton.

p.199[again]   Order John Young, Nathaniel Young, James Derr, Joseph German, William Stovall, William Hays and Hardy Hightower or any five of them view part of the road from Pulaski to Fayetteville which runs through Nicholas Holleys land and see if it be practicable to turn road agreeable to wish of sd Holley.

Order John Britton, Wm Kenneday, George Garrett, John Kenneday, James Derr, William New, Joseph German, James McCanless, Enoch Davis, Hardy Hightower, and Nicholas Holley or any five of them view part of road from Hightowers mill to Cockrells Gap near plantations of Robert R Alsup and John Kenneday and the ford of creek near Jesse Hackneys and see if it be practicable to turn sd road on other ground, and if proper to mark out same.

p.200[again]   John Manefee v James McCormack. A&B. Parties in proper persons;

dft assumed payment of all costs; plf directs suit be dismissed.

Pleasant Jones v William M Marr. Appeal. Parties in proper persons; dft confesses debt. Plf recovers $3.37½ debt; costs before magistrate and this court.

p.201 Appt George Coher overseer/road in room of Major Harralson resigned.

Court adjourned till tomorrow morning 9 Oclock.

John Dickey, Wm Mayfield, William Brown

p.202 Wednesday Decr 4th. Present John Dickey, William Mayfield, William Brown.

Reuben A Higgenbotham v William Ball. Case. Deposition of Clement C Clay and John M Taylor to be taken in Madison County, Mississippi Terr, on behalf plf.

Admrs/estate of Lewis Kirk decd returned account of sales of sd estate.

Appt Alexander Tinnen overseer/road in room of Jesse McAnally resigned.

p.203 John Paul Senr v Kinchen T Wilkinson. appeal. Jury Thos Markes, Wm Pullin, Jno Kenneday, Allen Abernathy, Mattw Johnston, Richd Darby, Gabriel Long, James S Haynes, Adam Bell, Peter Satterfield, Jos Riley, Nathan Davis. Dft recovers of plf his costs before magistrate as in this court expended.

Order John Hicks, Charles Buford, James Buford, Jesse Beasley, Elijah Anthony, Joseph Anthony, & Burton Beasley or any five of them to view that part of the fort Hampton road which lies between James Bufords and the Cedar Glade above Jesse Beasleys; see if it be proper to turn same, and if so, what damages Edmund J Bailey may sustain by the same.

p.204 Sampson McCown v William C Mayfield. Case. Parties in proper persons; final determination of case is refered to Jno Dickey, Nelson Patteson, Ralph Graves, Thos C Stone & William Henderson whose award is to be made judgment of Court.

Order of last Court appointing jury to view road near Elijah Anthonys plantation is hereby revived.

Appt Benjamin Wheeler overseer/Shelbyville road in room of Thomas Barton removed, with same district of hands.

Levin Dilling v James Payne. Trover. Thomas Billingsley and Thomas Johnston

p.205 defendants bail.

Abel Oxford v Charles Whitson. Case. Jury John Fry, David W Porter, Isaac Atkins, John Caldwell, James Wilkinson, Henry White, John Cook, John Vance, James Niell, James Kimbrough, Robert McDonald, Jacob Templin. Plf recovers of dft damages 6¼¢ besides his costs of suit.

p.206 William Hendry v Washington G L Foley. Case. Depositions of Jesse Foster and Thomas Creel of Mississippi Territory to be taken on behalf defendant.

Deed William Bradshaw sheriff of Maury County to Permenas Williams 5000 acres proven by Robert Mack and Robert L Cobbs.

Deed Maxamilian H Buchanon Sheriff to Major Harrolson 500 acres ackd.

p.207 Deed Maxamilian H Buchanon Sheriff to Major Harrolson 87 acres ackd.

Deed Commrs/Pulaski to Charles Perkins lott 26 ackd.

Deed Commrs.Pulaski to Henry Roberts lott 48 proven by John Keenan and Robert Kibble.

Deed Commrs/Pulaski to Henry Roberts lott 13 proven by John Keenan and Robert Kibble.

p.208 Deed Commrs/Pulaski to Henry Roberts lotts 228, 229, 230, 231 proven by John Keenan and Robert Kibble.

Admr/estate of Spencer Lyon decd returned additional account/sale.

Sampson McCown v William C Mayfield. Case. Referees met at house of Thomas

p.209   Smith; plf recovers of dft $17 and cost of suit. Signed by John Dickey, N Patteson, Ralph Graves, Thos C Stone, Wm Henderson.
John McCracken assee v James Terrell & William Purnell. Debt. Plf in proper person having assumed payment of all costs directs that this suit be dismissed.
p.210   On petition of Amy Temple, widow of John Temple decd setting forth that Jno Temple had land: 7 acres granted by Tennessee #8924 16th March 1816...on Reynolds creek...Josiah Temple...; 300 acres granted by Tennessee #3923 19th May 1812...Reynolds creek...; sd John Temple made a will from which Amy Temple widow dissented
p.211   under act of Assembly and betook herself to her legal allowance, and that she hath never received her dower in above lands. Order Sheriff to summon 12 disinterested freeholders to set off to Amy Temple one third of land including the mansion house and put Amy Temple in possession of same.
p.212   Court adjourned untill tomorrow morning 9 Oclock.

Thos K Gordon, James Bumpass, A Black

p.213   Thursday Decr 5th. Present Thomas K Gordon, Jas Bumpass, Alexander Black.
State v James McCormack. A&B on Jno Manefee. Dft in proper person pleads guilty. Fine $1 and pay costs of this prosecution.
State v William Adams. Gaming. Dft is not a citizen of this County; Nolle
p.214   Prosequi entered.
State v William Adams. Gaming. Judgment in favour of those entitled for all costs.
State v William Rose. Neglect/duty as overseer of road. Jury William Pullen, Allen Abernathy, Matthew Johnston, Richd Darby, Gabriel Long, James S Haynes, Adam Bell, John Fry, David W Porter, John Birdwell, Thomas Williams, John Porter say dft is not guilty as charged in Bill of Presentment.
p.215   State v William Rose. Dft being acquitted; judgment entered in favour of those entitled for costs in behalf of the State.
Power/attorney Henry Francis to Peter R Booker ackd.
Admr/Nicholas Akin decd returned inventory of sd estate.
Order/sale issued to Richard Briggs admr/estate of Nicholas Akin to sell perishable part of sd estate.
p.216   Deed John Samford to Richard Wright 41 acres ackd.
State v Joseph Hankins. A&B on Levi Fugate. Dft in proper person. Jury Thos Marks, Jno Kennedy, Jesse Kirkland, Parks Bailey, Henry Loyd, Saml H Dodson, Saml Criswell, Moses Grisham, Robt Read, Jas Simmons, Robt Anderson, Saml Cox fine dft guilty. Fine $5 and pay costs of this prosecution.
p.217   Admr of estate of Archibald Cunningham decd returned account of sale.
Order County trustee to pay Nathaniel Almon jailor $8.50 for boarding a Negro man Nace executed for murder of Mason Moss decd.
State v Charles Conniway, Jas Conniway, Richd Conniway, Edwd Conniway, Mark Miller. Riot. Noll prosequi entered. Charles Conniway assumes payment of all costs.
p.218   Wade Blazingame recognizance, condition he attend next Term to prosecute and give evidence behalf State against Wm Darnell for petit Larceny.
Blazingame Ham, Wm Blazingame, & Thos McBride recognizance, condition they attend next Term & give evidence behalf State agt Wm Darnell for Petit Larceny.
Wilson English recognizance, condition that his wife Sarah English appear
p.219   next term & give evidence against Wm Darnell for Petit larceny.
Admr/estate of William Shannon decd returned account of sale of sd estate.

DECEMBER 1816

Order of last Court apptg commissioners to settle with administrators of
Rees Porter, decd, is revived; report to be made to next Court.
Order Thomas Brown & Thomas B Haynie, constables, to attend next term.
p.220   State v Phelps Smith. A&B on Joab Campbell. Jury Wm Pullin, Mattw Johnston,
Allen Abernathy, Richd Darby, Gabriel Long, Adam Bell, Jno Fry, David W Porter, Jno
Birdwell, Jno Waldrop, Wm Graves, Geo Koher say dft is guilty. Fine $10 & pay costs
of this prosecution.
p.221   Jurors to next Circuit Court: Nelson Patteson, William Henderson, William
Mayfield, Buckner Harwell, Robert Buchanan, James McDonald, Willis McLaurine, James
Austin, Geo Brown, Jno Barnett, Jas Paine, Wm B Brooks, Thos Brown, Robert McNairy,
Robt Oliver, James Buford, John Yancy, Wm Rose, Jno Porter, John Phillips, William
Woods, Thomas K Gordon, Thomas Lane, John C Walker, George Malone, James Leitch.
Jurors to next County Court: Ralph Graves, William Neal, Harrison Hicks, Wm
Wells, Absalom Harwell, Jno Butler, Davis Brown, Micajah Ezell, Richd Harnett, Robt
Paine, Jesse McAnally, Samuel H Dodson, John Johnston, Henry S Steele, Alexander
Jones, Joseph Knox, Hamilton C Campbell, Claiborne McVay, Thomas Rea, Robert Ross,
p.222   Abner McGaha, Holman R Fowler, Richard McGee, Matthew Anderson, John New-
ton, Edmund J Bailey.
Constables Frederick Harwell & Thos Phillips to attend next Circuit Court.
Appointments to take lists of taxable property: Nelson Patteson in Capt
Wilkinsons company; Jarrat Manefee in Capt George Brown's company; Willis S McLaur-
ine in Capt Wilsons company; William Brown in Capt Thomas Browns company; Buckner
p.223   Harwell in Capt Brooks's company; James Dugger in Capt Poteets company;
Hardy Hightower in Capt Derr's company; William Henderson in Capt Cocks company;
Arthur Hicks in Capt Herralsons company; Jacob Byler in Capt Bylers company; John
p.224   Hillhouse in Capt Wisdoms company; Daniel Allen in Capt Hailes company;
George Malone in Capt Pickens's company; John C Walker in Capt Sheilds's company;
p.225   Britton Yarbrough in Capt Youngs company; Alexander Thompson in Capt McVays
company; Thomas Harwood in Capt Everetts company; Thomas Lane in Capt Allens compy.
State v William Adams. Gaming. Nole prosequi entered.
p.226   State v William Adams. Gaming. Judgment in favour of those entitled for
costs on the part of the State.
State v William Swanson. Bastardy. Dft in proper person assumes payment of
all costs. Judgment in favour of State entered up against him accordingly.
State v Abraham Crowson. Gaming. Dft not inhabitant of this State. Nole
p.--   prosequi entered accordingly.
State v Abraham Crowson. Gaming. Judgmt in favour of those entitled for
costs on the part of the State.
State v Abraham Crowson. Gaming. Dft not inhabitant of this State; Nole
prosequi entered accordingly.
p.--   State v Abraham Crowson. Gaming. Judgmt in favour of thos entitled to cost
in behalf of State.
Elijah Anthony v William Riddle & wife. Debt. Archibald Alexander a garnishee states Wm Riddle has laid some brick for him but as no settlement has taken
place he is unable to state what sum may be due sd Riddle. Nathaniel Moody garnishee states that Peyton Parham and Wm Riddle laid for him about one hundred
thousand brick but as the work which they undertook is not completed he is not
bound to pay anything untill it is. Therefore, order that Archibald Alexander and
p.227   Nathaniel Moody retain whatever may be due from them to Wm Riddle after deducting credits, subject to further order of Court.

Court adjourned till tomorrow morning 9 Oclock.

John Dickey, Wm Mayfield, A Black

p.228   Friday 6th Decr. Present John Dickey, William Mayfield, Alexander Black. State v William Rose. Neglect/duty as overseer of road. Counsel for State saith for manifest informality in bill of presentment he is unwilling further to prosecute the defendant; nole prosequi entered.

State v Wm Rose. Neglect &c. Judgment in favour of those entitled for costs on the part of the State.

p.229   Admrs/estate of Patrick Long decd returned inventory of the estate.

Order/sale issued to Jacob Tamplin & German Lester admrs/estate of Patrick Long decd to sell perishable part of said estate.

State v Butler Haile. A&B on [blank]. Dft came not. Judgment agt him for $400 according to tenor of his bail bond.

p.230   Licence Henry Hagen to keep an Ordinary for one year.

Licence Thomas Smith to keep an Ordinary for one year.

Order Wm Neale present overseer/road with hands under his direction keep in repair the Fayetteville road from Pulaski to top of ridge by Major Davises.

State v Butler Haile. A&B. James Braden bound for appearance of Butler Haile delivered him not. Judgment $400 according to tenor of his bail bond.

p.231   State v Butler Haile. A&B. John McCabe bound for appearance of Butler Haile delivered him not. Judgment according to tenor of his bail bond.

State v Henry Hester. Gaming. Jury Wm Pullen, Allen Abernathy, Mattw Johnston, Richd Darby, Gabriel Long, Jas S Haynes, Adam Bell, Jno Fry, John Birdwell,

p.232   Isham Brown, Jno Yarbrough, Robt Shane. Dft fined $5 & pay costs.

State v Henry Hester. Gaming. John Jones who was summoned to attend to give evidence behalf State agt Henry Hester came not; judgment according to tenor of his subpoena $125; scire facias issues returnable to next Court.

Admr/estate of Samuel Hurt Decd returned inventory of said estate.

p.233   Order/sale issued to Buckner Harwell admr/estate of Samuel Hurt decd to sell the estate of sd deceased; make return to next Court.

Appoint Early Benson guardian to Jordan Reasonover, Jeremiah Reasonover, Benson Reasonover, Hetty Bell Reasonover, Jacob Reasonover, Elizabeth Reasonover and Early Reasonover, minor orphans of John Reasonover decd.

Deed Gideon Pillow to Daniel Allen 200 acres ackd.

Deed Daniel Allen to William McCabe 100 acres ackd.

p.234   Deed Joseph McDonald to Robert McDonald 185 acres ackd.

Deed Robert McDonald to Jas Dugger 49½ acres ackd.

Grand Jury Bills/Presentment: State v German Lester; Same v Boyd Wilson; Same v James Carr.

Lester Morris, keeper of a cotton gin in this County, qualified and gave bond and security as inspector of cotton as Law directs.

State v German Lester. Neglect/duty as overseer of Street. Dft in proper

p.235   person pleads guilty. Fine $5 and pay costs of prosecution.

On motion of William Parker by attorney William Kelly & sd Wm Parker paid as security for Zacheus Hurt on 2 Novr 1816 to Maximalian H Buchanan sheriff $37.60 to satisfy judgment against sd Zacheus Hurt & sd Wm Parker his security in favour of Levi T Thompson admr of William T Thompson decd, therefore sd William Parker to recover of sd Zacheus Hurt afsd sum $37.60 with legal interest thereon from 2 Novr p.236 1816 till paid together with cost sof this motion.

On motion of William Parker by atty Wm Kelly, sd Wm Parker having paid as security for Zachs Hurt $6.47½ to Presley Ward agent for Robert & Wm Dickson on account of bond entered into by sd Zacheus Hurt & sd William Parker & others his securities for keeping within prison bounds of this County to which he was committed & from which bounds he departed without leave. Said Wm Parker recovers agt Zachs Hurt afsd sum together with costs of this motion.

p.237 State v Tobias Miller. Gaming. Dft arraigned and pleads not guilty.

State v Tobias Miller. Gaming. John Jones summoned to attend to give evidence behalf State agt dft came not. Judgment agt him for $125; scire facias issued against him returnable to next term of this Court.

Archibald Alexander v Zacheus Hurt. Motion. Plf by atty Alfred M Harris

p.238 suggests plf on 4 Aug 1816 paid at instance of Jacob and Abraham Byler agt Zacheus Hurt, and sd Archibald Alexander to Sheriff of this County $254.34 as security for sd Zacheus Hurt, and praying a jury might be impanelled to try sd facts. Jury David W Porter, Wm W Crittenton, Peter Satterfield, Jos McKerley, Jas Hammonds, James S Haynes, Jno Brashers, Wm B Brooks, Jas Paine, Thos Markes, James Goldsberry, Henry Roberts say sd plf paid. Whereupon on motion of plf by his atty

p.239 sd Archibald Alexander recovers of sd Zacheus Hurt $254.34 so paid as security afsd with legal interest thereon from 4 August 1816 till this time together with his costs by him about his motion in this behalf expended.

Court adjourned till tomorrow morning 9 Oclock.

John Dickey, Wm Henderson, N Patteson

p.240 Saturday Decr 7th. Present John Dickey, William Henderson, Nelson Patteson.

Commrs apptd last Court to allot to Mary Kirk widow of Lewis Kirk decd one years provision made return of their allotment.

Will of Mason Moss decd offered for probate by Joana Moss legatee therein named, whereupon James Moss the brother of the deceased appeared by attorney and opposed probate of sd will; necessary testimony to be produced at next Court.

Jury to mark a road from mouth of Richland creek towards Fort Hampton as far as State line make return they marked as agreeable to order. Order John Lucas

p.241 oversee sd road, having under his direction all hands living southwest of Temples road and south of Elk river to state line.

Order road from farm lane to Huntsville road lately viewed by comrs apptd for that purpose be opened; Nelson Patteson apptd overseer, and have under his direction the hands of James Patteson, Edward O Chambers, and Harrison Hicks.

Drury Joiner v Nathan Crenshaw. Certiorari. Motion of plf by atty: order proceedings before the Justice below be amended.

p.242 Drury Joiner v Nathan Crenshaw. Certiorari. [as above]

Thomas Murray v Nathan Crenshaw. Certiorari. On motion of William McCabe agent for plf by his atty; order proseecings before Justice below be amended.

Grand Jury Bills/Presentment: State v John Brown; Same v William Baty; Same v Hugh McDonald, Richd Conway, and James Conway.

p.-- Order William Mayfield, William Henderson, Robert Anderson, John Phillips, John Dickey, Tyree Rodes, Gideon Pillow and William Woods or any five view that part of the road near John Porter's plantation and see if it be proper to turn sd road agreeable to wish of sd John Porter on east or south side of Pigeon roost creek to intersect old road again on north or west of sd Porter's plantation.

Samuel F Glass v Nathaniel Allman. Debt. Dft in proper person cannot gainsay plfs action. Plf recovers of dft debt $100, damages of detention $6.25 & costs.
p.-- Maxamilian H Buchanon sheriff and Collector of Public & County Taxes
reports land not listed for taxation for 1816: [taxes due are here omitted]

Benjamin McCullock   50 acres west fork Bradshaws creek
Thomas Taylor Junr &   640 acres Pigeon roost cr granted by North Carolina #38
  James Taylor   and dated 14th July 1812.
Nathaniel Taylor   1000 including town/Pulaski grant #4 date 14th July 1812
Joel Lewis   331½ on Richland creek
Wm T Lewis heirs   1210 on west fork Bradshaws creek by grant
Henry Cearby   380 Richland creek held by deed
Henry Toomer   2020 both sides Robertsons fork granted by North Carolina
                           #24 July 14th 1812
William P Anderson   60 acres on Robertsons fork
p.--   Charles Ellis   200 acres Big Creek granted by No Carolina
Heirs of Thomas Polk   516 acres surplus quantity of 5000 acres tract granted to
                           Thos Polk on Richland Creek & Elk river
James Lewis   313 acres part of a 400 acres tract saved out of 2000 acre
                           entry on Elk River
Charles Gerard   225 acres on Robertsons creek
Thomas B Harrelson   120 acres part of 500 acres in name of Henry Cearby on
                           Richland creek
    ditto   25 acres part of tract of 250 acres name of Charles Gerard
                           on waters of Robertsons fork
    ditto   5000 acres on Bradshaws, Pigeon roost & Buchanans creeks
                           granted to Thomas Polk
Major Harrolson   87 acres part of 400 acres saved out of a 2000 acre entry
                           in name of James Lewis on Elk river
p.--   Major Harrolson 500 acres west of Elk river formerly sold in name of
                           Robert Lanier, Grant #1995.
John Nelson   5000 acres on Blue creek branch of Richland creek of Elk
                           River granted to sd Nelson grant #116 by virtue
                           of a warrant #1108 by state of North Carolina.
Edward Harris   86 acres Pigeon roost by grant
    ditto   70 acres Pigeon roost by grant
    ditto   14 acres Pigeon roost by grant
John Read   60 acres Richland creek by entry

Whereupon considered by Court that State and County recover against owners
or claimants of sd tracts of land respectively the amount of afsd double tax with
costs and charged due thereon; land to be sold for payment of tax, costs & charges.
p.-- Maxamilian H Buchanan Sheriff & Collector of State and County Tax reports
taxes ramain due on following tracts: [amount of taxes here omitted]

Rudy Estep   10 acres by entry on Reynolds creek
Robert Burton   5000 acres Big Creek
Joseph Greer   1000 acres Buchanons ck
James Conner   201 acres Robertsons fork
Francis Beard   25 acres Bradshaws creek
Richard Hightower   640 acres on Richland creek part of a 5000 acre tract
                           granted to Haywood
    ditto   400 acres Big creek now called Robertsons fork

111

DECEMBER 1816

```
      ditto              240 acres Bradshaws creek
Hightower & Hayes        360 acres Richland creek between Ezekiel and Thomas Polk.
      ditto              312 acres North of Armstrongs on Richland creek
p.--  ditto              300 acres Buchanans creek east of Martin Armstrong
Andrew Spratt            200 acres Robertsons creek
```

Considered by Court that State and County recover against owners or claimants of sd land respectively the amount of tax, costs & charges due thereon; land to be sold.

Grant letters/admn on estate of Polly Caldwell decd to John Caldwell.

Admr/estate of Polly Caldwell decd returned inventory of sd estate.

Order/sale issued to John Caldwell admr/estate of Polly Caldwell decd to sell estate of sd deceased, and make return thereof to next Court.

p.--   State v Anson Taylor. Gaming. Dft came not; judgment against him for $400 made absolute and that he pay costs.

State v Robert Taylor. Failing to produce Anson Taylor. Dft came not; judgment $400 made absolute against him and he to pay costs.

State v Matthias Richardson. Failing to produce Anson Taylor. [as above]

p.--   State v Anson Taylor. Gaming. Dft came not. Judgment against him $400 made absolute and he to pay costs.

State v Robert Taylor. Failing to produce Anson Taylor. [as above].

p.--   State v Matthias Richardson. Failing to produce Anson Taylor. [as above].

State v Anson Taylor. Gaming. [as above].

State v Robert Taylor. Failing to produce Anson Taylor. [as above]

p.--   State v Matthias Richardson. [as above]

State v James Kellet. Gaming. Dft came not. Judgment entered against him for sum $400 made absolute, and he to pay costs.

State v Robert McDow. Failing to produce James Kellet. Dft came not;

p.--   jugement against him for $400 made absolute and he pay costs.

State v James Kellet. Gaming. [as above]

State v Robert McDow. Failing to produce James Kellet. [as above]

State v James Kellet. Gaming. [as above]

p.--   State v Robert McDow. Failing to produce James Kellet. [as above]

State v James Kellet. Gaming. [as above]

State v Robert McDow. Failing to produce James Kellet. [as above]

p.--   State v James Kellet. Gaming. [as above]

State v Robert McDow. Failing to produce James Kellet. [as above]

p.--   Appoint German Lester guardian to Margaret Long, Jane Long, William A Long, and Polly A Long, minor orphans of Patrick Long deceased.

State v Levi Fugate. A&B on Joseph Hankins. Pleaded not guilty.

State v Bryant Smith. A&B on Joab Campbell. Sd Bryant Smith hath departed this life; order Nolle prosequi be entered.

State v Bryant Smith. Judgment entered up in favour of those entitled for costs on the part of the State.

p.--   On application of Parkes Bailey, order he be permitted to erect & keep a warehouse on his own lott in Pulaski for safekeeping of Tobacco &c.

State v Levi Fugate. A&B on Joseph Hankins. Joseph Hankins made default. Judgment against him $100; scire facias issued agt him returnable to next Term.

Order heretofore made appointing commrs to settle with M H Buchanon surviving admr/estate of Clayton S Buchanon is in all things revived.

p.--   Moses Pullin v Joseph Shadden & George Beard. Debt. Dfts came not. Plf recovers of dfts the sum of [blank]

112

MARCH 1817

Fanny Moore & James Wilkinson admrs v William H Ragsdale. Debt. Dft came
not. Plffs recover of dft $100 debt together with $18.42 damages of detention, and
p.-- costs of suit in this behalf expended.
Thomas Haynes v John Coleman. Appeal. Parties in proper persons. Dft cannot
gainsay plfs action; judgment of Justice below is in all things affirmed and plf
recovers of dft his debt afsd and his costs before the magistrate as in this Court.
John A King v James H Owen. Certiorari. Order dft appear next Term and give
additional security otherwise same will be dismissed.
p.-- Thomas B Haynie v William M Kerby. Command James Leitch bring up the proceedings below to next Term of this Court.
Oliver B Hayes & Richard Hightower caveators v Jeremiah Guilford Caveatee.
Daveat. Court not yet being advised what the Jury in this cause heretofore found,
this cause is ordered to be continued.
[here follow two blank pages]
Order Court be adjourned till Court in Course.

N Patteson, Thos K Gordon, A Black

p.-- Court of Pleas and quarter Sessions on Monday the 3d day of March. Present
William Mayfield, William Henderson, Joseph Rea, Esquires, Justices.
Commrs/Pulaski v Samuel Pearson & Zacheus Hurt. Debt. William Moore surren-
dered Zacheus Hurt to the Court.
Assignment of platt and certificate of survey from Solomon Burford to James
Smith 29 acres ackd.
Assignment of platt and certificate of survey from Solomon Burford to John
Austin 10 acres ackd.
p.-- Executors/will of Samuel Smith decd returned additional account/sales.
Excuse Richard McGee from serving on jury at present Term of this Court.
Appt John J Barber overseer/lower Elkton road in room of Henry Abernathy
resigned, having same district of hands.
Grant Ordinary Licence to Robert Oliver for one year.
Grand Jury: Ralph Graves foreman, Abner McGaha, Jno Newton, Harrison Hicks,
Micajah Ezell, Matthew Anderson, Richard Barnett, John Butler, Hamilton C Campbell,
William Neal, Holmon R Fowler, Davis Brown, Robert Paine.
Constable William R Davis qualified to attend Grand Jury at present Term.
p.-- Appt William H Cook and John Dickey Esqrs commissioners to settle account
current with Elizabeth Lee and William Lee admrs/estate of John Lee decd.
Deed John Callahan to William Callahan 100 acres ackd.
Deed John Cook to William H Cook 80 acres ackd.
Deed John Callahan to William M Marr 22½ acres ackd.
Admrs/estate of Joseph Moore decd returned account/sale of sd estate.
p.-- Deed William Sheppard to Henry F Steele 145 acres 90 poles proven to be act
of William Sheppard Junr agent for William Sheppard Senr by Wm H Cook & John Cook.
Deed Saml Polk to Jno Young 100 acres proven by Josiah Stovall & Jno Young.
Admr/estate of George Goff decd returned account/sale of Negro named Jack.
Appt Benjamin Essman overseer/Indian cr rd in room of Abram Brown resigned.
Appt Josiah Stovall overseer/rd in room of William Hayes resigned.

113

p.--   Appt Joseph Anthony overseer/Fort Hampton rd instead/Moses Grisham resignd.
Admr/estate of Ebby Cobb decd returned account of sale of sd estate.
Deed John Childress to Thomas K Gordon 200 acres proven by Nathan Farmer
and Robert McCullock.
Deed Thomas K Gordon to John McCanless 114 acres ackd.
Exrs/will of James Williams decd returned additional account of sale.
Deed John H Eaton to heirs and legatees of Nicholas Akin decd 150 acres was
p.--   proven by John Wilson and David McCullock.
Admr/estate of Nicholas Akin decd returned account of sale of sd estate.
Commrs apptd last Court to allot to Jane Akin widow of Nicholas Akin decd
one years provision made return of their allotment.
Order County trustee to pay John Eppler $30 for safekeeping of Malinda Cobb
an orphan child for one year ensuing the date hereof.
Appt Stephen Condry overseer/Big creek rd in roomof Israel Pickens removed.
Appt Elizabeth Smith guardian to Cynthia Smith and Susannah Smith minor
orphans of Samuel Smith decd.
p.--   Appt Ebenezar Petty gdn to Nancy Temple minor orphan of John Temple decd.
Appt Samuel Briggs gdn to Matilda Temple minor orphan of John Temple decd.
Appt Thomas K Gordon gdn to Eliza Temple minor orphan of John Temple decd.
Appt Baker P Potts overseer/road in room of [blank] Campbell removed.
Appt Thomas Harwood and Willis S McLaurine Esqrs commrs to settle accounts
of the estate of Alexander Laughlin with Brice M Garner and Jarrat Menefee admrs.
Appt Cary T Kelly overseer/road in room of John Littleton resigned.
p.--   Appt James Jones guardian to two children Henry T Jones and Mary Jane Jones
for purpose of receiving any legacy which may be coming to them[several illegible
interlineated words here]
Deed Archibald McKinney to Holman R Fowler 65 acres 31 poles proven by
Sterling C Robertson and John McCanless.
Deed Nathan Davis to Allen Abernathy 81½ acres ackd.
Deed William Polk to Lewis Brown 1516 acres proven to be act of Samuel Polk
agent for William Polk by oaths of Robert L Cobbs and Robert Mack.
Deed Lewis Brown to William King 225 acres ackd.
p.--   Order heretofore made apptg commrs to settle account current of estate of
Reese Porter deceased with administrators is in all things revived.
Appt Thomas Harwood and Jarrat Menefee Esqrs commrs to settle accounts of
estate of James Williams decd with Betsey Williams and Amos Williams exrs.
Order Tyree Rodes, Wm Woods, John Phillips, Wm Pullin, Washington G L
Foley, Robt Wilson and John Dickey or any five of them see what alterations ought
to be made in road by John Porters plantation beginning near Wm M Kerleys and to
near plantation of Washington G L Foley.
Grant Ordinary Licence to James M Ward for one year.
p.--   State v William Kyle. A&B on John Eppler. Dft in proper person pleads
guilty. Fine 6¼¢ and pay costs of prosecution.
John Edwards v John Maples. Case. Parties in proper persons; plf assumed
payment of all costs & directs suit be dismissed.
p.--   Henry Hagen & Peter Bass, Merchants &c v Ephraim Parham. Debt. John Taylor
and Edmund Cornelius surrender dft to Court; plfs by attorney pray dft in custody
of Sheriff which by the Court is ordered accordingly.
Henry Hagen & Peter Bass, Merchts v Ephrm Parham. Debt. [worded as above].
p.--   Appt Silas Flurnoy overseer of the Shelbyville road in the room of Samuel

Poteete resigned.

  State v James Adams. A&B on Robert Oliver. Dft in proper person pleads guilty. Fine 6¼¢ and pay cost of this prosecution.

  Deed William Sheppard to William Lee 195¼ acres proven to be act of William Sheppard Junr agent for william Sheppard Senr by James Tinnen and Robert Tinnen.

p.-- John Matthews v John Walthall. Debt. Dft in proper person cannot gainsay plaintiffs action. Plf recovers of dft debt $100, damages of detention $7, and costs by him about his suit in this behalf expended.

  Charlotty Ford v William Davis. Debt. Jacob Templin and German Lester summoned as garnishees and acting administrators of Halbert Allison decd which Garnishment was founded upon judgment which Charlotty Fort recovered against William [torn] alias William R Davis for the sum of [torn]

The last page or pages of this book are missing.

End of this Book.

Abstract of the

MINUTES OF THE CIRCUIT COURT FOR GILES COUNTY, TENNESSEE

1810 - 1816

p.1   At a Circuit Court begun & held on Monday the 10th day of December 1810 at the house of Lewis Kirk, being the second Monday. Present the honorable Thomas Stewart, Judge.
        The Sheriff of this county returned the names of the following persons summoned to serve as grand & petit during the present term of this court, to wit, Pleasant Moore, Peter Lyon Senr, James Hunt, Reese Porter Junr, Jacob Byler, James Knox, Walter Lock, Nathaniel Moody, John Jones, Robert Gordon, William Gideon, John Yancy, Nelson Patterson, Maximilian H Buckanan, Summerset Moore, Robert Steele, Charles Buford, William Woods, William Wells, John Williams, Allen Abernathy,
p.2   William McDonald, Samuel McKnight, Robert Buckanan, John McKnight, James McDonald, Jesse Westmoreland, Nathan Bass, Abner Cleveland, John Wilson, William McGuire, David Flint, James Tenin, Nathan Farmer, John Reasonover, Matthew Benthall, & John White of whom
1. Nelson Patterson foreman, 2 Nathan Farmer, 3 William Wells, 4 Matthew Benthall, 5 John Wilson, 6 William Gideon, 7 William McDonald, 8 Nathaniel Moody, 9 Samuel McKnight, 10 Allen Abernathy, 11 Jacob Byler, 12 John Williams, 13 John Jones, 14 David Flint, 15 John McKnight were elected & sworn a grant Jury & having received their charge withdrew to consider of their presentments.
        Marmaduke Williams & George C Witt Gent produced each in court a license to practice law in the several courts of law & equity in this State & took the oaths
p.3   to support the constitution of the United States & the constitution of the State of Tennessee & together with Felix Grundy Gent. took the oath of a counsellor or attorney & are therefore admitted to practice law as counsellors or attornies in this Court.
        It is ordered by the Court that Thomas H Benton Gent be appointed counsel for the state to prosecute on behalf of the state George Tucker for felony in the room of Alfred Balch who was previous to his being appointed solicitor general employed to appear as counsel for the said George Tucker.
        James Ashmore plt against Absolom Borin Deft. Appeal. This day came the
p.4   parties afsd by their attornies, and the Defendant by his attorney moved that the warrant had originally in this case be quashed which motion was argued & time is taken by the court to consider untill tomorrow.
        Thomas Ray who was bound in recognizance in the sum of $100 for his appearance here this day as prosecutor & to give evidence in behalf of the State against George Tucker for horse stealing, being solemnly called came not but made default whereby he has forfeited his recognizance. Therefore it is considered by the court that a writ of sci facias issue directing the Sheriff of this county to make known & returnable to the next term of this court.
p.5   Squire Bone who was bound in recognizance in the sum of $100 for his appearance hear this day as a witness to give evidence in bhealf of the State against George Tucker for horsestealling, being solemnly called came not but made default whereby he has forfeited his recognizance. Therefore it is considered by the court that a Sci facias issue directing the sheriff of this county that he make known &c returnable to the next term of this court.
        James McCarty who was bound in recognizance in the sum of one hundred dollars for his appearance here this day as prosecutor & to give evidence in behalf of the state against William Tary for horse-stealing being solemnly called came not but made default, whereby he has forfeited his recognizance: Therefore it is con-
p.6   sidered by the court that a Sci facias issue directing the Sheriff of this county that he make known to the said James McCarty that he be &c returnable to the

116

next term of this court.

Grand Jury indictments: Robert Allsup, breach/peace by assault & battery on Thomas Taylor a true bill; also against John Allsup, A&B on Thomas Taylor.

Court adjourned till tomorrow 10 oclock.   Thos Stuart

p.7   Tuesday 11th Decr 1810. Present Thomas Stewart Judge.

Deed Stephen Childress Sheriff of Williamson County to Joseph Love 335 acres proven by Oliver B Hays & Alfred Balch.

Deed Stephen Childers Sheriff of Williamson County to Joseph Love 160 acres proven by Oliver B Hayes & Aldred Balch.

Deed James Patton & Andrew Erwin by James Mitchel their attorney in fact to
p.8   James Reed 2500 acres proven by John Jones & Samuel Jones.

Deed Ho Tatum to John Jones 80 acres proven by Summerset Moore & William Parker.

James Ashmore agt Absolom Borin. Appeal. Dft's motion to quash warrant, plf
p.9   moves to amend warrant by inserting "whereas James Ashmore hath given information to me the subscriber a Justice of the peace for said county, that Absolom Borin on the [blank] day of [blank] 1809 at what is now the county afsd took up a certain estray sorrel mare at a place other than on his own land, contrary to an act of assembly, in such case made & provided, you are therefore commanded to summon the said Absolom Borin to appear before me, or some other
p.10   Justice of the Peace for said county, to answer the said James Ashmore in a plea of debt of twenty dollars &c" to which the Deft by his attorney objected. Dft recovers agt plf his costs; trial postponed till next term of this court.

p.11   Robert P Curren surviving partner of firm of Curren & Co agt John White. Appeal. Dft in proper person cannot gainsay plfs action; he doth owe plf $583.93½ debt and damages $42.04½ besides all costs. Plf recovers agt dft as afsd.

p.12   Den on the demise of Haywood & Turner agt Wamick & Doyle. Ejectment. Dft by
p.13   atty confesses the lease entry & ouster; to insist on title only at trial.

State agt Robert Allsup. A&B on Thos Taylor. Jury Pleasant Moore, Peter
p.14   Lyon Senr, Reese Porter Junr, Walter Locke, Robert Gordon, James Tennin, John White, Maxamilian H Buckanan, Summerset Moore, Charles Buford, William Woods, Robert Buckanan find dft not guilty; Dft recovers his costs agt plf Thos Taylor.

p.15   Den on demise of Haywood & Turner agt Wamick H Doyle. Ejectment. Grant plf leave to insert words "with force & arms" and he to pay sheriff his costs for serving the said writ.

Grand jury indictments: agt George Tucker for horse stealling, true bill;
p.16   agt William Tary for horse stealling not true bill; agt Thomas Taylor A&B on Robert Allsup true bill; & having nothing further to present, are discharged.

Appearance bond of James Reed with John Reed & Isaac Bond his securities, to Governor Willie Blount, $2000 and $1000 each respectively, to appear before
p.17   Judge of Circuit Court at house of Lewis Kirk in Decr 1811 to answer prosecution for forgery.

Benjamin George & Wyatt Tucker, bound $500 each for appearance of George Tucker brought him not; recognizances forfeited. Sci fa issues.

p.18   Appearance bonds of Thomas Ray, John Dickey, Squire Bone, Hezekiah J Balch, William Taylor, Hezekiah Boyd, to Gov Willie Blount, $200 each, to appear at next circuit Court on second Monday in June next at house of Lewis Kirk to give testi-
p.19   mony on behalf State agt George Tucker on a charge of horse stealing.

George Tucker, bound in sum $1000, came not but made default; forfeited his recognizance. Order sci fa issue; on motion of counsel for State, capias is awarded against sd George Tucker returnable to next term of this court.

p.20 Forfeitures yesterday entered agt Squire Bone, Thomas Ray, & James McCarty be held as nought, they paying the costs thereby incurred.

State agt John Allsup. Trial continued untill next term of this court.

p.21 State agt John Allsup. Atty for State no further prosecutes; Thomas Taylor the prosecutor assumes costs.

p.22 John A Wilson agt John McCabe. Debt. Dft came not. Plf recovers agt dft $290.50 debt, damages by detention $17.43, and costs. Plf has received of dft the whole amount of the debt & damages afsd; dft released.

p.23 Oliver B Hayes, Andrew Ervin & Thomas H Benton appearance bond to Governor Willie Blount, Hayes $500, Ervin & Benton $250 each, condition they appear at circuit court at house of Lewis Kirk Decr 1811, sd Hayes to prosecute, Erwin & Benton to give testimony in behalf State agt James Reed on charge of Forgery &c.

Petit Jury discharged.

p.24 Den on demise of Haywood & Turner agt James Grimes. Ejectment. James Grimes in proper person saith he cannot gainsay plfs action agt him but that he is guilty

p.25 of trespass & ejectment. Plf recovers agt dft his damages 1¢ & costs.

p.26 Reese Porter Senr agt Robert Brown. Case. Change of venue to next circuit court in Maury County.

Court adjourned untill tomorrow half past 9 oclock.   Thos Stuart

Wednesday Decr 12th 1810. Present the honorable Thomas Stewart, Judge.

p.27 James Hart agt John Yancy. Debt. Plf came not but made default. Therefore plf is nonsuited. Dft recovers agt plf his costs of defence expended.

Court adjourned till court in course.   Thos Stuart

p.28 At a Circuit Court begun & held at house of Lewis Kirk on Monday 10th June 1811. Present the honorable Nathaniel W Williams, Judge.

p.29 Mutual agreement made 28 Jany 1811 between Nathaniel W Williams Judge of the third Circuit and Thos Stuart Judge of the fourth circuit agreed to interchange ridings & preside in the counties of each others circuits from 9th February 1811 until 30 June year afsd pursuant to act of Assembly of 23 Novr 1809. Signed in the presents of H L White.

p.30 Grand & petit jurors: Tyre Rodes, James Forbes, John Dickey, John Baker Sr, Andrew Pickens, Saml Jones, David Jones, Henry Ross, Hamilton C Campbell, Thos Rea, Thomas Westmoreland, William Philips, Lewis Brown, Buckner Harwell Senr, Robert McNairy, Aquilla Wilson, John Barnett, William Abernathy, Thomas Whitson, Benjamin Long, Edmd J Baily, Elijah Anthony, Samuel Burney, James Kimbro, Adam Burney, John McKissick, William Hamby, Ralph Graves, Martin Flint, Richard Flint, John Rea, Gabriel Fulks, John Montgomery, John Lee, David W Porter, John Simmons, William Nut, James Hunt, Thomas Stuart.

p.31 Grand Jury: Ralph Graves foreman, John Dicky, William Philips, Thos Stuart, Hamilton C Campbell, Saml Burney, Thos Rea, Adam Burney, Wm Abernathy, Jno Montgom-

ery, Elijah Anthony, Robert McNairy, James Hunt, Samuel Jones, William Nutt.
John Lee discharged from further attendance as a juror.
John Rumover who failed to attend as a juror last December tendered his
p.32   excuse sworn to which was sustained & he dismissed.
Deed William Polk to Larkin Cleveland 300 acres proven by E Polk and A
Franklin.
John Den on demise of Haywood & Turner v Wamick H Dayle. Ejectment.
Nathaniel Moody appearance bail for deft delivered him.
Den on demise of James Greer, Robert, John, Thomas Bigham v Joseph Johns.
p.33   Ejectment. John Devazer appearance bail for dft delivered him. Nathaniel
Moody & John Lee to pay condemnation if he is convicted or render him to prison.
Haywood & Turner v Wamick H Dayle. Ejectment. Dft in proper person saith he
cannot gainsay plfs action agt him but that he is guilty of trespass & ejectment
p.34   as plf complains. Plf recovers agt dft his damages 1¢ & his costs of suit.
James Ashmore v Absolom Borin. Appeal. Parties in proper persons by mutual
p.35   consent & assent of court, suit is dismissed, each party pays half costs.
Joseph Kelly v Robert Allsup. TAB. Jury Tyre Rodes, Henry Ross, Thos Westmoreland, Lewis Brown, Edmond J Baily, James Kimbro, Wm Hambey, Martin Flint, Richd
Flint, Gabriel Fulks, David W Porter, John Simmons. Plf recovers agt dft damages
$13.62½ & costs.
p.37   Absolom Borin v Joseph Boyd. Case. Parties in proper persons leave matters
in difference to determination of Nathl Moody, George Malone, Miles Malone, Lemuel
Prewitt, Jno White Jr, Joshua Tacker & John Laird, their award the judgmt of Court.
John Den on demise of James Greer, Robert, John, & Thos Bigham v Richard
p.38   Fen. Ejectment. Joseph Johns made defendant in room of Richd Fen.
John Den on demise of Daniel Woods v Richard Fen. Ejectment. Sampson McCown
made defendant in room of Richd Fen.
p.39   John Den on demise of Daniel Woods v Richard Fen. Ejectment. William
Henderson made defendant in room of Richd Fen.
p.40   Wamack H Dayle discharged from custody.
Court adjd till to morrow 9 o clock.   Nath W Williams

Tuesday June 11th 1811. Present the honorable Nathaniel W Williams, Judge.
State v William Davis. Upon Recog. Matthew Cunningham prosecutor of charge
p.41   of horse stealing appeared. Prosecution dismissed, prosecutor in proper
person assumes all costs.
Isham Carter v William Hambey. Debt. Dft cannot gainsay plfs action, but
p.42   that he doth owe plf $77.56 debt, damages $9.11 & his costs. Plf recovers.
Daniel Woods v Sampson McCown. Ejectment. Plf no further prosecutes. Suit
p.43   is dismissed and recovers agt plf his costs of defence.
Daniel Woods v William Henderson. Ejectment. Plf no further prosecutes.
Suit dismissed. Dft recovers agt plf his costs about his defence expended.
p.44   Deed John Purviance to Samuel Woods 450 acres proved by David Woods and
William Woods.
p.45   State v Luke Osbourn. Perjury. Jury[above] find Luke Osbourn not guilty.
p.46   Grand Jury and Petit Jury discharged.
Scire facias to issue to Sheriff to make known to John Barnett, Buckner
Howel Senr, James Forbes, John Baker Senr, Andrew Perkins, David Jones, and Benjamin Long that they appear at next term of this court to shew cause why they did not

attend as Jurors at present term.
Court adjourned till tomorrow 9 oclock.   Nath W Williams

p.47   Wednesday June 12th 1811. Present, honorable Nathaniel W Williams, Judge.
Ordered Court adjourned till court in course.   Nath W Williams

p.48   Circuit Court at house of Lewis Kirk on Monday 9th December 1811. Present
the honorable Thomas Stuart, Judge.
        Ordered that court be adjourned to meet in one half hour at the Court-
house in the Town of Pulaski.
        Court met at the Court-house, Present the hon. Thomas Stuart, Judge.
        John & Robert Allen v Edmund J Bailey. Appeal. Plfs move Court affirm
p.49   judgt of court below. Plf recovers agt dft $808.06 judgt of court below
together with $52.52 being 12½ percent and costs of suit.
        Order William Mayfield discharged from attending as a juror at this term.
p.50   State v Andrew Pickins. Sci fa for not attending as a juror at June term.
Andrew Pickins in proper person who tendered excuse for non attendance; discharged
p.51   from payment of forfeiture on payment of all costs.
        State v David Jones. Not attending as a juror. Sd David by his brother who
tendered affidavit. Fine remitted on payment of all costs.
p.52   State v John Barnett. Not attending as juror. John Barnett in proper person
who tendered excuse; discharged from payment of any fine or costs.
        State v Buckner Harwel Senr. Not attending as a juror. Said Buckner in
p.53   proper person discharged from payment of forfeiture or costs.
        Joshua Tacker discharged from attendance as a juror at this term.
        State v James Forbes. Not attending as a juror. Jas Forbes in proper person
p.54   tendered excuse; discharged from payment of forfeiture or costs.
        State v Benjamin Long. Not attending as a juror. Sd Long tendered excuse
p.55   for nonattendance; discharged from payment of any fine or costs.
        State v Joseph Johns. Recognizance for hog killing. John Pate surrendered
dft in discharge of himself, and dft is ordered into custody.
        Grand & Petit Jurors: Somerset Moore, Joseph Lonn, Jesse Weathers, William
Casper, Jesse Beazley, William Mayfield, William Woods, Jacob Byler, Peter Lyon Sr,
p.56   Reese Porter Junr, John Hix, John McIninch, Nelson Patteson, Thos Goff, Wm
Dabney, Jas Ashmore, Mattw Benthall, Jno Forgry, Wm McDonald, Thos Philips, William
McGuin, Silas McGuin, Saml Montgomery, Saml Shields, Leander Shields, Humphry Tomp-
kins, Joshua Tacker, Joseph Knox, William Stanford, John Webb, Thos Marks, Quinton
Shanon, David Graham, William B Pepper, Lester Morris, Peter Swanson, Jordan McVay.
        Grand Jury: Nelson Patteson foreman, Wm Woods, Jos Lonn, David Graham, Saml
Montgomery, Jno McIninch[McIninit?], Wm McDonald, Jesse Beazley, Jno Webb, Jas Ash-
p.57   more, Quinton Shannon, Jos Knox, Jno Forgey, Wm Stanford, Lester Morris.
        James & Washington Jackson v James Reed & Absolom Borin. Debt. James J Ward
appearance bail for dft Reed surrendered him; John McCabe & Joshua Bond undertook
p.58   for dft. Jury Jacob Byler, Thomas Marks, Silas McGuin, Wm Cooper, William
Dabney, Somerset Moore, Matthew Benthall, Leander Shields, Jesse Weathers, John

Hicks, Saml Shields, Thos Goff. Plfs recover agt dfts $200 debt, & damages & costs.
p.59   Court adjourned untill to morrow half past 9 oclock.   Thos Stuart

Tuesday 10th December 1811. Present the honorable Thomas Stuart, Judge.
        John Allsup v Drury Stovall. Case. Trial postponed until next term. Depo-
p.60   sitions of Isham Lewis & Mary Lewis to be read in evidence on behalf dft.
Benjamin Philips v Gabriel Higginbotham. Debt. John Caldwell appearance
bail for dft surrendered him. Edmund J Bailey & Wm Crittington undertook for dft.
p.61   Grand Jury brought Bills of Indictment: against John Boyd for A&B on Reuben
Dickson true bill; against Richard Lonn true bill; agt John Harrinton true bill.
        Richard Luttrel v John McCabe. Appeal. Appealant having failed to bring up
the transcript of the record in this case in time, by his atty ordered transcript
p.62   be brought up & moved judgts of court below be affirmed. Plf recovers agt
dft & William Ball & James Reed his securities sd sum $86.50 the amt of judgment of
p.63   court below together with $3.18 being 12½ percent from time of rendering
judgmt & his costs of court below and his suit.
        William Eubanks by his friend v James Morgan. Covt. Jury Thos Marks, Silas
p.64   McGuin, Wm Cooper, Wm Dabney, Somerset Moore, Matthew Benthall, Leander
Shields, Jesse Weathers, John Hicks, Saml Shields, Thos Goff, Wm B Pepper. Dft recovers agt plf his costs about his defence expended.
        State v Polly White. Recognizance for murder. John White Junr surrendered
dft. Appearance bonds of John White Senr Thos White & Wm Johnson: Polly White
p.65 $1500, John Sr, Thos & Wm each $750.
        State v Richard Lonn. A&B on John Richardson. Richard Lann[Lonn?] in proper
p.66   person saith he is guilty. Fined $1 and costs of prosecution.
        Den on demise of James Greer, Robert, John & Thomas Bigham v Joseph Johns.
p.67   Ejectment. Plfs came not & are nonsuited; dft recovers agt plfs his costs.
        Clement C Clay produced license to practice law & took the oaths and is
admitted to practice law as a counsellor or attorney in this court.
        Court adjourned till tomorrow 10 oclock.   Thos Stuart

p.68   Wednesday December 11th 1811. Present the honorable Thomas Stuart, Judge.
        State v John Boyd. A&B on Reuben Dickson. John Boyd in proper person saith
he is guilty. Fined $2 and costs of this prosecution.
p.69   William Taylor bound for appearance of Polly Stags to prosecute John Stags
for breach/peace & to give evidence in behalf of State agt sd John Stags & to bring
in sd Polly, came not. Recognizance forfeited; scire facias issues agt Wm Taylor.
p.70   Henry Goodnight bound for appearance of Polly Stags to prosecute John Stags
for breach of peace and to give evidence agt John, brought her not; forfeited his
recognizance. Scire facias issues agt Henry Goodnight.
        John Herrinton bound for his appearance this day to answer charge agt him
p.71   for stealing came not. Scire facias issues agt sd Herrinton.
        John Yancy bound for appearance of John Herrinton brought him not, whereby
he forfeits his recognizance; scire facias issues.
p.72   Robert Wilson bound for appearance of John Herrinton [worded as above].
p.73   Gilford Dudly summoned personally to appear to give evidence in behalf
State agt James Reed in charge of forgery came not; scire facias issued agt him.
        Andrew Ervin bound for his personal appearance to give evidence agt James

p.74   Reed in a charge of forgery made default; scire facias issued against him.
Grand Jury brought Indictment agt Catherine Cox a true bill.

Thomas H Benton bound for personal appearance to give evidence behalf State
p.75   against James Reed, came not; scire facias issues against him.

William T Lewis bound personally to appear & give evidence behalf State agt
James Reed in charge for forgery came not; scire facias issues agt him.

p.76   William P Anderson summoned to give evidence in behalf/state agt James Reed
for forgery came not; scire facias issues against him.

p.77   State v Joseph Johns. James Reed & Thomas Goff who were bound for appearance of dft surrendered him & he is ordered into custody. Bond of Thomas Goff, John
Forgey & Walter Frazer & dft, condition sd Joseph Johns conduct himself civilly & be
p.78   of good behaviour toward all good citizens & particularly toward Elizabeth
Briggs for space of six months.

Grand Jury brought Indictment agt Benjamin Tutt a true bill.

John Overton, summoned to give evidence behalf State agt James Reed for
p.79   forgery, came not; scire facias issued against sd John Overton.

State v Benjamin Tutt. A&B on William Ferril. Sd Benjamin in proper person
saith he is guilty; fined $20 & costs.

p.80   Grand Jury returned Indictment agt Polly White not a true bill; having
nothing further, were discharged for further attendance at this term.

Polly White being led to the Bar in custody of the sheriff & pursuant to
her recognizance she moved the court by her counsel that inasmuch as the Grand Jury
had found the bill agt her for murder of her child to be not a true bill, that she
p.81   should be discharged. Polly is at liberty to depart.

Appearance bond, James Reed $1000, Absolom Borin, William W Walton &
William Nail $500 each, condition sd James Reed make his personal appearance from
day to day during next term of this court & answer charges against him.

p.82   James Hart v John Yancy. Debt. Dft in proper person saith he doth owe plf
debt, damages, & costs. Plf recovers $277.30 debt, damages $48.33½, & costs.

p.83   Forfeitures agt John Herrinton & his securities John Yancy & Robert Wilson
set aside and that they pay costs thereby incurred.

State v John Herrinton. Stealing a Bell Coller. Jury Silas McGuire[Mc-
Guin?], Wm Cooper, Wm Dabney, Somerset Moore, Matthew Benthall, Leander Shields,
Jesse Weathers, John Hicks, Samuel Shields, Thomas Goff, Wm B Pepper, Peter Swanson
p.84   find dft not guilty.

Deed Peter R Booker to Oliver Woods & John Woods 500 acres ackd.

p.85   David Stuart by his counsel Peter R Booker exhibited bill/Injunction to
stay proceedings on several judgments obtained by Zacheus Wilson & James C McRee
agt sd David. Writ/Injunction issues together with subpoenas upon complainants
giving bond & security for payment of the money.

Court adjourned till tomorrow 10 Oclock.   Thos Stuart

p.86   Thursday 12th December 1811. Present the honorable Thomas Stuart, Judge.

John Cunningham v Owen Shannon. Debt. Dft came not. Plf recovers agt dft
p.87 $815 debt, $351 damages of detention, & his costs of suit.

Richard Hightower v Peter Ussery. Covenant. Dft came not. Plf recovers agt
dft his damages by occasion of the nonperformance of the covenant; damages to be
enquired of by a jury at next term of this court.

p.88   Eaton Walker v Gabriel Bumpass. Deposition of Vincent Bennett of South

122

JUNE 1812

Carolina to be taken & read in evidence in this case in behalf of plf.
State v Catherine Cox. A&B on Pheaby Doolen. Jury Silas McGuire, William
p.89   Cooper, Wm Dabney, Somerset Moore, Matthew Benthall, Leander Shields, Jesse
Weathers, John Hicks, Saml Sheilds, Thos Goff, Wm B Pepper, Peter Swanson find dft
guilty. Dft fined $10 and costs of prosecution.
p.90   John Herrinton arraigned at the bar on indictment for petit larceny moved
court by his counsel moved that inasmuch as jury brought in verdict he is not
guilty of sd offense that he be discharged. John Herrinton is discharged.
       Absolom Borin v Joseph Boyd. Suit continued till next Term of this court.
       John Eppler v Gabriel Bumpass. Appeal. Court is of opinion that this court
p.91   has not jurisdiction of present case; cause struck off the docket.
       Scire facias issue against Thomas Philips, Humphry Tompkins & Peter Lyon
Senr who were summoned as jurors this term & failed to attend.
       Petit Jury discharged.
       John S Bailey v Gabriel Bumpass. Writ/Error from county court. Matters con-
p.92   tained in declaration are not sufficient in law for plf to maintain his
action agt dft. Judgment of court below is affirmed; dft recovers agt plf his costs
as well of the court below as his costs of suit in this behalf expended.
       Court adjourned till court in course.   Thos Stuart

p.93   Circuit Court at Court-house in Pulaski on Monday 8th June 1812. Present
the honorable Nathaniel W Williams, Judge.
       Grand & Petit jurors: Samuel Burney, Robert Wilson, William Hambey, William
Giddens, Zacheus Hurt, Adam Burney, Samuel Chambers, Edmund J Bailey, Oliver Woods,
Lewis Brown, Buckner Harwell Senr, William Wells, Parks Bailey, John Stephens,
Daniel Evans, John Campbell, George Malone, James Knox, James Ashmore, Jesse West,
p.94   Mansel Hall, Daniel Allen, John Lee, John Graves (C), Charles Buford.
       Grand Jury: Lewis Brown foreman, John Graves, John Lee, Mansel Hall, Samuel
Chambers, Daniel Evans, Zacheus Hurt, John Campbell, Parks Bailey, Robert Wilson,
Daniel Allen, George Malone, Buckner Harwell Sr.
       Robert Miller v Lawson Hobson. Appeal. Motion of plf by atty that judgment
p.95   of court below be affirmed. Plf recovers agt dft & Gabriel Bumpass & David
Campbell his securities the judgment $358.73 together with $11.34 being 12½
percent from judgmt untill this time, & his costs.
p.96   Power/attorney from Martin & Susanna Tongat, Zachariah & Jane Tongat, Mary
Fraser, Marget Fraser, James Fraser, William Fraser & Anna Fraser to John & Walter
Fraser was proven by oaths of Thomas B Hanie, John Lee & Stephen Samuel.
       Power/attorney from Martin & Susanna Tongat to Walter Fraser proven by
p.97   Thomas B Hanie, John Lee, & Stephen Samuel.
       Power/attorney from Marcus Mitchel to Nathaniel Parham acknowledged.
       State v Thomas Philips. Not attending as juror at Decr term. Thomas Philips
p.98   in proper person tendered excuse; discharged from forfeiture & costs.
       Edmund J Bailey is discharged from further attendance as a juror this term.
       Court adjourned till tomorrow 9 oclock.   Nath W Williams

123

DECEMBER 1812

p.99 Tuesday June 9th 1812. Present Nathaniel W Williams, Judge.
State v Humphry Tompkins. Not attending as Juror at Decr term. Humphry in
p.100 proper person tendered excuse; discharged from forfeiture on paying costs.
Reese Porter Sr v Robert & William Brown. Case. Plf no further prosecutes;
dft recovers agt plf his costs by him about his defence expended.
p.101 Benjamin Philips v Gabriel Higginbotham. Debt. William Crittington surrendered dft in discharge of himself. Jury Saml Burney, Wm Hambey, Wm Giddens, Adam
Burney, Oliver Woods, Wm Wells, John Stephens, Jas Knox, Jas Ashmore, Jesse West,
p.102 Chas Buford, Wm Crittington. Plf recovers agt dft debt, & damages, & costs.
p.103 John Allsup v Drury Stovall. Case. Tryal continued next term of this court.
Richard Hightower v Peter Ussery. Covenant. Trial postponed to next term.
Eaton Walker v Gabriel Bumpass. Case. Trial postponed untill next term.
p.104 Absolom Borin v Joseph Boyd. Rule for reference entered at June term set
aside. Remanded for trial at next term of this court.
State v James Reed. Recognizance. On Motion of Defendant by attorney, order
p.105 defendant discharged from his recognizance; he is at liberty to depart.
Thomas Humphreys bound by recognizance for appearance of Joseph Humphreys
is discharged from his recognizance.
Petit Jury discharged from further attendance at this term.
p.106 State v Peter Lyon. Not attending as juror Decr term. Peter Lyon in proper
person tendered excuse; discharged from forfeiture or costs.
p.107 State v Thomas H Benton. Benton in proper person [worded as above]
p.108 Den on demise of James Greer, Robert, John & Thomas Bighams v John McCabe.
Ejectment. Plfs failing to appear, suit dismissed; plfs pay costs.
Richard Hightower v Jacob Bogard. Covt. Parties failing to attend, suit is
dismissed.
Grand Jury discharged from further attendance at this term.
p.109 Court adjourned untill court in course.
                                                        Nath W Williams

p.110 Circuit Court for Giles County at Court-house in Pulaski, Monday 14th
December 1812. Present the honorable Archibald Roan, Judge.
Jurors: Volentine Huff, Saml McNight, Thos Marx, Wm McDonald, Robt McNairy,
Quinton Shannon, Richd McGee, John McCandless Sr, Charles Littleton, Jacob Crowson,
Isaac Atkins, James J Ward, Wm Marr, Wm Henderson, Jas McCraven, Robert Knox, Major
Harrolson, Richard Tutt, James Hunt, John Temple, James Starks, Stephen Anderson.
p.111 Grand Jurors: Thomas Marx foreman, Saml McNight, Robert McNairy, Stephen
Anderson, Volentine Huff, William McDonald, Wm Henderson, John McCanless, Quinton
Shannon, Richard McGee, James McCraven, Major Harrolson, Charles Littleton.
Bill/sale Zacheus Hurt to Samuel Hurt proven by E.J.Baily & Charles Buford.
Exempt James J Ward from surving as a juror at this term.
p.112 Writ/Habeas corpus issues directing sheriff to bring David Silman a
prisoner now confined in the jail of Williamson County.
Court adjourned till tomorrow 10 oclock.
                                                        Archibald Roane

Tuesday December 15th 1812. Present the honorable Archibald Roane, Judge.

124

Discharge Wm M Marr from attending as a Juror at this term.

p.113   Charles McCallister v James Reed & Absolom Borin. appeal. In making out the transcript in this case, Clerk omited that plea of payment was withdrawn; on motion of plf by atty & by consent of dfts atty, order transcript amended by inserting sd Plea of Payment withdrawn so that the case may rest on the demurer only.

Appearance bond of William Brown $150 to prosecute against Gabriel Joslin
p.114   for forgery.

John Allsup v Drury Stovall. Case. Jury John Temple, John McCrackin, John Yancy, Lewis Kirk, Ralph Graves, Buckner Harwel Junr, Henry Hogan, James Doren, John Griggory, Joseph McDonald, William Travis, William Kindle not agreeing, to be argued tomorrow.

p.115   Grand Jury indictment agt Gabriel Joslin, true bill.

Isham Lewis summoned to give evidence in behalf Drury Stovall at suit of John Allsup, came not; scire facias issues.

Discharge Robert Knox from attending as a juror at this term.

Grand Jury bill/indictment agt John Bryant, true bill.

p.116   Eaton Walker v Gabriel Bumpass. Case. Jury Thos Marx, Saml McNight, Robert McNairy, Volentine Huff, Wm Henderson, John McCanless, Jas McCraven, Quinton Shannon, Major Harrolson, Chas Littleton, Alexr Black, James Gideons. Plf recovers agt dft damages $134.81¼ and his costs of suit.

Court adjourned till tomorrow, 10 oclock.   Archibald Roane

p.118   Wednesday, Decemer 16th 1812. Present the hon. Archibald Roane, Judge.

State v Andrew Ervin. Not attending as witness Decr 1811 to give evidence behalf State agt James Reed for forgery. Deft is not found, came not. Execution
p.119   against dft for $250 the amt of his recognizance and also costs.

John Allsup v Drury Stovall. Case. Jury yesterday empannelled assess plfs
p.120   damages to 6¼¢.

State v John Bryant. Passing counterfeit money. John Bryant, labourer, appeared at the bar & was arraigned for sd offence, plead not guilty. Jury John Temple, Matthew Cunningham, Wm Jones, Jas Williams, Thos Smith, Gray Edwards, Enoch Bryant, Thos M Dement, Lewis Martin, Thos C Stone, John Yarbrough, Samuel Chambers
p.122   whereupon (night having come on) they disperse to come again tomorrow.

Order Sheriff to bring to court David Selman now in confinement to give evidence in case State v John Bryant.

Court adjourned till tomorrow 9 oclock.   Archibald Roane

p.123   Thursday December 17th 1812. Present the hon. Archibald Roane, Judge.

Charles McCallister v James Reed & Absolom Borin. Appeal. Plf recovers agt
p.124   dft $100 together with $9.43½ damages and his costs.

State v John Bryant. Passing counterfeit money. Jury yesterday empanelled
p.125   find dft John Bryant not guilty.

Grand Jury indictment agt David Selman, true bill.

p.126   State v David Selman. Horsestealing. David Selman, labourer, in custody of jailor arraigned & plead not guilty. Jury Wm R Cox, Early Benson, John Arnett, Saml Cooper, Wm B Pepper, John Reasonhover, Wm Brown, Pleasant Moore, William Smith, Jas
p.127   Leeth, Hugh Braton, Tyree Rodes find defendant not guilty.

Appearance bond $150 each, John Yancy to prosecute Samuel White and William

F Thompson & William Parker to give evidence in behalf State against Samuel White
p.128   in a charge exhibited against him for murder.

Joel T Rivers jailor of Williamson county allowed $78.62½ for boarding John
Bryant & David Silman prisoners arrested in Giles County and committed to the jail
of Williamson County.

p.129   Josias Kindred v Samuel Parmly. Appeal. Upon deliberation, it seems that
there is such a record in Wayne Circuit Court as plaintiff alledged. Plaintiff
recovers agt defendant $109.18½ as in declaration specified together with $24 & ¼¢
damages of detention of debt and his costs.

p.130   Appearance bond of William Brown to prosecute and give evidence against
Gabriel Joslin for forgery next term of this court.

John Allsup v John Birdwell. Appeal. Judgment of the court below be in all
p.131   things affirmed; defendant recovers against plaintiff & Thomas Allsup and
Wm Ball his securities $17.86½ costs of the court below & his costs in this behalf.

p.132   James Buford Sheriff & William R Davis allowed $43.84½ for conveying David
Selman a prisoner arrested in this county to Williamson County jail and for money
expended whilst in their custody after he was brought from the jail.

Scire facias issue agt Jacob Crowson, Isaac Atkins, Richard Tutt, James
Hunt & James Starks who failed to attend as jurors.

p.133   Court adjourned till tomorrow 10 oclock.   Archibald Roane

Friday December 18th 1812. Present the honorable Archibald Roane, Judge.

State v Guilford Dudley. Forgery. Sheriff returned on second scire facias
p.134   that defendant is not to be found; dft came not. State recovers against sd
Guilford Dudley $125 and costs.

John Kelso v William Ball. Debt. Depositions of John Key & others in
Amherst County and of James Dick & others of Prince Edward County, all in Virginia
p.135   to be taken and read in evidence in behalf of plaintiff.

Absolom Borin v Joseph Boyd. Case. Dft came not. Plf recovers agt dft his
damages; damages to be enquired of by jury at next term. Further ordered that
p.136   depositions be taken of John Jack of Pulaski County & Robert Hooten of
Warren County all of Kentucky to be read in evidence behalf of plaintiff.

Richard Hightower v Peter Ussery. Covt. Postponed to next term this court.

Grand Jury indictment agt John Bryant, true bill. Grand Jury discharged.
p.137   Petit Jury discharged from further attendance at this term.

Appearance bond of Washington Craft $250 and Robert Childers $150, Washington Craft to prosecute, Robert Childers to give evidence behalf State agt John
p.138   Bryant in the charge against him of passing counterfeit money.

State v John Bryant. Passing counterfeit money. Bryant committed to custody
of the Sheriff untill he should give two sufficient securities to be bound in the
p.139   sum of $2500 for his appearance at next term of this court.

Court adjourned till Court in course.   Archibald Roane

p.140   Circuit Court for Giles County held at the courthouse in Pulaski on Monday
12th April 1813. Present the hon. John F Jack, Judge, who produced a commission

APRIL 1813

under the signature of the governor of this State appointing him a judge.
Jurors: Samuel Shields, Robt Steele, John Hillhouse, Israel Perkins, John Dickey, Jacob Byler, Pleasant Moore, John Dabney, Nathaniel Moody, Samuel Jones, Nelson Patteson, James Dugger, Maxamilian H Buckhanan, Robt Buckhanan, Thos Westmoreland, Samuel Smith, Jarret Menefee, John Easley, John Temple, William Pennell, Buckner Harwell Senr, James Kimbro, Robt Reid, John Yancy, Richd Harwell.

p.141 Grand jury: Nelson Patteson foreman, Saml Shields, John Easley, Wm Pennell, Pleasant Moore, John Hillhouse, Robt Reid, Robt Stult, Jacob Byler, Jarret Menefee, Saml Jones, John Dickey, Buckner Harwell Sr.
Alfred Balch, the solicitor general, failing to attend, order that George Coulter be appointed solicitor in room of sd Balch at this term.
Exempt John Temple from attending as a Juror at this term, affidavit filed.
State v Jacob Crowson. Not attending as Juror at Decr term. Jacob in proper
p.142 person tendered his excuse; discharged from forfeiture and costs.
State v James Starks. [as above]
p.143 Joseph Kelly v John Menefee. Case. Edmond J Bailey & John McCabe undertook for defendant. Estate of dft attached at instance of plf is surrendered to him.
p.144 Thomas Kelly v John Menefee. Case. Edmond J Bailey & John McCabe undertook for dft. Estate of dft attached at instance of plf is surrendered to him.
John Kelso v William Ball. Debt. Plf by atty, affidavit being filed, order
p.145 trial postponed until next term of this court. Order made last term for taking depositions of John Key & others of Amherst County and of James Dick & others of Prince Edward county in Virginia be renewed.
Charles Boyles v Samuel Chambers. Appeal. Plf came not. Cause dismissed.
p.146 Judgment of court below is affirmed. Dft recovers agt plf his costs.
John Taylor v John McCabe. Appeal. Postponed untill next term. Depositions of John Mosely & Wm Philips of Jessamine County & of James Tygert, Thomas Robertson, & Burrel Jackson in Warren County, all of Kentucky, to behalf of defendant.
p.147 Samuel Black v John McCabe. Appeal. Postponed until next term. Depositions of Robert Forbis, Ephraim Maxa Fisher R Bennet & Henry Rennicks of Kentucky to be read in evidence behalf of defendant.
Court adjourned till tomorrow nine oclock.
                                                                      John F Jack

p.148 Tuesday April 13th 1813. Present the honorable John F Jack, Judge.
State v Samuel White. Murder. Alias Capias issues against defendant.
Exampt Samuel Smith from further attendance as a juror at this term.
p.149 State v Gabriel Joslin. Forgery. Appearance bond, Gabriel Joslin $500, John Black & Spencer Roach each $250.
p.150 Appearance bond, William Brown $250 to prosecute; William Mayfield, Thomas Bratton, William Smith & Nathaniel Moody $250 each to give evidence on behalf the State against Gabriel Joslin.
p.151 Absolom Borin v Joseph Boyd. Case. Defendant came not. Plf recovers agt dft damages; damages to be enquired of by a Jury at next term of this Court.
William Ball v John Scott. Appeal. Defendant recovers against the plaintiff
p.152 & George Cunningham his security $22.52 and his costs.
State v Richard Tutt. Non attendance as juror Decr term. Dft tendered his
p.153 excuse; exempted from payment of forfeiture or costs.
Wilton F L Jenkins v Henry Hagin. Detinue. Jury Israel Perkins, John Dabney, Nathl Moody, Jas Dugger, Maxamilian H Buckhanan, Robt Buckhanan, Thos West-

127

APRIL 1813

moreland, Jas Kimbro, John Yancey, Richd Harwell, John McCabe, John Barnett say dft
p.154   doth not detain Negro slave as in pleading alledged. Dft recovers against
plaintiff his costs about his defence in this behalf expended.
        Court adjourned till to morrow morning 9 oclock.   John F Jack

p.155   Wednesday April 14th 1813. Present the honorable John F Jack, Judge.
        Deed William McGee to John Hawkins 300 acres proven by Thomas Smith, Thomas
C Stone & Charles Sharpe.
        Wilton F L Jenkins v Henry Hagin. Detinue. Plf came not. Non suited. Dft
p.156   recovers against plaintiff his costs about his suit expended.
        Richard Hightower v Peter Ussery. Covenant. Postponed till next term.
        Harvey Johns v John McCabe. Appeal. Postponed until next term at plfs cost.
p.157   State v James Hunt. Not attending as Juror Decr 1812. Dft came not; order
p.158   execution agt dft for $5 together with costs of scire facias.
        State v Isaac Atkins. Non attendance as juror December. Alias Scire facias
issues against defendant.
        Grand Jury discharged from further attendance at this term.
        On motion of Alfred M Harris, order scire facias issue agt John Birdwell
who was prosecution bail of John Allsup in suit by sd Allsup against Drury Stoval.
p.159   State v John Bryant. Passing counterfeit money. Dft in proper person. Jury
Israel Perkins, John Dabney, Nathaniel Moody, James Dugger, Thomas Westmoreland,
James Kimbro, John Yancy, Richard Harwell, William Brown, Tyre Rodes, Lewis Kirk,
p.160   Moses McLamore find dft guilty as specified. Counsel for dft moved for new
trial; overruled. Granted appeal to Supreme court of Error & Appeals.
        John Bryant, John Grigory & Minor Winn appearance bonds to answer charge
p.161   against Bryant for passing counterfeit money.
        Washington Craft & Robert Childers appearance bonds, to give evidence
p.162   against John Bryant in charge of passing counterfeit money.
        John Yancy bond to appear at next court to prosecute Samuel White in charge
p.163   against him for murder.
        Court adjourned till court in course.   John F Jack

p.164   Circuit Court held Monday 11th October 1813. Present Bennet Searcy, Judge.
        Jurors: Duncan Brown, John Barnett, Richd Barnett, John Easley, Maximilian
H Buchanan, Samuel Smith, Jas McDonald, Drury Stovall, William Ezell, Saml McNite,
Leonard Morrow, Nathn Farmer, Thos Rea, Jno Robertson, John Hillhouse, John Dickey,
Robt Ross, George Hillhouse, Arthur Hix, Pleasant Moore, Somerset Moore, William
Mayfield, Gideon Pillow, John Elliott, John McNite.
p.165   Grand jurors: Maximilian H Buchanan foreman, Thomas Rea, John Dickey, Robt
Ross, Arthur Hicks, John Elliott, John Barnett, Samuel Smith, John McNite, Duncan
Brown, Leonard Morrow, William Mayfield, Drury Stovall.
        Absolom Borin v Joseph Boyd. Case. Jury James McDonald, William Ezell, Saml
McNite, Nathan Farmer, John Robertson, John Hillhouse, George Hillhouse, Somerset
Moore, John Graves, Brice M Mayfield, Charles Buford, Buckner Harwell Jr. Plaintiff
p.166   recovers agt dft his damages 6¼¢ besides his costs.

128

Elizabeth Smith by her friend v John Black & wife. Certiorari. Certiorari dismissed; plf recovers agt dft his costs by him in this behalf expended. Court adjourned till tomorrow 10 Oclock.   B Searcy

p.167   Tuesday 12th october 1813. Present the honorable Bennet Searcy, Judge.
William M Kirby v Douglass Blue. Appeal. Dft is the appealant. Judgment of court below confirmed. Plf recovers agt dft & Wm H Merrat[?] his security the sum p.168   of $50.03¾ with $4.16¾ being 12½ percent on amt of judgment of court below from rendition thereof untill this term, and his costs.
State v Gabriel Joslin. Forgery. John Black surrenders defendant; Sheriff p.169   took dft into custody. Jury James McDonald, Wm Ezell, Saml McNite, Nathan Farmer, John Robertson, Samuel Hurt, Zacheus Hurt, David Campbell, John Pate, Wm Pullin, Joseph Anthony, Thomas McKissack. Counsel for State no further prosecutes. p.170   Gabriel Joslin acquited of charge.
State v Andrew Erwin. Not attending as witness behalf State agt James Reed. Forfeiture set aside; sd Andrew pays costs of scire facias.
John Kelso v William Ball. Debt. Continued to next term; plaintiff to take p.171   depositions of James Dick & others in city of Richmond, of Thomas Pankey Martha Pankey & William Routon in Prince Edward & of John Key Thomas Key & others at Franklin Courthouse all in Virginia on behalf plaintiff. Defendant recovers agt plf his costs incurred by this continuance.
Grand Jury returned bill of indictment agt Parks Bailey, true bill.
p.172   Appearance bonds of Parks Bailey, Nathaniel Moody & Charles Buford, Parks Bailey $2000, Nathaniel & Charles $1000 each, charge of perjury.
Appearance bonds of James Reed, Alexander McCoy, Edward Lee & Samuel Jones, $500 each, Reed to prosecute, McCoy, Lee, & Jones to give evidence in behalf of the p.173   State against Parks Bailey in charge for Perjury.
John Taylor v John McCabe. Appeal. Postponed. Plf recovers agt dft the costs incurred by this continuance.
Samuel Black v John McCabe. Appeal. Suit dismissed by direction of plaintiff and defendant recovers plf his costs of defence.
p.174   Drury Stovall v Isham Lewis. Not attending as witness behalf Drury Stovall at suit of John Allsup. Plaintiff granted execution against dft for $125 & costs.
Leonard Brown v Nelson Patteson. Case. Continued until next term.
p.175   Gabriel Bumpass v Henry Scales. Appeal. Postponed on motion of dft.
Gabriel Bumpass v Nelson Patteson. Appeal. Postponed on motion of plf.
Bill/sale Solomon Asbell to Polly Asbell ackd.
p.176   Bill/sale Solomon Asbell to Betsey Asbell ackd.
Deed Commissioners of Pulaski to David Leech town lot 119 ackd.
Richard Hightower v Peter Ussery. Covt. Continued until next term.
Court adjourned till tomorrow 10 oclock.   B Searcy

p.177   Wednesday 13th October 1813. Present the honorable Bennet Searcy, Judge.
Harvey Johns v Jno McCabe. Appeal. Continued to next term on motion of dft.
p.178   Absolom Borin v Joseph Boyd. Case. Judgment rendered yesterday amended to insert that plaintiff recovers agt dft his damages & 6¼¢ for his costs.
Discharge petit jury from further attendance at this term.
p.179   Drury Stovall v John Birdwell. Sci fa agt him as prosecution bail of John

APRIL 1814

Allsup in suit Allsup agt Drury Stovall. Dft failing to appear, plf is granted execution agt sd dft for $40.66¼ & his costs of suit.

p.180 Joseph Kelly v John Menefee. Case. Plaintiff failing to attend, is nonsuited. Defendant recovers agt him his costs about his defence expended.

Thomas Kelly v John Menefee. Case. [as above]

p.181 Grand jury returned Indictment agt Gabriel Joslin, true bill. Grand jury is discharged from any further attendance at this term.

Capias issues against Gabriel Joslin returnable to next term of this court.

Scire facias issue against Pleasant Moore, John Easley & Richard Barnett delinquent jurors returnable to next term of this court.

p.182 Bill/sale Isaac Harday to Betsey [no surname stated] was proven by Joshua Wharton, the other subscribing witness thereto living out of the State.

Court adjourned till court in Course.   B Searcy

p.183 Circuit court for Giles County, Monday 11th April 1814. Present the honorable Thomas Stuart, Judge.

The courthouse being burnt, I therefore ordered that court be adjourned to meet at the house of David Martin immediately.

Court met at the house of David Martin in the Town of Pulaski.

State v Parks Bailey. Nathl Moody surrendered Parks Bailey to sheriff.

p.184 Discharge Thomas Westmoreland from further attendance as a juror.

Joel T Rivers, jailor of Williamson County, surrendered George Shawley a prisoner brought by him from Williamson county jail to custody of sheriff.

Jessee Vincent surrendered John A King to sheriff to answer charge against him for passing counterfeit bank notes.

p.185 Discharge Robert McDonald from further attendance as a juror at this term.

State v Richard Barnett. Not attending as juror Octr term. Sd Richard in proper person tendered excuse; discharged from payment of fine or costs.

p.186 Order first day of each term to try all issues on docket except ejectment which will be taken up on second day; third day for trial of criminal causes.

State v Isaac Atkins. Not attending as juror Decr 1812. Sd Isaac tendered

p.187 excuse; discharged from payment of fine or costs.

Deed Ho Tatum to Joshua Rickman 28 acres proven by George Cunningham and Thomas Westmoreland.

James Reed v William Robertson. Cer. Postponed until Wednesday; dft pays costs incurred by this continuance.

Andrew Jackson &c exors of Wm T Lewis decd v David Woods. Appeal. Motion by plfs that judgment of court below be affirmed and that plfs recover agt dft & his security $166.87½, 12½ percent on sd judgment, and costs of suit. Plfs recover agt dft & William Woods & Thomas C Stone sd sums.

p.189 Thomas Buford late sheriff returned names of jurors: Jacob Byler, Marcus Mitchell, Buckner Harwell Sr, Lewis Brown, Thos Westmoreland, Joseph Anthony, Elijah Anthony, Jas Bumpass, Robt McDonald, Alexr Barron, Robt Gordon, John White Jr, John Barnett, John McCrackin, Nathl Moody, Caleb Hill, Robert McNairy, John Clark, William Giddens, Jno Paul Sr, Peter Swanson, Ralph Graves, Jno Graves, Wm McDonald.

Grand jury: John Clark foreman, Ralph Graves, Caleb Hill, John Paul Senr,

APRIL 1814

Nathaniel Moody, William Giddens, Marcus Mitchell, Elijah Anthony, Robert Gordon, James Bumpass, John Barnett, Alexander Barron, John McCracken.
p.190   Court adjourned till tomorrow morning 9 oclock.   Thos Stuart

Tuesday April 12th 1814. Present the Honorable Thomas Stuart, Judge.
        State v Jno Bryant. Passing counterfeit money. Sheriff to bring dft to hear court pass judgment against him pursuant to verdict of guilty found at April term.
p.191   Joel T Rivers Williamson County jailer returned Adonijah Edwards on charge of having passed a counterfeit bill of the Nashville bank &c to give evidence in behalf the state against George Shawley on a charge against him for counterfeiting
p.192   & passing bank notes. Adonijah Edwards committed to custody of Joel T Rivers 20 Decr 1813 by David Shannon, and to be in custody of sheriff until he shall give evidence in behalf of the State against Shawly on charge afsd.
p.193   Deed/gift Larken Cleveland & Fanny his wife to German Lester proven by Samuel Jones and James Reed.
        State v Parks Bailey. Perjury. Jury Jacob Byler, Buckner Harwell Sr, Lewis
p.194   Brown, Jos Anthony, John White, Robert McNairy, Peter Swanson, John Graves, Wm McDonald, Thos Wells, Thos Marks, David Reed. Dft acquitted of charge agt him.
        State v John Easley. Not attending as juror Octr 1813. Sd John in proper
p.195   person tendered excuse; exonerated from payment of fine or costs.
        State v Pleasant Moore. Not attending as juror Octr 1813. [worded as above]
        Deed John & Oliver Woods to William Woods 500 acres proven by David Woods
p.196   and Robert Wilson.
        Richard Hightower v Peter Ussery. Covt. Continued till next term.
        Harvey John v John McCabe. Appeal. Jury David Woods, Robt Allsup, Alexr Jones, Wm B Brooks, John B Pendergast, Absolom Harwell, Richd Barnett, Robt Ander-
p.197   son, Chas Buford, John Waldrip, Alexr Tarply, Pleasant Moore assess plf's damages by reason on dft's nonperformance to $107 besides his costs.
        State v Parks Bailey. Perjury. Dft's attorney moved to tax prosecutor with costs; counsel for State objected, and was by court overruled.
p.198   Court adjourned till tomorrow morning 9 oclock.   Thos Stuart

Wednesday 13th April 1814. Present the Honorable Thomas Stuart, Judge.
        On motion of Alfred Balch counsel for State, order Sheriff bring to court John Shoemaker, witness to give evidence in behalf State against George Shawly to
p.199   answer for his contempt.
        State v John Bryant. Passing counterfeit money. Deputy Frederick Harwell brought John Bryant into court; Bryant taken into custody of the sheriff.
        James Reed v William Robertson. Appeal. On petition of deft that fair and impartial trial cannot be had in this county; order change of venue to the Circuit
p.200   Court for Bedford County.
        Gabriel Bumpass v Henry Scales. Appeal. Jury Jacob Byler, Buckner Harwell Sr, Joseph Anthony, John White Jr, Robert McNairy, Peter Swanson, John Graves, Wm Parker, Leonard Brown, John Thompson, Zacheus Hurt, John Yancey. Plf recovers agt
p.201   dft $11.17½ and his costs of suit in this behalf expended.
        Gabriel Bumpass v Henry Scales. Appeal. On affidavit of German Lester Clerk of county court setting forth that transcript is incomplete, that he omitted to insert claims of certain witnesses. Granted leave to insert sd claims.

131

p.202   Discharge Buckner Harwell Sr from further attendance at this term.

John Kelso v William Ball. Debt. Trial continued to next term on affidavit of Nelson Patteson agent for plf & that he pay costs incurred by continuance; deposition of John Key of [blank] county Ohio to be taken on behalf plf.

p.203   Gabriel Bumpass v Henry Scales. Appeal. Dft to shew cause for a new trial.

John Taylor assee of Saml Black v John McCabe. Appeal. Jury Henry Roberts, Alexr McDonald, John Harnett, David Campbell, Archd Alexander, Wm Smith, Lewis Brown, Wm McDonald, Gilbert D Taylor, Oliver Woods, Saml Smith, Jas Buford say dft

p.204   hath not paid so much of Kentucky money as is equal to $154.51¼, and assess damages to $31.67½ & further say dft has paid balance of Kentucky money. Plf recovers said sums and his costs of suit.

Fanny Cleveland who is party to Deed/gift from Larken Cleveland & his wife appeared in court & examined apart from her husband saith she executed same freely.

p.205   State v John Bryant. Passing counterfeit money. John Bryant in custody of Sheriff having heard evidence and argument of counsel and found guilty of charges

p.206   against him, fined $10 and pay costs of prosecution against him; imprisoned 30 days from this time in jail of Maury county and until he shall pay fine & costs.

p.207   Court adjourned until morning 9 oclock.   Thos Stuart

Thursday April 14th 1814. Preent the Honorable Thomas Stuart, Judge.

State v George Shawley[Shawby?]. Counterfeiting. Dft in custody of sheriff arraigned; trial tomorrow.

p.208   State v John A King. Passing counterfeit bank note. John A King yeoman in custody of sheriff is arraigned; trial at next term of this court. Dft to be jailed

p.209   in Maury County until October next when he stands trial.

John A King v Charles Payne & Jesse Vincent. Equity. Capias ad respondendum issues agt dfts returnable to next term of this court.

Charles Payne bound in recognizance $1000 for appearance this day to give evidence in behalf State against John A King on charge against him for passing bank note purporting to be a Kentucky bank note, came not. Scire facias issues.

p.210   Lewis Payne bound in recognizance $500 for appearance this day to give evidence behalf State agt John A King [as above]

Appearance bonds of Jessee Vincent, Samuel Smith, John Crowson, Isaac Atkins & Samuel Woods, each $500, to give evidence behalf State against John A King

p.211   at October Court.

Lewis Payne bound in recognizance $1000 for appearance of Charles Payne this day to give evidence against John A King brought him not, thereby forfeited his recognizance. Scire facias issues returnable to next term.

p.212   Jesse Vincent, recognizance $1000, appearance of Chas Payne[as above].

Jessee Vincent, recog $500 for appearance of Lewis Payne [as above].

p.213   Leonard Brown v Nelson Patteson. Case. Jury Lewis Brown, Jos Anthony, John White Jr, Robt McNairy, Peter Swanson, James Paul, John Hicks, Jas Buford, Jno Waldrip, John C Walker, Chas Buford, John Kinan. Dft recovers agt plf his costs.

p.214   Riley Finny summoned to give evidence behalf Leonard Brown agt Nelson Patteson came not. Scire facias issues against him.

William Brown v Gabriel Joslin. Cer. Jury John B Prendergast, John McCrack-

p.215   in, Henry Hagen, Wm McDonald, Saml Y Anderson, Leonard Brown, John Paul Sr, Quinton Shannon, Jas Doran, John Thompson, Jacob Byler, Henry Scales permitted to disperse until to morrow.

APRIL 1814

Court adjourned until tomorrow morning 9 oclock.   Thos Stuart

p.216   Friday 15th April 1814. Present the Honl Thomas Stuart, Judge.
William Brown v Gabriel Joslin. Certiorari. Order Robert Brashears be entered as security to bond given for prosecuting in place of John Black now released
for purpose of giving testimony behalf of defendant. Jury assess plf's damages to
$96 besides his costs.
p.217   State v George Shawley. Counterfeiting. George Shawley yeoman brought to
the bar in custody of sheriff. Jury Thomas Smith, Halbert Allison, Thomas C Stone,
Peter Swanson, Jacob Templin, William Hambey, John Waldrip, Jacob Byler, Thomas
Bratton, Edmond J Bailey, Joseph Lann Wm Pullin. Evening too far spent. Constable
p.218   William R Davis sworn to take charge of jurors, keep them together separate
& apart & from conversing from other persons whosoever & bring them together
tomorrow for the trial. George Shawley is remanded to jail.
So many of petit jurors as are not now engaged are discharged.
Court adjourned until to morrow morning 9 oclock.   Thos Stuart

p.219   Saturday April 16th 1814. Present the Honorable Thomas Stuart, Judge.
State v George Shawley. Counterfeiting. Dft bill of exceptions signed and
p.220   sealed by the court. Jury find dft guilty of fourth count and not guilty in
p.221   other counts of indictment. Court heard dfts counsel & motion overruled.
Order Sheriff convey George Shawley to Williamson County jail. Before first Monday
in September Sheriff shall reconvey sd George Shawley back to Pulaski and shall
p.222   hang the sd George Shawley by the neck until he be dead. Dft to pay costs
of this prosecution. Dft granted appeal to Supreme Court giving Michael Shawley and
John Shawley security.
p.223   State v Adonijah Edwards. Dft remanded to Williamson County jail.
James Huey bound in recognizance to give evidence this day against George
Shawley came not. Scire facias issues.
On Equity side of this court, order first day after each term shall be such
day except Sunday.
p.224   Leonard Brown v Nelson Patteson. Case. New trial, on plf's paying costs.
Plf & dft granted leave to amend declarations.
State v Parks Bailey. Dft acquitted, motion of counsel for state, order
judgt entered for State costs and certified to county Trustee.
p.225   Gabriel Bumpass v Henry Scales. Dft's motion for new trial overruled.
Gabriel Bumpass v Nelson Patteson. Trial continued to next term.
State v George Shawley. Account of Joel T Rivers, Williamson county jailer,
p.226   for keeping George Shawley & bringing sd Shawley and for bringing Adonijah
Edwards be allowed $84.
Court adjourned till court in course.   Thos Stuart

p.227[opening pages of this session are missing from the book]
Wednesday October 12th 1814.

133

Samuel Smith, John Crowson, Isaac Atkins, Samuel Woods bound to appear here this
day & give evidence against John A King, are bound to appear at April court to give
evidence agt John A King in a charge of passing counterfeit bank notes.

Thomas McKissack & Wm Mayfield, bound to appear here this day & give evidence in behalf State agt David Smith in charge of perjury appeared and are bound
to appear at April court to give evidence in behalf state agt David Smith.

p.229　Circuit Court 10th April 1815 at house of Isaac Smith in Pulaski. Present
the honorable Archibald Roane, Judge.

　Jurors: Tyree Rodes, Nelson Patteson, Jas Bumpass, Robt Buchanan, James Mc-
Donald, Saml Jones, Hardy Hightower, John Montgomery, Pleasant Moore, John Dickey,
Arthur Hicks, Wm Mayfield, Samuel Shields, Jarrett Menefee, Thos Harwood, Wm Price,
James Paine, Joel Lane, William McDonald, Nathaniel Moody, Charles Buford, Robert
p.230　McNairy, Robert Oliver, James Dugger.

　Grand Jurors: Nelson Patteson foreman, Jarrett Menefee, James Paine, James
McDonald, James Bumpass, Samuel Shields, Samuel Jones, Pleasant Moore, James Dugger, William Mayfield, Nathaniel Moody, John Montgomery, Thomas Harwood.

　Joel Carey gent produced a license to practice law & took the oaths of a
counseller or attorney and is omitted to practice in this Court.

　Direct the sheriff of Maury County to bring John Romack & Nancy Coventon to
p.231　this court, who are now confined in the public jail of sd county.

　Deed Robert John & Thomas Bigham to Daniel Woods & Gideon Pillow proven by
John McCabe and Richard H Allen.

　Richard Hightower v Peter Ussery. Covt. Suit discontinued. Dft recovers agt
plaintiff his costs about his defence in this behalf expended.

p.232　Deed Maximilian H Buchan sheriff to John Dewaaser 440 acres ackd.

　Juror John Dickey discharged from further attendance.

　Nathaniel Taylor v James Ashmore & Robert Campbell. Appeal. Petition of
plaintiffs agent sets forth at impartial trial cannot be had in this county. Order
p.233　trial adjourned to Bedford County.

　Nathaniel Taylor v James Ashmore. Appeal. [as above]

p.234　Appearance bond of Thomas Goff, Daniel Allen & William Brown, condition
that Thomas Goff appear in October to answer a charge of Assault & Battery.

p.235　Thomas Goff, Daniel Allen & William Brown[as above, charge of trespass]

p.236　Leonard Brown v Nelson Patteson. Case. Trial postponed until next term.

　Leonard Brown v Riley Finney. Not attending as witness behalf Brown agt
Patteson. Dft had departed this life. Suit revived agt executors or admrs of decd.

p.237　Deed Commissioners of Pulaski to John Paul lot 3 in sd town ackd.

　Deed Joel Lewis to Thomas Meredith 847 acres proven by Alfred Balch.

　Gabriel Bumpass, Tyree Rodes, Nathl Moody, Saml Jones, Maximilian N Buch,
p.238　as commissioners of Pulaski v Philip Parchman. Appeal. Jury Robt Buchanan,
Hardy Hightower, Arthur Hicks, Wm McDonald, Chas Buford, Robt McNairy, James Paul,
Quinton Shannon, Saml Chambers, John Paul, Wm Riddle, Wm B Brooks say dft hath not
paid his obligation nor any part thereof & assess damages to $27 & costs. Plfs by
p.239　atty moved that inasmuch as verdict was same as judgment of court below,
that plfs recover agt dft & his securities 12½ percent on sd judgment. Plfs recover

agt dft & Robert Wilson & William Ball his securities $200 debt and $9.45 damages.
Gabriel Bumpass, Tyree Rodes, Nathl Moody, Saml Jones & Maxamilian H Buch commrs/Pulaski v Philip Parchman. Appeal. Jury Robt Buchanan, Hardy Hightower,
p.240 Arthur Hicks, Wm McDonald, Chas Buford, Robt McNairy, James Paul, Quinton Shannon, Saml Chambers, John Paul, Wm Riddle, Wm B Brooks say dft hath not paid, assess plfs damages to $37.39 & costs. Plfs atty moved that inasmuch as verdict was
p.241 same as judgment of court below that plfs recover agt dft & his securities 12½ percent on judgment of court below. Plfs recover agt dft & Robert Wilson & Wm Ball his securities $277 debt, afsd damages, with further sum $16.45 on judgment of court below and their costs.
p.242 John Boyd v Edmund J Bailey. Appeal. Jury[above]. Plf recovers against dft
p.243 & Nelson Patteson & Wm Riddle his securities debt, damages, & costs in the court below and in this behalf expended.
Court adjourned till tomorrow morning 9 oclock.   Archibald Roane

p.244 Tuesday 11th April 1815. Present the honorable Archibald Roane, Judge.
John Kelso v William Ball. Debt. Thomas Harwood prosecution bail in room of Nelson Patteson whom the plaintiffs attorney wishes to introduce as an evidence.
William Kindell v Henry Scales. Appeal. Dft in proper person saith he can-
p.245 not gainsay plfs action. Plf recovers agt dft $40 & his costs.
Odell Garrett v Samuel Chambers. Eqty. Thomas McKissack & Robert Campbell exrs/will of Odel Garrett who hath departed this life since filing this cause. Con-
p.246 tract which complainant executed & on which dft hath recovered judgmt agt complainant is rescinded. Decreed by Court: injunction made perpetual, dft barred from proceeding on judgmt; contract on which dft recovered judgment is annulled.
p.247 Executors pay $4.50 part of the costs & defendant pay balance of costs.
James Perry gent. took oath of deputy sheriff & is admitted to duties.
John Kelso v William Ball. Debt. Jury Robt Buchanan, Hardy Hightower, Ar-thur Hicks, Wm McDonald, Chas Buford, Robt McNairy, Thos Bigham, Quinton Shannon,
p.248 Daniel Bentley, Gabriel Bumpass Junr, Martin Shadden, William Riddle are permitted to disperse until tomorrow.
Grand Jury bills/indictment: agt John Romack true bill; agt Nancy Coventon
p.249 true bill.
Tyree Rodes v Pleasant Moore. Ejectment. Plf orders suit discontinued. Plf recovers agt defendant his costs about his suit expended.
Jailer of Maury county brought John Romack & Nancy Coventon to custody of sheriff of this county.
p.250 Deed Commrs of Pulaski to David Abernatha lot 17 proven by William Ball and Charles C Abernatha.
Court adjourned untill tomorrow morning 9 oclock.   Archibald Roane

p.251 Wednesday April 3d[should be 12th] April 1815. Present Archd Roane, Judge.
William R Hess gent. produced commission from governor appointing him solicitor general in the room of Alfred Balch, resigned.
State v John Romack. Bigamy. Order change/venue to Maury cty October next.
p.252 Deed Commrs of Pulaski to John Tennin lot 222 ackd.
Grand Jury indictment agt Richard Allen & others, a true bill.
State v William McCabe, Thomas Johnson, Richard H Allen, Alexander Angus.

Burglary. Richard H Allen, yeoman, arraigned & plead not guilty. Trial continued.

p.253   Appearance bond of Richard H Allen $1000, to attend October court.

p.254   Bond of Daniel Allen, John McCabe, John Davidson, condition Richard H Allen appear at next term of this court to answer charge of Burglary.

State v Nancy Coventon. Horse stealing. Nancy Coventon spinster in custody of sheriff, arraigned & plead not guilty. Jury Stephen Anderson, Wm B Brooks, Jos

p.255   Dickson, Wm Riddle, Henry Hoggen, Archd Alexander, Wm Henry, Wm Bradly, Wm M Kirby, Charles Simpson, Thomas McKissack, John Boyd.

William Parker v Jesse Kirkland & Mayberry Helms. Eqty. Cause dismissed on motion of complainant by his counsel.

p.256   Bond of Elias Lunsford, $500, to appear at Octr court to prosecute behalf State agst Wm McCabe, Thos Johnson, Richd H Allen, Alexr Angus on charge/burglary.

Bond of Lewis Lunsford & Elias Lunsford, condition Lewis appear at October

p.257   court to give evidence in behalf of the state [as above]

Bonds of John Crowson, Isaac Atkins & Samuel Woods, condition they appear Octr Court to give evidence behalf State against John A King.

p.258   William Pillow & Mordecai Pillow v James Lindsey. Eject. Motion of plaintiffs attorney, suit dismissed; plf recovers agt defendant his costs of suit.

State v Gabriel Joslin. Forgery. Plurias capias issue against defendant.

p.259   David Smith on charge of forgery came not; scire facias issues.

Washington L G Foley recognizance for appearance of David Smith today but brought him not. Scire facias issue against Foley returnable to next term.

p.260   John Elliott recognizance for appearance of David Smith[as above]

State v Robert Paine. Appeal. Suit continued till next term of this court.

State v Charles Payne. Not attending agreeably to recognizance to give evidence against John A King. Sheriff returned second writ/scire facias that deft is

p.261   not found; dft came not. State granted execution agt dft for sum of $1000, the amount of recognizance together with costs in serving out sd scire facias.

State v Lewis Payne. For appearance of Chas Payne as witness behalf State

p.262   against John A King. Sheriff returned second writ/scire facias, dft not found. State granted execution against defendant $1000 and costs.

State v Jessee Vincent. For not bringing Lewis Payne agreeably to recognizance. Second writ; dft not found; State granted execution agt dft $500 & costs.

p.263   State v Lewis Payne. Not giving evidence against John A King. Exn granted.

p.264   State v Jessee Vincent. Not bringing Charles Payne to give evidence behalf

p.265   State against John A King. Execution granted for $1000 & costs.

Deed Commrs/Pulaski to William W Crittinton lot 76 ackd.

Deed Commrs/Pulaski to Matthew Cunningham lot 9 ackd.

p.266   Deed/gift Larken Cleveland to German Wright Lester proved by Alexr Jones.

State v William Ball. Appeal. Suit continued.

Bond of William Ball $300 condition he appear at next term of this court.

p.267   Bond of Nathaniel Moody $300, condition Wm Ball appear at next term.

p.268   Bond of Nathaniel Almon $100, to appear at next term to give evidence in behalf State against William Ball.

Bonds of William Mayfield, Reuben Smith, John Evans, Peggy Henry, Isabella Henry, $50 each, condition they appear at next term to give evidence in behalf of

p.269   State against David Smith.

Account of Joel T Rivers jailer of Williamson County for keeping of George Shawley $42.25; Shawley deemed insolvent.

p.270   Account of Maxamilian H Buchanan sheriff of this county for conveyance of

136

APRIL 1815

George Shawley & John A King to jail allowed for $23.69½.

Account of sundry persons serving as a guard in conveying George Shawley &
John A King to jail agreeably to order of this court, and for quartering during sd
term, allowed for sum of $44.02½.

p.271 John Kelso v William Ball. Debt. Juror withdrawn; jury discharged.

Spencer Roach v Hugh Gibson. Deposition of Richard Tutt in Christian County
p.272 Kentucky to be taken in behalf defendant. Also granted leave to take the
Note upon which this action is founded which is now filed in the Clerks office.

Court adjourned till tomorrow morning 8 Oclock.   Archibald Roane

p.273 Thursday April 13th 1815. Present the honorable Archibald Roane, Judge.

State v Nancy Coventon. Horse stealing. Jury sworn yesterday find Nancy
Coventon guilty.

p.274 Account of David Campbell jailer of Maury County for boarding Nancy
Coventon whilst confined for $89.50 is allowed.

William Magell, Lawson Hobson, Odell Garrett bound for appearance of
William Magell at this court; recognizance forfeited; scire facias issued.

p.275 State v Reuben Menifee. Certiorari. Dismissed.

Francis Adams v James Coursey. Appeal. Postponed until next term.

Gabriel Bumpass v Nelson Patteson. Appeal. Jury Hardy Hightower, Arthur
Hicks, Chas Buford, Robt McNairy, Wm F Cunningham, Mattw Den, Thos B Haynie, Mattw
Cunningham, Zacheus Hurt, John Keenan, Lester Morris, Saml Pearson. Plf recovers
p.276 agt dft damages $30 & costs of suit.

Grand Jury indictment agt Nancy Boner, true bill. James Dugger, Jarrett
Menifee, Thomas Harwood, James Bumpass four of sd jurors were discharged.

p.277 Appearance bond of John McCabe $500, to appear next term to prosecute Nancy
Boner on charge of perjury.

State v William McCabe, Thomas Johnson & Alexander Angus. Burg. Capias
issues against sd defendants returnable to next term of this court.

State v Charles Simpson. Riot. Dft in proper person; counsel for state no
p.278 further prosecutes; defendant is discharged from his recognizance.

State v William B Brooks. A&B on Washington Croft. Sd William in proper
person. Jury Jarratt Menifee, Jas McDonald, Saml Shields, Pleasant Moore, James
Dugger, Wm Mayfield, Nathl Moody, Jno Montgomery, Wm McDonald, John Clark, Marcus
p.279 Mitchel, John McCracken find dft guilty in second count and not guilty in
first court. Dft fined $1 besides costs.

Court adjourned till tomorrow morning 9 oclock.   Archibald Roane

p.280 Friday April 14th 1815. Present the honorable Archibald Roane, Judge.

State v William B Brooks. A&B on Washington Croft. Allow witnesses for
State the pay for one days attendance Octr term and two days at this term.

Nancy Boner, bound in recognizance to appear, made default. Scire facias
p.281 issues against her returnable to next term of this court.

Elias Lunsford bound $500 for appearance of Nancy Boner brought her not &
thereby forfeits his recognizance; scire facias issue.

Joseph Johns bound in recognizance $500 for appearance of Nancy Boner
brought her not; forfeits his recognizance; scire facias issue.

p.282 William Ball v Henry Scales. Appeal. Dft in proper person cannot gainsay

137

APRIL 1815

plfs action but that he doth owe $17.21¼ being the judgment of the court below besides costs. Plaintiff recovers against defendant and Nathan Davis his security also $1.73 the amount on judgment of court below at 12½ percent.

p.283   Deed, Commrs/Pulaski to John McCrackin lots 134 & 155 ackd.

John Dewaaser v Peter Fuquay. Ejectment. Alias Capias issues against defendant returnable to next October term.

State vs William Kile. Garnishment. Sheriff returned writ agt John Bryant, no property found; he garnisheed William Kile to appear this day to declare what p.284   property he had belonging to John Bryant; sd Wm came not. Sci fa issue.

Henry Scales v Bernard M Patteson. Appeal. Continued to October term. Jury discharged from further attendance.

Tyree Rodes v William Horn. Case. Suit dismissed, death of defendant having p.285   been suggested; plaintiff pays costs incurred.

Archibald Alexander v John Paul. Case. Suit dismissed by order of plaintiff who also pays costs.

John McCabe v John Taylor & Samuel Black. Eqty. Complainant by atty; dfts are not inhabitants of this State; ordinary process of this court cannot be served on them. Publication to be made in Nashville Whig commanding defendants John Taylor p.286   & Samuel Black to appear October next.

Tyree Rodes v Daniel T [blot.--ods]. Eqty. Dft summoned but came not. Trial next term of this court.

Henry Scales v Bernard M Patteson. Appeal. Parties in proper persons. Cause p.287   refered to determination of James Paine, Wm B Brooks, Jas Buford, Wm Wells at house of William Ball in Pulaski.

John A King v Charles Payne & Jessee Vincent. Eqty. Jessee Vincent is not p.288   an inhabitant of this State; order publication in Nashville Whig requiring Jesse Vincent to appear at next term of this court.

Bond of John Romack $300 condition he appear at Maury Circuit Court in October next to answer a change of Bigamy against him.

Bond of Henry Hagen & John Kenan $100 each condition John Romack appear at p.289   Circuit Court in Maury in October next to answer charge of Bigamy.

State v Nancy Coventon. Horse stealing. Dfts motion for arrest of judgment p.290   overruled; sd Nancy to be imprisoned six months & stand in the pillory two hours on 18th 19th & 20th May next between three & seven oclock in the afternoon & on the last day receive five lashes & be branded on the thumb of the left hand with the letters H T and that she pay costs. Sd Nancy is insolvant. Judgments entered p.291   against the county for costs of prosecution and claims of claimants.

Account of Isaac Smith for boarding John Romack & Nancy Coventon for $24 allowed.

Court adjourned till court in course.   Archibald Roane

p.292   Circuit Court for Giles County, Tuesday 10th October 1815, at the Courthouse in Pulaski. Present the Honorable William Kelly, Judge.

Leonard Brown v Nelson Patteson. Case. Cause postponed to next term; motion of dft by atty, order depositions be taken of William A Smith who is lying sick and William Ball who is about to leave the State.

138

p.293 John Paul v Kinchin F Wilkinson. Appeal. Judgment of court below
p.294 is in all things affirmed & plf recovers agt dft & Henry Hagen & Thomas Smith his securities $30.66½ judgment, $1.27½, and his costs.

Francis Adams v James Coursey. Writ/Error. Plf failing to appear, he is nonsuited; dft recovers agt plf his costs in court below as in this behalf.

p.295 Spencer Roach v Hugh Gibson. Certiorari. Jury Robert Paine Robt Buchanan Thos Steele Drury Allsup Wm Neel, Alexr Black Saml Y Anderson, Nelson Patteson, Wm Mayfield, Walter Locke, Wm Pickins, Robt Reed. Plf recovers agt dft & Charles Dever
p.296 his security $11.31¼ & his costs in court below & in this behalf.

Constable Jeremiah Parker exempted from further attendance this term.

John Den lessee of John Dewaaser v Joseph Johns. Ejectment. Postponed.
p.297 Jonathan Richards v Philmer Green. Appeal. Continued to next term.

Harvey Johns v John McCabe. Appeal. It was omitted to enter judgment on verdict of jury previously found, plf recovers agt dft & Nathaniel Moody & Richard Mcall his securities $107 damages assessed by jury at April term 1814 & costs.
p.298 John Kelso v William Ball. Debt. Postponed till next term. Depositions of William Routon, Wm White, Josiah Perkinson & Jno Chaffin of Prince Edward county Virginia at James Town & James Murphy, Wm H Cabal, Nelson Anderson & Stephen Watts of Amherst county Virginia at town of Warminster to be taken by justices.
p.299 Deed Joel Lewis to Thomas Meredith 847 acres proven by Daniel T Woods, same having been previously proven by Alfred Balch the other subscribing witness.

Nancy Odell v Benjamin Nail. Appeal. Postponed on affidavit of plaintiff.

John A King v Charles Payne & Jesse Vincent. Equity. On motion of complain-
p.300 ant's counsel, order bill dismissed as to defendant Payne.

Deed commissioners of Pulaski to Thomas Haynes lot 122 proven by Alfred M Harris & German Lester.
p.301 Deed commrs of Pulaski to Thomas Haynes lot 123 proven [as above]

Alfred M Harris v William G Corlen. Equity. Dft not inhabitant of this
p.302 State; publication to be made three weeks in Western Chronicle in Columbia requiring William G Corlen to appear at next term of this court in April next.

Tyre Rodes v Daniel T Woods. Equity. Bill charges complainant made contract
p.303 with dft & Gideon Pillow to convey by quit claim to dft & Pillow 333½ acres in Giles Co being part of 5000 acres granted to William Shepherd & Joseph Philips, beginning at Daniel Woods's NE corner...sd dft hath not paid the note; judgment obtained in County Court August 1813 for $82.84 debt and $6.62½ damages and $7.99 costs which remains wholly unpaid. Dft hath sold sd land to W G L Foley and put
p.304 Foley in possession of same. Dft to pay before January next $89.46½ and interest thereon at 6 per cent from last day August 1813 till paid together with costs in this and county court; complainant is thereupon to execute deed to dft. If Dft fails to pay, sheriff to advertize land and sell to highest bidder. Where-
p.305 upon complainant shall execute to purchaser title to sd land.

Court adjourned till tomorrow 9 oclock.   Wm Kelly

p.306 Wednesday October 11th 1815. Present the Honorable William Kelly, Judge.

Jonathan Richards v Philmer Green. Appeal. Deposition of Sampson McCown & Reuben Smith who are about to leave the state are to be taken at house of Isaac Smith in Pulaski in behalf defendant.
p.307 Exempt juror William Mayfield from farther attendance at this term.

Exempt juror John Jones from farther attendance at this term.

Jurors: William H Ragsdale, Humphry Tomkins, Aquilla Wilson, Wm Price, Robt Paine, Robt Buchanan, Thos Steele, Willis S McLaurin, Wm Maples, Drury Allsup, Wm Neel, Alexr Black, Ralph Graves, John Philips, Saml Y Anderson, Nelson Patteson, Wm Mayfield, Jno Dickey, Walter Lock, Joel Byler, Alexr Miller, Wm Perkins, Jno Jones. p.310[pages missing or misnumbered] State v Gabriel Joslin. Forgery. Order Plurias capias issue agt dft to Williamson County returnable to next term this court.

State v John A King. Passing counterfeit bank note. Counsel for State no further prosecutes. Dft discharged.

p.311　State v Charles Simpson & William Magill. Riot. Counsel for State no further prosecutes; dfts discharged.

p.312　State v Robert Paine. Appeal. Dft in proper person. Jury William Neel, Saml Cox, Augustine Carter, Saml Chambers, Wm Rose, Isaac Atkins, Richd Bently, William Graves, Thomas McKissack, Jessee Kirkland, William Lyon, Robert McLaurin.

p.313　Alexander Jones v Mary Heym[Heyrn?] Jones. Divorce. Dft came not.

Account of Maximilian H Buchanan sheriff for finding guard & conveying John Bryant (who was convicted for passing counterfeit money) to jail in Columbia for $11.84 is allowed.

p.315[page is misnumbered]　　　Grand Jury indictment against Brice M Mayfield, true bill; against Isaac Mayfield, true bill.

Elizabeth Stogdon v Benjamin Stogdon. Divorce. Elizabeth by counsel; Benjamin came not.

Court adjourned till tomorrow morning 9 oclock.　　　　　Wm Kelly

p.316　Thursday 12th October 1815. Present the Honorable William Kelly, Judge.

Appearance bond of Thos Goff, assault on Jno Dewaaser & malicious mischief. Bond of Wm Crittenton & Nathan Davis, condition the appearance at next term

p.317　of Thomas Goff for assault on John Dewaaser.

State v Nancy Boner. Not appearing Apl term 1815. Alias scire facias issue.

p.318　Alexander Jones v Mary Heyrn Jones. Divorce. Alexr by atty; Mary came not.

Elizabeth Stogdon v Benjamin Stogdon. Divorce. Elizabeth by attorney; Benjamin came not.

Appearance bond of William McCabe, Thomas Johnson & Alexander Angus condi-

p.319　tion they attend from day to day at this term.

Hugh McCabe, John McCabe, Daniel Allen, James Angus bond, condition Wm McCabe, Thomas Johnson, Alexander Angus appear day to day at this term.

Bond of John Dewaaser, condition he appear at next term to give evidence

p.320　against Thomas Goff for breach of peace by committing assault.

State v Washington G L Foley. Not bringing David Smith at Octr 1814 term. Exonerated from forfeiture but pay costs of scire facias.

Deed commissioners of Pulaski to heirs of Somersett Moore decd lots 148,

p.321　149, 78, 79 in Pulaski ackd.

State v Robert Paine. Appeal. One of jurors sworn yesterday is withdrawn and the rest of the jurors discharged.

State v William McCabe, Thomas Johnson, Richard H Allen, Alexander Angus.

p.322　Burglary. Jury Robt Buchanan, Enoch Byrant, Bernard M Patteson, Wm Brown, Thos Smith, John Thompson, John Birdwell, Wm Strawn, Isaac Reynolds Junr, Joseph

p.323　Johns, Nathan Davis. Defendants acquitted of charge.

State v David Smith. Not appearing Octr 1814. Alias scire facias issue.

p.324　State v Nancy Boner. Not appearing April term. Alias scire facias issue.

OCTOBER 1815

State v Elias Lunsford. Not bringing Nancy Boner agreeably to recognizance.
Alias scire facias issue against defendant returnable to next April term.
Court adjourned till tomorrow morning 9 oclock.   Wm Kelly

p.326   Friday October 12th 1815. Present the Honorable William Kelly, Judge.
        State v Nancy Boner. Perjury. Alias Capias issue against defendant.
        John McCabe v John Taylor & Samuel Black. Equity. Dfts not inhabitants of
this State, order order publication in Western Chronicle in Columbia requiring dfts
p.327   to appear at next term of this court in April next.
        Alexander Jones v Mary Hyrn Jones. Divorce. Alexr Jones by atty; Mary Hern
Jones came not. Order Alias subpoena issue agt Mary, & further that publication be
p.328   made in Western Chronicle in Columbia requiring Mary to appear & answer
petition of sd Alexander.
        Elizabeth Stogdon v Benjamin Stogdon. Divorce. Order Alias subpoena issue
agt sd Benjn returnable to next April term & publication in Western Chronicle requiring sd Benjamin to appear at next term of this court.
p.329   State v William Kile. Garnishment. Dft came not. Scire facias was made
known to dft; therefore State to have execution agt dft for $10 & $16.46½ & costs.
p.330   John Kelso v William Ball. Debt. Deposition of James Dick in Richmond
Virginia to be taken in benefit of plaintiff.
        John Den lessee of John Dewaaser v Joseph Johns. Ejectment. Deposition of
Kasper Mansco of Davidson County an infirm witness to be taken & read in evidence
in behalf plaintiff.
p.331   State v Daniel T Woods. Appeal. Dft in proper person. Jury John Philips,
Robt Buchanan, Francis Hicks, Enoch Bryant, Elisha Mayfield, John Reed, Isaac
Mayfield, Lester Morris, Green McCafferty, James H Williams, Gray H Edwards, James
p.332   L Hendry find dft guilty. Dft forever hereafter incapable of holding any
office or appointment in this government whether of honor or profit, shall be
incapable of giving testimony in any court of record, or serving as a juror, and he
to pay costs of this prosecution as well in court below as in this behalf expended.
        State v William Magill, Loson Hobson, Odell Garrett. Nonappearance of sd Wm
Magill at April term. Defendants exonerated from forfeiture but pay costs.
p.333   State v Joseph Johns. Not bringing Nancy Boner at April term. Dft exonerated from payment of forfeiture, pay costs of scire facias.
        State v Brice M Mayfield. Feloniously stabing. Jury Wm Neel, John Philips,
p.334   Nathan Davis, Charles C Bailey, Saml Chambers, Francis Hicks, Enoch Bryant,
John Reed, Green McCafferty, James H Williams, Gray H Edwards, James L Hendry. Dft
p.335   acquited of charge; prosecutor pays costs of this prosecution.
        Discharge juror Thomas Steele from further attendance at this term.
        State v John Kerby[Kerley?] A&B on Brice M Mayfield. Cause removed from
docket, this court having no jurisdiction of the case. John Kerby bound in recognizance to appear at the December county court for Giles County to answer a charge of
p.336   assault and battery.
        Bond of William M Kerby & John Walthel for appearance of John Kerby at next
p.337   County court for Giles for breach of peace by A&B on Brice M Mayfield.
        Brice M Mayfield recognizance, to prosecute in behalf State against John
Kirby in county court for Giles County December next.
p.338   William Crittenton recognizance [worded as above]
        Henry Scales v Bernard M Patteson. Appeal. Award of referees: convened at

p.339 house of William Ball in Pulaski; decision: Bernard M Patteson is to pay
Henry Scales $20 & costs; Jas Paine, James Buford, William B Brooks, William Wells.
Court adjourned till tomorrow morning 9 oclock. Wm Kelly

p.340 Saturday 14th October 1815. Present the Honorable William Kelly, Judge.
State v Brice M Mayfield. Feloniously stabing. Judgment entered yesterday
against John Kirby prosecutor for cost of prosecution. Sd order is rescinded.
Account of M H Buchanan sheriff of this county for persons guarding John A
p.341 King & George Shawley for $3 is allowed.
State v William Ball. Assault on Nathaniel Almon. Dft came not & thereby
forfeited his recognizance. Scire facias issue agt dft returnable to next term.
Green McCafferty stands in recognizance for appearance of William Ball at
p.342 this term brought him not, whereby he forfeited his recognizance.
Zacheus Hurt bound in recognizance for appearance of Wm Ball [as above].
John Den lessee of William Shepherd v James Tinnen. Ejectment. Defendant
p.343 came not. Plf recovers agt dft his term yet to come and recover against dft
in possession of the premises his costs about his suit expended.
Zacheus Hurt by counsel exhibited Bill/Injunction to stay proceeding on
judgment obtained by John Boyd against sd Zacheus in Giles County Court for $76
p.344 debt & damages with costs of suit. Writs/Injunction & subpoena issue upon
complainants giving bond & security.
State v Isaac Mayfield. A&B with intention to kill. Jury Humphry Tompkins,
p.345 Aquilla Wilson, Robt Buchanan, Drury Allsup, Wm Neel, Alexr Black, Saml Y
Anderson, John Dickey, Walter Lock, Wm Pickins, Robt Reed, John Knox say dft is
guilty of A&B but not with an intention to kill as in Indictment alledged. Court
has no jurisdiction of the offence whereof dft is found guilty, he is discharged.
p.346 John Page v James Terrel. Case. Plf came not. Plf is nonsuited; defendant
recovers agt plf his costs about his defence expended.
Court adjourned till court in course. Wm Kelly

p.347 Circuit Court for Giles County, april 8th 1816. Present the Honorable
Bennett Searcy, Judge.
Exempt Tyree Rodes from serving as a Juror this term.
David Craighead gent took oaths; is admitted to practice law in this court.
Jurors summoned: John Henderson, John Dabney, John C Walker, James Leach,
p.348 Alexr Thompson, Thos K Gordon, Oliver C Cleveland, Thomas Lane, Geo Malone,
Wm Cook, John Laird, Daniel Allen, Joseph Rea, John Hillhouse, John Dickey, Jacob
Byler, Buckner Harwell, Wm Brown esqr, Willis S McLaurine, James Dugger, James Mc-
Donald, Tyree Rodes, Robert Oliver, Hardy Hightower.
Grand Jurors: James Leach, John Hillhouse, Joseph Rea, Oliver C Cleveland,
William Cook, Thomas Lane, Thomas K Gordon, Willis S McLaurine, George Malone, John
Dabney, Buckner Harwell, James Dugger, Jacob Byler.
Bill/sale Zacheus Hurt to Edmond J Bailey four Negroes proved by Alfred M
Harris. Bill/sale Zacheus Hurt to Edmond J Bailey two Negroes proven by Alfred M
Harris.

APRIL 1816

p.349 Bill/sale Zacheus Hurt to Edmond J Bailey one Negro boy proven by Alfred M Harris.

Jonathan Richards v Philmer Green. Appeal. Jury John Dickey, James McDonald, John Philips, William Woods, Thomas Wilkinson, Robert Anderson, James
p.350 Agnew, Jason Hopkins, Robert McNairy, David Reed, Thomas H Meridith, Daniel Baker adjourned untill tomorrow.

Court adjourned till tomorrow morning 10 oclock.   B Searcy

p.351 Tuesday 9th April 1816. Present the Honorable Bennett Searcy, Judge.

Kinchon McVey to attend as constable in room of William R Davis who is not able to attend at this term.

Deed Commrs of Pulaski to Elisha Eldridge & Shadrack Nye lots 70 & 71 ackd.
p.352 Deed Commrs of Pulaski to German Lester lot 32 ackd.

Deed Commrs of Pulaski to William Fullerton lots 179 and 183 ackd.

Bill/sale David McMican to Gabriel Bumpass two Negroes proven by Andrew McMican.

Grand Jury bill/Indictment against William Magill a true bill.
p.353 John Walker v Edmond J Bailey. Appeal. Judgment of court below is affirmed, plf recovers agt dft and Thomas K Gordon & Thomas McKissack his securities the
p.354 judgment afsd together with his costs in court below and in this behalf.

Jonathan Richards v Philmer Green. Appeal. Jury not having agreed in their verdict, were adjourned till tomorrow.

Court adjourned till tomorrow morning 10 oclock.   B Searcy

p.355 Wednesday 10th April 1816. Present the Honorable Bennett Searcy, Judge.

Henry Roberts v Zacheus Hurt. Appeal. Considered by Court that the judgment
p.356 the court below be in all things affirmed and that the plaintiff recover against the dft & Archibald Alexander & William F Cunningham his securities $195.28 judgment with $7.79½ damages by delay & his costs in court below & this behalf.
p.357 State v Gabriel Joslin. Forgery. Plurias capias issue agt dft to Williamson County returnable to next term of this court.

Bond of William Brown, condition he appear at next term of this court to give evidence in behalf state against Gabriel Joslin on charge of forgery.
p.358 State v David Smith. Not appearing at October term 1814. Sheriff returned second writ that dft was not found. Dft came not. Execution granted to State for $100 the amount of his recognizance & the costs incurred.

State v Elias Lunsford. Not bringing Nancy Boner to April 1815 term. Dft
p.359 not found; & came not. Execution granted State for $500, his recognizance.

State v Robert Paine. Appeal. Dft in proper person. Dft's motion to dismiss appeal. Judgment of court below in all things affirmed, prosecutor Washington Croft to pay costs in court below.
p.360 Deed Commissioners of Pulaski to Robert Buchanan lot 19 ackd.

Deed Commissioners of Pulaski to Micajah Ezell lot 9 ackd.

Deed Commissioners of Pulaski to Dudley Smith lot 18 ackd.
p.361 Jonathan Richards v Philmer Green. Appeal. A juror withdrawn and rest of jurors discharged.

Levi Fugate bond $500 condition he attend from day to day this term to give evidence in behalf State against William Magill on charge of Murder.

143

APRIL 1816

p.362   Jane K Terrell v John Romack. Divorce. Jane by attorney; John came not.
       State v Thomas Goff. Appeal; indictment for assault on John Dewaaser.
Defendant in proper person pleaded not guilty. Jury John Anderson, James Simmons,
James Buford, William B Brooks, Wm Bratton, Nicholas Jackson, Payton Herring, Dudly
Smith, Micajah Ezell, William Ezell, Richard Johnston, William Brown.
p.363   Order Court adjourned till tomorrow morning 10 oclock.   B Searcy

p.364   Thursday 11th April 1816. Present the Honorable Bennett Searcy, Judge.
       State v William Magill. Murder. William Magill yeoman to the bar in custody
of sheriff and upon arraignment pleaded Not guilty. Change of venue ordered to next
p.365   Circuit Court held for Maury County.
       State v Levi Fugate. Murder. Order Giles County pay the several claimants
in this case all costs to which they are entitled.
       Bond of Peggy Simpson, condition she appear at next Circuit Court for Maury
county to give evidence in behalf State against William Magill on charge of murder.
p.366   Betsey Garrett, Susan McKissack, Wm Hendry, Arthur Hicks, Jonathan Berry,
Wm C Mayfield, John McKissack, Levi Fugate, Jas Stuart, Nathan Garrett, Robt Reed,
Charley Devers, Mary Dever, William M Kerby[Kerley?], German Lester, Tobias Miller,
John M Hobson, recognizance $500 each, to appear at next Circuit Court Maury Court-
house to give evidence in behalf State against William Magill charge of murder.
       Order accounts of Jonathan Berry, David Campbell, Jno Buchanan, Jas Stew-
art, Wm Hendry, Jno Dickey, Martha Magill, Polly Black, witnesses behalf State agt
p.367   Levi Fugate to be certified.
       Jane K Terrell v John Romack. Divorce. Jane by attorney; John came not.
Grant Jane leave to assume name of Romack which she had omitted in her petition.
       Bond of Thomas Goff & John Fulks, condition Thomas Goff appear at next term
p.368   term to answer charge against him of malicious mischief.
       John Dewaaser & William Dewaaser bond, condition they appear at Octr court
to give evidence against Thomas Goff for malicious mischief.
p.369   State v Thomas Gooff. Assault on John Dewaaser. Jury sworn yesterday say
dft is guilty. Motion of defendant for new trial.
       State v William Ball. Assault on Nathaniel Almon. William Ball in proper
p.370   person; State no further prosecutes; dft assumes costs of prosecution.
       State agt John Bryant. Fornication. John Bryant in proper person saith he
p.371   is guilty. Fined $2.50 and pays costs of prosecution.
       State against Jelly Pemberton. Fornication. Dft in proper person saith she
p.372   is guilty. Fined $2.50 and costs of this prosecution.
       State against William Ball. For not appearing last Octr term. Dft in proper
p.373   person tendered excuse for not attending; dft exonerated from payment of
forfeiture and that he pay costs of this scire facias.
       John McCabe against John Taylor and Samuel Black. Equity. Defendants not
appearing, set hearing ex parte at next term of this court.
p.374   Account of Peter Satterfield & John Anderson for guarding George Shawley
whilst a prisoner in Pulaski $1 each allowed.
       Grand Jury all but William Cook return indictment against William Magill, a
true bill, and withdrew.
       Thomas Wilkinson against Nelson Patteson. Appeal. Jury Daniel Allen, Robt
Bigham, Alexr Tarply, Robt Anderson, Joseph Johns, Adam Burney, Isaac Mayfield,
Major Haralson, James McDonald, John Kenan, Wm B Brooks, Wm W Crittinton adjourned

144

until tomorrow.

p.375   Alexander Jones against Mary Hyrn Jones. Divorce. Decreed by court that Bonds of matrimony existing between sd Alexander Jones & sd Mary Hyrn be entirely dissolved, and sd Alexander Jones recover against sd Mary Hyrn Jones his costs by him about his writ in this behalf expended.

p.376   Court adjourned till tomorrow morning 10 oclock.   B Searcy

p.377   Friday 12th April 1816. Present the Honorable Bennett Searcy, Judge.

Jane K Terrell otherwise called Jane K Romack against John Romack. Divorce. Petitioner by counsel; John came not. Order Alias subpoena against sd John Romack issue returnable to next term of this court to answer petition of sd Jane; other-
p.378   wise Court will proceed to hearing of sd petition ex parte.

Archibald McKissack recognizance, to give evidence in behalf State against William Magill in a charge of murder.

Daniel T Woods against Joseph Johns. Covt. Plf in proper person saith he
p.379   will not further prosecute. Dft recovers agt plf his costs of defence.

Thomas Wilkinson agt Nelson Patteson. Appeal. Plaintiff failing to prose-cute, plf nonsuited and dft recovers against plaintiff his costs of defence.

Account of David W Porter a witness in behalf State against Levi Fugate in Columbia allowed $3 and certified accordingly.

p.380   Deed George Coalter to John and Joseph Hodge lot[number blank] in Pulaski proven by Alfred M Harris and Robert Mack.

Elizabeth Stogdon by her friend against Benjamin Stogdon. Divorce. Peti-tioner by attorney. Opinion of court that facts stated in petition charging sd Ben-
p.381   jamin with acts inconsistant to matrimonial vows by wilful desertion & ab-sence without reasonable excuse for two years & upwards together with other facts, & sd Benjamin not appearing, decreed bonds of matrimony between Elizabeth Stogdon & Benjamin Stogdon be annulled, and sd Elizabeth Stogdon be divorced from bonds of matrimony, and that James Paine, Wm B Brooks, Robt Buchanan proceed to divide such
p.382   property now in possession of sd Elizabeth Stogdon which belongs to Benja-min Stogdon for her as her own right against claim of sd Benjamin; Micajah Ezell will pay the costs of this petition.

Leonard Brown against Nelson Patteson. Case. Jury Wilton F L Jenkins, Caleb White, Parks Bailey, Ambros Cobb, Jas McDonald, Robt Oliver, William B Brooks, Jno Dickey, Jno Birdwell, Saml Newton, John Webb, Jas Moore. Motion of plf; grant leave
p.383   to amend his declaration by erasing word James and inserting John; Juror withdrawn and jury discharged; trial continued to next term of this court.

Discharge juror James McDonald from further attendance at this term.

William C Oneal against Gideon Pillow. Cer. Grant plfs motion to dismiss
p.384   certiorari; plf recovers agt dft his costs in this behalf expended.

Nelson Patteson against Charles Smith & Josiah Alderson. Injunction bill. Injunction of complainant dissolved, but before dft have his execution at law agt complainant, further order dft give bond and security.

p.385   Edward O Chambers against John Boyd. Injunct bill. Complainant's injunction dissolved; before dft have execution at law agt complainant, order dft give bond & security. Otherwise to remain in full force against him & his securities.

p.386   Leonard Brown agt Riley Finny. Not attending as witness. Suit dismissed.

Order court adjourned till tomorrow morning 10 oclock.   B Searcy

APRIL 1816

p.387   Joseph Hankins recognizance, condition he appear next Circuit Court for
Maury County to give evidence behalf State against William Magill on charge murder.
        John A King against Charles Paine & Jessee Vincent. Equity. Decreed by
p.388   court that dft within two months give to complainant sd Negro girl Lucy and
surrender to complainant sd Bill of Sale and complainant pay dft $39 with interest
from fourteenth day of April 1814 till paid; if dft fail to deliver girl & bill of
sale, dft shall pay complainant $350 with interest; complainant pay costs in first
p.389   instance, & recover same of Jessee Vincent and have execution for same.
        Alfred M Harris agt William G Corlew[Corlen?]. Equity. Publication made
agreeably to statute, dft not appearing, hearing ex parte at next term this court.
        Grand Jury returned presentment agt William Lyon & others, same against
Nathaniel Moody, same against Rollin Tankesly same agt Henry Hagen, and withdrew.
p.390   State against Thomas Goff. Assault on John Dewaaser. Dfts cause for new
trial argued; not sufficient cause shewn. Dft fined $2 and pay costs of prosecution
as well in court below as in this behalf expended.
        John Den lessee of John Dewaaser against Joseph Johns. Ejectment. Order
order of last term awarding commission for plf to take deposition of Kasper Mansco
p.391   be renewed & directed to two Justices of peace in Sumner County.
        Grand Jury returned bills/indictment The State against Henry Hester a true
bill; same against Rollin Tankesly true bill; same against Benjamin Tut a true
bill; same agt Joseph Straughan true bill; same agt Balaam Straughan true bill;
same agt Henry Hagen true bill; same agt William Straughan true bill; same against
Nathaniel Moody true bill; same agt John A Dewaady true bill; and having nothing
further to present were discharged from further attendance.
        Order process issue against several persons against whom Grand Jury have
bound Bills/Indictment returnable to next term.
p.392   State against Orpha Black. Indictment. Orpha Black indicted for forcibly
carrying &c. Jury John Walker, Wm Henderson, John Coleman, Henry Roberts, John
Yancy, John Thompson, Richard B Walthal, Joseph McKerley, Samuel Y Anderson, Samuel
H Dotson, John Edwards, Samuel Pearson find dft guilty. Dfts atty moved to arrest
p.393   judgment. Motion overruled; dft fined $5 and costs of prosecution.
        Tobias Miller, Henry Hagen, John Guthrie, David Philips, recognizance, to
p.394   appear next term & give evidence behalf State against Nathaniel Moody &
others for unlawful gaming.
        Deed Commrs of Pulaski to Marckus Mitchell for lots 89 & 91 ackd.
        Order Sheriff of Giles County reconvey William Magill indicted of murder
back to jail in Maury County, and that jailer of sd jail receive sd Magill. Fur-
p.395   ther, if he be acquited of sd offence, that he be committed to custody of
sheriff of Giles County to give bail for appearance to answer charge of forgery.
        John Black & Orpha his wife bond, condition sd Orpha Black appear at next
Circuit Court holden for Maury County & give evidence behalf State agt William
p.396   Magill on a charge of murder.
        Order petit jury be dismissed.
        Leonard Brown against Nelson Patteson. Case. Renew order to take deposition
of William Ball in behalf defendant.
        Court adjourned till Court in course.   B Searcy

OCTOBER 1816

p.397 Circuit Court for Giles County at the Courthouse in Pulaski on 14th October 1816. Present the honorable Thomas Stuart, Judge.

Bill/sale Jane Allison to Jacob Templin and German Lester for a negro man Daniel proven by Nathaniel Almon & Harris Johnson.

Exempt Peter Swanson & Jarrat Menefee from further attendance at this term.

p.398 Jurors: John Dickey, Robt Buchanan, Jas Bumpass, Wm Brown, Jarrat Menefee, Arthur Hicks, Robt Oliver, Jno C Walker, Jno Henderson, Tyree Rodes, Saml Shields, Peter Swanson, Wm Henderson, Alexr Black, Wm Mayfield, Wm M Marr, Thos Welch, Danl Allen, James Cook, Duncan McIntire, Hardy Hightower, Thomas Harwood, Alexander Thompson, Britton Yarbrough.

Grand Jury: Tyree Rodes foreman, Robt Buchanan, Wm Henderson, Jas Bumpass, Samuel Shields, Thomas Welch, Alexander Black, William Brown, John C Walker, John Dickey, James Cook, Hardy Hightower, Arthur Hicks.

p.399 John Kelso agt William Ball. Debt. Continued untill next term.

Jonathan Richards against Philmer Green. Appeal. Continued until next term.

Nancy Odell against Benjamin Nail. Appeal. Suit dismissed, each party pays half the costs agreeably to their agreement.

p.400 Amy Custis against William Magill. Case. Plaintiff came not. Non suit; dft recovers against plaintiff his costs about his defence expended.

James Maxwell against Mary Maxwells administrators. Appeal. Postponed.

p.401 William Kelly & Tryon M Yancy gentlemen took oath of attorney and are admitted to practice as such.

Deed Commissioners of Pulaski to Francis Campbell lot #63 acknowledged by Tyree Rodes, M H Buchanan & Nathaniel Moody three of the commissioners.

Deed Commrs of Pulaski to James Goldsberry lots 25 & 24 ackd [as above]

p.402 Deed Commrs of Pulaski to Alexander Tarply lot 24 ackd [as above]

Deed Commrs of Pulaski to Allen Abernathy lot 90 ackd [as above]

p.403 Account of the division of property of Benjamin Stogdon now in occupation of Elizabeth Stogdon: Negro man Daniel, black man, 13 cattle, 16 hogs, bed and furniture, kettle, pot, Dutch oven, puter dish, 3 puter basins, tin pan, 6 tin

p.404 cups, 5 knives, 4 forks, 6 doz cups & saucers, 1 flax wheel, plough & gin, 3 weading hoes, 3 axes, 1 pair cotten cards, 1 grid iron, 5 books, 2 water pales, 1 tub. James Paine, William B Brooks, Robert Buchanan.

Thomas Yeatman against William Purnell. Appeal. Judgment of court below in all things affirmed; plf recovers agt dft & James Austin his security $1447.41, and

p.405 $51.70¼ interest, and his costs in court below as in this.

p.406 George Poyzer against William Purnell. Appeal. Plaintiff recovers against defendant & James Austen his security $1165.67 the amount of judgment of the court

p.407 below, with $52.58¾ interest, and his costs in court below as in this.

Leonard Brown against Nelson Patteson. Case. Postponed till next term.

James Tilford against Samuel Day. Case. Postponed till next term.

p.408 James Kimbrough against William Woods & Tyree Rodes. Appeal: Debt. Defendants in proper persons having previously withdrawn their plea, their attorney now begs for leave to put in a new plea; motion overruled. Judgment of court below is affirmed and plf recovers agt dfts & Gideon Pillow & John Porter $374.75 judgment and $16.91¼ interest, and his costs.

p.409 Polly Riddle against William Riddle. Divorce. Polly by atty; Wm came not.

Court adjourned till tomorrow morning 9 oclock. Thos Stuart

147

p.410   Tuesday October 15th 1816. Present the honorable Thomas Stuart, Judge.
Brice M Mayfield against Nathan Davis & Wm M Kerley. Appeal. Continued.
Brice M Mayfield agt Nathan Davis & Wm M Kerley. Appl. Continued.
p.410[again]   Deed Commrs of Pulaski to John Barnett lot #84 acknowledged by
Tyree Rodes, M H Buchanan, Nathaniel Moody three of sd commissioners.
Deed Commrs of Pulaski to John Barnett lot 85 ackd [as above]
Grand Jury Bill/Indictment against Benjamin Rutledge, true bill.
p.410[again]   Excuse juror Daniel Allen from further attendance at this term.
Robert L Cobbs gent took oath of attorney & is admitted to practice.
Account of Jonathan Berry for guarding Levi Fugate allowed, $17.62½.
Dudley Smith against William W Critintun. Appeal. Jury John Henderson,
Britton Yarbrough, Alexr Thompson, Samuel Chambers, Larken Mayfield, Isaac Smith,
p.411   Leonard Brown, Caleb White, Henry Hester, Saml Burney, Richd Bently, Edmond
Shelton say dft assumed as plf declared; further that the demand was from dft & not
from Gabriel Higginbotham, nor was it a property contract as dft alledged. Assess
plfs damage to $75.75 besides costs. Plf recovers sd damages & his costs.
p.412   Court adjourned till to morrow morning 9 oclock.   Thos Stuart

p.413   Wednesday October 16th 1816. Present the honorable Thomas Stuart, Judge.
Leonard Brown agt Nelson Patteson. Case. Deposition of William Cooper in
Mississippi Territory, Russels settlement, to be taken before Major William Russel,
in benefit of plaintiff.
p.414   John S Bailey & wife agt William Cooper & wife. TAB. Suit dismissed by
consent of the plaintiffs; defendant to pay the costs.
Deed Richard Hightower to Alexander McDonald 162 acres ackd.
Sheriff to bring into court Benjamin Rutledge now confined in jail to go
before Grand Jury to give evidence in behalf State against Philip Parchman.
p.415   Discharge Joana Moss who stands bound for appearance at this term.
Juror John White excused from further attendance at this term.
Sheriff of Maury County by Nimrod Porter his deputy brought John Pope and
Benjamin Rutledge who were confined in the Maury County jail, Pope for horse-
stealling and Rutledge for Negro-stealling.
p.416   Grand Jury Bill/Indictment against Philip Parchman, true bill.
Deed Commrs of Pulaski to Samuel Croft lot 92 ackd.
James Levesque, Joel West, Thomas Martindale & Dudly Smith recognizance,
p.417   Levesque $1000, others $500 each, appearance of Levesque this term on
charge of horsestealling.
John Den lessee of John Dewaaser and others against Joseph Johns. Eject.
Order dft as respects the Bighams who were heretofore admitted on demise enter into
p.418   common rule. Jury Alexander Thompson, Jno Henderson, Britton Yarbrough, Jno
Pate, Micajah Ezell, John Tucker, Prior Kile, Andrew Rogers, Joseph H Hodge, Henry
Roberts, Nathl Moody, Augustin Carter find dft guilty; assess plfs damages to one
cent besides costs. Plaintiffs recover against defendant their term yet to come in
the premises together with damages & costs. Writ/Possession awarded plaintiffs.
p.418 [again]   Order William McKinney bound for appearance to answer charge of
assisting in escape of the negro who murdered Mason Moss be discharged.
State against Gabriel Joslin. Forgery. State no further prosecutes. Claim-
p.418 [again]   ants on part of State recover against Giles County their costs.
State against Thomas Goff. Malicious mischief. Thomas in proper person.

148

Jury Wm M Marr, Thos Smith, Wm Ezell, Robt McCulloch, Matthew Anderson, Jno Yancy,
p.419   Nathan Davis, Tobias Miller, Wm Lyon, Henry Brown, John Caldwell, Saml Day
find dft guilty. On Motion of dft by atty, order him to shew cause why a new trial
should be had.
    Polly Riddle against William Riddle. Divorce. Polly by atty; Wm came not.
p.420   Court adjourned till tomorrow morning 8 oclock.   Thos Stuart

p.421   Thursday 17th October 1816. Present the honorable Thomas Stuart, Judge.
Appearance bond of Philip Parchman $1000 to answer charge against him as
accessory in stealing money.
    Bond of Nathaniel Moody, Daniel McIntyre & Drury Joiner, condition Philip
Parchman appear day to day at present term.
p.422   State agt Thomas Goff. Malicious mischief. Dft in proper person; new trial
cannot be had; rule entered yesterday is dismissed. Defendant imprisoned fifteen
minutes and fined $1 and pay costs of prosecution.
p.423   State agt Nancy Boner. Perjury. State no further prosecutes. Case dismissed
& claimants on part of State to receive costs to which they are entitled.
    State v Joseph Straughan. Gaming. Quashed for want of jurisdiction.
p.424   State agt William Magill. Forgery. Capias issue against defendant.
    State v John Pope otherwise called Cornelius Price. Horsestealing. Dft at
bar in custody of sheriff saith he is guilty. Dft to receive on bare back 8 lashes
p.425   & stand in the pillory 2 hours today, Friday, & Saturday, & be branded on
left thumb with letters HT and be imprisoned 15 days and until he pay the costs of
this prosecution; sheriff to proceed with execution of judgment immediately.
    James Maxwell agt Mary Maxwells administrators. Case. Dfts in proper per-
p.426   sons cannot gainsay plfs action against them. Plaintiff recovers against
defendants his damages $150; each party to pay half costs.
    Polly Riddle v William Riddle. Divorce. Polly by her attorney; William came
p.427   not. Alias subpoena issue agt Wm & publication made in Western Chronicle of
Columbia for four weeks requiring sd William to appear at next term to answer petition of sd Polly; otherwise court will proceed to hearing of sd petition.
    Deed commissioners of Pulaski to Alfred M Harris lot 7 ackd by Tyree Rodes,
Nathaniel Moody and M H Buchanan three of sd commissioners.
p.428   Deed Commrs of Pulaski to German Lester lots 128 & 129 ackd [as above]
    Deed Commrs/Pulaski to Barnustra[?] Hatchett lot 30 ackd [as above]
    Deed Commrs of Pulaski to Wm Ball lots 177 & 178 ackd [as above]
p.429   State v Benjamin Rutledge. Tempting slave to leave his masters service with
intent to send him out of the State. Order change of venue to next Circuit Court of
p.430   Maury County; defendant to be remanded.
    Henry Brown recognizance; to appear at next Maury Circuit Court to give
p.431   evidence in behalf State against Benjamin Rutledge.
    Joseph Dearing, John G Fowlkes, Peter Lyon, John Hilhouse, Joseph Rea,
Burrel H Peeples recognizance, to appear Maury Circuit Court to give evidence in
behalf State against Benjamin Rutledge.
p.432   State against Philip Parchman. Larceny. Philip Parchman yeoman stands
indicted as accessory in stealing money pleaded not guilty. Trial postponed.
    Philip Parchman, Nathaniel Moody, Daniel McIntyre & Drury Joiner recogni-
p.433   zance; Philip Parchman to appear at next term of this court.
    Grand Jury bill/indictment against Philip Parchman, a true bill.

OCTOBER 1816

James Levesque & his securities discharged from their recognizance.

Excuse juror Britten Yarbrough from further attendance.

p.434   State v Philip Parchman. Tempting slave to leave his masters service with intent to convey him out of the State. Trial postponed till next term of court.

Grand Jury returned Bill/Indictment against Littleberry Stone & Noble Stone, a true bill.

p.435   Philip Parchman, Nathaniel Moody, Parks Bailey, John Parchman, Henson Day recognizance, Parchman to appear at next term of this court.

p.436   Joseph Rea, John Hilhouse, Peter Ligon, John W Ligon, John G Fowlkes, George Malone, Claybourn McVey recognizance; condition they appear at next term this court & give evidence in behalf State against Philip Parchman.

Henry Brown recognizance, to appear at next term this court & give evidence

p.437   behalf State against Philip Parchman, indictment in stealing money.

Joseph Rea, John Hilhouse, Peter Ligon, John W Ligon, John G Fowlkes, George Malone, Claybourn McVey recognizance, they to appear next term to give evidence behalf State against Philip Parchman for tempting a slave.

Henry Brown recognizance, to appear next Term & give evidence behalf State

p.438   against Philip Parchman on indictment tempting a slave.

John B Long v Bernard M Patteson. Appeal. Dft cannot gainsay plfs action;

p.439   owes plf $224.71½ besides his costs. Plf recovers sd sum & costs of suit.

John B Long assee v Bernard M Patteson. Appeal. Trial postponed. Dft to have deposition of John B Long taken before 2 justices in Kentucky.

p.440   William Smith v William W Critintun. Appeal. Appeal. Dft cannot gainsay plf but owes plf $74.50 besides costs. Plaintiff recovers against defendant.

State v Noble Stone. Passing counterfeit bank note. Dft arraigned; pleads

p.441   not guilty.

Justices v Jno Yancy. Appl. Struck off docket, no appeal existing therein.

Court adjourned till tomorrow morning 8 oclock.   Thos Stuart

p.442   Friday 18th October 1816. Present the honorable Thomas Stuart, Judge.

State against Noble Stone. Passing counterfeit bank note. State no further prosecutes; indictment dismissed.

Gabriel Bumpass against John Griggory. Covt. Grant Plaintiff leave to amend his declaration, he to pay costs of this term.

p.443   Deed Commrs of Pulaski to William F Thompson lot 112 ackd by Tyree Rodes, M H Buchanan, Nathaniel Moody three of sd commissioners.

Deed Commrs of Pulaski to heirs of William F Thompson lots 114 115 ackd.

Deed Commrs of Pulaski to German Lester lot 24 ackd by commrs [above]

p.444   Bill/sale James Bumpass to M H Buchanan Negro woman & child ackd.

State v Balaam Straughan. Gaming. Indictment quashed; want of jurisdiction.

State v Henry Hagen. Gaming. Indictment quashed for want of jurisdiction.

p.445   State v Nathaniel Moody. Gaming. Quashed for want of jurisdiction.

State v Rowland Tankersley. Gambling. Quashed for want of jurisdiction.

State v Benjamin Tutt. Gambling. Quashed for want of Jurisdiction.

State v Henry Hester. Gambling. Quashed for want of Jurisdiction.

p.446   State v William Straughan. Gambling. Quashed for want of Jurisdiction.

State v John A Dewoody. Gambling. Quashed for want of Jurisdiction.

State agt John McCracken. Gambling. Quashed for want of Jurisdiction.

State v John Jones. Gambling. Quashed for want of Jurisdiction.

OCTOBER 1816

p.447 State v Joseph Shadden. Gambling. Quashed for want of Jurisdiction.
State v Thomas Smith. Gambling. Quashed for want of Jurisdiction.
State v Nathaniel Moody. Gambling. Quashed for want of Jurisdiction.
State v William Lyons. Gambling. Quashed for want of Jurisdiction.
p.448 State v William Ball. Gambling. Quashed for want of Jurisdiction.
Grand Jury Indictment agt Littleberry Stone & Noble Stone, true bill.
Grand Jury Indictment agt Joseph Moore, true bill.
Grand Jury Indictment agt Joel Rutledge, not a true bill.
Excuse juror Hardy Hightower from further attendance this term.
p.449 John Den on demise of Pallis Neel against Micajah Ezell. Eject. Jury
Alexander Thomson, James Neel, Robt McCulloch, Wm Martin, Jno Calahan, Saml Mont-
gomery, Tobias Miller, Samuel Peirson, Edmond J Bailey, Robin Brown, Charles C
Abernathy, Henry Hester find defendant not guilty of trespass & ejectment.
p.450 Court adjourned till tomorrow morning 8 oclock.   Thos Stuart

p.451 Saturday 19th October 1816. Present the honorable Thomas Stuart, Judge.
Account of David Campbell jailer of Maury County for boarding John Pope in
jail afsd allowed $65.50.
Bill/sale David McMican to Gabriel Bumpass two Negros proven by John
Henderson.
State v John Pope. Horsestealling. Insolvency of defendant, order claimants
p.452 on part of State to recover against the county their costs.
Account of Nimrod Porter deputy sheriff of Maury County for guarding of
John Pope in Pulaski until he could surrender him, is allowed $3.68¾.
John Den lessee of Pallis Neel v Micajah Ezell. Eject. Motion of Plf, order
rule for him to shew cause why he ought to have a new trial in this case.
State v Joseph Moore. Passing counterfeit bank note. Capias is awarded agt
p.453 said defendant, returnable &c.
William Waters, Samuel Day & Nathan Farmer recognizance, to appear next
term to give evidence behalf State against Joseph Moore.
Excuse juror John Henderson from further attendance this term.
p.454 State v Noble Stone. Passing counterfeit bank note. Pleaded Not Guilty.
Trial continued to next term of this court.
Noble Stone & Solomon Stone recognizance; Noble Stone sum $10,000 & Solomon
$5000, condition sd Noble Stone appear at next term of this court to answer indict-
p.455 dictment for passing counterfeit bank note.
William Waters, Samuel Day & Nathan Farmer recognizance, to give evidence
behalf State against Noble Stone.
p.456 David Woods compt v William T Lewis's executors. Equity. Order Injunction
be dissolved; complainants councel has leave to amend his bill; bill retained for
further decision thereupon to be had.
Account of Nathaniel Alman jailor of this county for boarding &c of James
Levesque whilst confined, allowed, $20.
p.457 William Noblett & wife v John Boyd. Appeal. Trial continued to next term.
Andrew B Moore v Gabriel Bumpass. Appeal. Trial continued to next term;
deposition of Samuel Neely in Spartenburgh district, South Carolina, to be taken in
behalf defendant.
p.458 State v Littlebury Stone. Passing counterfeit bank note. Capias awarded
against defendant.

151

State v Joel Rutledge. Grand Jury returned on Bill Indictment, not a true bill. Order claimants on part of State to recover costs against the county.

p.459   Sheriff to take Benjamin Rutledge now in county jail to Maury County jail, the jail in this county being deemed insufficient.

State agt James Levesque, Grand Jury returned Not a true bill. Levesque was discharged; claimants to recover costs against Giles County.

p.460   John McCabe v John Taylor & Samuel Black. Equity. Continued to next term.

Nelson Patteson v Charles Smith & Josiah Alderson. Equity. Complainants bill dismissed and he to pay his costs, and defendant Smith to pay his own costs and costs of defendant Alderson.

p.461   Gabriel Bumpass v John Greggory. Covt. Trial continued to next term.

Joseph Perkins v Harrison Hicks. Appeal. Trial postponed on dfts affidavit.

Alfred M Harris v William G Corlen[Corlew?]. Equity. To be heard exparte before Hon Thos Stuart Circuit Judge now presiding. On 1st August 1814 defendant

p.462   executed to complainant a mortgage on Negro boy Frederick about two or three years old to secure payment of $50 due complainant for services rendered as attorney for dft, payable on 1st Feby 1815; no part of debt yet paid; Complainant hath redeemed sd Negro boy from two other mortgages of prior date to the one to himself, one of which was given to Lunsford M Bramlet Esqr to secure payment of $25 due 1 Sept 1814, the other to Ephraim Parham to indemnify him agt payment of costs of a suit against Vance Greer in Lincoln County Court in which sd Parham was

p.463   security for prosecution; suit dismissed by sd Corlen at his costs to the amount of $4.25 have been paid by sd complainant as well as sum due Bramlet, no part has yet been paid; further, sd complainant obtained possession of sd Negro boy on first week in August 1815 & hath kept him from that time until this & fed & clothed him well. Said Negro boy is yet too small to be of any service, and also sum of $20 per annum would be a reasonable compensation for keeping & cloathing sd

p.464   boy. Order that unless dft shall within three months pay costs of this suit and pay complainant $50 with interest thereon from 1 February 1815, and further sum of $25 paid to Bramlet on mortgage with interest thereon from 1 Sept 1814, and also whatever sum may be due complainant for keeping & cloathing sd boy at rate of $20 per annum from 10 August 1815, and also $4.25 paid of complainant on Parhams

p.465   mortgage with interest from 15th Sept 1815, that mortgage to complainant be forever foreclosed, and Sheriff proceed to advertise and sell sd Negro Frederick to highest bidder for ready cash & apply proceeds to payment of costs of this suit and secondly to satisfaction of the several sums herein decreed to complainant and surplus if any deposited with Clerk of Court for benefit of William Corlew[Corlen?]

p.466   and further order that should sd negro boy due within the three months that sd complainant may have execution agt sd Wm G Corlew for sums herein decreed to him against sd Corlen. Thos Stuart, Judge.

William Dusy[?] assee vs John Paul. Appeal. Jury: Tyree Rodes, Robt Buchanan, Wm Henderson, Jas Bumpass, Samuel Shields, Thomas Welch, Alexr Black, Wm Brown, John C Walker, John Dickey, James Cook, Arthur Hicks. Plf recovers against dft and Elias Tidwell & Andrew Paul his securities $185.73 amount of judgment of court as

p.468 $14.27 for detention thereof & his costs in court below and this.

John Den in demise of Pallis Neil v Micajah Ezell. Eject. Plaintiff ought not have a new trial, rule to shew cause dismissed. Bill of exceptions made part of record. Plf granted appeal to Supreme Court of Errors & Appeals.

p.469   Deed Commissioners of Pulaski to Thomas Wilkinson for lot 27 in Pulaski acknowledged by Tyree Rodes, M H Buchanan, Nathaniel Moody.

Account of Nimrod Porter deputy Sheriff of Maury County for bringing & guarding John Pope to Pulaski is allowed for sum of $10.

p.470   Order that court be adjourned till court in course.   Thos Stuart

End of this book.

BALEY, Charles 60 William 55
BALL, William 3 22-28 30 32-34 37 40 41
45-47 50 51 57 65 69 71 73 77 78 81 82
84 87 90 94 106 121 126 127 129 132
135-139 141 142 144 146 147 149 151
BAPTIST CHURCH 52
BARBER, John 113
BARNET/BARNETT, John 7 33 35 56 63 70
76-82 86 88 91 96 99-101 108 118-120
128 130 131 148 Richard 19 45 49 52 70
75 77 113 128 130 131 Susannah 19
Thomas 9 William 5
BARNS, George 5 Joshua 5
BARRON, Alexander 7 19 84 91 95 96 130
131 John 19 84 88 William 88
BARTON, John 83 105 Thomas 69 106
Widow 69
BASS, Nathan/Nathaniel 23 26 51 52 84
85 91 95 100 116 Peter 43 114
BATEY, Thomas 97 William 18
BATY, William 110
BAUER, Nancy 44
BEAL, Thomas 6 59 60
BEAN, Francis 79 Henry 39
BEARD, Francis 43 44 50 53 55 87 111
George 97 112
BEASLEY, Burton 31 43 106
Jesse 64 77 106
BEATY, William 14 33 72
BEAZLEY, Jesse 120
BEDFORD COUNTY 131 134
BEEN, Henry 7
BEESON, Benjamin 92
BELCHER, Craven/Cravens 70 72
BELL, Adam 75 104 106-109 Robert 60
BENNET, R 127
BENNETT, Benjn 68 Joseph 68 Vincent 122
BENSON, Benjamin 44 51 Captain 7 17 39
Drew 16 Earley/Early 8 44 46 47 56 62
73 84-86 88 90 91 93 94 96-98 109 125
BENTHAL/BENTHALL, Mathew/Matthew 9 15
54 56 116 120 121 122 123
BENTLEY/BENTLY, Captain 39 46 Daniel
135 Richard 38 44 55 56 69 70 75 81 94
100 140 148
BENTON, Thomas 116 118 122 124
BENTSON, Captain 9
BERRY, David 41 James 26 38 44 85 Jona-
than 1 37 46 103 144 148
BERT, Christopher 1
BESHEERS, John 52
BESHERS, John 34

BEST, Christopher 1
BIGHAM, John 3 9 119 121 124 134 Robert
71 73 93-95 98 104 119 121 124 134 144
Thomas 88 119 121 124 134 135 -- 148
BILLINGSLEY, Thomas 106
BIRD, Samuel 39
BIRDWELL, Jane 63 John 19 23 25 26 30
36 37 38 54 55 63 71 80 104 107 108 109
126 128 129 140 145 Joseph 75 Robert 10
63 75 76 William 76
BLACK, A 62 74 88 90 94 96 113 Alexan-
der 10 23 29 35 38 39 47 56 59 62 79 81
83 89 91 93 95 97 98 102 107 109 125
139 140 142 147 152 John 3 7 12 16 62
63 71 77 82 127 129 133 146 Orpha 7 20
81 82 146 Polly 144 Robert 65 80 82 84
85 86 87 88 90 91 93 102 Samuel 127 129
132 138 141 144 152
BLASENGAME/BLAZINGAME, Ham 107 John 1
56 62 73 Thomas 1 Wade 90 100 107
William 90 100 107
BLOUNT, Willie 117 118
BLUE, Douglass 5 10 11 32 53 62 129
BLYTHE, Andrew 21 William 85
BOATWRIGHT, Thomas 93
BOGARD, Jacob 52 53 124   -- 98
BOGLE, Robert 32
BOILS, William 53
BOLDING, William 55
BOLEN, Joseph 75 William 75
BOLIN, Joseph 53
BOLING, Joseph 65 William 81
BOLLING, Joseph 53 78 William 78
BOND, Isaac 19 41 103 117 Joshua 120
William 37 45
BONE, Azariah 5 Squire 116 117 118
BONER, Nancy 44 70 83 137 140 141 143
149
BOOKER, Peter 18 30 84 107 122
BORAN, James 33
BOREN, Absolom/Absolum 8 15
BORIN, Absolom 116 117 119 120 122 123
124 125 126 127 128 129
BOTTOM/BOTTOMS, William 19 85 96
BOWLING, William 82
BOYD, Elijah 92 Francis 67 Hezekiah 117
John 5 6 11 19 20 21 24 25 29 34 35 36
43 47 50 56 65 68 69 73 80 86 91 92 121
135 136 142 145 151 Joseph 8 119 123
124 126 127 128 129
BOYLES, Charles 127
BRADEN, James 109 John 65

BRADFORD, Ira 84
BRADLEY, Samuel 63 William 51 55 56 58
59 61 136 -- 50
BRADSHAW, William 30 106 -- 42 creek
14 42 45 55 67 73 111 112
BRAMLETT, L 93 104 Lunsford 10 70 75 82
85 99 152
BRANDON, Richard 102
BRANNON, Alexander 73
BRASHEAR/BRASHEARS, Jeral 5 Robert 133
BRASHER/BRASHERS John 56 71 98 110
Robert 1 58 59
BRATON, Hugh 125
BRATTON, Paul 5 Thomas 47 50 71 93 127
133 William 23 99 144
BRECKENBRIDGE, James 80 98
BRECKENRIDGE, George 11 James 81
BRIDGEWATER, Isaac 96
BRIGGS, Elizabeth 122 Richard 2 46 51
81 82 89 94 99 103 107 Samuel 99 114
BRIGHT, James 3 9 42 52 80 81 87 -- 5
BRITTIAN, Thomas 55
BRITTON, John 105 Thomas 21
BROOKS, Captain 45 81 108 William 9 12
13 56 65 66 71 75 78 79 83 97 101 108
110 131 134-138 142 144 145 147
BROWN, Aaron 17 28 38 52 64 73 79 88
Abraham 17 64 87 Abram 113 David 28
Davis 68 94 108 113 Duncan 19 30 33 35
38 49 71 102 128 Edward 65 80 84 85 91
96 Elizabeth 95 George 10 16 37 52 62
81 91 108 Henry 149 150 Isam 63 Isham
17 32 44 45 52 53 64 75 76 95 109 James
3 5 16 17 27 52 60 74 86 87 95 96 John
28 95 110 Leonard 23 31-34 57 58 66 88
101 102 129 131-134 138 145-148 Lewis 2
6 7 9 12 19 23 27-32 34 73 77 83 114
118 119 123 130-132 Mathew 12 Robert
118 124 Robin 151 Rolan/Roben/Rolin/
Rowland 13 14 18 20-24 95 Rolly 44 Rowland 71 75 95 100 Rowlin 17 19 Sterling
45 51 Thomas 57 68 69 77 81 88 91 93 99
102 108 William 3 6 7 12 13 20 23 31-33
36 37 43 50 55 56 58 63 65 68 69 71 72
80 102 105 106 108 124-128 132-134 140
142-144 147 152
BROWNING, Charles 64
BROWNLOW, James 64 William 86
BRYANT, Enoch 68 71 83 101 102 125 140
141 John 2 18 47 57 58 59 61 71 72 89
90 94 125 126 128 131 132 138 140 144
BUCH, Maximilian 134 135

BUCHAN, Maximilian 134
BUCHANAN, Clayton 98 Jesse 93 John 17
62 93 144 M 2 20 142 147 149 150 152
Maxamilian/Maximillian 7 9-11 17 44 73
77 93-95 98 109 111 128 136 Robert 7 10
11 19 20 23 33 51 52 56 65 66 78 79 82
98 108 134 135 139 140 141 142 143 145
147 152 creek 14 17 74 85 111
BUCHANNON, John 34 M 31 32 Robert 77
creek 33
BUCHANON, Clayton 59 112 Jesse 91 John
74 M 58-60 80 81 93 99 112 Maxamillion
24 36 41-43 62 74 75 101 106 111 Robert
39 63 65 66 76 81 91 William 69 81
creek 41 42 43 111
BUCKALOO, Ezekiel 72
BUCKANAN/BUCKANON, CLAYTON 3 Maximilian
116 117 140 Robert 116 117 140
BUCKHANAN, Maximilian 127 Robert 127
BUD/BUDD, Samuel 6 39
BUFORD, Charles 1 24 26 39 56 63 80 91
95 98 99 101 106 116 117 123 124 128
129 131 132 134 137 J 2 James 2 3 5
11 14 22-24 28 35 56 61 63 64 67 76 77
84 91 93 94 101 106 108 126 132 138 142
144 Spencer 99 Thomas 130
BULLMAN, Thomas 17
BUMPASS, Doctor 10 17 24 72 Gabrael/
Gabriel 3 9 10 17 37 45 47 49 50 58 71
74 75 85 94 95 98 122-125 129 131-135
137 143 150-152 Hartwell 95 James 2 7
10 13 15 16 19 22-25 30 35 38 39 45 47
54 61-64 67 68 76 77 79 80 81 91 98 104
107 130 131 134 137 147 150 152
BUNCH, David 27 28 James 23 56 69
BUNCOMB HEIRS 3 41
BUNDY, David 123
BUNN, Etheldred 80
BURFORD, Solomon 113
BURGES, Harris 55 trace 37
BURNETT, Adam 16 Benjamin 83 Richard 95
BURNEY, Adam 8 9 55 86 118 123 124 144
James 32 Saml 34 50 61 118 123 124 148
BURNS, James 85 86
BURTON, Robert 87 111 Samuel 23 87
BUTLER, Captain 10 39 46 51 John 9 13
30 40 48 56 62 73 80 88 105 108 113
ford 17
BYLER, Abraham 15 84 110 Captain 39 46
81 86 108 J 88 Jacob 7 10-12 19 21 28
39 46 56 62 64 65 78 80 84-87 89 108
110 116 120 127 130-133 142 Joel 140

156

BYLERS POWDER MILL 23
CABAL, William 139
CABE, John 7 11
CALAHAN, John 52 151
CALDWELL, James 36 52 68 94 John 20 26
29 35 49 58 75 88 106 112 Madison 91
Polly 112 William 2 11 16 26 52 65 71
73 75 84 91 104
CALLAHAN, John 88 113 William 113
CALLOWAY, William 76
CALTON, Robert 88
CAMPBELL, Alexander 1 Captain 7 9 11
David 8 9 38 47 49 50 53 60 65 66 68-70
123 129 132 137 144 151 Francis 147
George 4 87 Hamilton 32 33 56 62 73 84-
89 93 94 108 113 118 Hugh 23 26 50-52
72 85 86 91 95 Joab 99 108 112 John 3 5
32 66 123 Robert 8 11 13 22 32 41 42 56
57 74 81 83 134 135 William 13 18 20 32
34 65 71 72 -- 114
CANNAMORE, Jacob 44
CANNON, William 5
CANON, John 87
CANTRILL, Stephen 55
CAPURAN, Thomas 3
CARDIN, Larkin 17 20 31
CAREY, Joel 134
CARLTON, Robert 52 88
CARR, James 109
CARROL, Charles 99
CARSON, John 87
CARTER, Augustine 24 101 140 148 Isham
119 Jabez 101 Landen/Landon 4 14 74
CARWOOD, William 5
CASH, Benjamin 84 Francis 29
CASPER, William 120
CASTLEMAN, Andrew 93
CASWELL, Samuel 63
CAVNAS, Nedom 11 Thomas 11
CEARBY, Henry 42 74 111
CHAFFIN, John 139
CHAMBERS, Edward 36 57 64 65 77 78 110
145 Samuel 16 21 61 66 68 71 81 83 123
125 127 134 135 140 141 148   -- 67
CHAPMAN, Benjamin 3 55 John 3 55 60
Thomas 55 William 47 54 55 60
CHATMAN, Thomas 64
CHEATHAM, Thomas 79
CHEEK, Randal 63 Valentine 63
CHESHER, Benjamin 95
CHILDERS, John 14 Robert 126 128
Stephen 117

CHILDRESS, John 4 18 41 48 86 114
Stephen 117
CHILDS, Francis 4 14
CHISHER, Benjamin 83
CHOATE, Valentine 58
CHRISTIAN COUNTY, Kentucky 47 83 137
CHRISTOPHER, Christopher 86
CLACK, John 7 13 23 26 30 47 89 101
Spencer 13 19 23 24 43 46 47 50 57 58
60
CLAIBORNE/CLAIBOURNE, Ferdinand 21 22
30 62 Mary 21 22 30 62 McCajah 62
Micajah 21 30 Thomas 21 22
CLARK, Andrew 10 69 Jesse 10 John 7 15
19 89 130 137
CLARKE, Robert 31 Thomas 26
CLAY, Clement 106 121
CLEAVELAND, Carter 49 Larkin 49
CLEVELAND, Abner 116 Carter 41 46 83
102 Fanny 41 46 131 132 Larken/Larkin
25 119 131 132 136 Oliver 41 46 80 102
103 142
COALTER, George 60 77 80 82 145
COBB, Ambros 145 Avelina 87 Ebby 87 114
Malinda 114
COBBS, Robert 106 114 148
COCK/COCKE, Captain 81 108
William 65 67 80
COCKRAN, William 4
COCKRELLS GAP 45 55 64 67 76 87 105
COCKS, Captain 39 45
CODY, Jacob 57 95
COHEA, Perry 20
COHER, George 106
COLE, Abraham 49 96 99 Amelia 49 50
Doctor Franklin 49 50 Milley 49 50 61
COLEMAN, John 113 146
COLLIER, Wilson 50 90
COLVILLE, Lusk 8
CONDEN/CONDIN, Larkin 14 18 19 21-24 31
CONDRAY/CONDRY, Stephen 4 114
CONN, -- 47
CONNER, James 41 73 111 Lewis 88 91
CONNIWAY, Charles 95 107 Edward 93 107
James 107 R 98 Richard 93 107
CONNWAY, James 68 Richard 19 60
CONWAY, Charles 24 30 32 43 56 57 67 85
90 91 Edward 89 James 56 67 101 110
Richard 15 56 58 67 101 110   -- 67 68
COOK, Hugh 31 James 147 152 John 80 105
106 113 Lemuel 101 William 47 54 80 81
87 90 91 96 102 105 113 142 144   -- 57

COOKE, David 62 James 91 John 62 Lemuel 62 William 36 77
COOPER, Edmond 45 Joel 105 Lavinah 75 Levi 15 20 75 77 83 Levina 83 Robert 105 Saml 55 65 125 William 120-123 148
CORLEN, William 139 146 152
CORLEW, William 146 152
CORNELIUS, Edmund 105 114
CORNISH, Thomas 66 67 William 66 67
COTTON, Robert 49 68
COULTER, George 50 127
COUNTS, John 6 7 12
COURSEY, James 7 13 22 23 137 139
COVENTON, Nancy 134-138
COVEY, Polly 93
COX, Captain 47 Catherine 122 123 Daniel 5 Phenice 88 Robt 69 84 Samuel 6 12 23-25 31 39 41 47 49 62 66 71 88 99 107 140 William 55 59 65 66 71 90 125
COXE, Robt 84 Samuel 56 80 81 Wm 80 89
CRAFT, Jesse 75 76 Washington 126 128
CRAIG, James 102 John 51 Samuel 3 18 William 72
CRAIGHEAD, David 142 John 88
CREAMER, William 7 16 19 22
CREEK NATION 3 12 13
CREEL, Thomas 83 106
CREESY, Bennett 17 87
CREMER, William 12
CREMORE, William 12
CRENSHAW, Freeman 72 76 88 Nathan 110 Rebeccah 67 Thomas 13 67
CRISWELL, Samuel 26 27 28 33 47 54 69 94 96 107
CRITINTUN, William 148 150
CRITTENTON/CRITTINTON, Henry 62 66 John 5 32 33 40 47 52 67 William 5 12 17 20 47 48 50 61 66 68 71 79 82 91 93 95 99 101 110 136 140 141 144
CRITTINGTON, William 121 124
CROCKET/CROCKETT, Archibald 38 44 48
CROFT, Samuel 33 Washington 7 9 13 14 18 25 49 50 51 137 143
CROOK, David 71 95 96 97
CROSS, Benjamin 17 97 Henry 17 37 97 Shadrack 38 87
CROWSEN, Jacob 12
CROWSON, Abraham 38 108 Gilly 76 Hightower 66 76 Isaac 38 72 101 Jacob 5 6 36 48 50 56 68 70 124 126 127 Jane 36 38 John 4 27 36 38 66 71 72 132 134 136 Jonathan 36 38 Mary 27 36 38 45 66 76

94 Mason 101 Moses 27 38 66 76 94 97 99 Richard 27 36 38 94 Thomas 38 William 27 36 38 45 66 76 77 94 98 99
CRUTCHER, Thomas 3 8 84 94
CUBLEY, William 47 53
CUMBERLAND COUNTY, Virginia 18
CUMMINS, Robert 22
CUNNINGHAM, Archibald 68 69 95 97 107 Charity 97 Elijah 91 George 127 130 James 51 88 96 104 John 122 Matthew 76 119 125 136 137 William 20 22 40 95 97 105 137 143
CURREN, Robert 117
CUSTIS, Amy 147
CYLER, Thomas 54 64 84
CYRUS, Henry 61 79 80
DABNEY/DABNY, J 27 30 John 1 4 10 11 22 23 30 38 39 44 47 53 54 59 64 72 76 80 97 102 127 128 142 William 1 8 22 23 27 30 48 57 120 121 122 123
DANY, Hugh 37
DARBY, Richard 62 106 107 108 109
DARNELL, William 90 92 98 100 107
DARY, Hugh 37
DAVIDSON, Andrew 4 Ephraim 83 John 88 136 William 44
DAVIDSON COUNTY 141
DAVIS, Daniel 4 Edward 19 30 31 68 69 Enoch 7 45 51 55 56 64 76 87 105 John 7 19 29 70 Joseph 85 86 Major 109 Micajah 66 Nathan 3 19 22 23 29 31 33 34 55 56 59 63 64 73 88 100 104 106 114 138 140 141 148 149 Thomas 2 William 8 12 15 19 20 23 28 94 104 113 115 119 126 133 143
DAY, Henson 150 Samuel 88 147 149 151
DAYLE, Wamick 119
DEARING, Berry 25 98 Joseph 149 William 25 31
DEARMAN, Solomon 21 31 67 Thomas 21 67
DEERY, -- 16
DEMENT, Thomas 125
DEN, Matthew 137
DENTON, Edwin 57
DERR, Captain 108 James 105
DEVAZER, John 119
DEVENPORT, Robert 87 102
DEVER/DEVERS, Charles 31 57 58 81 88 100 139 Mary 144 Charley 144
DEW, Matthew 6 22 41 46 47 65 66 80
DEWAADY, John 146
DEWASER/DEWAASER, John 17 18 31 33 52 69 88 94 134 138-141 144 146 148

William 17 18 31 33 69 144
DEWOODY, John 150
DICK, James 126 127 129
DICKEY/DICKY Alexander 5 John 2 3 6-8
11-13 15-17 19 21-25 27 28 30 39 41 43
50 54 56 57 62 75-77 80-82 84 91 93-95
98-101 105-107 109 110 113 114 117 118
127 128 134 140 142-145 147 152
DICKINSON, John 21
DICKSON, David 14 17 68 82 James 1 26
62 63 98 Joseph 14 17 26 31 46 47 56
62 63 65 66 67 68 71 97 136 Reuben 121
Robert 83 110 William 83 110
DILLING, Levin 105 106
DILLON, John 71 72 Polly 72 Thomas 66
DISMUKE, Paul 38
DOCERES, James 27
DODSON, Elisha 65 67 75 Mary 69 Raleigh
69 79 Samuel 57 58 65 67 82 86 107 108
William 72 -- 67
DOGGET/DOGGETT, Miller 86 88 98
DOHERTY, George 4 73 John 4 -- 26 38 44
DONALD, William 26
DONALDSON, Alfred 60 Andrew 4 James 1
75 105 Polly 105 Stokely 14
DOOLEN, Pheaby 123
DOOLIN, Sally 8 16 20 21 43
DORAN/DOREN, James 47 93 94 103 125 132
DOTSON, Green 45 Samuel 146
DOWDLE, Robert 33 39
DOWNS, James 32
DOYLE, -- 117
DRAKE, John 15 42 80 81
DUDLEY, Guilford 126
DUDLY, Gilford 121
DUGGER, James 2 22 23 25 39 44 46 52 56
63 66 68 74 80 108 109 127 128 134 137
142
DULIN, William 4
DUNCAN, John 91 Samuel 87
DUPREES, James 88
DUSY, William 152
EARNEST, George 29 35 64 Mary 35 64
EASLEY, Charles 53 65 John 2 5 10 27
36 46 49 53 56 65 96 127 128 130 131
EAST, Joseph 4 14
EATON, John 21 27 30 54 62 102 114
Mira 21 22 30
EDDY, Josiah 39
EDWARDS, Adonijah 131 133 Gray 7 8 20
23 31 36 47 50 55 56 65 66 71 125 141
John 40 41 69 114 146

EGNEW, James 32 55
ELDRIDGE, Elisha 143
ELLIOTT, Andrew 23 59 70 76-80 82 92
Hugh 74 John 9 19 32 53 56 59 60 62 73
128 136 Suvion 74
ELLIS, Charles 111 John 87
ELLISON, Frank 45 Halbert 34 Holbert 43
45 55 Margaret 45
ELLISS, John 7 21 45 55 78 88 96
ENGLISH, Sarah 90 100 107
Wilson 100 107
EPPLER, John 100 114 123
ERVIN, Andrew 118 121 125
ERWIN, Andrew 16 17 27 52 94 117 129
Robert 101
ESSMAN, Benjamin 41 113
ESTEP, Eba 43 Eby 37 Isabella 43
Rudy 111
ESTESS, Eby 37
EUBANKS, William 121
EVANS, Daniel 123 James 52 98
John 8 26 55 136
EVERETT, Captain 108 Larkin 81
EVETS, Samuel 46
EVETTS, Moses 3 55
EZEL/EZELL, Micajah 9 47 50 80 108 113
143-145 148 151 152 Timothy 1 23 37 51
55 57 William 14 17-24 128 129 144 149
EZZELL, Micajah 29 70 76 77 80 Timothy
26 44 56 58 60 69 81 William 38 44 70
75 87
FAIN, Samuel 52
FANE, Nicholas 69
FANIE, Samuel 86
FANNING, George 28 29 John 28 29 Joseph
10 William 104
FANNON, William 67
FARIS, John 4
FARMER, Nathan 27 28 38 44 65 84 87-91
93 114 116 128 129 151 Stephen 88
FARNNEY, William 5
FARRIE, Samuel 86
FAULKS, Gabriel 31
FENNER, Robert 41
FERRELL, William 20 22
FERRIL, William 122
FINCH, Joshua 17 44 Mary Ann 97 105
FINNEN, James 93
FINNEY/FINNY, James 67 79 89 93 100
Riley 32 40 132 134 145
FIPPS, Benjamin 1 Jorden 5 Joseph 5
FISH, Tabitha 95 Wm 24 47 48 51 95 105

FISHER, Ephraim 127 -- 88
FITCH, Joshua 17
FITTS, Walker 66
FLAT/FLATT, Benjamin 5 David 1 5 25 63
77 78 95
FLETCHER, Thomas 85
FLINT, David 10 14 17 19 22 116 Martin
118 119 Richard 23 118 119
FLOURNOY/FLURNOY, Silas 71 72 114
FLYNT, Abijah 65 Hasten 71 Martin 25
71 Mereday 25 26 Perry 25 52 Rich-
ard 17 25 38 39 Sally 71 Susannah 71
FOLEY, W 139 Washington 3 29 31-40 49
50 51 57 59 61 67 83 94 105 106 114 136
140
FOLLIS, Abram 4 John 4 William 68 71 82
FORBES, James 23 51 52 118 119 120
FORBIS, Robert 127
FORD, Charlotty 115 J 52 James 38
FORGEY, John 3 7 11 120 122
FORGRY, John 120
FORK, Charlotty 19
FORMER, Henry 42
FORT, Charloty 19 20 23 94 115
FORT HAMPTON 64 77 88 99 106 110 114
FOSTER, Ambrose 17 32 63 76 89 Jesse 1
94 106 Mary 89 Rachel 100 Thomas 89
William 89
FOULKS, Herod 34 37 59 82 John 71
FOWLER, Holman 108 114 Holmon 70 75 113
FOWLKS, Gabriel 19 31 35 Herod 31 38
61 95 John 86 88 149 150
FRALEY, Caleb 66
FRANCIS, Henry 107
FRANKLIN, A 119
FRANKLIN COUNTY, Virginia 129
FRANKS, Edmund 78 Leanna 10 Marshall 78
Martin 15 Thomas 85 93
FRASER, Anna 123 James 62 84 102 123
John 102 123 Marget 123 Mary 123 Walter
45 62 91 95 Walton 123   Wm 45 62 123
FRASIER, James 103 John 103
FRAZER, Walter 101 122
FRAZIER, John 4
FREE PERSONS OF COLOR, Benjamin 25
Betty 6, Jacob 93
FRILEY, Caleb 7 13 18 47 Martin 2 19 30
FRY, John 52 106 107 108 109
FUGATE, Levi/Levy 97 98 99 107 112 143
144 145 148 Nancy 103 Randal 103
FUGET, Andrew 1
FULKS, Gabriel 118 119 John 144

FULLERTON, William 3 6 7 9 13 86 143
FUQUA, Isham 66 Jesse 66 Peter 66
FUQUAY, Peter 138
GALASPIE, Jeremiah 3
GAMBLE, John 4 Thomas 26
GARNER, Brice 4 9 44 85 97 114 Fresh 5
John 4
GARRETT, Betsey 144 George 87 96 103
105 James 79 John 45 46 57 Nathan 144
Odel/Odell 32 33 50 53 135 137 141
Polly 53 William 70 75 Willie 87
GATLIN, Edmond/Edmund 1 55 86
GAUHA, Abner 44
GAYNES, William 29
GEE, Lucas 97
GEORGE, Benjamin 117
GEORGIA (state) 66
GERARD, Charles 111
GERCO, Jeremiah 5
GERMAN, Joseph 8 15 43 45 53 55 78 81
95 105
GERRARD, Charles 41
GIBSON, George 33 37 38 41 43 60 72 83
Hugh 19 137 139 Isaac 72 Jilley/Jilly
71 72 John 56 63 65 68 69 71 72 Samuel
72 Trion 7 Tryon 67 76 77 87
GIDDENS, James 3 99 William 1 7 57 65
67 69 80 123 124 130 131
GIDEON/GIDEONS, James 125 William 116
GILBERT, John 31 64 Nancy 101
GILL, Thomas 105
GILLESPIE, Elizabeth 53 Jeremiah 53
GLASGOW, Robert 96 Thomas 4
GLASS, Samuel 111
GLOVER, Joshua 5
GOFF/GOOFF, George 25 27 75 103 113
James 25 27 65 John 25 27 75 103 Peggy
25 27 Thomas 1 7 15 17-19 29 31-33 36
98 120-123 134 140 144 146 148 149
GOLDSBERRY, James 90 110 147 John 37
GOLDSBURY, John 8
GOODEN, Michael 64
GOODNIGHT, Henry 121
GORDON, Captain 7 11 17 John 17 38 45
55 91 R 27 30 Robert 3 7 15 22 27 30
45 47 54 55 69 82 88 93 116 117 130 131
Thomas 23 38 47 54 57 66 69 76 80 81 83
96 97 99 100 102 104 107 108 113 114
142 143   -- 55
GOUGH, John 16
GRACE, Levin 25 Lemon 76 Lumm 76
GRAHAM, David 4 120 James 18 39 52 77

William 40 51 61
GRAVES, Eliza 9 Fanny 48 51 73 Frances
9 93 94 Jacob 5 John 6 7 13 22 23 26 37
38 40 48 50 51 52 61 65 72 73 79 80 85
87 88 101 123 128 130 131 Polly 9 40 51
Ralph 1 3 6 7 9 12 23 24 26 33 34 50 56
61 63 70 80 89 94 101 106-108 113 118
125 130 140 Sally 9 48 51 73 93 94 Sol-
omon 72 William 3 6 7 14 17 89 108 140
GRAY, William 69
GREEN, Lewis 41 Philmer 8 9 35 59 61 93
139 143 147 William 72
GREENWOOD, Thomas 91
GREER, James 119 121 124 Joseph 4 14 41
74 111 Thomas 42 74 Vance 152
GREGGORY/GREGORY, John 9 13 15 23 31 34
66 84 85 88 89 90 93 152
GRIFFIN, Spencer 44
GRIFFIS, -- 88
GRIGGORY/GRIGORY, John 125 128 150
GRIGS, John 55 Nicholas 3 55
GRIMES, James 118
GRISHAM, Moses 107 114
GRISSOM, Moses 47 50
GROVE, H 52 Henson 52
GRUNDY, Felix 116
GUDRELAN, Charles 85 91
GUERELAN, Charles 85
GUILFORD, Jeremiah 42 74 102 113
GUNTER, Hawkins 69
GUTHRIE, John 146
HACKNEY, Jesse 96 105
HADDEN, Hugh 5 Samuel 5 Thomas 5
HADLEY, Joshua 55 60 74 93 94
HAGEN, Henry 8 10 12 15 20 21 24 26 28
30 36 38 40 43 49 57 58 61 83 89 101
104 109 114 132 138 139 146 150
HAGIN, Henry 127 128
HAILE, Butler 68 79 109 Capt 77 81 108
HAINIE, Thomas 13 Widow 15
HALE, Butler 56
HALL, James 48 Mansel 123 Thomas 3 6 7
HAM, Blasengame 90 100
HAMBLEN/HAMBLIN, John 8 20 21 43
HAMBEY/HAMBY, William 13 41 43 68 118
119 123 124 133
HAMILTON, Moses 58 76
HAMLIN, John 16
HAMM, John 51 52
HAMMONDS, Isam 58 69 James 110
John 58 69 72
HAMMONS, James 22 John 20

HAMPTON, Noah 49 68 Reuben 66
HANIE, Thomas 123
HANKINS, Joseph 97 99 107 112 146
Polly 97
HANN, Thomas 5
HANN--, James 78
HANNA, James 76 John 9
HANNAH, James 32 33 51 57 58 70 77 79
80 82 John 7 9 10
HANNUM, Washington 18
HANSON, Robert 68
HARALSON, Major 144
HARDAY, Betsey 130 Coleman 5 Isaac 130
HARDEN, Joseph 105
HARNETT, John 132 Richard 108
HARRALDSON, Major 45
HARRALSON/HARRELSON, Major 17 106
Thomas 111
HARRINTON, John 121
HARRIS, Alfred 1 2 10 18 30 35 43 56 62
64 70 72 75 85 98 103 104 110 128 139
142 143 145 146 149 152 Edward 111
James 1 -- 13
HARRISON, George 37 41 50 56 62 71 74
93 John 49 68 Robert 49
HARROLSON, Major 14 18-24 56 88 106 111
124 125
HART, James 118 122 Joseph 31
HARTY, Dennis 19
HARVEY, Alexander 72 Andrew 4 Harvey 4
Robert 72 William 72
HARWELL, Absalom 33 35 37 68 108 131 B
28 Buckner 7 8 23 26 29 30 33 35 37-39
41 43-46 52 55 56 70 80 81 89 95 102
104 108 109 118 120 123 125 127 128
130-132 142 Captain 7 11 Coleman 54 60
Featherston 65 66 Fred 17 Frederick 38
46 51 108 131 Gardener/Gardner 49 54
Herbert 54 55 James 8 26 37 43 Nancy 54
60 Richard 37 94 127 128 Rolly 54 88
Rowley 54 Sally 94 Samuel 38 48 49 54
55 60 76 77 Sarah 55 Shadrack 37 38 44
70 75 Thomas 29 50 65
HARWOOD, Thomas 10 23 27 39 51 57 80 85
87 91 97 105 108 114 134 135 137 147
HATCHETT, Barnustra 149
HAWKINS, John 10 19 25 30 34 45 57 88
128
HAYES, Oliver 113 117 118 William 113
-- 102 112
HAYNE, Andrew 78
HAYNES, Andrew 9 35 70 76 77 79 80-82

James 9 26 35 36 38 106 107 109 John 35
Joseph 4 Thomas 113 139
HAYNIE, Mrs 18 Thomas 28 36 37 50 62 65
81 87 90 95 108 113 137
HAYS, Oliver 117 William 50 53 105
HAYWOOD, John 41 42 -- 4 14 111 117-
119 creek 79
HELMS, Franky 105 Maberry 83 Mayberry
136
HEMPHILL, Samuel 27 28
HENDERSON, Captain 7 12 James 86 John
7-11 16 23 37-39 41 44-47 53 54 72 73
80 81 84 87 91 97 104 142 147 148 151
Nathan 31 53 54 Robert 64 Sally 53
William 1 11 26 28 45 50 55 61 63 64 66
67 70 75 77 84 91 102 104 106-108 110
113 119 124 125 146 147 152
HENDRY, James 141 William 40 41 43 51
57-59 61 65 67 68 71 73 84-90 93 94 102
105 106 144
HENRY, Isabella 136 Peggy 144 William
33 40 50 136
HERN, Mary 141
HERRALDSON/HERRALSON, Captain 39 46 81
108 Major 82
HERRING, Payton 144 Peyton 69
HERRINGTON/HERRINTON, John 5 121-123
HESKINS, Andrew 5
HESS, William 135
HESTER, Henry 109 146 148 150 151
HEYM, Mary 140
HEYRN, Mary 140
HICKS, Arthur 23 28 39-41 46 49 50 54
56 57 74 78 91 103 108 128 134 135 137
144 147 152 Charlotte 48 Francis 39 59
68 141 Harrison 11 12 34 38 59 89 93 94
108 110 113 152 John 8 12 13 26 33 35
48 56 59 89 98 103 104 106 121 122 123
132 Mary 59 Parkey 59 Sally 59
HIGGINBOTHAM, Gabrael/Gabriel 47 72 121
124 148 Reuben 40 41 47 77 87 106
HIGGS, Simeon 4
HIGHSAW, Andrew 43
HIGHTOWER, H 50 Hardey 39 Hardy 7 8 10
39 40 45 47 48 53 55 65 67 74 76-80 85
91 103 105 108 134 135 137 142 147 151
Reuben 96 Richard 4 14 31 36 41 42 46
48 62 64 84 96 97 111 113 122 124 126
128 129 131 134 148 -- 14 102 112
mill 45 55 64 67 76 78 87 105
HILL, Caleb 7 10 14 17 130 Captain 7
18 David 62 John 86

HILHOUSE, John 149 150
HILLHOUSE,George 23 84-91 93 94 128
John 3 6-8 11-13 15 16 24 29 32 39 45
56 62 66 67 75-77 80 84 98-100 108 127
128 142 Robert 5
HINSON, Alexander 84
HIX, Arthur 128 John 120
HOBBS, Christopher 78 79 Solomon 5
HOBSON, Isaac 85 91 93 99 John 144 Law-
son 15 32 56 77 85 Loson 123 137 141
HODGE, John 145 Joseph 145 148 Rhoda 99
Rhody 86 Welcome 86 Wellcome 97 99
HODGES, James 53
HOGAN, Henry 125
HOGGEN, Henry 136
HOGUE, George 72 John 72
HOLLEY, Nicholas 105
HOLT, William 15 20 55 56 79 80
HOOD, Alexander 10
HOOKER, Ann 66 67 Nathan 1 27 32 66
Richard 32 66
HOOKS, James 55 65
HOOSER, Isaac 42
HOOTEN, Robert 126
HOPKINS, Jason 91 98-102 143
HORN, Nancy 44 48 56 William 39 44 48
56 138
HOWARD, Shadrack 36
HOWE, William 47
HOWEL/HOWELL, Buckner 119 120 127
John 2 4 -- 5
HUDSON, Thomas 74
HUDSPETH, Charles 34 50 51 53 54 61 63
HUEY, James 133
HUFF, Valentine/Volentine 52 124 125
HUGGINS, Phillup 10
HUGHES, John 11 52 88
HUGHS, Daniel 76 John 62 63
HUMPHREYS, Joseph 124 Thomas 124
HUNNECUT, Robert 31
HUNT, James 4 116 118 119 124 126 128
HUNTSVILLE 17 110
HURT, Elizabeth 12 Judith 57 Samuel 23
24 57 89 90 98 104 109 124 129 Zacheus
12 22 28 34 36-38 40 41 43 48 51 65 72
76 80 84 104 109 110 113 123 124 129
131 137 142 143
HURTSVILLE 24
HUTCHESON, Coleman 64
HUTCHINSON, James 4 John 4
HYNES, Andrew 85
HYRN, Mary 141 145

ILLINOIS TERRITORY 83
INDIAN LINE 17 24
INDIANA 105
INGRAM, Silvanus 97
IRELAND, James 36
ISAAC, Abraham 69
ISAACKS, Jesse 82 100
ISHAM, John 68
ISOM, John 25 37 38
JACK, John 126-128
JACKSON, Andrew 3 8 84 94 130 Burrel
127 General 28 James 120 Nicholas
144 Washington 120
JAMES, S 27 Thomas 49 William 98
JAMISON, -- 72
JENKINS, Thomas 4 Wilton 14 17 86 127
128 145
JERMAN, Joseph 11 50
JESSAMINE COUNTY, KENTUCKY 127
JEWELL, John 4
JOHN/JOHNS, Harvey 128 129 131 139
Joseph 21 46 47 57-59 64 73 88 94 101
104 105 119-122 137 139-141 144-146 148
JOHNSON, Harris 147 Isaac 47 100 Thomas
135-137 140 William 4 121
JOHNSTON, Alexander 25 Daniel 25 Harris
83 Isaac 10 43 54 58 59 83 99 102 103
James 11 John 11 33 60 87 105 108
Littleton 100 Matthew 11 32 60 63 87
106-109 Nancy 102 103 Richard 60 80 87
144 Robinson 25 Thomas 105 106
JOINER, Drury 97 110 149 Eli 33 39
JONES, Alexander 6 8 9 55 66 88 92 108
131 136 140 141 145 Alston 86 Charlotte
85 95 David 36 46 56 66 68 69 83 90 91
118-120 Henry 114 James 114 John 8 37
45 56-59 83 85 87 90 95 109 110 116 117
139 140 150 Leonard 5 Mary 5 85 114 140
141 145 Pleasant 88 106 Rebeccah 77
Robert 85 S 58 Samuel 7 11 22 30 39 43
45-47 52 54 59 66 80 85-87 117-119 127
129 131 134 135 Thomas 100 101 William
3 6 29 34 48 52 53 71 87 89 90 125 Willie 5 Willson 77 Wilson 66 71 77 89
JORDAN, Archer 53 Robert 69
JOSLIN, Gabriel 71 74 125-127 129 130
132 133 136 140 143 148
KEARBY, William 45
KEARLY, William 29
KEARNEY, Guston 25 27 36 78 95
KEELING, Edward 72 George 73
KEENAN, John 17 18 19 20 21 22 23 25 43

66 82 83 106 137
KEENON, John 50
KEILEY, William 19
KEITH, Andrew 7 26
KELLET/KELLETT, James 92 112
KELLY, Cary 114 John 25 29 32 49 57
Joseph 31 32 69 71 78 119 127 130
Thomas 32 127 130 William 95 96 99 109
110 138-142 147
KELSO, John 126 127 129 132 135 137 139
141 147
KELTET/KELTIT, James 92 93
KELTNER, George 4
KENADY/KENEDY, John 50 67
KENAN, John 14 66 138 144
KENDELL, William 68
KENEDAY, John 96 William 96
KENLEY, William 24
KENNEDAY, John 11 21 56 63 78 87 105
106 William 105
KENNEDY, John 7 16 55 107
KENTUCKY 47 67 83 105 126 127 132 137
KERBY, John 79 82 141 Wm 113 141 144
KERLEY, William 3 4 22 23 26 37 54 105
114 141 144 148
KERNEY, Guston 2
KETTELL, James 92
KETTIT/KETTET, James 92 93
KEY, John 126 127 129 132 Thomas 129
KIBBLE, Robert 106
KILBURNE, Solomon 79
KILE, Prior 148 William 138 141
KILLAM, Custus 67
KILLEBRU, Thomas 15 20
KILPATRICK, Daniel 67
KIMBRO, Elisha 16 20 27 James 19 25 78
79 118 119 127 128 Nathaniel 4
KIMBROUGH, Elijah 80 Elisha 26 28 99
James 2 32 35-38 41 43 44 52 68 82 84
86 87 101 106 147 John 6 Robert 3
KINAN, John 132
KINDALL, William 18
KINDEL/KINDELL, Moses 64 William 13 30
34 35 58 61 69 82 92 135
KINDLE, William 3 6 7 19 20 23 24 25 34
57 61 100 125
KINDRED, Josias 126
KING, John 113 130 132 134 136-140 142
146 William 114
KIRBY, John 141 142 William 129 136
KIRK, Lewis 2 3 6 7 19 21 22 26 33 34
37 38 44 50 60 61 82 97 99 101 106 110

116-118 120 125 128 Mary 99 101 110
KIRKLAND, Jesse 8 50 68 83 107 136 140
KIRKLIN, Jesse 32
KNOX, James 14 17 70 71 75 116 123 124
John 56 142 Joseph 1 23 26 54 71 72 108
120 Robert 124 125 William 5
KOHER, George 108
KYLE, Pryor 71 79 William 60 72 100 114
LACEFIELD, John 5
LAIRD, John 23 25 31 32 34 52 57 80 98
119 142
LAMB, Isaac 25 Jesse 53 70 103
LANCASTER, Aaron 2 3 5 Eli 4 Thomas 4
LANE, Joel 9 25 39 134 Martin 25 57 80
103 Thomas 25 44 64 80 81 103 108 142
LANIER, Robert 4 14 111
LANN, Isaac 3 33 35 89 90 Joseph 3 14
17 19-22 24 33-35 50 66 85 104 133
Richard 68 86 121
LARK, Elizabeth 69 71 72 Julius 71
LAUGHLIN, Alexander 9 97 114
LAWN, Joseph 18
LEACH, James 77 80 142
LEE, Alizabeth 45 Edward 63 129 Eliza-
beth 44 48 113 John 9 44-46 48 53 55 65
113 118 119 123 Simpson 19 22 55 68 70
77 William 44 63 87 105 113
LEECH, David 129 Humphreys 5
LEETH, James 125
LEITCH, James 88 108 113
LEITH, James 4
LEMMONDS, Peter 50
LEMMONS, Peter 5 72
LESTER, Fountain 32 47-49 67 74 88 97
Fountin 47 G 65 German 1 2 6 10-12 15
17 21 24-26 28 31 40 41 44 49 55 70 87
98 101 105 109 112 115 131 136 139 143
144 147 149 150 Harriett 47 Harriott 67
Henry 6 John 42
LEVESQUE, James 148 150 151 152
LEWIS, Andrew 71 Charles 62 Charlotte
21 22 27 30 Isham 121 125 129 James 4
14 54 72 111 Joel 73 111 134 139 Levi 1
Margaret 21 22 30 Mary 121 Micajah 21
27 30 42 62 Robert 2 Samuel 5 W 3 27 94
William 3 4 8 14 21 25 30 41 42 54 62
73 111 122 130 151
LIGON, John 150 Peter 150
LINCOLN COUNTY 7 11 44 152
LINCOLN COUNTY, North Carolina 40 52 61
LINDSEY, James 7 9 10 26 136 Lemuel 71
72 Samuel 4 54 William 83

LINN, John 17
LINSEY, Lemuel 47
LITTLEJOHN, Silas 67
LITTLETON, Charles 67 80 124 125 John
67 114 gap 67
LIVINGSTON COUNTY, Kentucky 105
LOCH, Walter 56
LOCK/LOCKE Walter 7 9 11 15 23 71 116
117 139 140 142
LOCKHART, Benjamin 78 Elizabeth 34
James 78 John 78 Matthew 78 Samuel
78 98 Thomas 78 William 78 -- 42
LOCKHEART, Samuel 4 42
LOFTIN, Thomas 100
LONG, Benjamin 118-120 Gabriel 106-109
James 69 71 72 Jane 112 John 92 94 150
Margaret 112 Partrick 91 Patrick 100
105 109 112 Polly 112 William 86 112
LONN, Joseph 120 Richard 121
LOOFTIN, George 47
LOONEY/LOONY, Joseph 75 104
LORANCE, Martin 11 60
LOVE, Gilly 76 Joseph 72 76 87 117
Mary 87
LOWERY/LOWRY, Adam 42 48
LOYD, Henry 37 80 99 100 107 Woody 93
LUCAS/LUCUS, John 66 67 99 110
LUKER, Joseph 47 54 81 97
LUM, John 17
LUNENBURG COUNTY, Virginia 97 101
LUNN, Joseph 19
LUNSFORD, Elias 136 137 141 143 Lewis
44 70 83 136 Mahulda/Mahuldah/Mahulday
44 70 83
LUTTREL, Richard 121
LYON, Peter 1 4 70 76 78-82 116 117 120
123 124 149 Robert 1 88 92 103 Spencer
84 106 William 23 46 89 90 140 146 149
LYONS, Peter 77 William 36
LYTLE, William 42 44 45
MABRY, William 6
MacANALLY, Jesse 47
MacCAFFERTY, Green 50
MacCOLLUM, Daniel 49
MacGEE, Samuel 50
MACH--, Robert 98
MACININCH, John 47
MACK, Robert 13 30 34 80 106 114 145
MacNIGHT, John 47 50
MADDERWOOD, Levi 5
MADERELL, Shaderick 5
MADISON COUNTY 10

MADISON COUNTY, MISSISSIPPI TERRITORY
40 47 51 96 99 106
MADRY, Buckner 55 James 64
MAGEE, Mary 79
MAGELL/MAGILL, Martha 82 144 William
137 140 141 143-147 149
MAJORS, William 5
MALONE, George 8 9 19 20 28 30 57 80
108 119 123 142 150 Miles 119
MANEFEE, Jarrat/Jarret 2 7 76 97 105
108 John 8 52 68 71 73 78 79 105 107
Reuben 2 3 5 6 77 William 37
MANIFEE, James 98 Jared 9 Jarret/Jar-
rett 35 39 45 76 81 91 John 32 36 55 57
69 72 99 100 W 45 ford 2 10
MANSCO, Kasper 141 146
MAPLES, Holloway 94 John 114 Josiah 2
27 William 14 16 17 27 56 80 83 98 140
MARK, Thomas 63
MARK--, Captain 81
MARKER, Thomas 44
MARKES, Capt 39 46 Thomas 44 83 106 110
MARKS, Captain 11 Thomas 11 12 57 84
107 120 121 131
MARLOR, Jesse 93
MARLOW, Jesse 45 65 67 83 89 100
John 67   -- 67
MARR, William 21 22 23 48 64 66 76 85
86 88 91 106 113 124 125 147 149
MARTIN, David 130 Lewis 125 Richard 72
William 23 151   -- 16
MARTINDALE, Daniel 63 Thomas 148
MARX, Captain 7 Thomas 56 124 125
MASTERSON, John 4 Lazarus 5 Thomas 22
MATTEN, George 16
MATTHEWS, James 99 John 115
MAURY, Thomas 101   -- 36 37
MAURY COUNTY 25 44 86 103 106 118 132
134 135 137 138 144 146 148 149 151 153
MAXWELL, David 51 52 69 81 85 88 103
James 41 73 147 149 John 45 55 58 64 81
83 93 Mary 10 16 104 147 149 Thomas 31
36 37 45
MAYFIELD, Brice 3 13 19 22 23 82 85 91
93 99 100 128 140-142 148 Campbell 11
12 38 Elisha 13 24 37 93 141 Isaac 22
34 79 82 98 140-142 144 Larken/Larkin
23 29 30 34 37 41 50 100 148 William 3
7 12 16 17 19 22 23 25 29 33 35 38-40
43 48 49 52 56 59 61 62 66 67 72 74 75
77 81 82 84 90 91 98 101 106 108-110
113 120 127 128 134 136 137 139 140 144

147
McALL, Richard 139
McANALLY, Jesse 46 47 60 67 106 108
John 19 30 79 William 79
McANDLESS, Samuel 69
McANINCH, John 49
McANNALLY, John 21
McBRIDE, Thomas 1 56 62 73 90 107
McCABE, Hugh 140 John 7 44 48 58 70 71
86 89 109 118 120 121 124 127-129 131
132 134 136-141 144 152 William 33 34
109 110 135 136 137 140
McCAFFERTY, Green 24 29 41 43 68 71 72
79 80 81 82 83 84 94 141 142
McCALLISTER, Charles 125
McCALLUM, Daniel 38
McCANDLESS, James 87
McCANLESS, James 105 John 15 114 124
125
McCARLEY, Ezekiel 32 33 Thomas 26 89 90
McCARTY, James 116 118
McCEARLY, Thomas 23
McCLANAHAN, William 96
McCLANNAHAN, James 84
McCLURE, Fanny 64 76   Wm 48 53 64 76
McCOLLOCH, James 53
McCOLLUM, Daniel 51 56-58 60 80
McCONN, Sampson 19 66
McCOOL, Joseph 5
McCORMACK, Absolom 60 James 65 95 98
99 100 105 107 Joseph 6 Ruth 1
Samuel 95 Stroud 17 87
McCOUN, Sampson 101 105
McCOWN, Sampson 50 60 92 106 119 139
Samson 23
McCOY, Alexander 129
McCRACKEN/McCRACKIN, John 2 6 7 43 51
62 85 86 90 104 107 125 130 131 132 137
138 150 William 70
McCRARY, Andrew 5
McCRAVEN/McCRAVENS/McCRAVIN, James 1 24
26 34 38 44 53 55 84-91 93 94 124 125
McCULLINS, -- 7 11
McCULLOCH, David 55 James 55 Robert 55
59 149 151
McCULLOCK, Benjamin 73 111 David 3 88
102 114 James 3 102 103 Robert 3 114
McCUTCHEN, Andrew 72 James 83
McDANIEL, James 68 69 Robert 60
McDONALD, Alexander 20 26 35 38 43 44
64 84 85 91 94 97 132 148 Hugh 110
James 7 11 17 23 38 39 44 46 70 71 80

165

81 95 108 116 128 129 134 137 142-145
John 4 14 34 68 69 91 96 97 Joseph 1 38
44 102 109 125 Robert 7 97 106 109 130
William 1 7 31 35 39 44 55 64 75 81 84
91 116 120 124 130 131 132 134 135 137
McDONNALD, Elexander 44 James 44 Wm 44
McDONNELL, James 97
McDOW, Robert 66 92 93 112
McGAHA, Abner 108 113
McGANHA, Abner 44
McGAUGHEY/McGAUGHY, Abner 70 88
McGEE, Elizabeth 63 Mary 32 79 Richard
15 31 54 63 108 113 124 Samuel 43
William 128
McGEHEE, Richard 18
McGILL, James 59 William 19 22 29 31 32
33 81
McGUIN, Silas 120-122 William 120
McGUIRE, Silas 122 123 William 116
McININCH, John 120
McININIT, John 120
McINTIRE, Daniel 98 Duncan 10 35 38 44
64 77 97 147 Malcomb 98 branch 31
McINTYRE, Daniel 149 Duncan 47 54 78
81 85 88 91 95 104 105
McIVER, John 7 25 37 42 74
McKENNEY, William 91
McKENNY, Rolin 49
McKERLEY, Ezekiel 32 Joseph 110 146
Thomas 50 53 54 63
McKEY, Henry 48 91
McKINNEY, Alexander 4 72 84 Archibald
102 114 Elizabeth 20 George 84 James 84
John 84 102 Robert 4 Rolen 4 Roland/
Rowland 19 26 29 30 35 58 65 68 101
William 1 101 148
McKINNSY, William 10
McKINNY, George 26
McKIRLEY, Ezekiel 24
McKISSACK, Archibald 3 15 22 31-33 37
40 46 51 70 71 83 90 145 John 13 27 37
48 55 80 89 91 95 144 Thomas 8 9 27 32
33 50-53 72 77 129 134-136 140 143
Susan 144
McKISSICK, John 29 31 49 118 Thomas 31
William 31
McKNIGHT, John 45 116 Samuel 45 58 116
McLAMORE, Moses 128
McLAURIN, Robert 65 140 Willis 140
McLAURINE, Robert 65 William 56 80 108
114 142
McLEMORE, Amos 31 Moses 31 Richard 59

McMECKEN, David 93
McMECON, Robert 34
McMEEKIN, Robert 17
McMEKIN, Andrew 10
McMICAN, Andrew 143 David 143 151
McMICKEN, Andrew 26 73 104 David 41 45
63 Robert 24
McNAIRY, Robert 7 13 14 20 23 39 56 63
65 67 68 71 91 95 108 118 119 124 125
130 131 132 134 135 137 143
McNEAL, Thomas 4
McNEES, James 101
McNEIL, Thomas 93 William 3 24
McNIGHT, John 38 44 46 47 49 64 67 82
87 96 102 Samuel 51 55 56 58 64 96 124
125
McNITE, John 6 17 128 Samuel 17 57 128
129
McPETERS, Andrew 13 19 32 34 40 41 47
49 50 88 90
McREE, David 4 9 14 24 28 34 42 48 97
James 4 9 14 24 28 34 48 97 122
McVAY, Captain 39 46 81 108 Claiborne
108 Claibourn 12 Claibourne 23 Clay-
bourn 99 Kenson 19 44 Jordan 120
McVEY, Claybourn 150 Kinchon 143
McWHERTER, Moses 89 92
MEADE, Lemuel 76
MEADOWS, Anderson 64 Elijah 64 Isaac 64
74 104 Lileston 70 75 103 Patsey 103
Rebeccah 70 75 103 Talitha 103
MELTON, Elijah 1 Elisha 33 51 52 Henry
105
MENEFEE/MENIFEE, Jarrat/Jarret 76 87
114 127 134 137 147 John 9 63 127 130
Reuben 6 137
MERCER, Edward 76 Nathaniel 79 93
MEREDITH, Thomas 56 62 83 134 139 143
MERRAT, William 129
MESSER, Nathaniel 57 68
METCALF, William 63
MILLAR, Alexander 46 John 51 88 96
Tobias 27 28 34 81
MILLER, Alexander 6 11 13 14 17 18 19
22 56 140 Andrew 6 11 John 5 Mark 107
Robert 123 Tobias 13 66 104 110 144
146 149 151
MILROY, John 60
MILTON, Elijah 50
MINFREE, Matthias 101
MINOR, Henry 56
MISSISSIPPI TERRITORY 40 47 51 96 99

106 148
MITCHEL/MITCHELL, James 26 84 87 101
117 Jesse 99 Marckus/Marcus 6 7 9 30
36 68 76 77 91 93 96 98-102 123 130 131
137 146 Thomas 77
MONTCRIEF, Matthew 91
MONTGOMERY, Jacob 65 John 25 39 96 118
134 137 Samuel 88 120 151
MONTGOMERYS GAP 9 32 63 87 95 96
MONTOREFT, Mathew 45
MOODY, Isaac 21 Jonathan 10 44 98 N 58
Nathaniel 1 2 7 9 11 12 15 16 21 23 25
27 28 37 39 43 45 49-52 63 70 99 101
103 108 116 119 127-131 134-137 139
146-152 Thomas 52 98
MOON, Moses 58 80
MOORE, Allan 27 32 33 34 Andrew 98 151
Asa 3 55 60 100 101 Charlotte 22 24 28
41 47 48 Fanny 102 103 113 French 3 55
James 23 29 82 89 90 95 145 Japtha 60
Jeptha 3 5 55 Joseph 102 103 113 151
Lamb 55 Pleasant 7 8 10-13 15 16 25 28-
33 35 37-41 43 48 51 57 59 61 62 68 70
72 74 81 116 117 125 127 128 130 131
134 135 137 Somerset 1-3 6-9 22 24 35
41 48 120-123 128 140 Sommersett 28
Summerset 116 117 Thomas 82 William 98
113 creek 9 16
MORE, Charlotte 24 Sommerset 24 Wm 1
MORFET, Shaderick 5
MORGAN, Henry 5 James 121
MORPHOS, James 60
MORRIS, Lester 12 23 27-29 31-34 56 62
73 83 99 102 109 120 137 141
MORRISON, James 4 14 John 89
MORROW, Leonard 128
MORTON, William 5
MOSELY, John 127
MOSS, James 110 Joana/Joannah 104 110
148 Mason 19 30 101 104 107 110 148
MURFREE, Hardy 4
MURPHEY, Archd 83 Hardy 14 Joseph 38
MURPHY, James 139 Joseph 36 64
MURRAH, William 2 6 20 21 45 62 87
MURRAY, tHOMAS 110
MURRY, William 12 29
MYERS, John 81 83 98 105
NAIL, Benjamin 139 147 Nicholas 41
William 9 122
NAILE, Benjamin 18 51 55 63 95 102
Nancy 18 Nicholas 48 51 57 89
Reuben 95 102

NAVE, Henry 62 75 89 John 56
NEAL, Andrew 36 James 10 99 Pallas 42
William 4 14 23 26 38 44 57 108 113
NEALE, William 56 64 69 109
NEEL, James 151 Pallis 151 Wm 139-142
NEELY, Samuel 151
NEIL, Andrew 53 James 10 Pallis 152
William 87
NEILE, James 18 96
NEILL, Potter 85
NELSON, John 16 59 74 75 104 111 Lydia
59 Robert 42 William 16
NEW, Pleasant 1 41 43-45 50 53 61 64 87
96 William 44 50 53 55 64 78 104 105
NEWELL, James 46 74 84
NEWLAND, Captain 7 Henry 41 45 83
Jesse 81 83 98 105
NEWLIN, Captain 11 Henry 19 103
NEWTON, John 22 23 80 108 113
Samuel 51 52 145 creek 102
NICHOLS, Joshua 64
NIEL/NIELL, James 49 99 106 Pallis 64
NIXON, William 19
NOBLET/NOBLIT, Wm 11 16 19 21 34 151
NODD, John 5
NORMAN, John 32
NORTH CAROLINA 10 21 30 40 42 44 51 61
74 78 83 86 102
NUT/NUTT, William 23 26 118 119
NYE, Shadrack 143
ODELL, Nancy 55 139 147
OHIO 132
OLIVE, Abel 9 25 45
OLIVER, Robert 3 6 7 23 36 39 50 55 62
64 80 81 84 85 91 108 113 115 134 142
145 147
ONEAL, William 65 145
ORANGE COUNTY, North Carolina 10
OSBOURN, Luke 119
OSBURN/OSBURNE, Benjamin 49 96 99 Fanny
6 Frederick 6 Nathan 83 Peggy 6
OVERTON, John 122
OVERTON COUNTY 43
OWEN, James 113
OWENS, James 72 Patsey 6 12 21
Smallwood 72 William 72
OXFORD Abel 33 34 39 48 61 99 106 Isaac
23 28 44 55 98 John 4 60 88 Samuel 5
PACKSTON, Captain 47
PAGE, John 142
PAIN, James 47
PAINE, Charles 146 Hardin 37 38 James

29 37 39 57 61 68 71 78 79 101 102 105
108 110 134 138 142 145 147 John 95
Joseph 4 Lewis 79 Robert 9 12 13 56 89
99 102 108 113 136 139 140 143 Rosannah
79 Thomas 4 William 45
PALL, John 28 29
PANKEY, Martha 129 Thomas 129
PARCHMAN, John 150 Philip/Phillip 2 20
32 36 41 47 57 58 60 75 76 79 81 83 98
105 134 135 148-158
PARHAM, Ephraim 44 45 114 152 James 7
Nathaniel 123 Peyton 108 William 78
PARKER, Jeremiah 33 39 46 56 91 102 139
William 8 26 36 37 38 70 71 78 80 81 83
84 85 100 109 110 117 126 131 136
PARMLY, Samuel 100 126
PARTAIN, Hightower 79 87
PARTEN, Hightower 52 67
PARTIN, Hightower 64 95 Leonard 87
PARTRICK, Ephraim 64
PATE, John 11 24 29 80 120 129 148
PATRICK, Ephraim 64 76 Samuel 95
PATTERSON, James 34 N 30 Neil 87 Nelson
26 30 33 47 116 135 148 Niel 96 Noel 65
PATTESON, Bernard 2 3 6 38 41 65 66 71
92 94 101 138 140 141 142 150 James 14
23 67 78 93 104 110 N 25 62 74 76 82
107 113 Nelson 2 6-8 10-19 21-24 38 39
43 44 47 49 51 54-56 59-61 63-65 68 70
72 73 75 77 80 81 83 85-87 95 98 101
104 106 108 110 120 127 129 132-135
137-140 144-147 152
PATTON, James 117 William 96
PAUL, Andrew 100 152 James 34 37 40
132 134 135 John 7 14 17 24 27 28 32
33 36 37 38 43 44 61 62 66 106 130 132
134 135 138 139 152
PAXTON, Captain 7 11 39 45 81 James 1
36 64 Samuel 36 50 62 64 87
PAYNE, Charles 132 136 138 139
James 93 97 106 Lewis 132 136
PEARSON, Samuel 38 43 44 60 68 84 98
113 137 146
PEELER, Hiram 4
PEEPLES, Burrel 149
PEIRSON, Samuel 151
PEMAY, Jonathan 5
PEMBERTON, Jelly/Jilley 61 71 72 144
PENDERGAST, John 131
PENDLETON, Charles 72
PENNELL, William 127
PENNINGTON, Jacob 4

PENRAY, Jonathan 5
PEPPER, William 13 56 62 73 96 98 99
102 120-123 125
PERKINS, Andrew 119 Captain 7 Charles
99 106 Constantine 95 Elizabeth 43
Israel 127 128 Jacob 4 14 Joseph 52 152
Saml 43 52 63 Thomas 42 74 William 140
PERKINSON, Josiah 139
PERRY, James 6 26 44 53 135 Jeremiah 25
35 43 John 25 31 53 54 57 65 68 69 71
80 95 96 103 William 58 71 80
PETTIWAY, Hinchey 101
PETTWAY, -- 36 37
PETTY, Ebenezer 96 114
PEYZER, George 85 86
PHILIPS, Benjamin 121 124 David 146
Esquire 24 John 98 140 141 143 Joseph
139 Thomas 19 120 123 William 2 118
127 -- 13
PHILLIPS, Captain 7 12 39 46 81 James
72 John 56 58 65 67 68 99 108 110 114
Thomas 29 32 33 46 56 61 69 86 87 108
William 1 4 23 26 27 29 31 35-38 42-45
49 54 57 64 69 77 78 86-90 95 96 102
PICKENS/PICKINS, Andrew 10 11 16 19 30
60 76 81 118 120 Captain 12 39 46 65 81
108 Israel 7 10-13 19 51 52 75-77 114
James 15 33 35 John 10 19 75 Joseph 94
Robert 86 William 1 10 11 16 56 76 77
91 139 142
PILLOW, Abner 74 86 Ann 38 Giddeon/
Gideon 3 18 19 23 31 38 50 65 73 76 82
84 99 109 110 128 134 139 145 147 Mordecai 84 136 William 25 136
PLUMMER, William 22
POLK, E 119 Ezekiel 50 102 112 Samuel 4
30 56 73 113 114 Thomas 4 42 73 74 102
111 112 William 28 56 97 102 114 119
PONTIN, Hightower 95
POPE, John 148 149 151 153
PORTER, David 8 9 27-29 31 38 48-50 56
63 65 66 68 70-72 77 99 106-108 110 118
119 145 Elias 28 29 James 55 77 Janette
99 John 21 27 61 66 70 83-85 87 88 90
91 93 94 99 107 108 110 114 147 Joseph
95 Nelly 99 Nimrod 148 151 153 Rees/
Reese 21 27 55 95 99 108 114 116-118
120 124 Robt 4 Sally 95 Thomas 42 --18
POSTIN, Nancy 9 15
POSTON, Nancy 34
POTEET, Captain 108 George 4 Samuel 96
POTEETE, George 53 Job 53 Samuel 115

POTTER, John 4
POTTS, Baker 91 114
POWELL, John 1 7 20 50
POYZER, George 147
PRATER, Andrew 89 100
PRATHER, Andrew 4
PRATT, Jesse 69
PRENDERGAST, John 1-3 12 22 46 54 84
132
PREWITT, Lemuel 119
PREWETT/PREWITTS GAP 21 29 73 79 98
PRICE, Cornelius 149 Isaac 4 14 42
James 83 103 William 10 38 39 45 47 48
56 57 72 84 100 103 105 134 140
PRIDE, William 84 87-94
PRINCE, William 5
PRINCE EDWARD COUNTY, Virginia 126 127
129 139
PULASKI COUNTY, Kentucky 126
PULLE, Edmund 28
PULLEN, William 31 63 80 87 107 109
PULLIN, Moses 60 96 112 William 40 60
79 93 101 102 106 108 114 129 133
PURNELL, Adaline 25 Amanda 25
Hortensius 25 William 2 7 24 25 42 46
49 51 55 85 86 96 99 107 147
PURVIANCE, John 42 119
PURVIS, Isaac 49 58 66
PURYEAR, Daniel 75 76
QUINN, Amos 55 65 James 55 65
RAGSDALE, Edward 99 William 4 10 25 47
56 67 73 75 77 78 99 101 103 104 113
140
RAINEY, James 59
RALEY, James 74
RAMSEY, Richard 74 75 Samuel 52 53 64
96 William 45 66
RANDOLPH COUNTY, North Carolina 83
RANEY, Zebulon 94
RAWSON, Charles 43
RAY, John 10 Thomas 27 116-118
REA, John 63 72 118 Joseph 32 33 35 56
62 73 77 80 81 96 97 113 142 149 150
Ritta 101 Thomas 23 28 29 31-34 52 108
118 128 William 32
READ, Captain 7 12 46 David 13 19 50
James 4 14 19 27 36 41 46 47 John 15 20
50 Levinah 103 Robert 56 107 Samuel 103
Thomas 20
REASONHOVER, Frances 96 98 103 John 17
52 80 86 97 103 125
REASONOVER, Benson 109 Early 109 Eliza-

beth 109 Hetty 109 Jacob 109 Jeremiah
109 John 109 116 Jordan 109 Polly 103
REDDISH, William 99
REDDUS, James 57 58
REDERS, William 53
REDDLE, -- 98
REDLE, John 95
REDUS, William 53
REECE, Robert 32
REED, David 22 49 131 143 James 4 95
117 118 120-122 124 125 129-131 John
117 141 Reed 45 139 142 144
REESE, Robert 105
REEVE, Joseph 64
REID, Robert 127
RENNICKS, Henry 127
RESENHOVER, John 10
REYNOLDS, Isaac 7 19 20 22 57 62 81 140
John 5 creek 14 87 107 111 island 31
RHEA, Abner 99 104 John 36 76 96
Thomas 51 91 95
RHODES, Tyree 10 80
RICHARDS, Jonathan 8 28 29 35 59 61 139
143 147 Mathew/Matthew 21 28 29
RICHARDSON, John 121 Maj 64 Matthias
92 112 May 26 Muntilear 76 William 88
RICKMAN, Joshua 52 130
RICHMOND VIRGINIA 129
RIDDLE, John 104 Mary 96 Polly 40 51
73 85 147 149 William 9 22 24 36 37 40
51 59 61 73 80 82 85 96 108 134 135 136
147 149
RIDDLES, Mary 101 William 101
RILEY, Joseph 31 35 60 106 Samuel 32 33
RITCHIE, Thomas 85 Widow 67
RIVERS, Joel 126 130 131 133 136
Robert 91 94
ROACH, Spencer 1 19 127 137 139
ROADES/ROADS, Tyree 29 31 39
ROAN/ROANE, Archibald 124-126 134 135
137 138
ROBARDS, Henry 50
ROBERTS, Henry 7 36 40 41 56 57 58 68-
72 76 80 96 100 103 106 110 132 143 146
148 John 3 55 Levi 51
ROBERTSON, Charles 10 64 97 David 23
Eldridge 18 57 93 James 38 62 63 75
John 33 35 56 70 75 128 129 Joseph 26
86 Martha 62 63 75 Sterling/Stirling
18 85 93 114 Thomas 127 Tyree 4
William 19 41 130 131 creek 67 112
fork 14 41 42 60 73 74 88 111

169

ROCKBRIDGE COUNTY, Virginia 24
RODES, Hasel 100 Hazel 82 Tyre/Tyree 15
21-23 33 34 37-39 48-51 56 58 84 86 91
99 110 114 118 119 125 128 134 135 138
139 142 147-150 152
RODGERS, McNiece 4 Paul 5 Samuel 4
William 4
ROE, Joseph 31 100
ROGERS, Andrew 52 148
ROMACK, Jane 145 John 61 86 134 135
138 144 145
ROOPS, John 31
ROOSS, John 31
ROPER, Joseph 53
ROSACK, William 5
ROSE, Samuel 58 69 William 56 63 65 66
78 107 108 109 140
ROSEN, John 5
ROSS, Henry 51 118 119 John 15 Robert
72 108 128 -- 79
ROUTON, William 129 139
ROWE, Joseph 50 64
ROWSEY, John 26 67
RUBEY/RUBY, James 42 Tho 5
RUCKER, -- 85
RUDDLE, William 40
RUFF, George 23
RUMOVER, John 119
RUSSEL/RUSSELL, John 10 79 86 Wm 148
RUST, William 5
RUTLEDGE, Benjamin 148 149 151 Joel 151
152 William 5
SALLY, Joseph 5
SAMFORD, John 36 54 55 107
SAMUEL, Anthony 28 57 62 Benjamin 5
John 13 44 Stephen 96 123
SANDERS, Benjamin 41 47 77 George 49
SAPPINGTON, John 27
SATTERFIELD, Peter 83 96 98 106 110 144
SAUNDERS, George 96 99 Hubbard 87
SAWYERS, William 2 19 30
SCALES, Henry 2 6 8 20 23-25 37 38 40
41 48 71 82 129 131-133 135 137 138 141
142
SCOTT, Edney 15 18 George 15 Jacob 44
John 5 127 M 69 Robert 79 Samuel 15
54 creek 87
SCRATCH, Enoch 31
SEAL/SEALE, Anthony 70 76 77 82
SEALS, Anthony 1 78-81 Eli 75
SEARCY, B 146 Bennet 128-130 142-145
SEAY, Mary 54 55 68 Rebeccah 54 55 68

SELMAN, David 125 126
SEQUERS/SEQUIRS, Abraham 51 68
SHADDEN, John 67 93 Joseph 34 58 66 67
72 94 104 112 151 Martin 32 33 37 48 58
61 65 67 92 135 -- 67
SHADDON, Martin 9 24 50
SHANE, Robert 13 34 109
SHANNON, David 5 131 Owen 122 Quinton
19 23 26 30 38 44 54 71 84-91 93 94 120
124 125 132 134 135 William 95 107
SHANON, Quinton 120
SHARPE, Carlus 5 Charles 128
SHAWBY, George 132
SHAWLEY/SHAWLY, George 130-133 136 137
142 144 John 133 Michael 133
SHEILDS, Captain 108 George 80 Leander
33 Samuel 7 19 39 43 48
SHELBYVILLE 15 18 64 67 81 94 106 114
SHELTON, Edmond 148 Edmund 74 75 77 89
90 91 93 97 98 103 Elisha 57 79
Thomas 5 6 7
SHEPHERD, William 139 142
SHEPPARD/SHEPPERD, Wm 15 84 113 115
SHERLEY, George 5
SHIELDS, Captain 39 47 George 19 96
Leander 35 120-123 Samuel 9 23 25 27 30
38 48 91 96 120-123 127 134 137 147 152
SHIP, M 88
SHOEMAKER, John 36 52 131 ferry 49
SHOULTS, John 72
SILMAN, David 124 126
SIMMONS, James 55 84-91 93 94 100 102
107 144 John 118 119 Lemuel 5 59 Martha
45 Mary 86 Solomon 86 Winnifred 45
SIMMS, John 38 Walter 5 42 60 -- 9
SIMPSON, Charles 19 22 32 33 50 53 87
136 137 140 George 42 Peggy 87 144
Thomas 75 William 7
SIMS, David 11 John 68
SINGLETON, Theophilus 72
SLAVES: Amelia 49 Anarchy 87 Daniel 147
Doctor Franklin 49 Frederick 152 Grace
75 Jack 103 113 James 44 Joe 36 John 2
Lucy 146 Mary 87 Milly 49 Nace 101 107
Ned/Neddy 80 Rhody 76
SMALLWOOD, John 5 54 90
SMART, John 4
SMITH, Austin 63 78 84 Bryant 112
Captain 7 11 12 39 Charles 65 145 152
Cynthia 114 David 21 33 73 134 136 140
143 Dudley/Dudly 40 66 79 80 82 143 144
148 Elizabeth 59 74 75 114 129 Isaac 19

46 52 62 134 138 139 148 James 5 42 88
113 John 50 Joseph 10 Owen 91 Phelps
108 Reuben 15 50 63 65 136 139 Samuel
10 16 17 27 30 31 38 45 66 74 75 113
114 127 128 132 134 Susannah 114 Thomas
3 6 8 12 13 15 17 20 22 24 25 28 30 32
34 35 36 40 43 47 49 51 52 55 57 58 68
107 109 125 128 133 139 140 149 151
William 17 20 23 28 33 66 84 88 99 100
101 125 127 132 138 150
SNIPES, Phillip 72
SNOW, Eli 22 69
SOLOMON, Jordan 53 75
SOUTH, Joseph 32
SOUTH CAROLINA 123 151
SPARTENBURGH, South Carolina 151
SPENCER, -- 18
STAGS, John 121 Polly 121
STANDFORD, George 53 John 53 Thomas 29
William 25 38 44 57
STANFORD, George 54 Thomas 4 William 9
120
STANLEY, John 5
STAPLES, William 52
STARK, Captain 45 James 10 36 53
STARKE, James 49 96 99
STARKES, Captain 39
STARKEY, Joseph 91
STARKS, Abram 5 Captain 7 11 37 James
10 124 126 127 John 5 Joseph 5 Wm 5
STEEL, Henry 87 Robert 5 William 6
STEELE, Henry 14 17 26 66 96 108 113
Robert 7 25 56 73 116 127 Thomas 56 65
139-141 William 3 7 11 51 61 67 71 101
STEGALL, Elizabeth 40 Lucinda 40
STEPHENS, John 14 17 123 124
STEPHENSON, Robert 19 William 5
STEWART, David 1 5 24 34 38 44 53 60
102 James 3 5 10 103 144 Lazarus 33
Richard 25 48 Thomas 32 48 116-118
William 89
STINSON, Alexander 26 87
STOGDON, Benjamin 140 141 145 147
Elizabeth 140 141 145 147
STOKES, John 36 72
STONE, Littleberry/Littlebury 150 151
Noble 150 151 Solomon 10 151 Thomas 13
15 18 19 21-23 26 31 33-35 37 47 50 51
59 62 65 73 100-102 106 107 125 128 130
133
STOVAL/STOVALL, Drury 14 17 28 52 121
124 125 128 129 130 Joseph 64 Josiah 10

64 75 84 113 William 8 11 16 17 105
STRAUGHAN, Balaam 83 89 90 146 150
Joseph 146 149 William 57 68 83 91 105
146 150
STRAWN, William 140
STROTHER, John 5 9 87 -- 3 branch 69
STUART, David 122 James 144 Laz 1
Thomas 98 117 118 120-123 130-133 147-
153 branch 98
STULT, Robert 127
STURT/STUAHT, Thomas 52
SULIVAN COUNTY 10
SUMNER, Thomas 99
SUMNER COUNTY 146
SWAIN, William 76 87 103
SWANSON, Peter 7 33 60 91 97 105 120
122 123 130-133 147 William 105 108
TACKER, John 7 26 Joshua 119 120
TAIT, Samuel 104
TAMPLIN, Jacob 109
TANKERSLEY/TANKERSLY, Roland/Rowland 83
90 92 150 Rolen 5 Rollin 146
TARPLEY, Alexander 12 18 19 47 48 57 65
66 67 80 Eliza 70 Thomas 37 40 68-70 80
TARPLY, Alexander 99 102 131 144 147
TARY, William 116 117
TATUM, Ho 117 130
TAYLOR, Anson 89 92 112 George 8 20 43
Gilbert 20 24 25 65 132 Hardin 20 James
42 74 111 John 28 77 106 114 127 129
132 138 141 144 152 Jonathan 44 Joseph
5 Lewis 5 Nathaniel 8 22 42 74 111 134
Robert 5 6 13 20 68 80 86 91 92 112
Thomas 15 42 55 66 68 74 111 117 118
William 95 117 121
TCHOAT, Charles 71 77 Letty 77
TEMPLE, Amy 107 Eliza 114 James 5 14 36
95 99 John 1 2 8 9 31 36 37 45 51 65 69
78 88 107 114 124 125 127 Josiah 63 107
Matilda 114 Nancy 114 road 110
TEMPLEN, Jacob 38 46 47 49 55 93
TEMPLIN, Jacob 50 70 101 102 105 106
115 133 147
TENIN, James 116
TENISER, Robert 88
TENNEN/TENNIN, James 47 50 117 John 135
William 48
TERRELL, James 107 142 Jane 144 145
William 81
TERRY, Henry 51 55 56 57 58 59 61
THOMAS, Isaac 36 William 73
THOMPSON, Alexander 69 80 91 104 108

142 147 148 Beriah 53 Calvin 53 Duncan
72 Ebenezer 53 John 6 33 36 37 40 63 67
131 132 140 146 Levi 53 73 94 109 Nancy
53 Oliver 5 William 28 37 40 41 53 59
73 94 109 126 150
THOMSON, Alexander 93 94 151 John 77
THURSBY, Edward 5 14
TIDWELL, David 48 Eli 14 17 19 28 31-34
37 43 89 90 100 102 Elias 23 27-29 88
152 Elizabeth 48 Ely 47 Gazeway 48
Isaac 48 Millinton 50 Nancy 48
Permelia 48 Vinson 48
TILFORD, James 147 John 84
TINNEN, Alexander 106 James 18 38 46
47 65 67 115 142 John 27 32 Robert
115 point 79
TOLLIS, William 47
TOMKINS, Humphry 140
TOMPKINS, Humphrey 14 17 56 100 Humphry
120 123 124 142
TONGAT, Jane 123 Martin 123 Susanna 123
Zachariah 123
TOOMER, Henry 74 111
TORMER, Henry 42
TRAVIS, William 5 125
TREMBLE, James 78 79 105
TRIGG, A 65 Will 65
TRIMBLE, James 2
TRUMBULL, James 5
TUCKER, George 116-118 Henry 6 John 148
Wyatt 117
TURNBOW, Andrew 32
TURNER, Hamner 93 John 21 Robert 88
William 96 -- 117 118 119
TUT/TUTT, Benjamin 59 69 122 146 150
Richard 5 124 126 127 137
TUTTLE, David 56 Solomon 9 88
TYGERT, James 127
USSERY, Peter 52 53 75 122 124 126 128
129 131 134 Thomas 75 William 52
VANCE, John 44 45 87 88 99 106
VANHOOSER, Isaac 102
VERNON, Amos 49 96 99
VICKERS, Green 88
VINCENT, Jesse 130 132 136 138 139 146
VINSENT, Jesse/Jessee 15 39
VINSON, Daniel 32 Eliab 16 17 -- 31
VIRGINIA [state] 18 24 62 65 97 101 126
127 129 139
W--, William 78
WAKE COUNTY, North Carolina 86
WALDRIP, John 131-133

WALDROP, John 22 28 58 101 102 108
WALKER, Eaton 122 124 125 Henry 52 53
62 78 J 88 James 7 18 80 John 11 24 34
77 80 81 89 91 98 101 108 132 142 143
146 147 152 Thomas 86 Widow 98 -- 52
WALLACE, Joseph 6 28 31 William 77
WALTERS, George 62 103
WALTHAL/WALTHALL, John 86 103 115
Richard 101 146
WALTHEL, John 141
WALTON, Jesse 46 Keller 102 William
46 122 Willis 46
WAMICK, -- 117
WARD, J 2 James 9 40 45 46 80 94 114
120 124 Presley 97 110
WARREN COUNTY, Kentucky 126 127
WASHINGTON, Thomas 22 47
WATERS, Alston 60 98 Daniel 43 74
George 45 53 55 78 95 William 151
WATSON, William 17 52 95 96
WATTERS, George 16 62 75
WATTS, Stephen 139
WAYNE CIRCUIT COURT 126
WEAKLEY, Robert 21 42 72
WEAKLEYS CREEK 1 31 46 63 74 102
WEATHERS, Jesse 1 55 56 102 120-123
WEAVER, Zebedee 99
WEBB, Jesse 33 John 23 27-29 31 32 34
57 120 145 Julius 26 27 Larken/Larkin
10 17 38 44 45 64 87 99 Thomas 26 27
William 79 81 88 90 99
WEBSTER, Catherine 10 William 10
WEIR, Samuel 91 95
WELCH, John 28 30 56 Nicholas 7 18 34
39 50 77 Sarah 39 Thomas 10 23 27 39
66 91 147 152 William 7 9 28 33 34 39
48 61 92
WELLS, James 74 John 75 Ransom 23 37
38 95 100 Thomas 13 60 71 99 131
William 2 9 11 22 30 37 39 53 73 77 80
82 108 116 123 124 138 142
WEST, Elzey 86 Jesse 3 6 7 65 67 123
124 Joel 6 148
WESTMORELAND, Jesse 20 23 116 Reuben
64 Sally 47 67 104 Thomas 1 7 9 10 12
17 20 22 23 28 30 38-40 46-48 52 67 76
104 118 119 127 128 130
WHARTON, Joshua 130
WHEELER, Benjamin 55 106 John 10
WHITE, Caleb 13 22 55 56 59 68 90 96
145 148 Capinan/Capusan 22 Carol 33
Chapman 42 47 88 92 Daniel 19 48 51

Elijah 80 Elisha 91 Elizabeth 74 75 89
H 118 Henry 84 106 J 42 John 1 3 7 74
75 84 91 116 117 119 121 130 131 132
148 Polly 121 122 Samuel 125-128
Simpson 75 Thomas 121 William 5 63 69
74 88 93 139 -- 47 mill 46
WHITESIDE, Jenkins 55 71 81
WHITSETT, William 95
WHITSON, Charles 99 106 Thomas 5 14 118
WILBOURN, Solomon 32
WILBURN, Solomon 32
WILCHER, Henry 17 27
WILCOCKSON, David 18
WILCOX, David 45
WILKINSON, Captain 81 108 James 29 37
38 50 76 77 102 106 113 Kinchen/Kin-
chin 24 61 106 139 Thomas 8 12 13 15 19
22 23 31 34 39 55-57 60 61 68 73 90 100
143-145 152
WILKISON, Thomas 12 13 39
WILLIAMS, Amos 65 72 73 95 114 Andrew
95 Betsey 65 72 73 114 George 63 77 81
82 Isaac 64 76 James 5 10 20 23 48 63
72-76 95 103 105 114 125 141 Joel 5
John 9 54 57 73 83 96 98 99 116 Lorenzo
36 Marmaduke 116 Moses 5 Nathaniel
118-120 123 124 Permenas 106 Pleasant
36 Rebeccah 63 77 81 82 96 Robert 9
12 13 14 47 80 Sally 75 76 Sarah 36
Simon 63 71 Stephen 55 65 Thomas 52
65 71 72 99 107 William 95
WILLIAMSON COUNTY 2 116 124 126 130 131
133 136 140 143
WILLIS, Plummer 22 39
WILLS, John 70 Thomas 34
WILLSON, Captain 81 James 66 Robert 2
33 81
WILSFORD, John 5
WILSON, Acquilla 49 Aquila/Aquilla 14
17-24 33 35 38 45 56 76 89-91 102 118
140 142 Boyd 109 Captain 97 108 Isaac 2
26 29 James 45 52 66 90 John 14 55 102
114 116 118 Matthew 60 66 90 Maxwell 66
90 Richard 5 Robert 8 9 19 22 35 51 75
114 121-123 131 135 Zacheus 122 -- 5
WINN, Eliza 89 John 76 Minor 6 17 32
63 76 128 Minos 38 Nancy 89 Polly 17
89 Rachel 89
WINNINGHAM, Abel 83
WINTERBOWER, George 9 63 Jacob 9
WINTERS, James 29
WISDOM, Captain 108 William 7 23 26

WISENER, John 53 64 78 95
WISENOR John 103
WISNER, John 18
WITT, George 116
WOOD, Thomas 89
WOODS, Daniel 3 18 24 25 29 33 34 36 39
48-51 55 64 71 73 81 82 94 101 105 119
134 139 141 145 David 3 6 19 33 34 46
93 94 99 119 130 131 151 Israel 5 John
122 131 Oliver 20 29 36 39 50 51 122-
124 131 132 Samuel 2 9 36 45 47 49 76
85 119 132 134 136 Thomas 100 101
William 14 16 22 27 30 44 48 65 67 70
73 75 84 86 96 99 101 108 110 114 116
117 119 120 130 131 143 147
WOODWARD, Jeremiah 36 93
WRIGHT, Christopher 23 27 87 Elijah 72
Hezekiah 42 James 25 John 87 97 Richard
107 Samuel 1 16 64 Winlock 72 branch 72
YANCEY, John 128 131
YANCY, Alfred 13 14 88-92 98 100 James
89 John 10 12 22 23 29 31 33 37 40 44
46 48 50 51 54 56 57 59 61 62 64 73 77
89 90 93 94 108 116 118 121 122 125 127
128 146 149 150 Philip 6 Tryon 147
YARBORO, Ambrose 25 Britton 25
YARBOROUGH, Ambrose 63 Brittain 63 67
Britton 45 55 70
YARBROUGH, Britton 75 91 104 108 147
148 150 James 69 John 109 125
YARUM, Joseph 97
YEATMAN, Thomas 85 86 147
YOUNG, Archibald 25 48 63 70 75 97
Captain 7 9 17 39 67 81 108 Jesse 53
John 7-9 16 30 41 48 50 52 53 61 64 87
105 113 Nathaniel 43 45 50 53 100 105
YOUNGBLOOD, Aaron 5 Henry 5
ZOLLICOFFER, George 82

Heritage Books by Carol Wells:

Abstracts of Giles County, Tennessee: County Court Minutes, 1813–1816 and Circuit Court Minutes, 1810–1816

CD: Tennessee, Volume 1

CD: Tennessee, Volume 2

Davidson County, Tennessee County Court Minutes, Volume 1, 1783–1792

Davidson County, Tennessee County Court Minutes, Volume 2, 1792–1799

Davidson County, Tennessee County Court Minutes, Volume 3, 1799–1803

Dickson County, Tennessee County and Circuit Court Minutes, 1816–1828 and Witness Docket

Edgefield County, South Carolina Probate Records, Boxes One through Three Packages 1–106

Edgefield County, South Carolina Probate Records, Boxes Four through Six Packages 107–218

Edgefield County, South Carolina: Deed Books 13, 14 and 15

Edgefield County, South Carolina: Deed Books 16, 17 and 18

Edgefield County, South Carolina: Deed Books 19, 20, 21 and 22

Edgefield County, South Carolina: Deed Books 23, 24, 25 and 26

Edgefield County, South Carolina: Deed Books 27, 28 and 29

Edgefield County, South Carolina: Deed Books 30 and 31

Edgefield County, South Carolina: Deed Books 32 and 33

Edgefield County, South Carolina: Deed Books 34 and 35

Edgefield County, South Carolina: Deed Books 36, 37 and 38

Edgefield County, South Carolina: Deed Books 39 and 40

Edgefield County, South Carolina: Deed Book 41

Edgefield County, South Carolina: Deed Books 42 and 43, 1826–1829

Edgefield County, South Carolina: Deed Books 44 and 45

Genealogical Abstracts of Edgefield, South Carolina Equity Court Records

Natchez Postscripts, 1781–1798

Rhea County, Tennessee Circuit Court Minutes, September 1815–March 1836

Rhea County, Tennessee Tax Lists, 1832–1834, and County Court Minutes Volume D: 1829–1834

Robertson County, Tennessee Court Minutes, 1796–1807

Rutherford County, Tennessee Court Minutes, 1811–1815

Sumner County, Tennessee Court Minutes, 1787–1805 and 1808–1810

Williamson County, Tennessee County Court Minutes, July 1812–October 1815

Williamson County, Tennessee County Court Minutes, May 1806–April 1812